MEANING, FORM, and BODY

MEANING, FORM, *and* BODY

edited by
Fey Parrill
Vera Tobin
Mark Turner

CSLI
PUBLICATIONS
Center for the Study of
Language and Information
Stanford, California

Printed in the United States
14 13 12 11 10 1 2 3 4 5

Library of Congress Cataloging-in-Publication Data

Meaning, form, and body /
edited by Fey Parrill, Mark Turner, and Vera Tobin.

p. cm.

Includes bibliographical references and index.

ISBN 978-1-57586-595-9 (cloth : alk. paper)
ISBN 978-1-57586-594-2-X (pbk. : alk. paper)

1. Language and culture. 2. Human body and language.
3. Semantics. 4. Connotation (Linguistics)
I. Parrill, Fey, 1976- II. Turner, Mark, 1954-
III. Tobin, Vera, 1975- IV. Title.
P35.M38 2009
306.44–dc22

2009035409

CIP

∞ The acid-free paper used in this book meets the minimum requirements of the American National Standard for Information Sciences—Permanence of Paper for Printed Library Materials, ANSI Z39.48-1984.

CSLI was founded in 1983 by researchers from Stanford University, SRI International, and Xerox PARC to further the research and development of integrated theories of language, information, and computation. CSLI headquarters and CSLI Publications are located on the campus of Stanford University.

CSLI Publications reports new developments in the study of language, information, and computation. Please visit our web site at
http://cslipublications.stanford.edu/
for comments on this and other titles, as well as for changes and corrections by the author and publisher.

Contents

Preface

FEY PARRILL, VERA TOBIN, & MARK TURNER

1 Introduction

The edited volume resulting from the first Conference on Conceptual Structure, Discourse, and Language (CSDL) states that the intention of the conference was to bring together researchers from both cognitive and functional perspectives (Goldberg, 1996). This is an excellent goal.

Both cognitive and functional (or usage-based) approaches share the assumption that language happens within a social and conceptual context, and that grammar is motivated by use. Cognitive approaches force us to confront the fact that language is part of general cognition, while usage-based approaches keep us grounded in the real phenomena of language. Bringing the two approaches together has resulted in powerful demonstrations of the value of taking real language data and building towards a theoretical framework that has explanatory power (witness the success of construction grammar).

The CSDL conference has a special status for two of the editors of the volume: CSDL-5 was the first academic conference they attended, and the unified approach to language they found there deeply inspired them both. The tenth conference is now approaching, and the field of linguistics has changed substantially since the inaugural meeting in 1995. It is therefore worth considering the extent to which the original goal has been achieved, whether it has shifted, and what it should be for future conferences. In this preface, we will describe the themes that link the papers in this particular volume, but we will also reflect on the future of this conference.

Meaning, Form & Body.
Fey Parrill, Vera Tobin, and Mark Turner (eds.).

2 Changes in the field of linguistics that affect CSDL

The first CSDL conference—at which one of the editors of the current volume spoke—occurred in 1994, in San Diego. In that era, the International Cognitive Linguistics Association (ICLA) was still relatively new: ICLA was established during a conference held in 1989 in Germany. That conference was retroactively named the first ICLC, but the first conference announced as a conference of the ICLA was held in 1991, in Santa Cruz, California. In the 1990s, there were few venues in which to present research that was still seen as non-traditional and often marginal. Cognitive linguistics is now a thriving approach to the study of language. Fredrick Newmeyer's (2003) paper in Language explicitly points out that a shift has taken place in the field towards cognitive and usage-based approaches, and that this shift has been welcomed by other disciplines, especially psychology. The size of the ICLA conference (ICLC) and the diversity of research presented there both testify to the success of the cognitive approach.

One consequence of the success of cognitive linguistics in general, however, is that CSDL—ostensibly a union of cognitive and functional approaches—has become in effect the North American ICLC. In 2005, the Conceptual Structure, Discourse, and Language Association (CSDLA) became an affiliate of the International Cognitive Linguistics Association, in recognition of the fact that CSDL is a major forum for presentation of cognitive linguistic research.

Cognitive and functional, or usage-based, approaches are naturally allied. Indeed, it may be difficult to separate them. However, members of the CSDL research community should consider whether usage-based approaches are still fully represented at CSDL, and whether this unique feature of the conference should be prioritized. If cognitive linguists are no longer being exposed to research from a functional and usage-based approach, cognitive approaches increasingly run the risk of overlooking any number of significant facts about language as it is used, relying on potentially misleading or incomplete data, and losing sight of the range and sources of linguistic variation.

CSDL has been affected by a second shift within the field of linguistics: a movement towards the development and inclusion of methods for conducting laboratory experiments. The principal method of science is theory—that is, generalization over data. The data must be empirical, rather than imaginary. Science requires a second, all-important, empirical step: the worth of the scientific theory is to be determined by how well it captures data not used in the development of the theory, including data that do not yet exist. For most of science—astronomy, geology, evolutionary descent of species—data are robustly available, in what are by definition ecologically valid environments, and they can be gathered. Coming up with good generalizations—Newton's laws of motion, for example—is the crucial step. Scientific generalization over language data was very nearly the exclusive method used by early cognitive linguistics. But experiments are necessary to elicit data that are not plainly and indisputably available, and to help us choose between well-thought-out theories whose implications conflict on points for which there is no suitable naturally-occurring data to support one over the other. In choosing Einstein's mechanics over Newton's, we point to the orbit of Mercury: data gathered, but not from an experiment.

Recently in cognitive linguistics, the method of scientific generalization-and-evaluation has come to be supplemented with methods for conducting laboratory experiments. This marriage of experimental procedures with methods of scientific generalization has been fruitful. The use of methods from psycholinguistics to evaluate theoretical frameworks has provided further evidence that cognitive approaches are on the right track. As always, it is a struggle to keep the laboratory experiments free of the standard weaknesses: experimenter effects, elicitation via abnormal affordances in the laboratory, invalid linguistic environments, invalid motivational structures for subjects, inadequate statistical measures, and so on. It seems to us that cognitive linguistics has embraced the need to design laboratory experiments in ways that finesse or at least manage these potential limitations.

Experimental procedures are only one tool for doing research, and don't provide the only answer to a question. They can lead to, as Wallace Chafe puts it, "...a preoccupation with unnatural data and disregard for even the most obvious properties of conscious experience" (1994, p. 20). A shift towards experimental methods may also have the effect of alienating those who use observational methods, collect naturalistic data, or whose research centers on case studies or detailed analyses of small samples of language, and such researchers may be less likely to submit papers to CSDL.

Functional and usage based approaches have a long tradition of using empirical methods, particularly in corpus studies, and there have been many exciting advances in corpus linguistics in recent years. However, corpus studies may induce a focus on data—which are themselves inert—rather than theory. The laudable advances in statistical analysis that characterize some of the best recent work in corpus linguistics may also threaten to eclipse qualitative methodologies, which provide important information about sociological and dialectical variation, as well as other contextual factors affecting language use and structure.

What cognitive linguistics needs above all is the work of good minds, engaged in active, intelligent research and in conversation with one another. It will be so much the better if these good minds have available to them as many methods as possible for testing their thoughts. In our view, cognitive linguistics currently has the opportunity to pursue an integration of good theoretical, quantitative, qualitative, and experimental research, the whole being stronger than the parts, and cognitive linguistics in the current moment is engaged with the framework for this integration.

3 Recommendations

The goal of uniting cognitive and functional or usage-based approaches is a worthy one. Concrete steps can be taken to prioritize this goal, and we believe these efforts would have a salutary effect on both the organization and future research.

It is noteworthy that CSDL 8, 9, and 10 will all have been hosted in departments of cognitive science. Hosting the conference in a department of linguistics might encourage a balance in the representation of different methods, including both theoretical and quantitative work. In addition, the call for papers should explicitly note the goal of the conference, and should include the phrase *usage-based*. It has been absent in recent years, including the call for papers circulated by the current editors. Finally, at the time of this writing, the proposal for the next CSDL indicates that the conference will center on experimental methods. Such a conference would be an asset to the field, as it would help to ensure that researchers interested in exploring those methods have an opportunity for training. However, it might be of value to the field as a whole to have a future conference that provides training and focus on non-experimental methods. These methods are at the heart of our field.

4 This volume

The ninth conference on Conceptual Structure, Discourse, and Language was held October 18-20, 2008, at Case Western Reserve University in Cleveland, Ohio, under the theme "Meaning, Form, and Body." It focused on two central, related research areas in the study of language. The first is the integration of form and meaning, and the second is the relationship between language and the human body—topics that intersect naturally, as in the study of grammatical constructions, conceptual integration, and gesture.

An obvious starting point for a volume that proposes to say something meaningful about the relationship between language and bodies is an investigation into the relationship between linguistic representations and perceptual experience. This collection thus begins, in its first chapter, with a vigorous argument that direct perceptual simulation indeed plays a pervasive and fundamental role in all language comprehension. Sarah Anderson and her collaborators present several pieces of experimental evidence for sensorimotor involvement in the processing of even the seemingly amodal linguistic operator of negation. Moving in the opposite direction, Caleb Everett's study of event classification in speakers of Brazilian Portuguese and Karitiâna provides evidence for the effect that grammatical categories can have on speakers' perception of objects in the world.

The construction of linguistic perspective is another tantalizing arena for exploring the importance of embodied experience for meaning construction and linguistic structure. In his chapter, Adam Głaz argues that Vantage Theory, which connects linguistic behavior to speakers' fundamental embodied experience of their own orientation in space and time, can serve as a psychologically plausible and useful approach to this phenomenon. His analysis extends Vantage Theory's range of application beyond its original confines of color categorization and brings it to bear on the rhetoric of political discourse.

The bodies of speakers play complicated roles in two papers that investigate the boundaries and interactions between "gestural" and "linguistic" performance in the same communicative modality. The studies presented in Marcus Perlman's chapter suggest that speech rate often functions as an iconic vocal gesture accompanying (indeed, inseparable from) speech, perhaps arising from underlying sensorimotor simulations. Leland McCleary and Evani Viotti, meanwhile, analyze an extended narrative in Brazilian Sign Language and argue that idiosyncratic, gestural, or otherwise nonverbal elements play a larger role in signed discourse than generally recognized in the linguistics literature. The body tells secrets the conscious mind does not know in Svetlana Gorokhova's study of slips of the tongue, in which linguistic performance may provide unexpected clues about the activation processes that lie behind language production as well as language comprehension. Finally, the body also takes center stage in Judit Simo's cross-linguistic study of body part metaphors in Hungarian and American writing about chess, an unusually thorough and detailed catalog of metaphors in which the human body serves as the source domain.

The study of metaphor and metaphoric blends continues to figure prominently in the research represented at both the CSDL conference and in this volume: Vito Evola examines the idiosyncratic use of conceptual metaphors in the speech and gesture of two individuals discussing their personal religious beliefs. Anna Pleshakova provides a conceptual blending account of a recently emergent and wildly popular metaphor used in Russian media to refer to corrupt officers of law enforcement agencies, "werewolves in epaulettes." At the border of the blending-metaphor interface, Karen Sullivan and Eve Sweetser address the long-standing question of when, and whether, "Generic is Specific" blends should be considered metaphors at all. Vera Tobin's analysis of English constructions for expressing causation and change also makes use of blending theory, though its focus is on conceptual compression, rather than the relationship between metaphors and blends.

Other cognitive accounts of individual constructions make up a significant portion of this collection. Ron Langacker's analysis of the construction day after day extends a discussion he began, in brief, over ten years ago. This detailed account deploys the tools of Cognitive Grammar to demonstrate how a construction can indeed fit into the general patterns that characterize English grammar, despite defying the apparent constraints of constituent structure. Carol Moder and Naoki Otani, in two separate chapters, also consider sets of constructions in English, both from a usage-based standpoint. Moder's chapter takes on expressions using like to introduce a noun phrase, observing that previous accounts in cognitive linguistics have placed an emphasis on metaphoric uses that is not borne out by the relative frequency of these uses in natural language (making her paper an interesting and useful counterpoint to the several papers on metaphor in this volume). Otani discusses discourse-organizing functions of the particle aside, using a combination of quantitative and qualitative corpus analysis to put together an account of the grammaticalization of these constructions in contemporary American English.

Several other papers take a similarly close look at lexical items in languages other than English. Tuomas Huumo and Jari Sivonen present the case of the Finnish deictic verbs *tulla* ("come") and *mennä* ("go"), and their complicated, only partially metaphorically motivated, historical extension to abstract senses. Nina Yoshida considers another closely linked pair of lexical items, Japanese *mono* and *koto*, and their semantic extensions in constructions marking deontic and epistemic stance. Hélène Mazaleyrat and Audrey Rudel discuss the French adjective *curieux*, the conceptual motivations for its different primary senses, and its sensitivity to different constructional contexts. Takeshi Koguma's chapter proposes a new account of nominative/genitive conversion in Japanese, using Cognitive Grammar to explain both historical phenomena and existing constraints in a single framework.

5 Procedural details

Proposals to present a paper at the conference were submitted to a process of selection governed by blind peer review. After the conference, presenters were invited to submit their papers to a process of selection for inclusion in this volume, also governed by blind peer review. This volume is the result of those successive processes.

References

Chafe, W. (1994). *Discourse, Consciousness, and Time: The Flow and Displacement of Conscious Experience in Speaking and Writing*. Chicago: University of Chicago Press.

Goldberg, A. (Ed.). (1996). *Conceptual Structure, Discourse, and Language*. Stanford: CSLI.

Newmeyer, F. J. (2003). Grammar is grammar and usage is usage. Language, 79(4), 682-707.

1

On the Temporal Dynamics of Negated Perceptual Simulations

SARAH E. ANDERSON, STEPHANIE HUETTE, TEENIE MATLOCK, & MICHAEL J. SPIVEY

Some language theorists have suggested that the comprehension of negated statements, such as "The theory is not fully developed," involves different processes from non-negated propositions. However, those processes may vary when measured by memory methods versus comprehension methods, and by the number of alternative possibilities afforded by the negated statement. In the context of comparing various theoretical accounts of sensorimotor embodiment in language comprehension, we discuss experimental results that demonstrate a bias toward the affirmative in memory, as well as results that provide support for direct perceptual simulations (unmediated by the affirmative version) of negated sentences.

1 Language as a Trajectory Through Neural State-Space

In the latter half of the 20th Century, the dominant theoretical framework for understanding language processing was based on Boolean-logical internal representations (e.g., Chomsky 1957; Marcus 2001; Pinker 1994; Pylyshyn 1980). The amodal linguistic symbols conceived by these theorists are entirely divorced from: a) the sensory modalities through which linguistic input is delivered, and b) the motor constraints of the body through which linguistic output travels. However, as the century came to a close, many theoretical accounts of language instead began to rely on those very sensorimotor groundings for building their representations (e.g., Langacker

Meaning, Form & Body.
Fey Parrill, Vera Tobin, and Mark Turner (eds.).

1987; Lakoff & Johnson 1980; Talmy 2000). The notion of image-schematic representations of language – spatially arrayed iconic units of meaning that often carry with them some temporal dynamics – acquired support not only from the grammatical intuitions of trained linguists, but also from statistical analyses of language corpora (Grondelaers, Speelman, & Geeraerts 2007) and from the pooled intuitions of naïve experimental participants (e.g., Gibbs & O'Brien 1990; Gibbs, Ström, & Spivey-Knowlton 1997; Richardson, Spivey, Edelman, & Naples 2001). Over the past decade, a whirlwind of experimental findings has revealed many connections between linguistic knowledge and sensorimotor primitives, even in real-time comprehension tasks (e.g., Barsalou 1999; Barsalou, Breazeal, & Smith 2007; Bergen, Lindsay, Matlock, & Narayanan 2007; Glenberg & Kaschak 2002; Meteyard, Bahrami, & Vigliocco 2007; Nazir, Boulenger, Roy, Silber, Jeannerod, & Paulignan 2007; Pecher & Zwaan 2005; Richardson, Spivey, Barsalou, & McRae 2003; Zwaan, Stanfield, & Yaxley 2002). In fact, as more and more evidence accrues that many areas of cortex exert functional bidirectional influences among one another in real-time (e.g., Fuhrmann Alpert, Hein, Tsai, Naumer, & Knight 2008; Kveraga, Ghuman, & Bar 2007; Motter 1993; Pulvermüller 1999; Spence & Driver 2004; see also Sporns, Chialvo, Kaiser, & Hilgetag 2004), it becomes less and less likely that internal patterns of neural activity that implement linguistic representations could possibly avoid being instantaneously coupled with related patterns of neural activity in sensory and motor cortices. Essentially, the temporal continuity with which perceptual, cognitive, and motor representations interact with one another, combined with the spatial contiguity of partially-overlapping representations in state space, make the sensorimotor embodiment of language an inevitable fact (Spivey 2007).

Inspired by Elman's (1990) treatment of simple recurrent networks that learn linguistic sequences, one can conceptualize the dynamics of a language-processing neural network (real or artificial) as forming a trajectory through the state space of the network. If each neuron is treated as a dimension, then the firing rates of all the neurons at any given time slice form a set of coordinates that index a location in the state space. Therefore, a string of words in a sentence necessarily forms a string of locations: a trajectory. Similar sentences (lexically, semantically, and syntactically) will produce similar trajectories in nearby regions of state space. Likewise, very different sentences will produce very different trajectories in separate regions. Importantly, sensorimotor features can be integrated into a simple recurrent network (Howell, Jankowicz, & Becker 2005), allowing embodiment effects to be infused in those trajectories. Thus, rather than the comprehension of a sentence being represented as a string of discrete symbols bracketed or tree-branched into a precise hierarchical structure, the subtleties of phonological, semantic, syntactic, and embodiment constraints may be encoded together in the continuous dynamics of the state space (e.g., Elman 2004; Tabor & Hutchins 2000).

The debate over the relative importance of amodal symbols versus sensorimotor primitives in language is likely to reach a crescendo in the coming years. A key battleground – or perhaps a busy shared workbench – for this debate may turn out to be the *negation of linguistic propositions*. Although many linguistic propositions easily lend themselves to perceptual symbols grounded in sensation and action (Barsalou 1999), negation operators may not so easily avail themselves to that rather analog format of representation. Nonetheless, negation operators perform an extremely powerful cognitive operation, and thus, warrant analysis. After all, it can profoundly transmogrify one's outlook on life when a sentence changes from "There are cookies in the cupboard" to "There are no cookies in the cupboard." Where else in cognition can one so radically and sharply alter the meaning of a concept with the simple flick of a word?

In the rest of this paper, we will discuss more traditional ways of describing negation as a two-step process before exploring a new way of describing negation as a continuous trajectory through state space. Under this latter view, the trajectory of a negated sentence through state space that shares many locations, or words, with the path of its affirmative counterpart could easily exhibit some graded uncertainty and competition between these possible routes. Next we will explore empirical findings related to misremembering negated sentences (section 4), evidence supporting the perceptual simulation of negated binary alternatives (section 5), and evidence for the direct perceptual simulation of these negated binary alternatives (section 6). The final section urges further investigation of the mechanism by which a negated sentence is perceptually simulated, and presents a preliminary neural network that is being applied to this topic.

2 Negation as a Two-Stage Process

Negation is fundamental in everyday communication. Throughout the course of a typical day, people frequently have to report where things are *not* located, for instance, "Your keys are not on the table" or "My car is not in the garage." They must also describe events that are *not* happening, for instance, "The Patriots are not playing tonight" or "Your car will not start." Despite the ubiquity of negated statements, surprisingly little is known about how they are processed and what their conceptual structure is relative to their affirmative counterparts.

Psycholinguists have examined the comprehension of negated statements. One of the main findings is that people are slower to read negated sentences than they are to read affirmative sentences because they are more complex (see Barres & Johnson-Laird 2003; Carpenter & Just 1975; Clark & Chase 1972; Mayo, Schul, & Burnstein 2004). Such findings have provided invaluable insights into sentence processing, but many important questions about processing remain. For example, is the increased complexity of negation due to multiple processing stages or to something else, such as an increase in the number of possibilities afforded by negation? Also, how do negated statements influence everyday cognition? Are negated statements remembered any differently from non-negated statements, and if so, how? Are negated sentences comprehended differently than non-negated sentences? The present goal was to further consider negation's influence on memory and sentence comprehension.

Negation has been of interest to philosophers and language theorists for centuries (for review, see Gilbert 1991), but only recently has it received close attention in the experimental laboratory. Early cognitive work on processing suggested that negated statements about spatial relations were processed differently from similar affirmative statements. For instance, participants in Clark and Chase (1972) were presented with sentences followed by pictures and then asked whether the sentence was true or false of a corresponding picture. For example, a "true" trial might consist of the sentence, "The star is above the cross," followed by a picture with a star above a cross, accurately depicting relationships expressed by the sentence. On average, participants responded true or false more quickly to a picture following an affirmative sentence such as, "The star is above the cross," than to a negative sentence such as, "The star is not above the cross." The findings demonstrated that affirmative and negated sentences are processed differently. In particular, it was suggested that the increased processing time of negated sentences may have resulted from first processing core proposition information about the spatial relation (e.g., star above cross) and second processing negated information about that proposition (e.g., star not above cross).

Likewise, linguistic negation is often viewed—even by embodiment advocates—as implemented in the form of a digital logical operation applied to an analog perceptual simulation (Kaup, Zwaan, & Lüdtke 2007). For example, Kaup et al. propose what they call the *two-step simulation hypothesis of negation*. According to this hypothesis, a negated sentence like "Johnny has no talent at singing" is first represented via a perceptual simulation of the affirmative version. So one would briefly imagine Johnny singing quite nicely. However, about one second later, this perceptual simulation would be replaced by the negative version, in which Johnny is singing poorly. Their evidence for this account comes from several experiments.

Let us start with Zwaan, Stanfield, and Yaxley (2002), who asked participants to read sentences and then to decide whether or not a subsequent picture was mentioned in the sentence they had just read. When a sentence such as, "The eagle was in the sky," was presented, participants were quicker to respond that a picture of an eagle with outstretched wings had been mentioned in the previous sentence than when they saw a picture of an eagle with folded wings. These results support claims that participants construct an image to represent the sentences they read; this in turn makes that image more accessible and leads to quicker subsequent responses to that image. Such images, constructed through the partial activation of the neurons used to actually perceive or interact with the objects, are called perceptual simulations. When the test picture matched the image that had been mentally created, reaction times were faster than if the test picture did not match the state of the object described in the text. These data provide evidence that comprehending language is grounded in perceptual representations, at least in some cases.

While perceptual simulations seem capable of explaining the comprehension of affirmative sentences, negated sentences may not be handled in the same way. Kaup, Yaxley, Madden, Zwaan, and Lüdtke (2006b) presented participants with sentences like, "The eagle was not in the sky," and asked them to make judgments about whether a subsequently presented picture was mentioned in the sentence they had just read. If participants perceptually simulate negation in the same way they simulate affirmative sentences, then participants should be quicker to respond "yes" to pictures that match the sentence, i.e., an eagle with its wings folded. The experimenters found that when participants read negated sentences, response times to a picture that matched the affirmative version of the proposition (an eagle with wings spread) were faster than pictures that actually match the negated sentence. This suggests that a perceptual simulation of the affirmative situation was being created in response to negated sentences. Although the mechanism responsible for these differences in processing negated sentences is not determined or discussed in terms of modal or amodal representations, these results imply that the process of negation itself is handled differently from other aspects of sentence processing and not through perceptual simulation.

3 Negation as an Alternative Trajectory

Similar to the pattern of results reported so far, negated and affirmative sentences seem to be handled differently in lexical decision tasks as well (e.g., Hasson & Glucksberg 2006; Kaup 2001; MacDonald & Just 1989). For example, in three probe recognition experiments, MacDonald and Just

(1989) showed that probes like "bread" exhibit reduced priming when they correspond to nouns that were negated in the preceding sentence, e.g., "Almost every weekend, Elizabeth bakes no bread but only cookies for the children." However, priming for associated probes, like "butter" for that sentence, was not reduced. Thus, the process could, in principle, be described as follows: A negated noun such as "no bread" initially activates the [bread] concept, which then spreads its activation to associated concepts (e.g., [butter]). Soon thereafter, however, the [negation] concept manages to dampen the activation of the [bread] concept, so that when it is probed it exhibits reduced priming. Thus, it is tempting to conclude that when you read a phrase like "no bread," you *first* think about bread (and its related concepts), and *then* you think about what the phrase actually communicates: the absence of bread.

However, that stage-like sequential way of conceptualizing the process could be misleading. It could just as well be the case that the negation concept and the bread concept become simultaneously active, and the negation concept gradually modifies the bread concept (via lateral connections) to instantiate it as referring not to the default sense of "the presence of bread" but instead to "the absence of bread." In this way, the bread concept cannot help but spread its initial activation to its associated neighbors that are nearby in semantic state space, simply because it takes some time for the negation concept to fully exert its inhibitory influence on the bread concept via a form of conceptual blending process (e.g., Coulson 2001; Fauconnier & Turner 2002).

A commonality can perhaps be found between our notion of a trajectory through state space and Fauconnier's (1994) mental spaces framework, where he suggests that negated statements set up alternative counterfactual spaces in which the positive version of the statement holds true (see also Mok, Bryant, & Feldman 2004). Here, and throughout this paper, factual simply implies converging with the actual state of affairs in the environment, while counterfactual implies *not* converging with the state of affairs in the environment. One can imagine a gradual instantiation of both of these *mental* spaces at the same time (affirmative and negative), as a sentence unfolds over time, i.e., "There are no cookies in the cupboard." Such a gradual formation of these two alternative mental spaces could be equivalently described as traversing in *state* space toward the midpoint of both the affirmative-statement region in space (where the cookies are in the cupboard) and the negated-statement region in space (where the cookies are not in the cupboard). If the state-space trajectory that embodies this time-dependent construction of the two mental spaces were to have a general graded bias toward the affirmative side of all such paired alternatives, then one would see exactly the tendency toward affirmation that is observed across a wide swath of the cognitive psychology literature (e.g., Clark & Chase 1972; Fiedler, Walther, Armbruster, Fay, & Naumann 1996; Johnson-Laird & Byrne 2002; McKinstry, Dale, & Spivey 2008; Wason 1961).

This description of a kind of *conceptual* ambiguity resolution shares some properties with the early lexical ambiguity resolution literature (e.g., Swinney 1979; Tabossi, Colombo, & Job 1987; Tanenhaus, Leiman, & Seidenberg 1979). In that early work, cross-modal priming tasks produced data suggesting that there might be an initial context-independent stage of word recognition (e.g., accessing both the noun and verb senses of "rose"), which is then followed by a second stage that performs the contextual integration (e.g., selecting only the verb sense of "rose," because it was preceded by "The man"). For example, if the word "bread" on its own can, in principle, be used to denote the presence or the absence of bread, then preceding it with the word "no" functions something like a context. Kawamoto's (1993) neural network simulation clearly demonstrated how a lexical ambiguity naturally activates its manifold meanings, and a preceding context will take some time to gradually dampen the contextually inappropriate meaning(s). Thus, one need not be forced to postulate a two-stage account of lexical or conceptual ambiguity resolution. The data may not require a first stage of processing that, upon hearing or reading a word, "accesses" a default set of context-independent representations (such as the two meanings of an ambiguous word, or the default (affirmative) version of a concept), and then a second stage that integrates context (such as semantic constraints that select one meaning of an ambiguous word, or logical constraints that negate the affirmative version of a concept). Kawamoto's model provides a compelling existence proof of how the trained associations between an input and its internal representations will automatically activate those representations when the input is received, and preceding (still active) context will just as automatically, *but not instantaneously*, modify those representations by inhibiting the inconsistent aspects and facilitating the consistent ones. In this scenario, despite there not being two separate stages of processing, there will always be some brief period of time during which certain contextually inappropriate aspects of the target input will nonetheless be partially active due to spreading activation, such as [petals] for "The man rose," [butter] for "no bread," and [eagle in the sky] for "The eagle was not in the sky."

4 Memory for Negated Sentences

In recent work, we have been exploring the degree to which this partial activation of the affirmative version of these very same negated statements can linger in memory and potentially supplant the correct information. We adapted twelve stimulus item pairs from Kaup et al. (2006b), and presented them to 290 participants at the University of California, Merced. Each critical sentence was preceded by a context such as "Jennifer didn't know where the airplane was. So she went to ask her friend". Then, the final sentence was negated or affirmative, as in "The airplane was (not) in the sky". Four items were presented to each person on paper, early in a packet containing other irrelevant tasks. After reading the four sentences, participants were instructed to remove and destroy that page of the packet. Later in the packet, visual depictions were presented of two contextual alternatives for each item, e.g., a line drawing of a plane flying (with motion lines) and another of a plane parked by a hangar. For each pair of images, participants were instructed to circle the one that corresponded to the original statement they had read.

When sentences were affirmative, participants circled the correct image 73% of the time. However, when the sentences were negated, participants circled the correct image only 59% of the time. This difference was robustly significant, t (283) = 4.9, p<.0001. Thus, more than 40% of the time, people were misremembering a negated statement as its affirmative counterpart. This observation shows that these kinds of negated sentences do much more than speed up reaction times to images of affirmative propositions. These negated sentences have a conspicuous habit of being confabulated into their affirmative propositions – reliably more so than vice versa.

If understanding negated sentences involves two-steps, an initial affirmative instantiation of the event followed by a formal negation of it (Kaup et al. 2007), then it would appear that sometimes that second step does not quite take effect. Alternatively, a trajectory through state space that already shares many locations (i.e., words) in common with a similar path could easily exhibit some graded uncertainty between these possible routes upon revisitation. Importantly, this trajectory account would not require an intermediate process, between the affirmative and negated stages, that employs a formal logical operation applied to an analog perceptual simulation. The state-space trajectories embody and implement the perceptual simulations, and the capacity for negation in such a system is an intrinsic part of the continuous dynamics endowed to it during its learning of how words like "no" and "not" are used. Determining whether the two-step account or the continuous-trajectory account better accommodates the data is our goal for current and future work.

5 Negation of Binary Alternatives

While it may be the case that negation is simply processed differently from the perceptual simulation generated by affirmative sentences (due to an extra stage of processing), perhaps the experimental materials of Kaup et al. (2006b) were not able to capture the perceptual simulation of the negation. Support for this possibility comes from research in verbal aspect. Madden and Zwaan (2003) set out to demonstrate that differences in verbal aspect produce processing differences in narrative reading. In one experiment, participants were asked to choose a picture of an event after reading a sentence containing either a simple past verb or a past progressive verb. They found that participants were more likely to choose a picture showing a completed action, rather than a picture showing intermediate action, after reading a sentence containing a simple past verb, but found no differences between pictures chosen when participants read a sentence containing a past progressive verb. Similarly, in a second experiment, participants were quicker to respond to pictures showing completed action after they had read a sentence containing a simple past verb than when they had read a sentence containing a past progressive verb. No such latency differences were found, however, when participants read sentences containing past progressive verbs and then saw pictures of intermediate action. Like affirmative and negated sentences, these results suggest that perhaps simple past verbs are comprehended through perceptual simulation and that comprehension of past progressive verbs are understood differently.

However, rather than embracing this alternative, Madden and Zwaan (2003) suggested that the lack of effect in the past progressive condition was due to different readers representing the ongoing action at various stages of completion. Simple past verbs place emphasis on the end state of the action, which typically corresponds to only a single state, while past progressive verbs place emphasis on the ongoing nature of the verb. With the past progressive, the participant may be simulating a number of locations. Madden and Zwaan suggested that this pattern of results indicates that different aspectual forms lead to subtle comprehension differences. (For related work, see Anderson, Matlock, Fausey, & Spivey 2008; Ferretti, Kutas, & McRae 2007; Magliano & Schleich 2000; Morrow 1985.) Therefore, even though the past progressive verbs are being perceptually simulated similarly to the way the simple past verbs are, the static picture that participants are asked to respond to simply does not match the particular point in the ongoing motion they are simulating.

By the same token, it may be the case that when participants hear or read a negated sentence, they do create a perceptual simulation of the negation, but the pictures they are asked to respond to do not capture well the perceptual simulation. Whereas an affirmative sentence in these experiments identifies a particular state for the noun that is responded to more quickly when presented visually, the negated sentences do not. For example, when "the eagle is in the air," its wings are necessarily open to accommodate flying. However, when "the eagle is not in the air," there are a number of different things it could be doing other than sitting with its wings folded. It could be walking on the ground, or standing and eating, etc. Therefore, when hearing a negated sentence of this sort, participants may be simulating the eagle in the air not because perceptual simulations are incapable of implementing negation on their own but instead because the alternative simulations are too numerous and too diffuse. If this is the case, then constraining the possible simulations to only two possibilities for a given object, one corresponding to the affirmative proposition and one to the negated proposition, should further inform this research.

Correspondingly, Kaup, Lüdtke, and Zwaan (2006a) investigated the way participants perceptually simulate sentences like those used in the earlier negation research (Kaup, et al. 2006b), but created materials that were binary, or had contradictory predicates, such as "The door was not closed." In Kaup, et al. (2006a), participants read these binary sentences in a self-paced reading paradigm, and then after a blank interval of either 750ms or 1500ms, they saw a picture of an object that they had to name as quickly as possible. In the 750ms delay condition, negated sentences followed by pictures matching the affirmative state of affairs or the negated state of affairs showed no difference in response latencies. At that point in time after reading the negated sentence, neither an affirmative perceptual simulation (of a closed door) nor a negated perceptual simulation (of an open door) was uniquely activated. By contrast, in the 1500ms delay condition, when the target sentence was negated, responses to pictures matching the actual (negated) state of affairs were significantly faster than pictures depicting the affirmative version of the proposition.

Thus, quite unlike the case with "The eagle was not in the sky" (Kaup et al. 2006b), it appears that participants did not show evidence of forming a uniquely activated perceptual simulation of the affirmative version of these negated binary-state sentences. Instead, they seemed to go directly to perceptually simulating the actual state of affairs (of an open door) after reading "The door was not closed." However, Kaup and colleagues (2006b) do not delve into the exact nature of the mechanism involved. Again, they make no speculation as to whether modal or amodal representations better accommodate these and earlier data (Kaup, et al., 2006a). In addition, it is puzzling that this effect was a bit late (obtaining only after 1500ms delay) compared to the affirmative sentences, which showed priming for their matching pictures in the 750ms delay condition. Moreover, it is worth noting that Kaup et al. (2006a) used a different method (picture naming) than Kaup et al. (2006b) used (sentence-picture verification).

6 One-Step Perceptual Simulations of Negated Sentences

In our own ongoing studies, we have been testing a set of binary-state sentences (similar to those of Kaup et al. 2006a) but with the original sentence-verification methodology used by Zwaan et al. (2002) and by Kaup et al. (2006b). Additionally, we used an intermediate interval of 1000ms, allowing us to test for evidence of a relatively early prominence of the perceptual simulation corresponding to the actual state of affairs, and not its erroneous affirmative version, after a negated sentence.

Thirty Cornell University undergraduates were part of in an experiment with sixteen target sentence pairs, such as "The coin is (not) heads up." Sixteen filler sentences, half of which were affirmative and half of which were negated, were also constructed. Two pictures were created for each target frame: a picture matching the affirmative proposition of the frame, and a picture matching the negation of that proposition. For example, for the sentence frame, "The coin is not heads up," the picture corresponding to the (affirmative) proposition would be a heads-up coin (see Figure 1a) and the picture corresponding to the negation would be a tails-up coin (see Figure 1b). All of the images were black and white ink drawings. All of the pictures were scanned onto the computer in the same size to control for discrepancies between the objects.

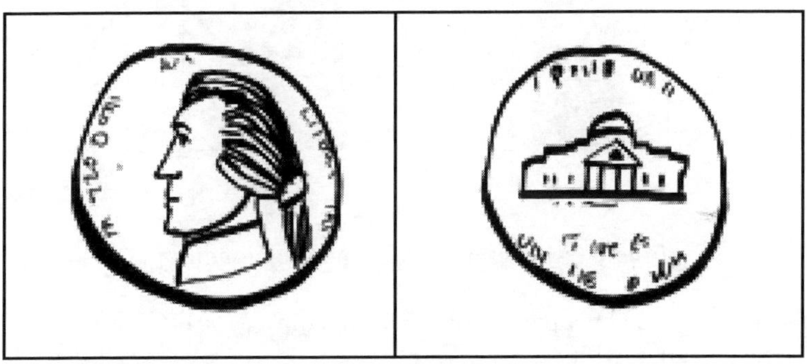

Figure 1: Example visual probes that would follow, "The coin is heads up," or "The coin is not heads up," respectively.

Participants first read a sentence located in the center of the screen. They pressed the spacebar when they had understood the sentence. A fixation cross appeared in the center of the screen for 1000ms, and then a picture appeared. Participants indicated whether the pictured object had been mentioned in the previous sentence by pressing a "yes" or a "no" button. The correct response to all experimental trials was "yes" because in every case the pictured object (whatever its state) was indeed mentioned in the preceding sentence. The correct response to all the filler trials was "no." To encourage attentive reading, half of the trials were followed by comprehension questions. There was a significant interaction of Sentence and Picture, $F(1,29)= 4.308$, $p<.047$. See Figure 2. With affirmative sentences, the non-negated proposition-based pictures (e.g., "The coin was heads up" followed by a picture of a heads-up coin) were responded to more quickly, M = 1245ms (SD = 85), than negated-propositional pictures ("The coin was

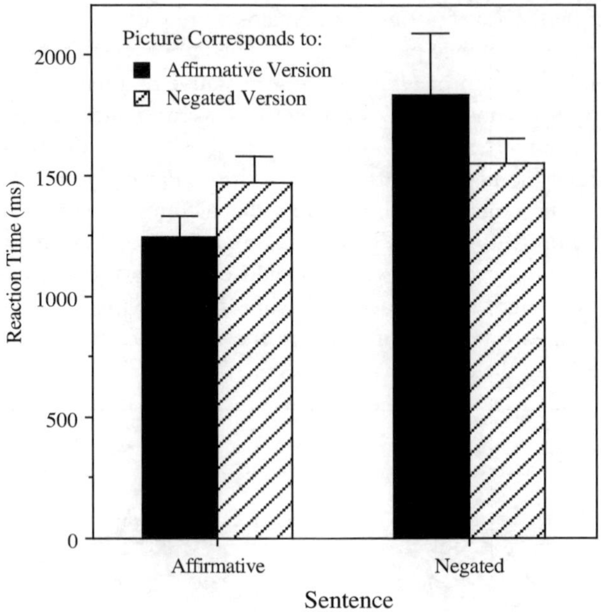

Figure 2: Reaction time values per condition.

heads up" followed by a picture of a tails up coin), M = 1467ms (SD = 113). These results align with earlier perceptual simulation research (Zwaan, et al. 2002). Additionally, negated sentences followed by negated propositional pictures ("The coin is not heads up" followed by a picture of a tails up coin) were responded to more quickly, M = 1550ms (SD = 100), than negated sentences followed by propositional pictures ("The coin is not heads up" followed by a picture of a heads up coin), M =1829ms (SD = 255). These results confirm the findings of Kaup et al. (2006a) with the statistical interaction that had previously been elusive. Crucially, they provide evidence suggesting that an early perceptual simulation of the appropriate state of affairs may be generated for negated sentences, as long as the negated property points to an alternative that is precisely defined, as it is in descriptions that have binary alternatives.

In examining the simple effects, the pictures following affirmative sentences, $M = 1467$ms ($SD = 619$), were responded to significantly faster than those following negated sentences, $M = 1245$ms ($SD = 465$); $t(29) = 2.08, p<.05$. This result is in keeping with earlier research, like that of Clark and Chase (1972) and McKinstry et al. (2008), indicating that affirmative sentences and events tend to be easier to comprehend than negated sentences. Indeed, it may be that extra bit of processing time for a negated sentence that is required in order to allow the appropriate perceptual simulation to rise to prominence – with the erroneous affirmative version competing but not necessarily occupying its own initial stage of processing.

7 General Discussion

Previous research suggests that negated propositions are processed differently from affirmative propositions. They seem to be more complex to comprehend and encode and also seem to have different impacts than affirmative proposition processing on more specific areas of cognition. In memory, considering a proposition that is initially falsified may lead to it later being recalled as an affirmative proposition (Fiedler, et al., 1996), suggesting that negation may be fragile in memory. The results of our own memory experiment here coincide with that conclusion.

The real-time comprehension of negated sentences may also involve processes accompanying the perceptual simulation that are different from those involved in affirmative sentences (Kaup, et al. 2006b). However, if a circumstance is constrained into binary alternatives, a perceptual simulation of the state of affairs denoted by a negated sentence may result (Kaup, et al., 2006a). Accordingly, our materials were designed to reflect *binary state* propositions. This way, affirmative and negated forms each referred to only one possibility. A statistical interaction of picture type with sentence type supports the hypothesis that perceptual simulations are used for comprehending these binary-state negated sentences, and may not need to go completely through an affirmative-version stage before being converted into depicting the actual state of affairs.

The findings reported here are promising for the development of a theory that allows embodied representations to perform their own negations themselves, as it were. For example, perhaps the words "no" and "not" can function as powerful contextual modifiers, quantitatively stronger than (but not qualitatively different from) other contextual modifiers such as adjectives and quantifiers. If so, then they can be learned in the state space of a neural network just like other words, and may be able to perform their negations of properties and events by diverting the trajectory through that state space in meaningful ways. This work will also need to address other forms of sentential negation. As Kaup (2001) notes, different forms of negation may be processed differently. For example, the sentence "The coin is not heads up" has a very different meaning than the sentence, "There is no heads up coin," even though both involve negation.

Simulations, and data visualizations, of this kind of process will be crucial if embodied accounts of language (Barsalou et al. 2007; Glenberg & Kaschak 2002; Spivey 2007) are to have a chance at describing sentence comprehension without having to resort to using rules and symbols for the tricky parts (Dale 2008; Louwerse 2008; Mahon & Caramazza 2008). Further experimentation, as well as computational simulations, will bring us to a clearer understanding of the cognitive processing involved in interpreting negation.

However, it is still unclear exactly what the mechanism is by which a negated sentence's initially counterfactual perceptual simulation (of the affirmative version of the sentence) gets converted into the factual perceptual simulation of the actual state of affairs denoted by the sentence (Kaup et al. 2006a). (Here again, factual refers to the convergence with the state of the environment, while counterfactual refers to non-convergence with the environment.) Explication of this mechanism is likely to require computational modeling. To this end, we have begun some preliminary explorations with a simple recurrent network (Elman 1990). In addition to the word-prediction relation between 91 input word-nodes to 91 output word-nodes, our model includes 63 perceptual features on the output layer that are prominent properties of the relevant perceptual simulations (see also Howell et al. 2005). Thus, combined with its learning to predict the next word in a sentence, this network also learns to activate the appropriate set of features for the perceptual simulation associated with the sentence. After training in this network model, the only difference between an affirmative sentence and a negated sentence is that the input from the negated sentence has the word "not" immediately preceding its critical adjective (e.g., flying, not flying, heads-up, not heads-up).

In its current incarnation, this model does not have sufficiently fine-grained temporal dynamics to exhibit the gradual transition (following the end of the sentence) from an initially counterfactual perceptual simulation of a negated sentence to a factual one (Kaup et al. 2007). However, already in these preliminary explorations of negated sentences, the model is exhibiting a form of "partial conversion" from the counterfactual perceptual simulation (as impelled by the critical adjective itself) toward the factual perceptual simulation (due to the word "not" acting as a context for that critical adjective). For example, Figure 3 shows the activation of the Face output node (for the heads side of a coin) and the Feathers output node (for the tails side of a coin), as "The coin is..." is fed into the network. Naturally, for "...heads-up," the Face node is .91 active and the Feathers node is .03 active; and vice versa for "...tails-up." However, things are less straightforward for the negated versions of those two sentences, as the contextual influence of the word "not" can only do so much. For the "...not heads-up" sentence, the Face node is appropriately reduced to .28 active, and the Feathers node is .63 active. Although the "...not tails-up" sentence is not as successfully inverted as that, it is definitely exhibiting substantial reduction of the Feathers feature due to the word "not." Further

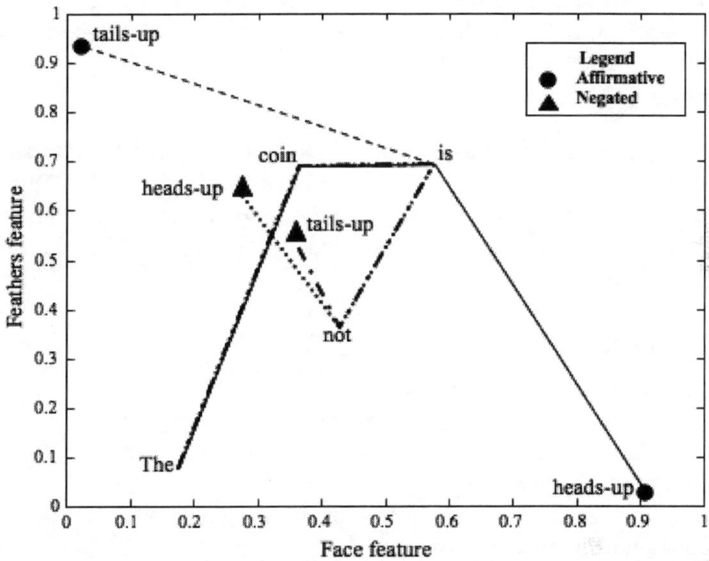

Figure 3: The perceptual simulation feature nodes for Face and for Feathers reveal the alternative trajectories for affirmative and negated sentences.

explorations with versions of this model may provide insight into how it is that an adjective like "flying" or "heads-up" cannot help but initiate some activation of its features, with a preceding "not" exerting a partial and/or gradual modification of that perceptual simulation.

Finally, rather than summarily accepting the position that "negation cannot be represented explicitly in a perceptual representation" (Kaup & Zwaan 2003, p.445), perhaps there is still some hope for a purely embodied account of negation that does not rely on a rule-based operation. Although a static image may not be able to explicitly represent negation, the change over time in a temporally dynamic perceptual simulation (implemented as a continuous trajectory through state space) may be able to represent negation for sentences like, "The were no cookies in the cupboard." Crucially, rather than a two-step sequence of static images, one that has the cookies in the cupboard and then one where they are gone, perhaps one can imagine a dynamic perceptual simulation where the cupboard is seen with a ghostly presence of cookies (as the sentence unfolds over time), and the cookies either then fade into nothingness (for the negated sentences) or then fully materialize (for the affirmative sentences). Moreover, that ghostly presence of the sentence's topic may have a subtle bias toward materialization rather than fading, and this might explain the general bias toward affirmation. In such a scenario, it is the derivative over time in this perceptual simulation (rather than any single freeze frame) that can explicitly represent negation.

Author Note

Sarah E. Anderson, Department of Psychology, Cornell University. Stephanie Huette, Teenie Matlock, and Michael J. Spivey, Cognitive Science Group, University of California, Merced. We are grateful to Simone Zuares for help with data collection. This work was supported by NSF grant BCS-0912496 to MJS.

References

Anderson, S. E., Matlock, T., Fausey, C., & Spivey, M.J. 2007. On the Path to Understanding On-line Processing of Grammatical Aspect. *Proceedings of the 30th Annual Conference of the Cognitive Science Society,* 143-148. Mahwah, NJ: Lawrence Erlbaum Associates.

Barres, P.E. & Johnson-Laird, P.N. 2003. On Imagining What Is True (And What Is False). *Thinking and Reasoning* 9:1-42.

Barsalou, L. W. 1999. Perceptual Symbol Systems. *Behavioral and Brain Sciences* 22:577-660.

Barsalou, L. W., Breazeal, C., & Smith, L. B. 2007. Cognition as Coordinated Non-Cognition. *Cognitive Processing* 8:79-91.

Bergen, B., Lindsay, S., Matlock, T., & Narayanan, S. 2007. Spatial and Linguistic Aspects of Visual Imagery in Sentence Comprehension. *Cognitive Science* 31:733-764.

Carpenter, P.A., & Just, M.A. 1975. Sentence Comprehension: A Psycholinguistic Processing Model of Verification. *Psychological Review* 82:45-73.

Chomsky, N. 1957. *Syntactic Structures*. The Hague: Mouton.

Clark, H.H., & Chase, W.G. 1972. On the Process of Comparing Sentences Against Pictures. *Cognitive Psychology* 3:472-517.

Coulson, S. 2001. *Semantic Leaps: Frame-shifting and Conceptual Blending in Meaning Construction*. Cambridge: Cambridge University Press.

Dale, R. 2008. The Possibility of a Pluralist Cognitive Science. *Journal of Experimental Theoretical Artificial Intelligence* 20:155-179.

Elman, J. L. 1990. Finding Structure in Time. *Cognitive Science* 14:179-211.

Elman, J. L. 2004. An Alternative View of the Mental Lexicon. *Trends in Cognitive Sciences* 8:301-306.

Fauconnier, G. 1994. *Mental Spaces*. New York: Cambridge University Press.

Fauconnier, G., & Turner, M. 2002. *The Way We Think: Conceptual Blending and the Mind's Hidden Complexities*. New York: Basic Books.

Ferretti, T. R., Kutas, M., McRae, K. 2007. Verb Aspect and the Activation of Event Knowledge in Semantic Memory. *Journal of Experimental Psychology: Learning, Memory, & Cognition* 33:182-196.

Fiedler, K., Walther, E., Armbruster, T., Fay, D., & Naumann, U. 1996. Do You Really Know What You Have Seen? Intrusion Errors and Presuppositions Effects on Constructive Memory. *Journal of Experimental Social Psychology* 32:484-511.

Fuhrmann Alpert, G., Hein, G., Tsai, N., Naumer, M. J., & Knight, R. T. 2008. Temporal Characteristics of Audiovisual Information Processing. *Journal of Neuroscience* 28: 5344-5349.

Gibbs, R. & O'Brien, J. 1990. Idioms and Mental Imagery: The Metaphorical Motivation for Idiomatic Meaning. *Cognition* 36:35-68.

Gibbs, R., Ström, L., & Spivey-Knowlton, M.J. 1997. Conceptual Metaphors in Mental Imagery for Proverbs. *Journal of Mental Imagery* 21: 83-110.

Gilbert, D. T. 1991. How Mental Systems Believe. *American Psychologist* 46:107-119.

Glenberg, A. M., & Kaschak, M. P. 2002. Grounding Language in Action. *Psychonomic Bulletin & Review* 9:558-565.

Grondelaers, S. Speelman, D. & Geeraerts, D. 2007. Lexical Variation and Change. *The Oxford Handbook of Cognitive Linguistics*, eds. D. Geeraerts & H. Cuyckens, 988-1011. Oxford: Oxford University Press.

Hasson, U., & Glucksberg, S. 2006. Does Understanding Negation Entail Affirmation? An Examination of Negated Metaphors. *Journal of Pragmatics* 38:1015-1032.

Howell, S. R., Jankowicz, D., & Becker, S. 2005. A Model of Grounded Language Acquisition: Sensorimotor Features Improve Lexical and Grammatical Learning. *Journal of Memory and Language* 53:258-276.

Johnson-Laird, P.N. & Byrne, R.M.J. 2002. Conditionals: A Theory of Meaning, Pragmatics, and Inference. *Psychological Review* 109:646-678

Kaup, B. 2001. Negation and Its Impact on the Accessibility of Text Information. *Memory & Cognition* 29:960-967.

Kaup, B., Zwaan, R.A., & Lüdke, J. 2007. The Experiential View of Language Comprehension. How is Negation Represented? *Higher Language Processes in the Brain*, eds. F. Schmalhofer, & C.A. Perfetti, 255-289. Mahwah, NJ: Erlbaum.

Kaup, B., Lüdtke, J., & Zwaan, R.A. 2006a. Processing Negated Sentences With Contradictory Predicates: Is a Door That Is Not Open Mentally Closed? *Journal of Pragmatics* 38:1033-1050.

Kaup, B., Yaxley, R.H., Madden, C.J., Zwaan, R.A., & Lüdtke, J. 2006b. Experiential Simulations of Negated Text Information. *The Quarterly Journal of Experimental Psychology* 60:976-990.

Kaup, B., & Zwaan, R.A. 2003. Effects of Negation and Situational Presence on the Accessibility of Text Information. *Journal of Experimental Psychology: Learning, Memory, and Cognition* 29:439-446.

Kawamoto, A. H. 1993. Nonlinear Dynamics in the Resolution of Lexical Ambiguity: A Parallel Distributed Processing Account. *Journal of Memory and Language* 32:474-516.

Kveraga, K., Ghuman, A. S., & Bar, M. 2007. Top-down Predictions in the Cognitive Brain. *Brain and Cognition* 65:145-168.

Langacker, R. W. 1987. *Foundations of Cognitive Grammar: Theoretical Prerequisites*. Stanford, CA: Stanford University Press.

Lakoff, G., & Johnson, M. 1980. *Metaphors We Live By*. Chicago, IL: University of Chicago Press.

Louwerse, M.M. 2008. Embodied Representations Are Encoded in Language. *Psychonomic Bulletin and Review* 15:838-844.

MacDonald, M.C., & Just, M.A. 1989. Changes in Activation Levels with Negation. *Journal of Experimental Psychology* 15:633-642.

Madden, C.J., & Zwann, R.A. 2003. How Does Verb Aspect Constrain Event Representations? *Memory & Cognition* 31:663-672.

Magliano, J.P., & Schleich, M.C. 2000. Verb Aspect and Situation Models. *Discourse Processes* 29:83-112.

Mahon, B.Z., & Caramazza, A. 2008. A Critical Look at the Embodied Cognition Hypothesis and A New Proposal for Grounding Conceptual Content. *Journal of Physiology - Paris* 102:59-70.

Marcus, G. F. 2001. *The Algebraic Mind: Integrating Connectionism and Cognitive Science*. Cambridge, MA: MIT Press.

Mayo, R., Schul, Y., & Burnstein, E. 2004. "I am not guilty" vs "I am innocent": Successful Negation May Depend on the Schema Used for Its Encoding. *Journal of Experimental Social Psychology* 40:433-449.

McKinstry, C., Dale, R., & Spivey, M.J. 2008. Action Dynamics Reveal Parallel Competition in Decision Making. *Psychological Science* 19:22-24.

Meteyard, L., Bahrami, B., & Vigliocco, G. 2007. Motion Detection and Motion Words: Language Affects Low-level Visual Perception. *Psychological Science* 18:1007-1013.

Mok, E., Bryant, J. & Feldman, J. A. 2004. Scaling Up to Mental Spaces. *Proceedings of the Second Workshop on Scalable Natural Language Understanding,* ed. R. Porzel, 41-48. East Stroudsburg, PA: Association for Computational Linguistics.

Morrow, D.G. 1985. Prominent Characters and Events Organize Narrative Understanding. *Journal of Memory and Language* 24:304-319.

Motter, B. C. 1993. Focal Attention Produces Spatially Selective Processing in Visual Cortical Areas V1, V2, and V4 in the Presence of Competing Stimuli. *Journal of Neurophysiology* 70:909-919.

Nazir, T.A., Boulenger, V., Roy, A., Silber, B., Jeannerod, M., and Paulignan, Y. 2007. Language-induced Motor Perturbations During the Execution of a Reaching Movement. *Journal of Cognitive Neuroscience* 18:1607-1615.

Pecher, D., & Zwaan, R. A. 2005. *Grounding Cognition: The Role of Perception and Action in Memory, Language, and Thinking*. Cambridge: Cambridge University Press.

Pinker, S. 1994. *The Language Instinct: The New Science of Language and Mind.* London: Penguin.

Pulvermüller, F. 1999. Words in the Brain's Language. *Behavioral and Brain Sciences* 22:253-279.

Pylyshyn, Z. W. 1980. Computation and Cognition: Issues in the Foundations of Cognitive Science. *Behavioral and Brain Sciences* 3:111-169.

Richardson, D. C., Spivey, M. J., Barsalou, L. W., & McRae, K. 2003. Spatial Representations Activated During Real-time Comprehension of Verbs. *Cognitive Science* 27:767-780.

Richardson, D., Spivey, M., Edelman, S., & Naples, A. 2001. "Language is Spatial": Experimental Evidence for Image Schemas of Concrete and Abstract Verbs. *Proceedings of the 23rd Annual Conference of the Cognitive Science Society*, 845-850. Mahwah, NJ: Erlbaum.

Spence, C. & Driver, J. (eds.) 2004. *Crossmodal Space and Crossmodal Attention.* Oxford: Oxford University Press.

Spivey, M. 2007. *The Continuity of Mind.* New York: Oxford University Press.

Sporns, O., Chialvo, D. R., Kaiser, M., & Hilgetag, C. C. 2004. Organization, Development and Function of Complex Brain Networks. *Trends in Cognitive Sciences* 8:418-425.

Swinney, D. 1979. Lexical Access During Sentence Comprehension: (Re)Consideration of Context Effects. *Journal of Verbal Learning and Verbal Behavior* 18:645-660.

Tabor, W. & Hutchins, S. 2000. Mapping the Syntax/Semantics Coastline. In *Proceedings of the 22nd Annual Conference of the Cognitive Science Society,* 511-516. Mahwah, NJ: Erlbaum.

Tabossi, P., Colombo, L. & Job, R. 1987. Accessing Lexical Ambiguity: Effects of Context and Dominance. *Psychological Research* 49:161-167.

Talmy, L. (2000). *Toward a Cognitive Semantics*. Cambridge, MA: MIT Press.

Tanenhaus, M.K., Leiman, J.M., & Seidenberg M.S. 1979. Evidence for Multiple Stages in the Processing of Ambiguous Words in Syntactic Contexts. *Journal of Verbal Learning and Verbal Behavior* 18:427-441.

Wason, P. C. 1961. Response to Affirmative and Negative Binary Statements. *British Journal of Psychology* 51:133-142.

Zwaan, R.A., Stanfield, R.A., & Yaxley R.H. 2002. Language Comprehenders Mentally Represent the Shape of Objects. *Psychological Science* 13:168-171.

2

Language-Mediated Thought in 'Plural' Action Perception

CALEB EVERETT

1 Introduction

In the past decade and a half, there has been a resurgence of research into the subject of linguistic relativity. This research has resulted in an impressive array of evidence demonstrating manners in which a speaker's thought patterns can be constrained by his or her native language. Such relativistic effects are often subtle, and do not necessarily buttress the strong version of linguistic relativity referred to by many as the Sapir-Whorf hypothesis, which was most famously delineated in Whorf (1956), but can be traced back in one form or another at least several centuries, in the work of Humboldt, Vico and Verner, among others. (Cf. Koerner 1992)

The recent resurgence of investigations into linguistic relativity has been guided by an experimentally-oriented approach to uncovering effects of language-mediated thought on cognition. The research is by necessity crosslinguistic in nature, and is also characterized by research foci that span a variety of semantic domains. Specifically, the work has sought to demonstrate that the ways in which a variety of semantic domains are reified in particular grammars have demonstrable effects on the performance of speakers of the relevant languages on non-linguistic tasks. For example, experimental evidence has demonstrated that language-specific categories of spatial topology may influence speakers' perception

Meaning, Form & Body.
Fey Parrill, Vera Tobin, and Mark Turner (eds.).

of the space around themselves and other referents, in a wide variety of languages (cf. Levinson and Wilkins 2006). Similarly, recent work on Amazonian languages has provided strong empirical evidence for linguistic relativity in the domain of mathematics (cf. Gordon 2004 and Pica et al. 2004). To cite another example, Konishi (1993) presents evidence for effects of grammatical gender categories on speakers' perception of certain objects. Even the semantic domain of color words, which was once thought to reflect cognitive universals that vitiated some of the central tenets of linguistic relativity, has been re-analyzed with novel experimental methodologies, and these studies are strongly consistent with some form of language-mediated thought. (Davidoff et al. 1999, Gilbert et al. 2006) For a more detailed survey of some of the basic areas of inquiry in the recent linguistic relativity literature, I refer the reader to Boroditsky (2003).

One area that has received little attention in the current literature is event classification. Given the centrality of verb classification and argument structure to grammar, and given that the attention of humans naturally gravitates towards dynamic actions/events and the concomitant agents of such events (see e.g. Robertson and Suci 1980), one could argue that it is particularly interesting to consider whether there is evidence for language-mediated effects on event perception. Put another way, any demonstrable language-mediated influences on something as basic as event perception would arguably be particularly noteworthy, since such effects could not be claimed to be marginal or tangential to the core of cognitive and linguistic processing. Recent work (Bohnemeyer et al. 2007) on the semantic typology of motion events has demonstrated that there is a remarkable variety of strategies of perceptual segmentation of motion events evident in crosslinguistic data. Other work has systematically investigated the cross-linguistic differences in the ways in which events of cutting and breaking are coded linguistically (Majid et al. 2007). Such studies are consistent with the existence of different patterns of event construal reified in grammars, but do not explicitly support linguistic relativity since they do not provide evidence of linguistic influences on speakers' performances in non-linguistic tasks. Boroditsky (2001) provides convincing evidence that disparate temporal metaphors employed in English and Mandarin affect the perception of time, and consequentially of events, by speakers of these languages. While her study strongly supports the case for language-mediated thought, however, it relates to *event* perception in a rather oblique fashion.

The pilot study described below seeks to make inroads into the investigation of linguistic relativity in a very restricted and little-studied semantic distinction in an Amazonian language. Despite the limited distribution of the distinction in question, I would like to suggest that it is a potential source for demarcating a clear case of language-mediated thought in the broader domain of action or event perception. The ultimate purpose of the study is to provide preliminary evidence for linguistically-based differentiations in the patterns of event construal across two subject populations. The existence of such patterns is consistent with the hypothesis that the construal and discrimination of events may be affected in subtle ways by language-mediated thought, and suggests the need for future work seeking to uncover language-mediated influences on action perception.

More specifically, the preliminary work described below is concerned with uncovering differences in the perception between 'plural' actions and 'singular' actions, via subjects' participation in a brief triad discrimination task. These subjects included native speakers of two unrelated languages, Brazilian Portuguese and Karitiâna. The latter language does not mark nominal number distinctions via common means such as verb agreement and noun inflections. Significantly, however, Karitiâna distinguishes between 'plural' verbs and 'singular' verbs in the case of a number of frequently described actions, as described in 3. The goal of the study is to try to determine whether the categorization of certain verbs as 'plural' verbs in Karitiâna leads speakers of the language to perceive certain actions differently (when contrasted with Portuguese speakers' perceptions), depending on the number of participants involved in a given action. In other words, for Karitiâna subjects, are certain 'plural' actions conceptually discriminated, vis-à-vis non-'plural' actions, in a way that they are not by Portuguese subjects?

I should note from the outset that the work described below represents the initial portion of an inchoative and ongoing investigation, and is taken to be representative of future work on the subject. While the results provided in 5 are highly suggestive of a particular form of linguistic relativity in the domain of event perception, they require replication. Furthermore, the methods described below are currently being refined and extended, as described in section 6, in order to provide a more complete delineation of the relevant sort of linguistic relativity.

2 Overview of 'plural' actions

Prior to discussing the relevant data collected in the field, it is worth providing background on the semantic domain of action number, since it is both rare and easily conflatable with another semantic domain, namely that of nominal number. Nominal number is a category that exists in most languages in one form or another, and is frequently indexed through a plural affix on nouns. However, it may also be indexed through plural/singular agreement marking inflected on a verb form. For example, consider the following Portuguese clause:

1.	Os	jogador-es	morrer-am.
	Def.masc.plural	player-plural	die-Past.3rd plural agreement
	'The players died.'		

In this case, we see that there is a plural subject. The plurality of this subject is indexed in a variety of different ways, on all three words in the clause. The article chosen reflects both gender and number, while the subject itself is inflected with a plural suffix. Finally, the verb agrees in number via a number/person suffix. Crucially, however, despite the fact that the verb inflects for number, it is the number of the noun that is being indexed. This sort of nominal number is of course common typologically.

As has been noted in the literature (Durie 1986, Corbett 2000), however, a number of languages also reveal a distinct semantic category of 'verbal' number. Verbal number is fairly widespread in North American languages (cf. Mithun 1988a), but is also found in Semitic, Khoisan, and Dravidian languages. It is also evident in a few Papuan and Amazonian languages.

Corbett (2000:243-264) posits a further distinction within the larger category of verbal number. Some languages, he notes, distinguish between verbs that are singular and others that are plural, and the latter forms are generally understood to represent repeated occurrences of a particular action. This sort of 'event' verbal number, or pluractionality, is evident in the following contrasted clauses from Chadic:

2a.	naa	aikee	su
	I	send	them

2b.	naa	a''aikee	su
	I	send.plural	them

In 2a, only one event of sending is denoted, while in 2b the speaker implies that more than one event of sending occurred.

A second type of verbal number is evident in language, however, and it is this second type that we are concerned with here. This type is termed 'participant' verbal number by Corbett. In languages in which this distinction surfaces, two different verbs may be employed to describe an action that is denoted with one verb in most languages. In languages with participant verbal number, however, the choice of verb depends on whether one or more participants are involved in the given action. Superficially, this distinction may appear similar to the nominal number distinction indexed on certain irregular verb pairs in languages like English (e.g. *S/he is* vs. *they are*). However, there is a clear *verbal* semantic distinction in the relevant cases, so that the verb used with a number of participants is conceived of as a different action altogether, when contrasted with the verb used when only one participant is involved in the depicted action/event.

One clear illustration of such a distinction is evident in Klamath (Mithun 1988a:214-215). As an example of the participant verbal number distinction in this language, consider that there are four words for 'give'. These include *l*^{v}*oy*, 'to give a round object,', *n*^{e}*oy*, 'to give a flat object,' and *k*^{s}*voy*, 'to give a live object.' Crucially, however, they also include *ʃ/ewan/*, 'to give several objects,' and this latter verb is employed whether the objects in question are live, inanimate, round, or flat. Corbett (2000:248) notes that the latter verb 'illustrates clearly that some verbs require objects of particular types, and that being numerous is just one of these possible types.' As Mithun (1988a) notes, the purpose of forms such as *ʃ/ewan/* is not simply to enumerate entities, as in the case of verbal agreement with a plural argument, but to quantify in a more central way the effect of particular actions or events.

Cases of participant verbal plurality typically entail a completely different lexical root than their singular counterparts, and are *not* inflected forms of other verbs. This is evidenced by the fact that verbs with plural participant number may not even have a singular counterpart. For instance, consider the English verb *scatter*. This verb is employed when a number of participants are departing a particular scene with some alacrity (or when one participant disperses multiple participants). It is unclear what the singular variant of *scatter* might be. The same might be said for the verb form of *stampede*. In fact, such words are arguably instances of participant verbal number in English.

While participant verbal number is less common than event verbal number (i.e. pluractionality), it does surfaces in languages such as Huichol, Ainu, Karok, Mikasuki, and, as we will illustrate shortly, Karitiâna. In most of these cases, however, participant verbal number surfaces for only a handful of verbs, since the distinction is not part of a broader number agreement paradigm, but reflects altogether different ways of categorizing particular events according to whether they necessarily involve one or many participants.

3 Lack of number inflection Karitiâna

Karitiâna is a Tupí language spoken natively by approximately 300 people in the state of Rondônia, Brazil. It has been described in a number of recent works, including Storto (1999) and Everett (2006, 2008, forthcoming a). These studies have sought to describe a number of typologically-remarkable features of the language, most significantly the remarkable variety of surface nasal forms in the language. Everett (2006) also describes basic patterns of voice and grammatical relations in the split-ergative language. What we are concerned with here, however, is the status of number marking in the language. In general, nominal number marking is absent in the language. For example, there is one third-person pronoun, which is ambiguous for number[1]:

3. i na-okɨ-t i
3 NSAP[2]-kill-NFUT 3
'S/he/they killed him/her/them.'

First person and second person pronouns do evince a number distinction, as we see in the following example with a 2nd person plural pronoun:

4. a:tʃa na-okɨ-t i
2PL NSAP-kill-NFUT him/her
'You all killed him/her.'

Significantly, however, non-anaphoric NPs do not inflect for number. Furthermore, verbs do not agree in number with their argument NPs. These facts are evident in clauses such as the following, which allow for any of the four readings in the absence of discourse-contextual cues:

5. ɲõnso naka-mĩ:-t taso
woman NSAP-hit-NFUT man
'The woman hit the man.' 'The woman hit the men.'
'The women hit the man.' 'The women hit the men.'

---

1 This pronoun is also ambiguous for gender and case. Other pronouns do reflect grammatical relations in subtle ways (cf. Everett 2006), though all pronouns in the language are ambiguous for gender.

2 Morpheme abbreviations: NSAP: Non-speech-act-participant, used when the absolutive argument of a verb is a 3rd person referent. NFUT: Nonfuture tense. INT: Intransitive verb root. PROG: Progressive aspect. S: Singular. PL: Plural. AL: Allative.

6. õmbakɨ na-okɨ-t borotɨ
jaguar NSAP-kill-NFUT paca
'The jaguar killed the paca.' 'The jaguar killed the pacas.'
'The jaguars killed the paca.' 'The jaguars killed the pacas.'

7. õmbakɨ naka-ɨ:-t epe o
jaguar NSAP-eat-NFUT tree round.thing
'The jaguar ate the fruit.' 'The jaguar ate the fruits.'
'The jaguars ate the fruit.' 'The jaguars ate the fruits.'

Karitiâna does have a robust set of numerals and quantifiers, however, and these may be used post-nominally to modify a given noun. However, as we see in 8 in such cases the head of the NP remains uninflected.

8. taso otadnamɨ̃n na-ohi:t-Ø
man four NSAP-fish-NFUT
'Four men fished.'

Data such as these demonstrate that number marking is generally absent in the language. There are no singular, dual, or plural inflections on nouns, and verbs do not generally agree with nouns in terms of number. There are some unusual exceptions to this latter tendency, however, namely cases in which verb aspect suffixes must agree with the singular or plural status of an NP. Progressive aspect suffixes in Karitiâna may be optionally attached to the verb. These aspect suffixes also reflect the posture and number of any animate (human or otherwise) absolutive argument of the verb[3]. Consider the following example of a clause with a verb inflected for progressive aspect:

9. õmbakɨ i-pɨtʔɨ-**tɨso/tɨ̃so/tɨ̃ka**-t
jaguar INT-eat-PROG.SG-NFUT
'The jaguar is eating.' (Standing, seated, or active, respectively)

Clause 9 is understood to denote a situation in which one and only one jaguar is eating an unspecified animal (for this reason an intransitive form of the verb 'eat' is used). If more than one jaguar is involved in the eating of

[3] The five progressive aspect markers that also conflate number and posture semantics are evident in 9-10b. They are discussed in greater detail in Landin (1984:229-230) and Everett (2006:277-279). Their relevance here is restricted to their role in marking absolutive number agreement.

a given animal, then the same verb is inflected with a different progressive marker, which also varies according to the posture of the jaguars:

10a.	õmbakɨ	i-pɨtʔɨ-**tɨsɨp**-Ø
	jaguar	INT-eat-PROG.PL-NFUT
	'The jaguars are eating.' (Laying down, inactive)	

10b.	õmbakɨ	i-pɨtʔɨ-**ŋgi**-Ø
	jaguar	INT-eat-PROG.PL-NFUT
	'The jaguars are eating.' (Standing, active)	

In clauses 9-10b, we see that there is a weak form of number agreement in Karitiâna. However, this agreement is non-obligatory, and in cases such as 11 in which the progressive marking is absent the number of the absolutive argument is not retrievable apart from context.

11.	õmbakɨ	i-pɨtʔɨ-t
	jaguar	INT-eat- NFUT
	'The jaguar(s) is/are eating.'	

This section has served to demonstrate that, with the exception of the non-obligatory number agreement conflated with aspectual and body-posture semantics, number inflection is generally absent in Karitiâna morphology. Clauses with semantically singular NPs typically have the same form as clauses with semantically plural NPs. Of course, in most cases in discourse, the number of the participants involved is resolved by contextual/referential cues, or alternatively by quantifiers or numerals (cf. Everett 2006:315). Nevertheless, the grammar of the language itself has fairly limited means of expressing number distinctions, and the means available do not include any sort of nominal inflection. Despite the general absence of nominal number in Karitiâna, however, there are several clear cases of 'participant' verbal number, as outlined in the following section.

4 'Plural' verbs in Karitiâna

There are at least five common verb pairs in Karitiâna that reflect differences in participant verbal number. There may be other such pairs in the language, however the five pairs in question, described below, are the only examples I am familiar with at present that unambiguously instantiate the phenomenon under investigation here. Crucially, these verb pairs refer to very basic actions and are extremely frequent in recorded transcriptions of discourse. There is also evidence for event verbal number or pluractionality in the language, particularly in certain reduplicated forms (cf. Müller and Shanchez 2008), though such pluractionality is fairly limited in scope. Event verbal number lies outside the present locus of attention, however.

What we are interested in are verb pairs such as that evident in 12a and 12b, in which entirely different lexical roots are employed in order to describe the same basic event types (at least to English speakers), which differ in terms of the number of participants entailed.

12a. ɲõnso naka-tat-Ø o:pok akan pip
woman NSAP-go-NFUT white.people village AL
'The woman went to the city.'

12b. ɲõnso naka-hot-Ø o:pok akan pip
woman NSAP-go.PL-NFUT white.people village AL
'The women went to the city.'

While it may be tempting to analyze the verb form in 12b as an irregular plural version of the form in 12a, such an analysis seems specious in the light of the fact that there is no verb agreement for number in Karitiâna, apart from the idiosyncratic progressive/body posture suffix set. The fact is that Karitiâna grammar treats the events in 12a and 12b as different events altogether (a conclusion buttressed by the preliminary experimental data in 5). The same can be said of the verb pair in 13a and 13b, as well as that in 14a and 14b, respectively.

13a. õwã, ĩnã i-pɨkɨna-Ø hiɾinã
child small/short INT-run-NFUT fast
'The short child ran fast.'

13b. õwã, ĩnã i-piʔoɾot-Ø hiɾinã
child short INT-run.PL-NFUT fast
'The short children ran fast.'

14a. ɨ-ta-ɨɾɨt-Ø ɨ̃n
1S.ABS-SAP-come-NFUT 1S
'I came/arrived.'

14b. ɨj-ta-mbɨkɨt-Ø ɨ:tʃa
1PL.ABS-SAP-come.PL-NFUT 1PL
'We came/arrived.'

In 13a and 13b, we see that entirely different verbs are used to denote scenes in which there is one participant, or in which there are multiple participants, running. (This might be analogous to a case in English in which we described one cow running, or cattle stampeding.) In 14a and 14b, we see once again that the English verb for 'coming' has more than one corresponding verb in Karitiâna, depending on the number of participants involved in the depicted action.

There are at least two other frequent verb pairs in Karitiâna that appear to reflect participant verbal number. There are two verbs for 'flying', *tãm* and *tẽŋ*. The former verb is used in those cases in which one event participant is flying, while the latter verb is used when there is more than one participant flying. Interestingly, however, the verb *tẽŋ* also implies something akin to scattering, i.e. it is a verb that is used for instance if a number of bats disperse together from a cave. Such semantic connotations also support the conclusion that verb pairs such as *tãm* and *tẽŋ* do not simply differ according to number agreement. Instead, they have different semantic connotations, involving primarily (but not entirely) differences in participant verbal number.

The final verb pair that I have examined in depth, which appears to reflect a participant number distinction, involves two verbs glossed in English as 'taking', *o:t* and *pi:t*. The former verb is used in cases in which someone is taking one thing, while the latter verb is used in cases in which someone is taking several things. Crucially, the latter verb does not denote serial occurrences of taking. Instead, it is employed if one person takes for example an entire stalk of bananas. The former verb would be used if a person were taking only one banana. The semantic distinction involved in this pair is perhaps fairly intuitive, since there are many things that are often taken in groups (e.g. grapes, papers, beads) while other things are typically taken individually (e.g. a bow, a pan, a tapir).

In the following section I present some preliminary experimental data related to these verb pairs, towards the aim of demonstrating that actions and events denoted by such verbs are discriminated/perceived differently by Karitiâna speakers, when contrasted to speakers of Portuguese, even in non-linguistic contexts. The data focus on the verb pairs evident in 12-14, as well as the two verbs for flying mentioned above. The verb pair denoting events of taking is not considered further, since for the purposes of this initial study I restricted my attention to intransitive verbs.[4]

Recall that the ultimate purpose of investigating the events denoted by the verb pairs described in this section is to learn whether any language-influences on event discrimination surface in non-linguistic tasks. The evidence of such influences would provide evidence for some sort of linguistic relativity in the domain of action perception. As was mentioned above, while there is growing evidence of linguistic relativity in the literature, only a fragment of this evidence impinges on the dynamic processes of action perception.

5 Pilot study: methods and results

In this section I describe a pilot study, along with its suggestive results. There are several ways in which the methods used in the pilot study are being extended and developed for experimental work to be carried out in the near future. These methodological refinements are discussed in section 6.

In order to test whether the presence of participant verbal number in Karitiâna affects the non-linguistic construal of relevant events, a series of abstract non-linguistic stimuli were designed. These stimuli consisted of four sets of three drawings each. Each set of drawings related to a particular event type that is clearly associated with a frequent verb pair in Karitiâna instantiating the phenomenon of participant verbal number. The four relevant verb pairs in question are described in the preceding section, and correspond roughly to the English verbs 'to go', 'to come/arrive', 'to fly', and 'to run'.

The stimuli were designed in order to fit the general methods of a triad-discrimination task. In other words, for each set of three drawings, two drawings differed according to two parameters. In this case, the two parameters were number of participants and type of participants. For example, as we see in figure 1, the drawing on the left depicts three human-like participants arriving at a building, while the drawing on the right depicts a situation in which a four-legged animal arrives at the building. These two drawings differ in terms of participant number and participant type, then. The middle drawing of the set differs from the drawing on the left according to participant number, and differs from the drawing on the right in terms of participant type. For this reason, this and the other three sets of drawings in figures 2-4 were utilized in the action discrimination

[4] Given that all of the verbs examined here were intransitive, it is unclear if or how Karitiâna speakers perceptions of object plurality are influenced by verbal number in the language.

task. In the case of each set of drawings, participants could in principle group the middle drawing with either of the two remaining drawings, depending on the discrimination strategy employed. The expectation was that, for these sets of stimuli, Karitiâna speakers might group the drawings according to participant number more frequently than Portuguese speakers. This expectation is plausibly motivated by our understanding of the specifically-relevant categories of participant verbal number in Karitiâna. For example, in the case of the drawings in figure 1, the events with one participant but different participant types could potentially be described with the same verb (evident in 14a above), while a description of the scene with more than one participant would require a separate verb entirely (evident in 14b above). Analogous reasoning would apply to the drawings in figure 2 (see 12a and 12b above), figure 3 (see discussion of verbs for 'flying' in Karitiâna above), and figure 4 (see 13a and 13b above).

Figure 1. Stimuli for first triad discrimination task.

Fourteen native Portuguese speakers and eight Karitiâna speakers participated in this preliminary study. The study was undertaken in the city of Porto Velho, Brazil, in May of 2008. A number of other speakers have agreed to participate in a more extensive series of follow-up experiments in the summer of 2009.

The discrimination task proceeded as follows. Subjects were tested individually with the four basic triads, which were presented in randomized order. For each triad, the subjects were presented with the three drawings, each of which was scaled to fit a normal printer-size paper. The drawings were laid out on a desk in front of each subject, in the manner in which they are presented in figures 1-4 (though the order of the top two drawings was randomized). Subjects were told that, while the drawings themselves were static, they represented scenes in which certain figures were moving in the direction of the arrow (if present). The subjects were asked to take the middle drawing, which could be categorized with one of the other two drawings depending on discrimination strategy chosen, and place it with the drawing that most closely resembled the scene of the middle drawing. After the subjects made their decision, they were presented with the next set of three drawings. Subjects were asked to make their decisions silently and as rapidly as possible.

Figure 2. Stimuli for second triad discrimination task.

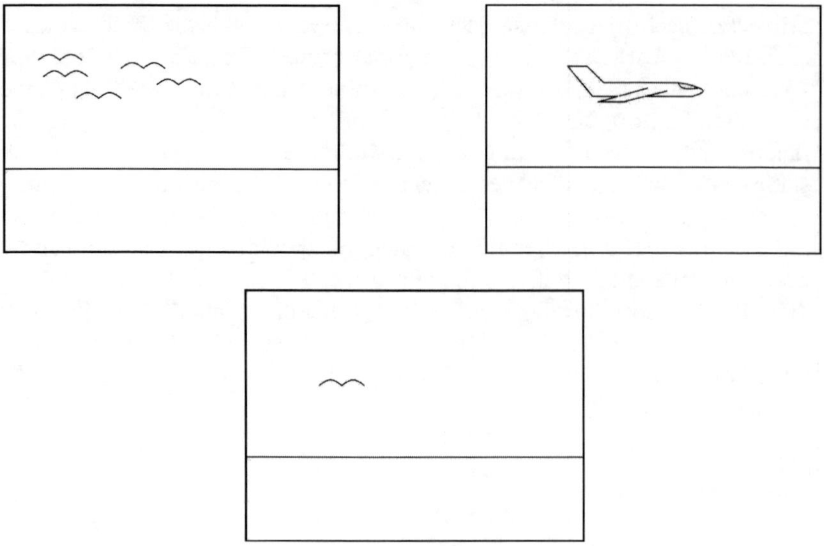

Figure 3. Stimuli for third triad discrimination task.

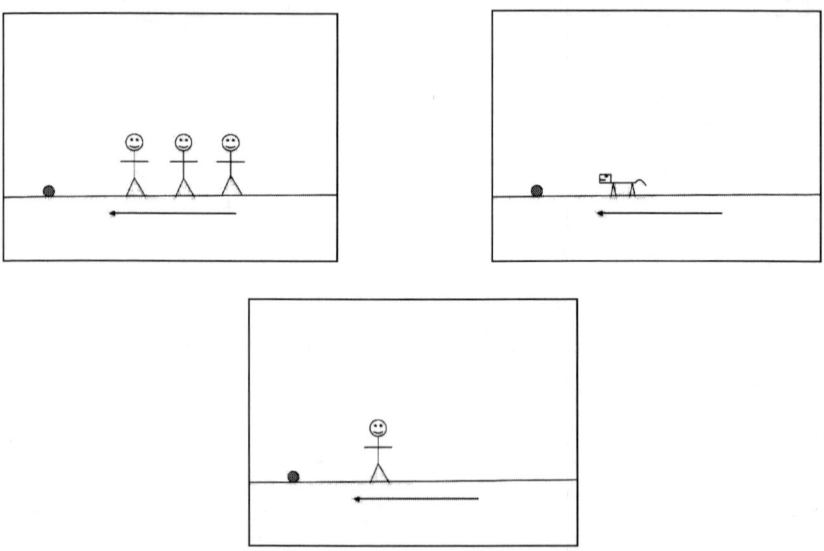

Figure 4. Stimuli for fourth triad discrimination task.

It is also worth noting that all subjects were instructed in Portuguese. While all of the Karitiâna-speaking subjects spoke Karitiâna natively as a first language, they were also able to communicate in Portuguese, with varying degrees of fluency. The purpose of providing instructions in Portuguese, and to asking subjects to carry out the task silently, was to avoid overt linguistic influences on the task. For example, if Karitiâna speaking subjects described the drawings in Figure 1 out loud, they might quickly realize that there is a greater phonological resemblance between the verbs used to describe the middle drawing and the drawing on the right. This phonological resemblance could then be used in order to complete the task, but would tell us little about any more general perceptual discrimination patterns associated with action perception. (See Boroditsky 2001 for similar comments.)[5] Given that the tasks were not conducted in Karitiâna, and that subjects were asked to remain silent and perform each task quickly, we can be somewhat confident that any patterns in the data are the result of general discrimination strategies.

The subjects generally required less than five seconds for each discrimination task, and this was true of both pools of subjects. After the author provided the subjects with brief instructions and when it was clear to the subjects that they were to group the two depictions that were most similar over all, the tasks were completed. It should also be noted that the tasks were conducted after the subjects had assisted the author with a lengthier series of tasks for unrelated studies on acoustic phonetics (Everett 2008, Everett forthcoming b).

As we see in table 1, the overall results of this preliminary study of action perception in Karitiâna are remarkably consistent with a relativistic sort of account. Specifically, we see that the eight Karitiâna speakers generally employed the strategy in which they grouped event depictions according to the number of participants in a given drawing. The converse generally held for the fourteen Portuguese speakers who participated in the study. The crosslinguistic differences were significant. The differences surfaced for all four sets of drawings.

---

[5] One reviewer correctly points out that employing Portuguese in the instructions could have resulted in some sort of contact effect of Portuguese on the Karitiâna subjects. If so, however, this would result in a greater similarity between the results of the two subject populations, and would weaken rather than strengthen any relativistic claims.

Table 1. Response rates according to discrimination strategy.

	Number of participants	Type of participants
Portuguese	18 (32%)	38 (68%)
K	26 (81%)	6 (19%)

Fisher's exact test, $p<0.001$

To be clear, the data in table 1 suggest that Karitiâna speakers tended to group the middle drawings in figures 1-4 with the drawings that depicted scenes with different actor types but with the same number (one) of actors. Put differently, Karitiâna speakers tended to construe the actions depicted in the left-most drawings in figures 1-4 as though they were most distinct from the remaining two drawings. This is most likely due, I would argue, to the fact that the events depicted in these left-most drawings are in each case potentially represented with a completely distinct Karitiâna verb that denotes a different participant verbal number. In other words, the events in these drawings are perceived as entirely different events, when contrasted with the other events. This conclusion is supported by the data from the Portuguese speakers, who do not have distinct verbs denoting such 'plural' events, and also more frequently grouped the middle drawings in figures 1-4 with the left-most drawings in these figures. (Recall however that in the actual stimuli the order of the top drawings was randomized.) The Portuguese speakers typically rely on participant type to discriminate the three drawings, apparently since in Portuguese the events depicted in the three drawings of each respective triad could be described via the same verb.

6 Discussion of follow-up study

The results of the task described in section 5, as well as the linguistic data for Karitiâna described in 3 and 4, are generally consistent with an interpretation under which a certain typologically-unusual linguistic category, namely participant verbal number, affects the way in which Karitiâna speakers construe particular actions. While the results in 5 are suggestive, however, they are of course very preliminary at this point. The study described above requires replication, extension, and methodological refinement before stronger conclusions on the matter can be made.

One way in which this study will be improved upon in a follow-up study, scheduled for July 2009, is via the implementation of a broader range of stimuli. The stimuli in figures 1-4 are obviously static in nature, and were designed in the field. A series of real-life images and videos will be implemented in the follow-up studies. Subjects will be presented with video triads, including videos of humans (both Karitiâna and non-Karitiâna) performing certain actions, and will once again be asked to discriminate stimuli in order to test whether perceptual patterns such as that described in section 5 surface in the perception of more dynamic data. Dozens of such stimuli involving an assortment of action participant types in a number of different contexts are presently being developed.

Furthermore, the follow-up study will include a wider assortment of static stimuli such as those in figures 1-4. Crucially, these will include depictions of actions that are unrelated to the four above actions described via 'plural' verbs in Karitiâna. As Paul Kay (personal communication) notes, the relativistic interpretation of the data in section 5 would be further buttressed if there were evidence that Karitiâna speakers group stimuli related to non-'plural' verbs in a different manner than the way in which they group the above stimuli related to 'plural' verbs. Under the present interpretation of the data it would be surprising if they do not, given that number plays such a minor role in Karitiâna grammar. This issue nevertheless merits further attention, since the prediction is that the attention to number for speakers of this language is dependent on whether a 'plural' verb is employable in the depiction of a given event.

The stimuli currently being developed for the more comprehensive study also include triad pairs that vary inversely according to the animacy of the relevant stimuli. As one anonymous reviewer insightfully notes, participant animacy may influence discrimination strategies in different ways across subject populations. One way to control for this will be to have a triad analogous to that in figure 4, along with another triad that is reversed according to animacy, i.e. the stimuli with plural participants (similar to the top-left drawing of figure 4) would contain non-human referents. Such triads could help to tease apart possible animacy effects on discrimination patterns. While there is no clear linguistic or cultural motivation for suspecting that Karitiâna and Portuguese speakers are influenced in different ways by participant animacy, such factors should nevertheless be controlled for.

Finally, the study will be improved by utilizing a second control population of English speakers, along with a pool of Portuguese speakers. If the action discrimination patterns evident in the responses of Karitiâna speakers differ significantly from those of the English and Portuguese speakers, but the latter two groups do not differ significantly from each other, the relativistic interpretation will be further supported.

7 Conclusion

It is worth stressing that, while the findings presented in section 5 are admittedly tentative and will soon be investigated in greater detail, they are remarkably consistent with a relativistic interpretation.

Participant verbal number of the sort described above is interesting in and of itself. It is unusual typologically, and its presence in Karitiâna is particularly interesting in the light of the fact that Karitiâna grammar generally ignores nominal number, whether in verbal agreement or nominal inflection patterns. Participant verbal number is perhaps most interesting, however, because it is an area that allows us to test fairly specific predictions made by a relativistic approach to perceptual discrimination. As described above, recent crosslinguistic studies related to a wide variety of semantic domains have suggested strongly that the language one speaks affects their construal of the world around them in a variety of subliminal yet pervasive ways. Most of the recent literature, however, relates to speakers' discriminations and construal of relatively static facets of perception, i.e. non-actions. There is relatively little work on possible relativistic effects on the perceptions of actions. Furthermore, the general focus of this study, the perception of 'plural' actions in languages with participant event number, is unattested in the literature. Perhaps future work on Karitiâna, as described in the preceding section, and future work on other languages with similar patterns of event number will provide us with a new inroad into the investigation of relativistic phenomena. Ultimately, the little-known linguistic phenomenon described in this paper may serve as a fecund source for novel inquiries into the role of language-mediated thought in the domain of action perception.

Author note

Caleb Everett is an assistant professor of anthropological linguistics at the University of Miami.

References

Bohnemeyer, Jürgen, Nicholas Enfield, James Essegbey, Iraide Ibarrentxe-Antunano, Sotaro Kita, Friederike Lüpke, and Felix Ameka. 2007. Principles of event segmentation in language: The case of motion events. *Language* 83:495-532.

Boroditsky, Lera. 2001. Does language shape thought?: Mandarin and English speakers' conceptions of time. *Cognitive Psychology* 43:1-22.

Boroditsky, Lera. 2003. Linguistic relativity. In Nadel L, (Ed.) *Encyclopedia of Cognitive Science*, 917-921. MacMillan Press: London.

Corbett, Greville. 2000. *Number*. Cambridge: Cambridge University Press.

Davidoff, Jules, Ian Davies and Debi Roberson. 1999. Colour categories in a stone-age tribe. *Nature* 398: 203-204.

Durie, Mark. 1986. The grammaticization of number as a verbal category. *Berkeley Linguistic Society*, 12:355-370.

Everett, Caleb. 2006. Patterns in Karitiâna : Articulation, perception, and grammar. Houston: Rice University PhD dissertation.

Everett, Caleb. 2008. Locus equation analysis as a tool for linguistic fieldwork. *Language Documentation and Conservation* 2:185-211.

Everett, Caleb. Forthcoming a. Negation and the untransitive category in Karitiâna. *Proceedings of the 35th Annual Meeting of the Berkeley Linguistic Society*.

Everett, Caleb. Forthcoming b. Aspects of Tupí-Karitiâna vowels. *Anthropological Linguistics*.

Gilbert, Aubrey, Terry Regier, Paul Kay and Richard Ivry. 2006. Whorf hypothesis is supported in the right visual field but not the left. *Proceedings of the National Academy of Sciences of the United States of America* 103.2:489-494.

Gordon, Peter. 2004. Numerical cognition without words: evidence from Amazonia. *Science* 306:496-499.

Koerner, E.F. Konrad. 1992. The Sapir-Whorf hypothesis: A preliminary history and bibliographical essay. *Journal of Linguistic Anthropology* 2:173-198.

Konishi, Toshi. 1993. The semantics of grammatical gender: A cross-cultural study. *Journal of Psycholinguistic Research* 22:519-534.

Landin, David. 1984. An outline of the syntactic structure of Karitiana sentences. In R. Dooley (Ed.) *Estudos Sobre Linguas Tupi do Brasil*. Brasilia: SIL.

Levinson, Steven and David Wilkins, eds. 2006. *Grammars of Space*. Cambridge: Cambridge University Press.

Majid, Asifa, Melissa Bowerman, Miriam Van Staden and James Boster. 2007. The semantic categories of cutting and breaking events: A crosslinguistic perspective. *Cognitive Linguistics* 18:133-152.

Mithun, Marianne. 1988a. Lexical categories and the evolution of number marking. In M. Hammond and M. Noonan (Eds.) *Theoretical Morphology*, 211-234. New York: Academic Press.

Müller, Ana and Luciana Sanchez-Mendes. 2008. Pluractionality in Karitiana. *Proceedings of SuB12, Oslo*, 442-454.

Pica, Pierre, Lemer, Cathy, Izard, Veronique & Dehaene, Stanislas. 2004. Exact and approximate arithmetic in an Amazonian indigene group. *Science* 306: 499-503.

Robertson, S.S. and G.J. Suci. 1980. Event perception in children in early stages of language production. *Child Development* 51.

Storto, Luciana. 1999. Aspects of a Karitiâna Grammar. Boston: Massachusetts Institute of Technology PhD dissertation.

Whorf, B. L. 1956. *Language, Thought and Reality: selected writings of Benjamin Lee Whorf*, ed. J.B. Carrol. Cambridge, MA: The MIT Press. Bloomfield, L. 1933. *Language*. New York: Holt.

3

A Multimodal Analysis of Individuals' Beliefs and Metaphors in Words, Gestures and Drawings

VITO EVOLA

People cross-culturally claim to have various types of spiritual or religious experiences: visions of God or the Virgin Mary, of angels and saints, voices and presences that somehow guide and inform, sensations of being at one with the world. Other people have less sensational experiences, like the sense of 'knowing' that there is an afterlife, of 'feeling' that they are constantly at a cross-road where they must choose 'good' over 'evil'. And then there are others still, who deny the possibility of a Superior Transcendental Being, and nonetheless are in a society where gods and demons, heavens and hells surround them indirectly through those who—expressly or not—are 'believers'.

If religion was once relegated as a problem for theologians, now, with science more than ever bringing us closer to the outskirts of the universe and deeper in the cells of humans, the very fact that people should even believe in such 'other-worldly' concepts may seem a contradiction or evidence of common 'ignorance'. Nonetheless religion plays such a crucial role even in the lives of many scientists. For believers there is no conflict, and people cross-culturally, as we will see, make certain contradictions 'fit' in their belief system and are cognitively capable of making sense of visions, auditory hallucinations, or of other 'worlds'. Religion, and culture in general, is not a ready-made social product; it is a process in which the individual actively participates. As Forman (1999: 39) has noticed, Constructivists have argued that mystical experiences are a sort of 'reconditioning of conscious-

Form, Meaning, and Body.
Fey Parrill, Vera Tobin, and Mark Turner (eds.).

ness', that the concepts proposed by religious systems condition *a priori* a believer's experience, but the description of phenomenological experiences in religion, and most likely elsewhere in culture, is contingent and not necessary. Although, for example, a religious system may propose a metaphor such as GOD IS A FATHER, I will provide clues which indicate that this becomes just one conceptual slot or role whose values are filled in by the interpreters (for example 'vengeful' vs. 'loving'), more according to people's dynamic interaction with their world than just passively via culture.

This chapter does not want to tackle problems regarding religion per se. Although I will describe some conceptual phenomena dealing with spiritual and religious experiences in believers, the focus is on abstract thought and how it is conceptualized, manifested, and communicated by humans and the relationship between language and abstract thought, like religious ideas and spiritual experiences. Abstract concepts differ from other concepts 'out there in the world' for the very fact that what is abstract is something that cannot be immediately perceived in a physical sense. What happens when people talk about something they have never experienced through bodily perceptions, like abstract ideas of GOD, HEAVEN, GOOD and EVIL? How are these concepts construed in the minds of the individuals and their collectivity?

After justifying my object of inquiry, I will provide the motivations behind the choice of anthropomorphized metaphors for God in Hebrew and Christian Scriptures, which represent Divine authority for these believers. I will then present data from a series of interviews with two Christians, a street-preacher and a mission house-mother,[1] and analyze how my informants interpret these metaphors and represent others multimodally in their speech, gestures and artwork. Before concluding, I will investigate incongruities and incompatibilities of some metaphors with my informants' conceptual systems, which are not caused by religious culture (both are Christians), but because of the individual's personal knowledge of how the world works.

The metaphors used by my informants indicate that the language used in religious discourse is experientially based on their encyclopedic knowl-

---

[1] I appreciate one of my anonymous reviewers' pointing out that these sources of data are very different to what is more generally found in the metaphor studies literature in that they are not traditional, common Christians: 'The examples we see there almost always come from sources that are high in social and cultural capital: published prose and poetry, the spoken discourse of university students, and the introspection of researchers. Even those studies that do go against this trend (for example, Núñez and Sweetser's work on Aymara) deal in unmarked, mainstream usages across an entire language. The interviewees in this study are both operating in less secure sociological spaces, and their discourse communities and semiotic frameworks intersect with but are not fully ratified by institutional structures.'

edge of their own personal worlds and stimulated by cultural constructs only up to a certain point. Some of these metaphors are based on universal properties of the human conceptual system, others are more culturally based, but all of them heavily depend on the way these people interact with their own worlds. For this very reason some believers' ways of reasoning, almost impossible for others even of the same religious system, have an internal logic serving to manage what may appear to some as real-world contradictions.

To be sure my object of study is spiritual experiences and concepts, but the focus is more on the semiotic, the cognitive, and the social, with language and multimodal communication being the manifestation of these concepts. The framework I use is what I have dubbed 'Multimodal Cognitive Semiotics' (Evola 2009), which intends to emphasize certain aspects of the semiotic process which often go unaddressed, in particular the role of social context in the hermeneutic process, drawing from more recent tendencies within the Cognitive Linguistics community which appreciate communication as part of a broader socio-cultural system and not as something to be studied in isolation. In truth Multimodal Cognitive Semiotics is nothing new per se, but it intends to approach language and communication more broadly according to both production- and interpretation-oriented processes which are inherent to the symbolic mode of relationship, by combining traditional semiotics with contemporary methods from Cognitive Linguistics and other human and social sciences (*inter alia* Bourdieu 1990; Brandt & Brandt 2005; Clark 1996; De Certeau 1984; Fauconnier & Turner 2002; Goodman 1978; Goodwin & Duranti 1992; Hanks 1995; Kendon 2004; Kockelman 2005; Lakoff & Johnson 1999; McNeill 1992; Peirce 1955; Tomasello 2001). Moreover this framework takes into account the affordances and limitations of the various modes used in linguistic and non-linguistic representation. In this perspective meaning emerges from an individual's practice (Bourdieu 1990) within the immediate or the more ambient context, where that particular meaning is interpretable *because of* the context, which includes the individuals' personal experiences and encyclopedic knowledge of the world. Thus, meaning is not something that resides in the world, but phenomenologically meaning is construed by a sign-agent's interaction with the world as he or she knows it. Moreover, a semiotic sign may include various layers of meaning, which become relevantly salient during the interpretational process, which of course depend on context as well. To apply a metaphor of my own, semiotics and hermeneutics are two sides of the same door of meaning, and context is the key.

1 Why might descriptions of spiritual experiences be of interest to linguistics?

But why even use spiritual experiences as an object of cognitive and linguistic inquiry? The reply is two-fold.

Spiritual experiences are *similar* to all other human experiences: Each and every experience is lived through the body, whether it is reading words on a page or having a divine vision. These experiences are based on concepts and categories, which bridge the mind and the world, and are constructed by our interaction with and encyclopedic knowledge of the world (Rosch 1999). Many scholars from Merleau-Ponty (1945) on would agree that perception of any type is not passive reception of data, but an action-oriented restructuring of the world. As subjects we have a continuing identity of ourselves, and memory plays an important role by reconstructing past events on our present context and not simply by retrieving data stored like a computer might do. This continuous reconstructing of past experiences gives way to coherence and plausibility in our narratives, relating them to future plans and goals, creating a 'narrative self' (cf. Flanagan 2002; Turner 1996). In this sense cognitive sciences see the self, or the person, as an ecological system, a multileveled psychosomatic unity (Murphy 1999), and the framework I use here maintains that because both human persons and their environment are constantly changing, conceptual integration (Fauconnier & Turner 2002) must be a continual and dynamic process. Each experience, whether it is meeting a friendly face for the first time or having an epiphany of what you should be doing in a given situation, is never experienced if not relationally and contextually, because as humans we embody all our experiences, including the most abstract.

However, spiritual experiences are *different* from other experiences: Within spiritual experiences, what 'appears' paradoxically is often different from what really 'is', yet people have a sense of great conviction, to use the term following William James (1902), most likely because of the way the narrative self works. Intuitively spiritual, mystical or religious experiences do seem to have a different quality from other 'secular' experiences. The effects of visions, revelations and divine encounters often have great impact on the persons experiencing them, both psychologically and socially (Evola 2005). Usually there is a sense of self (awareness), cognition (revelation, knowledge) and emotions. People change their lifestyles because they undergo a revelation, and the effects often endure time (something that otherwise only happens because of some physical or directly social causation, like a trauma). Subjects often describe these experiences as objectively real; likewise, more 'intense' experiences are considered 'ineffable': People in fact use metaphors to communicate and represent these experiences, albeit with a sense of insufficiency.

My definition here of a spiritual experience is any phenomenon which can be interpretable in relation to the transcendent, for example feeling the presence of God in one's everyday life or having visions. I present relative data of believers who claim to have had various types of spiritual experiences, and there is no reason to believe that their accounts regarding their system of beliefs are not sincere. As the anthropologist de Certeau (1984: 178; emphasis his) wrote, 'As a first approximation, I define "belief" not as the object of believing (a dogma, a program, etc.) but as the subject's investment in a proposition, the *act* of saying it and considering it as true.'

2 Metaphors We Pray By

DesCamp and Sweetser (2005) analyze a total of 44 metaphors from the Hebrew scriptures and 50 from the Christian scriptures, for example GOD IS A FATHER, GOD IS A SHEPHERD, A ROCK, and so forth. Their analysis points towards relational metaphors between God and humans, for example Father-child, Lord-servant, and so on, which show 'a two-way, loving relationship, with asymmetric power but symmetric love' (p. 233).

Elsewhere I have claimed that one very pervasive conceptual metaphor of the Bible is the blend GOD IS A LOVER (Evola 2004). This metaphor permeates the *Šîr Haššîrîm*, or the *Song of Songs*, as well as Psalm 45. In this metaphor, God and devotee are seen as LOVER and BELOVED, and there is complete symmetry, even if illusionary or temporal for the devotee, to the point that the devotee, because of his or her experience of mystical union, can profess 'I am God.' What is interesting about the *Song of Songs* is that God is never mentioned once, which is probably why this metaphor was not taken into consideration in the aforementioned essay; yet, at least as far back as Rabbi Akiba in the 2nd century, this book was already traditionally seen as an allegory of the love of God, and many saintly figures have used this conceptual metaphor to talk about the Divine Love and Mystical Union (for instance the Spanish mystics Teresa de Ávila and Juan de la Cruz). The same conceptual metaphor manifests itself in other theistic religious systems such as Judaism, Islam and Hinduism and is arguably a typological literary universal (cf. Hogan 2005).

This does not mean that this particular metaphor is acceptable or conceptually present for all devotees. In the following pages I will present some evidence for the fact that each individual believer has a 'preferred' way of representing God, motivated by their own life experiences and the degree of authority attributed to their sources (cf. Evola 2005). But it does seem rather surprising that eroticism should be used to talk about God at all. This is not platonic love: it is the typical language used in the poetry of passion, where the beloved lusts for the kisses and caresses of the lover, fearing separation, giving up one's own family and social dignity to be forever with the lover. In fact there is a whole genre of mystical literature, cross-culturally, which is based on erotic metaphors, and many consider these writings as examples of great expression, not only of poetry, but also of devotion.

One could argue that one contradiction is the fact that a religious system, whose laws concerning sexuality are so rigorous and whose punishments are so harsh, would even admit more or less explicit descriptions of those same acts to talk about the Sublime. In fact, believers should not even talk about God and the Divine in terms of a human source domain. After all they could employ other non-anthropomorphic domains, like clothing or mechanical objects, especially when for so many religious systems[2] it is a sin to represent God, and even more so as a human. The reasons lie in human cognition.

Divine agency is very often seen in terms of the most complex object that humans knows of, and that is themselves. The cognitive system of humans automatically infers many operations to avoid an overload on itself, and it recruits information from all its resources. '[A] lot happens beneath that Cartesian stage, in a mental basement that we can describe only with the tools of cognitive sciences' (Boyer 2001: 18). People know a lot about themselves, much more than other things in the world, and human beings become the easiest source for information to produce inferences. One might say that God was created in man's image, and it is an anthropological universal that supernatural beings are considered to have a mind (*ibid.*: 143-144), and this places man much closer to the Divine than to the animal on the Great Chain of Beings.

A human-like God is nonetheless, in Justin Barrett's words, 'theologically correct' (1999). Devotees of Eastern or Western religious systems would say that God has a lot of human-like qualities. For Christians the Divine became human by taking on the flesh of Jesus of Nazareth, or for Hindus by becoming an avatar like Krishna. Yet one must agree that these 'humanized gods' are not quite *like* other humans (in fact one of the ways the God is often described is through the *via negativa*, or the path of negation). The God presented in the Bible or the Qur'an has a mighty hand, and His eyes see everything, but these are metaphors of His omnipotence and His omniscience. In a way devotees must juggle with two different mental spaces (Fauconnier & Turner 2002): one is a human-God, to which they can

[2] Some variants of Abrahamic religious systems (e.g. Islam, Judaism) strictly forbid making images of God, and some (e.g. Amish and Mennonites) even prohibit images of any living creature, based the teachings of *Exodus* 20: 4.

relate; the other, which builds on the first, is a supernatural-God, far more different from what they can ever imagine. Muslims are warned that God is beyond anything one might devise by the way of concept or definition: a concept which is half way between the *via remotionis* and literalists' anthropomorphism (Bausani 1980: 16-17), and this could be considered true also by other religious systems. Although God has revealed Himself in and through the Holy Word in human language, the devotee constantly shifts between knowing and not being able to know. Devotees, thus, are 'capable of God',[3] being able to understand this Transcendental Idea, despite His infinite qualities, but only in terms of humanity and considering Him as one of themselves, albeit the Ultimate Perfection of Humanity.

Since the case studies I present here are of Christians, I focus my attention on Christian and Biblical language, which nonetheless is analogous in many regards to the language used by other theistic religious systems. People choose to represent God based on tradition (or authority), but also on the individuals' knowledge and experience of themselves and their world. A group of people, like the Inuit, who had never seen sheep in their everyday arctic world could never have understood the metaphor GOD IS A SHEPHERD, which is why the first missionaries translating the Bible substituted it with GOD IS A REINDEER HERDER, and what gets sacrificed is not the Lamb of God, but the White Seal Pup of God (Douglas-Fairhurst 2002: 283).

3 GOOD IS UP/BAD IS DOWN

The most pervasive metaphor in moral, religious and spiritual thought and representation in my data is GOOD IS UP/BAD IS DOWN, which is an extension of the MORE IS UP/LESS IS DOWN image schema. Humans have all experienced this fundamental image schema since infancy: whenever there is more water in a glass the level goes up, or when one stacks things in a pile, the more things get stacked up, the higher the pile gets. In most Western cultures there is also the idea that MORE IS BETTER, thus GOOD IS UP. Ancient Romans, for example, would give thumbs up or down to approve or disapprove. Indeed the GOD IS GOOD metaphor (and therefore UP) is probably the most profuse and consistent one in my data cross-modally. 'Our Father' is up in the heavens, and people who have had out of body experiences say they see things while in this peaceful state from 'hovering above' the real world. Most people deictically point 'up' in reference to God, and 'down' for the devil, and in Paul's Letter to the Corinthians he admonishes, 'let him

---

[3] Bonaventure (*Comm. Quat. Libr. Sent.* I, 3, II) cites Augustine of Hippo, '*Eo mens est imago Dei, quo capax Dei est et particeps esse potest.* – The more the mind is an image of God, the more it is capable of ('able to fit') God and able to participate in Him' (*De Trin.* XIV, 11).

Figures 1a & 1b: “Draw yourself” (left) and “Draw God” (right): Although the person drawing wanted to replicate the same drawing (a dot in the center of the page), “God” was placed in a higher space compared to “self”, unintentionally representing the GO(O)D IS UP metaphor.

who thinks he stands take heed lest he fall’ (*1 Cor* 10: 12). Medieval European architects played with this conceptual metaphor, in that the architecture of Gothic churches included slender, pointy rooftops. The church, first as a building and then metonymically extended to those who pray in it, is the *locus* where the faithful go to ‘lift’ their souls to ‘reach the heavens’.

In my research, this metaphor of GOOD IS UP in one way or another was consistently used in speech, gesture and the drawings. For example, even when drawing Paradise (which would already be an ‘up’ space), people would draw God in the upper part of their pictures, and almost always to the right, following another conceptual metaphor GOOD IS RIGHT/BAD IS LEFT as described in Casasanto (in press).

This metaphor is present also in non-linguistic representation. For example, consider the drawing of one informant when I asked him to draw a picture of himself (Fig. 1a), and compare this to his drawing of God (Fig. 1b), which is analogous, but drawn in a slightly higher position, although his aim as he told me was to replicate the exact same drawing.

This is sound evidence that as with any type of experience, common or less common, people’s perception is always embodied. Indeed, people maintain their *habitus* (in a Bourdieuian sense), through which society and culture is impressed on the individual, not only in mental habits, but even more corporeal ones, including gesture as I will describe below.

4 The MORAL ACCOUNTING metaphor

Lakoff and Johnson (1999) contends that much of our moral reasoning is rooted in metaphors, among which the MORAL ACCOUNTING metaphor. Our knowledge of ACCOUNTING is laminated onto the metaphor WELL-BEING IS WEALTH (so, for example, one might say that a millionaire who loses his family is a ‘poor guy’). This is conceptu-

Figure 2: Edward’s vision of paradise

ally at the basis of the Catholic notion of indulgences and of many representations of paradise: You pray somewhere or do something so to get into heaven more readily.

In one of my case studies, I asked my informant, Edward, to draw his vision of Paradise (Fig. 2). Edward is a self-proclaimed 'street preacher' who calls himself an 'apostle of Christ'. In summary, he was mapping onto his vision of the afterlife all the commodities he did not have in this world by conceptualizing WELL-BEING as WEALTH. In his drawing, his 'piece of paradise' included a house on a piece of land, with a river and waterfalls near it. What is particularly interesting is that in his drawing the house was for him and his wife (even though in this world he does not even have a girlfriend), and his house has a chimney and a garage nearby where to keep his 'many cars'. His view of paradise is made of the projection of a wealthy and stable life on earth, but transposed in paradise.

In April, 2008, police raided the compound of a Mormon sect in Texas, seizing more than 400 children. A news article[4] reported that the mothers opened up to the media after a week, trying to convince authorities to have their children back. A Mormon studies expert testifying in favor of the Mormons said in an interview, 'To really enjoy heaven, you have to be married and you have to have your kids with you. Everything experienced on Earth will be in its more perfected form in heaven.' This is the same metaphoric concept, which for the Mormon mothers is more than just metaphoric. Getting their children back was not simply for maternity's sake, but for eternity's sake.

Following this reasoning, just like on earth you have to earn your way to have a home, the same can be said about paradise. By doing morally positive actions in this world or, like Edward says, 'doing the right thing', he would be repaid, and his earthly suffering is a sort of investment for the afterlife.

This metaphor is generally pervasive in religious reasoning, for example when Christians say that 'Jesus Christ died on the Cross to pay our *debt* of sin.' For Eastern belief systems, keeping account of the individual's moral actions is the way that Karma is maintained, and this concept is present in many other religious systems: there is an investment and a payback, if you do something good, something good will happen back.

Within certain Christian Charismatic and Pentacostal traditions, a teaching dubbed 'Prosperity theology' is preached, adhering to the idea that an authentic religious belief and behavior in a person will result in their material prosperity. Through prayer and by giving a tithe to the church, God will

---

[4] McLaughlin, E.C. 2008. "Experts: Sect opens up to retrieve children, hasten heaven" *CNN*. (April 28) http://www.cnn.com/2008/CRIME/04/28/flds.openness/index.html

repay ten-, if not hundred-fold. The promise is that God will make a way for the poor to be happy, which often equates to financial stability. One YouTube video[5] shows Prosperity preacher Rev. Creflo Dollar of Atlanta, Georgia, who follows the charismatic way of preaching typical of the Bible Belt, addressing his congregants, 'I cames here to get this message <u>to</u> you / I came here to bring you somethin' / that's gonna deliver you outta this <financial bondage> / I came here to get you somethin' / that's gonna step you outta where you are right now, / and you'll <u>never</u> be the same again!'[6]

Returning back to Edward, what exactly is 'doing the right thing' for him? In Figure 3 is what he says about it in his own words and with a gesture analysis (see transcription legend, *infra* §8). For Edward, people have

Figure 3: Edward and Judgment Value Polarity in Co-Speech Gestures

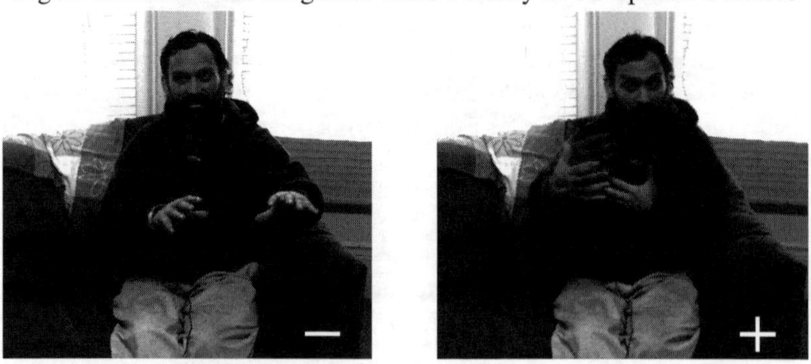

Edward: The right thing (00:26:50 – 00:27:02)

1. Well / to put a short / ah: short story together it's just
2. where people choose [and do THIS /][a]
3. in ah words [peop- other people tryin' to do / ↑ THE [RIGHT] THING /][b]
4. so ><u>e::verybody's</u>< [over here doin' %grunt-"THIS" / the <u>devil</u> thing][c]

[a,c] **'This/The devil thing' (NEGATIVE)**	[b] **'The right thing' (POSITIVE)**
Downward	Upward ('do the [RIGHT] thing')
Outward palms (exclusion)	Inward palms (inclusion)
Centrifugal	Centripetal

[5] From http://www.youtube.com/watch?v=VMSRjgzBrxc.

[6] Beyond the fascinating conceptual blend of 'financial bondage' (the Bible only refers to 'spiritual bondage'), I wish to underline the sociological implications behind the usage of the MORAL ACCOUNTABILITY metaphor. As Jonathan Watson has noticed this metaphor encourages congregants who got dicey mortgages to believe 'Well, it was thanks to God that the bank ignored my credit score, and God blessed me with my first house.' The results, he says, are 'disastrous, because [these preachers] pretty much turned parishioners into prey for greedy brokers.' In Van Biema, D. 2008. "Foreclosures: Did God Want You to Get That Mortgage?" *Time* (October 03) http://www.time.com/time/printout/0,8816,1847053,00.html

to choose to do 'the right thing' or 'the devil thing'. His co-speech gestures reveal much more than what he says. In this extract, it is interesting to notice how he embodies the metaphor GOOD IS UP/BAD IS DOWN, especially on the word 'right' when his right hand jerks upward. The 'the devil thing' is not the right thing, so it is excluded and put to the side, whereas he includes himself in 'right thing'.

The gesture Edward makes when talking about 'the right thing' is in a metonymic relationship with other instances of the same gesture throughout our interview. At times it may seem a little idiosyncratic, but it is not if considered part of a system which includes his language practice and his beliefs. His gesture is as if he is holding something, and in fact the first time he performs this gesture was in reference to the Bible almost three minutes into the interview. In Table 1 is a list of Edward's metaphoric/metonymic extensions of his 'Bible gesture'. Semiotically speaking, the sign is the same, but what it represents differs, thus giving rise to a 'polysemic gesture'.

Table 1: Metonymic and metaphoric extensions of Edward's 'Bible gesture'

- The Bible (indefinite object)
- A Bible, i.e. a particular edition (definite object)
- The books of the Bible (partonomy)
- Reading the Bible (embodied action)
- 'This is the way the world works'
- A spiritual guide, the 'something more' he was looking for in his life
- The 'right thing' to be taught and learned
- Prayer/praying
- Christ

The first time he performs this 'Bible gesture', less than three minutes into the interview, he uses it four times in 33 seconds all with different 'meanings'. Moreover, when he talks about prayer, he is using the MORAL ACCOUNTING schema.

Edward: Performing the first Bible gestures (00:02:57 – 00:03:30)

1. I was [reading the Bible] I need somethin' more so I figured [this is it] /
   Embodiment of action **Deixis**
2. 'n then / ya know / the Bible thing was: where*/
3. ya know i' was a* ya know
4. you have to get the [right books so they got like] /
   Partonomy
5. ya know so many different books you gotta find the right book
6. so it was like struggle 'n then /
7. *Now do you think prayer is important?*

8. ↑ Yeah /
9. *Ok, why?*
10. Cuz it always does something for you /
11. So what I found out is / if you don't pra:y
12. somebody's not gonna be looking out for you /
13. so [if you pray /] the:n they're gonna hear the prayer
Prayer
14. and they're gonna be lookin' around 'n doin' something for you

This network of associations—Bible, prayer, Jesus, 'the right thing', 'the way the world works', 'the something more'—may seem obvious, but this is only because they are so entrenched in the conceptual systems of many Westerners. However they are contingent, and not necessary. They are fruit of Edward's experiences and interaction with *his* own world. Indeed non-Christians would deny these associations, and perhaps even some other Christians might wish to argue with them. What is interesting, though, is that Edward did not manifest these associations either consciously or intentionally, rather his gestures provided a backdoor to Edward's conceptual system by embodying his system of phenomena and beliefs.

5 One God, Two Fathers: STRICT FATHER VS. NURTURING PARENT

I will now concentrate on one fundamental metaphor in Christianity, which is GOD IS A FATHER, and how this metaphor plays out in two of my interviewees.

We have already met Edward, so let me present an older lady who goes by the name of 'Mama'. Mama is an African-American lady 'over 60' who runs a mission for the homeless. Her mother was not present from early on, and she talks about her father, a very large man, who liked to drink and who had many wives and other families. Even so, her father was very nurturing, and she loved him very much. When he died, she was alone and homeless, and she started stealing, doing drugs, and being sexually promiscuous. Nonetheless, she always felt the presence of God in her life, guiding and protecting her.

For Mama, God is like a father, and in many ways like her real father. As a matter of fact, every time but once during our interview when Mama discussed God using fatherly terms, she then mentioned her own father shortly after, sometimes without rhyme or reason. This could simply indicate that when she thinks and talks in terms of this metaphor, her source domain is saliently present. For example in the following extract Mama talks about how as a youth, she and her friends had been doing drugs and were driving along a bridge. All of a sudden she yelled to stop the car, and luckily she did otherwise they were going to die, but she did not know what made her scream 'stop.'

Mama: Mentioning her father (00:14:18 – 00:14:29)

1. and then I realized that it was somebody bigger than me. /
2. ↓ Cause I thought that I was biggest, ya know? /
3. my father was big, ya know? /
4. 'n the::n [...]

In this other excerpt, Mama confesses how she was ready to stop doing drugs, so she abandoned herself to God. Notice she mentions three things that were everything for her: at one point it was her father, then it was being a drug addict (like her father), and finally now, God the Father is her everything.

Mama: The only thing I got (00:16:10 – 00:16:40)

1. ↓I prayed to <God I know I'm doin' wro::ng> #
2. 'n I know gyou don't want me to u:se dru:gs #
3. ↑and I actually I really don't want to use 'em either #
4. but Father $^{(2.5)}$ I'm tired / it's the only thing I got #
5. but I didn't know He: was the only thing I really had #
6. 'n the:n so: /
7. I loved my father so much ↓ He took my father from me ‡
8. and that led me $^{(1.5)}$ by myself

Lakoff (1996) describes the STRICT FATHER Model and the NURTURING PARENT Model in political reasoning, a dichotomy useful for religious reasoning as well (see Table 2).

Table 2: Parent Models (Lakoff 1996)

STRICT FATHER	VS. NURTURING PARENT
• Hierarchical relationship	• Two way communication
• Power/ Authority	• Empathy/ Responsibility
• Reward/ Punishment	• Personal earning or loss

In Mama's religious conceptual system, her earthly father maps onto her heavenly Father. One was physically big, and the Other is big, powerful.

Throughout our interview it is clear that she is able to go beyond her father's faults, remembering how he guided and protected her and was indeed a nurturing parent; via conceptual integration, her view of God the Father is analogous.

Edward's conceptual system, on the other hand, presents an example of the STRICT FATHER Model. His biological father was a drug-addict, and he does not talk very highly of him during our interview, yet it is clear that Edward feels his loss.

In the following extract, which reveals his source domain FATHER, I asked Edward if he had ever seen God, and at the end he gives a vivid description of his vision. His gestures would be analogous to another of his drawings of God. It is interesting that, although he was initially talking about Christ's Father, he became emotional, and it seems as though he was talking more about the source domain of EARTHLY FATHER than the target domain of HEAVENLY FATHER.

Edward: Father and Son (00:15:14 – 00:16:20)

1. Yeah I have but /
2. That guy's* he's kinda tight so %laugh:
3. He's like / kind of a meanie or %laugh-"whatever" %laugh
4. *Who's this?*
5. The Lord Jehu or / Christ's father $^{(1.5)}$
6. So he* he's / yeah he does {that} so /
7. *Now what's the difference*
8. *between the Father and the Son?*
9. %sniff $^{(1.5)}$ %exhale / He's almighty /
10. He create* / ya know / he could take something and
11. make this into an animal %laugh:
12. He's a cr'ator /
13. He's a great man ($^{3.5}$-%cry) but when it come to /
14. being like a man he doesn't %laugh-"do it very well I'm thinking" /
15. ↓ cuz I know he made me suffer a lot
16. ↑ And then they'll use this long suffering >{this} suffering
17. th: suffer long suffer he's like<
18. He could be a better ↑ man /
19. So: the difference is Christ is pro'ly /
20. The difference is the same but / he's a li'l more compassionate
21. ↓ <than his father> $^{(1.5)}$
22. So he's a good man bu:t he needs to show more compassio- ya know
23. He needs to do a li'l more so /
24. *Now you're saying man, is he a man like you and me?*
25. ($^{1.0}$-%laugh) ↑ Yeah,
26. I seen a vision of him /
27. ↓ like I seen a little scene like the powers

28. he's like ah <he's a man> /
29. (2.0) so he's like (1.0) all grown tan man /
30. (2.0) and then he's: just like just like that so he's like
31. if you seen a guy that was tan like hair /
32. he's just like that

What is revealing is that he mapped the relationship of God the Father and God the Son onto his own relationship with his biological father. Similar concepts have a special cognitive role in devotees, because they become highly relevant in their everyday lives and not only in their conceptual system, but more profoundly, in their system of beliefs.

6 Incompatible metaphors and source domain lamination

During my interviews, after I identified the main metaphor used to talk about God, I introduced other metaphors in the discourse and tried to see which caught on and why. I will provide examples which indicate that when another conceptual metaphor was introduced, it was either rejected because the source domain could not coexist with the interviewees concept of the target domain (i.e. the encyclopedic knowledge and real-life experiences pertaining to that concept could not prompt plausible mappings), or the source domain was laminated onto the interviewee's habitual source domain, highly motivating the mappings when speaking in terms of the target.

Because Mama during our interview was quite good at citing and referencing the Bible, I asked her to talk about the *Song of Songs*, attributed to King Solomon, and to explain the imagery of the lover and the beloved. When I asked Mama if she could see God as being a lover, or even as a husband, she accused me of blasphemy: there was an incompatibility of domains in her conceptual system based on her life experiences.

Mama: God is not a lover (01:04:33 – 01:05:31)

1. *In the book of Solomon, could it be?*
2. >yeah: 's a book of Solomon<
3. *ok, where it talks about two lovers,* (2.5) *the bride, and the groom /*
4. (1.5) ↑ God is the groo:m
5. *ok, so you can see how some people see*
6. *God as being like a lover, like being a boyfriend, or being a husband, or being a groom*
7. he's th:e husband >of the church< /
8. *ok*
9. yeah, 'at's the way you look at that
10. you don't look at that in a /

11. <he’s my lover / he comes to me at night and we have s:ex> /
12. no that’s >very, very ↑ u:nchristian talk<
13. I don’t even talk like that

I want to remind that Mama’s culture suggests the GOD IS A LOVER metaphor, and although she possibly was aware of *Song of Songs* (5: 2), she ultimately interpreted the metaphor based on *her own* experiential knowledge of the source domain (her idea of LOVER cannot be applied to God). It reads:

> I slept but my heart was awake.
> Listen! My lover is knocking:
> ‘Open to me, my sister, my darling,
> … my hair [is damp] of the night.’

Other metaphors besides GOD IS LORD, CREATOR and FATHER analogously seemed implausible according to her conceptual system.

As for Edward, he basically refused any alternative metaphors for God other than GOD IS A FATHER. When asked if God is a ‘mother’ he only accepts this view in that God is a creator, and says ‘but as far as anything like that…nah.’ When asked if God is a ‘lover’, he replied without thinking ‘he’s not!’ On a different note, but in complete accord with his epistemic stance, the following extract documents how he replied when I asked him to tell me if God can be thought of as a ‘doctor’:

Edward: God is a doctor (00:21:23 – 00:22:00)

1. $^{(\sim1.0)}$ Doctor::: $^{(1.5)}$ ye:ah he does do that
2. >So he’ll pinch your fee::t or he’ll hurt your tee:th
3. So he’ll give you um like a- <a ↓ cu:re>
4. ↑ So he’s like a doctor >like you’re sayin’<
5. So what he’ll do is >hurtcha<
6. Cuz he’s havin’ his little vengeance on ya cuz you sinned
7. So I {knew} right from wrong / like ya know /
8. Don’t mess with my stuff and then I mess with it and then he’s gonna
9. %yell-“ow:” %laugh: %laugh-“he’s gonna hurtcha” /
10. So he’ll fix your tee:th /
11. Er ya know you’re like you have a: >a:arth- somewhe- he’ll go /
12. hurt it ‘n then< /
13. So yeah he’s like that ↓ like you’re sayin’
14. <Like a f:ather> kinda thing /

Edward tries to elaborate the metaphor of GOD IS A DOCTOR, but because his fundamental metaphor is so salient for him, he laminates the two source domains and at the end even reverts back (almost hesitantly) to GOD IS A FATHER, a tough, uncompassionate father, unlike his own, a real ‘meanie’.

7 Some considerations on entrenched and incompatible metaphors and domains

To conclude, a culture may suggest a conceptual metaphor, but ultimately the meaning construed will be founded on individuals' experiential and encyclopedic knowledge of their personal worlds. People's views about themselves and the world around them are deeply entrenched in their conceptual systems, which are created by their experiences and their bodily interactions with the world, whether it is having to do with gravity in the case of UP and DOWN, or what their individual and social concepts (like FATHER) are. When people talk about religious and spiritual concepts, they are revealing a great deal about the way they are, their world, and the way they interact with it.

The more entrenched a frame of mind is, the less plastic it is, and this is confirmed by the neurosciences which claim that it is difficult to break down and reconstruct certain synaptic structures of the brain. Our basic way of seeing things are often incompatible or at best seep through in the lamination when a new frame or a new conceptual metaphor is introduced, whether it be in the form of speech, gesture or drawings. The clues for this here presented is consistent with other data I collected from another dozen of informants who define themselves as Jewish, Muslim, Monotheistic, Pagan, New Age, Reiki, and so forth, and not only Christians.

One conceptual metaphor does not give way to another one immediately, and according to psychoanalytic studies, it is possible to substitute conceptual metaphors and frames of mind, but only with a great deal of effort. Studies in psychoanalysis indicate that when a subject affected by depression states "I don't know which way to go, I don't see a way out", the conceptual metaphor LIFE IS A MAZE can be therapeutically (but laboriously) modified with a similar metaphor, that is LIFE IS A JOURNEY, having drastic implications for the patient's view of life and the world (Casonato 2003). The primary source domain of our habitual conceptual metaphor, I would say, will always motivate any other laminated domain mappings or blends especially for such meaningful concepts like personhood or belief systems.

Moreover, speech alone does not provide all the information. Conceptual metaphor certainly tells a great deal about the way we think the world works, but a lot more needs to go into the conceptual integration networks. Gesture studies has proven to be another powerful instrument, which should demonstrate how useful it can be for discourse analysis, psychoanalysis and various types of counseling, just to mention a few. Speech, gesture and drawings, each semiotic mode has its characteristic affordances and limitations, but when used together as with Multimodal Cognitive Semiotics, they can paint a more complete picture of what we are looking for, whether it be a person's concept of God or of one's self.

8 Transcription Legend

*	speaker self-interrupt, self-correction or restart
:	prolonged or stuttering
#	breath pause
‡	palato-alveolar click release
%	non-speech sound; *e.g.* %laugh, %sneeze
-	abrupt halt in utterance
/	unfilled speech pause, <1.0 seconds
(1.5)	unfilled speech pause in seconds
↑	rising pitch
↓	falling pitch
>text<	enclosed speech delivered more rapidly than usual
<text>	enclosed speech delivered more slowly than usual
{text}	uncertain speech
text (underlined)	emphasis
[	beginning of gesture phrase
]	end of gesture phrase
CAPS	main stroke of gesture phrase
bold	comment on gesture

Author note

Università degli Studi di Palermo (Italy)

Special thanks to Alan Cienki and my two anonymous reviewers for their comments on a previous draft of the paper, and to my friends and colleagues for their observations and support.

References

Barrett, J.L. 1999. Theological correctness: Cognitive constraint and the study of religion. *Method & Theory in the Study of Religion, 11*, 325-339.

Bausani, A. 1980. *L'Islam*. Milan: Garzanti.

Bourdieu, P. 1990. *The Logic of Practice*. Stanford: Stanford University Press.

Boyer, P. 2001. *Religion Explained: The Evolutionary Origins of Religious Thought*. New York: Basic Books.

Brandt, L. & Brandt, P.A. 2005. Making sense of a blend. A cognitive-semiotic approach to metaphor. *Annual Review of Cognitive Linguistics, 3*, 216-249. Amsterdam/Philadelphia: John Benjamins Publishing Company.

Casasanto, D. (in press). Embodiment of Abstract Concepts: Good and bad in right- and left-handers. *Journal of Experimental Psychology: General*.

Casonato, M. 2003. *Immaginazione e metafora. Psicodinamica, psicopatologia, psicoterapia*. Bari-Roma: Laterza.

Clark, H. 1996. *Using Language*. New York: Cambridge University Press.

De Certeau, M. 1984. *The Practice of Everyday Life*. Berkeley: University of California Press.

DesCamp, M.T. & Sweetser E.E. 2005. Metaphors for God: Why and How Do Our Choices Matter for Humans? The Application of Contemporary Cognitive Linguistics Research to the Debate on God and Metaphor. *Pastoral Psychology, 53*, 3, January 2005.

Douglas-Fairhurst, R. 2004. *Victorian Afterlives: The Shaping of Influence in Nineteenth-Century Literature*. New York: Oxford University Press.

Evola, V. 2009. *Multimodal Cognitive Semiotics and Metaphor in Spiritual and Religious Discourse*. Doctoral dissertation. Università degli Studi di Palermo.

Evola, V. 2005. Cognitive Semiotics and On-Line Reading of Religious Texts. A Hermeneutic Model of Sacred Literature and Everyday Revelation. *Consciousness, Literature and the Arts, 6*, 2, August 2005.

Evola, V. 2004. Blending the Erotic and Divine in Mystical Literature. *Language, Culture and Cognition Conference*. University of Portsmouth (UK).

Fauconnier, G. 1985. *Mental Spaces*. Cambridge, MA.: MIT Press.

Fauconnier, G. & Turner M. 2002. *The Way We Think*. New York: Basic Books.

Flanagan, O. 2002. *The Problem of the Soul: Two Visions of Mind and How to Reconcile Them*. New York: Basic Books.

Forman, R.K.C. 1999. *Mysticism, Mind, Consciousness*. New York: State University of New York Press.

Goodman, N. 1978. *Ways of Worldmaking*. Indianapolis: Hackett Pub Co. Inc.

Goodwin, C. and Duranti A. (eds) 1992. *Rethinking context: Language as an interactive phenomenon*. Cambridge: Cambridge University Press.

Hanks, W.F. 1995. *Language and Communicative Practices*. Series Critical Essays in Anthropology. M. Bloch, P. Bourdieu and J.L. Comaroff, (eds.) Boulder: Westview Press.

Hogan, P.C. 2005. Verbal art and the human mind: notes on a research program in cognition and culture. *Consciousness, Literature and the Arts, 6*, 2, August 2005.

James, W. 1985. *The Varieties of Religious Experience*. USA: Longmans, Green, and Co., 1902; Penguin American Library.

Kendon, A. 2004. *Gesture: Visible action as utterance*. Cambridge, MA: Cambridge University Press.

Kockelman, P. 2005. The semiotic stance. *Semiotica, 157*, 1/4, 233–304.

Lakoff, G. 1996. *Moral Politics*. New York: Basic Press.

Lakoff, G. & Johnson M. 1999. *Philosophy in the Flesh: The Embodied Mind and Its Challenge to Western Thought*. New York: Basic Books.

McNeill, D. 1992. *Hand and mind: What gestures reveal about thought*. Chicago: The University of Chicago Press.

Merleau-Ponty, M. 1945. *Phénomènologie de la perception*. Paris: Gallimard. *Phenomenology of Perception*. Trans. Colin Smith. London: Routledge & Kegan Paul, 1962.

Murphy, N. 1999. Supervenience and the downward efficacy of the mental: A non-reductive physicalist account of human action. In Russell, R.J., Murphy, N., Meyering, T.C. & Arbib, M.A. (eds.). *Neuroscience and the Person: Scientific Perspectives on Divine Action*. Vatican City: Vatican Observatory. 147-164.

Peirce, C.S. 1955. *Philosophical Writings of Peirce*, Justus Buchler (ed.). New York: Dover Publications.

Rizzuto, A.-M. 1979. *The Birth of the Living God: A Psychoanalytic Study*. Chicago: The University of Chicago Press.

Rosch, E. 1999. Reclaiming Concepts. In R. Nunez & W.J. Freeman (eds.) (1999). *Reclaiming cognition: The primacy of action, intention and emotion*. Thorverton, Eng.: Imprint Academic.

Tomasello, M. 2001. *The Cultural Origins of Human Cognition*. Cambridge: Harvard University Press.

Turner, M. 1996. *The Literary Mind*. New York: Oxford University Press.

4

Candidates Construct Vantages

ADAM GŁAZ

A major tenet of Cognitive Linguistics is the perspectival nature of language. Given a sample of linguistic usage plus information about the pertinent circumstances in which it was produced, one should be able to reconstruct the mental position of the speaker, assumed for making a projection of a given scene or event, as well as correlating this position with the circumstances. I attempt to perform such reconstruction by couching an analysis of two political speeches within the terms of Robert E. MacLaury's (1995, 1997, 2000, 2002) Vantage Theory.

1 Vantage Theory

At a time when there is no shortage of descriptive models, to propose one more may seem superfluous. Yet, Vantage Theory (henceforth also VT), an off-mainstream cognitivist account of categorization mainly in the color domain, is a model that gives one hope for substantial gains from the endeavor. Although in a preliminary form it has been available in print for almost a quarter of a century (MacLaury 1986; application to specific data but with little theoretical apparatus in MacLaury 1991), and in a more complete form for about fifteen years (roughly since MacLaury 1995), its impact on linguistics has been relatively inconspicuous. Admittedly, it has been used, often with substantial modification, in a variety of linguistic analyses (cf. especially a special issue of *Language Sciences*, 2002, vol. 24 (5–6), as well as another, forthcoming special issue of the journal), but remains largely unknown and possibly unattractive to a wider community of cognitive linguists because of its rather complex theoretical side and non-

Meaning, Form & Body.
Fey Parrill, Vera Tobin, and Mark Turner (eds.).

obvious application to domains other than color.[1] The aim of the present proposal is to show that VT can shed light on questions of the speaker's/conceptualizer's perspective or point of view (for the sake of the discussion at hand I use the two terms interchangeably; cf. end of this section for more comment). More specifically, I will attempt to show the connection between two aspects of discourse, its content and form, and the processes of conceptualization (derivable from those of categorization). The processes are modeled in specific ways as constructs called *vantages* (cf. below). Although space limitations prevent me from comparing VT with other cognitivist accounts of perspectivization, I do not necessarily view the latter as worse or inadequate. Rather, VT is claimed to be compatible with other cognitivist models, though enriching them with novel observations[2] and more directly linked with what it views as the very essence of categorization. It allows the researcher to attribute linguistic behavior to independently established cognitive processes of non-discrimination, synthesis and analysis, and those to yet more fundamental processes of recognizing and emphasizing similarity and difference (cf. below). In short, it models links between linguistic and cognitive behavior.

Vantage Theory arose from the dissatisfaction of its author, Robert E. MacLaury (d. 2004), with models of categorization available in the 1980s, such as Rosch's prototypes (e.g. Rosch 1978 and many other publications) or Zadeh's (1965) fuzzy sets. Having collected huge amounts of data from interviews with about 900 speakers of 116 Mesoamerican languages, MacLaury identified a hundred or so regular categorizing behaviors. Assuming that they constitute a coherent set, it was impossible to account for them in terms of the models available at the time. (For a list of these regularities see Appendix VII of MacLaury 1997.)

MacLaury's method of data elicitation (MacLaury 1997: 73–81, 434–48) include three kinds of interviews with the use of Munsell Color Chart, an array of 320 color tokens arranged in forty columns according to hue and eight rows according to brightness (all chips are maximally saturated), plus ten achromatic tokens ranging from black to pure white. The interview types are: naming, mapping, and focus selection. In the naming task, the subject is asked to give a term for each of the 330 color chips, presented to him/her in isolation (against a grey background to reduce the influence of context) and in random order. The responses are noted, so that when the chips are displayed as a chart, category boundaries can be marked. In the

[1]A list of these applications can be found in Głaz and Allan forthcoming.

[2]A comparison of Vantage Theory and Langacker's Cognitive Grammar is offered in Głaz 2009. Some ideas on how VT can enrich our understanding of certain processes typically explained within the theory of blending are offered in Głaz 2007.

mapping task, the subject is presented with the arranged set and asked to put a grain of rice on each chip he/she would refer to with a given term. The procedure is repeated for every term used in the naming task. Finally, the subject is asked to select the best example (focus) of each color category he/she has identified.

The categories constructed in the three types of interview need not coincide. Even more importantly, a speaker can refer to the same color category with different terms during a single interview, sometimes without being aware of doing so. Color categorization, MacLaury concludes, consists in constructing a *vantage*, i.e. a point of view on a category, the category as a whole being an assembly of the vantages constructed by a given conceptualizer. Vantage Theory, therefore, attempts to account for what these vantages are, how they are constructed, how they relate to one another, etc.

At a deeper level, it is claimed that categorization is grounded in the fundamental human experience of spatiotemporal orientation. In space, people orient themselves by coordinating the axes of up-down, left-right, and front-back. Because of the complexity of the surrounding, the axes operate on different levels and the human subject can find his or her way through them by arranging the percepts into a series of interdependent figure-ground alignments. MacLaury thus describes a simple case of locating a newspaper on a table in the living-room:

> To find the newspaper, one must locate the living room in reference to the house, the table in reference to the room, and the newspaper in reference to the table. People constantly zoom in and out during the waking day when they enter and leave structures, confine or diffuse their attention, locate objects or wend their way from place to place. (MacLaury 1995: 243–4)

One must now add to it the temporal dimension, experienced as motion and affecting not only the perceived object but also the perceiving subject. As a result, judgments of different subjects affected by motion in different ways will also differ. Says Albert Einstein:

> I stand at the window of a railway carriage which is travelling uniformly, and drop a stone on the embankment, without throwing it. Then, disregarding the influence of the air resistance, I see the stone descend in a straight line. A pedestrian who observes the misdeed from the footpath notices that the stone falls to earth in a parabolic curve. I now ask: Do the "positions" traversed by the stone lie "in reality" on a straight line or on a parabola? ... The stone traverses a straight line relative to a system of coordinates rigidly attached to the carriage, but relative to a system of coordinates rigidly attached to the ground (embankment) it describes a parabola. With the aid of this example it is clearly seen that there is no such thing as an independently existing trajectory, but only a trajectory relative to a particular body of reference. (Einstein 1920: 9–10)

Therefore, events such as movements of bodies are not passively perceived "as they are": the perceptions are actively (though subconsciously) constructed from a (spatiotemporal) point of view. These points of view, in turn, are identifiable through the perceived behavior of objects. In other words, if the parabolic and straight trajectories are "given," one can on their basis compute the respective spatiotemporal locations of the observers.

MacLaury uses these conclusions in his conception of categorization. As with spatiotemporal events involving motion, categories do not exist in any objective shape but are viewed and constructed by subjects as projections from viewpoints. It is these projections that are available to external observers and it is on their basis that one can define the viewpoints.

Furthermore, MacLaury postulates that the analogy is actually performed by the conceptualizer in an instinctive and subconscious manner.[3] The spatial axes are translated into fixed reference points (in MacLaury's terminology: fixed coordinates), while motion is translated as reciprocally balanced degrees of attention, on the part of the conceptualizer, to *similarity* or *difference* (mobile coordinates) between the fixed reference points and other stimuli. If in space-time motion assumes extreme values from inertia to the speed of light in vacuum, in categorization the similarity-difference cline ranges from identity to total disparity (cf. Figure 1).

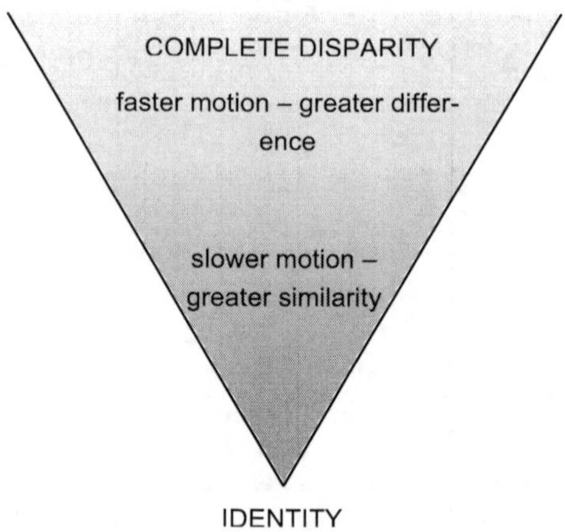

Figure 1. Equivalences between motion and the mobile coordinates of attention to similarity or difference in spatiotemporal analogy

---

[3]The final years of Robert MacLaury's research were, among others, devoted to specifying the exact nature of this analogy. The author left a preliminary account of his work (MacLaury 2003) but did not manage to argue the case in print in the form which he had planned.

The similarity-difference relationship is a continuum. A greater degree of attention to one of these coordinates at the expense of the other results in what I call, somewhat modifying MacLaury's terminology, *viewing modes*, which can be of three basic types. The first is the *non-discriminatory mode*, when similarity is strong and the cognitive distance between items reduces; as a result, the category is seen as a homogeneous mass. It has no clear-cut boundary and gradually shades into other categories. Towards the other end of the spectrum is the *analytic mode*, resulting from greater attention to difference, which protracts the cognitive distance between items inside the category. The conceptualizer is able to identify individual items (or groups of items), as well as distinguishing the category from others by means of a clear-cut boundary. The third type, the *synthetic* or *systemic mode*, again results from stronger attention to similarity but is constructed against the background of previously analyzed components. The role of that mode is to link the separate entities identified by attention to difference into "an abstraction, a theory, or a systemic understanding" (MacLaury 1997: 291). In that mode, attention to similarity allows the viewer to establish connections between entities: they are no longer isolated units but constitute an integrated whole.

But the viewing modes are not self-contained and independent; rather, they combine into larger constructs which I have above referred to as projections and which in VT are called *vantages*.[4] Vantages are arrangements of viewing modes. They can be of two major types: *dominant* and *recessive*. Each involves a zooming process, as shown in Figure 2.

[4]MacLaury treats vantages as points of view, which is misleading because of the association of the latter with a "point" as a location. It is perhaps closer to MacLaury's intention to regard them as "projections" or "perspectives," which involve point of view but also coherent complexes of cognitions.

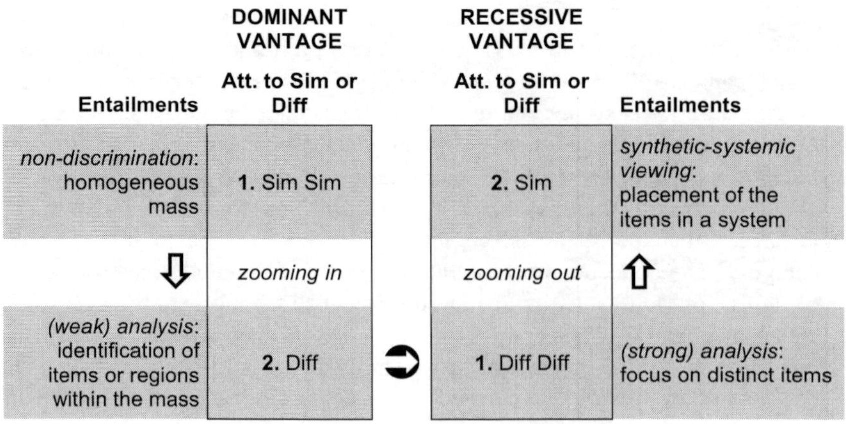

Figure 2. Viewing modes in vantages

The dominant vantage starts with strong emphasis on similarity (marked by double Sim), which *entails*[5] lack of discrimination, and then it progresses to stronger attention to difference. Because similarity is the predominant force in the vantage, attention to difference can only cause weakly analytic viewing: some entities or regions can be viewed as distinct but only in a coarse-grained fashion. In the recessive vantage, the conceptualizer starts with strong attention to difference (double Diff), which protracts the cognitive distance between the items and facilitates focusing on any of them as a distinct entity. Finally, the conceptualizer zooms out by emphasizing similarity more, which allows him/her to place the distinct items in a larger system. In other words, the dominant vantage is a process of zooming in from non-discriminatory to weakly analytic viewing, while the recessive vantage is a process of zooming out from strongly analytic to synthetic/systemic viewing.

Observe that attention to either similarity or difference at the expense of the other parameter can result in different entailments, depending on the place of a given viewing mode in the overall arrangement. Thus, very strong attention to similarity on the first level of the dominant vantage entails non-discriminatory viewing but (weaker) attention to that coordinate on the second level of the recessive vantage entails systemic viewing, not only because it is relatively weaker, but because it operates against the indi-

[5]*Entailment* in Vantage Theory is "a consequence or necessary accompaniment" of a particular choice (of emphasis or coordinate arrangement) (MacLaury 1997: 517). Entailments are observable behaviors deriving from hidden cognitions.

vidually identified entities in its background. Also, attention to difference on level 2 of the dominant vantage entails weakly analytic viewing: the predominating strength of similarity in that vantage does not leave much room for action. But on level 1 of the recessive vantage, difference reigns supreme and allows the conceptualizer to view the entities within the category as individualized and distinct.

Let me conclude this section with a note on the nomenclature. In VT vantages are treated as points of view but in a sense broader than the ordinary understanding of the term: not only as (physical or mental) *locations* but also *ways* of looking and conceptualizing. Suggestions therefore have been made to use the term *perspective* for the purpose, as a more appropriate one (cf. also note 4). For reasons of space, I here leave the resolution of the terminological issue for another occasion and use the terms *point of view*, *viewpoint* and *perspective* interchangeably. However, greater terminological precision should certainly be sought.[6]

2 Data

In the remainder of the paper I attempt to apply the descriptive framework of VT[7] to specific data, namely to one speech delivered by each of the US presidential candidates in the 2008 elections: by Barack Obama on January 29, 2008 in El Dorado, Kansas, and by John McCain on May 15 the same year in Columbus, Ohio. More precisely, I will concentrate on the central parts of each speech, which have the same function: to sketch the policy of the given candidate when and if he is elected president (see Appendix). After the analysis I will try and relate its results with the social makeup of the communities in the two places.

The basic statistics are as follows: the speeches are comparable in length (the total word count for Obama's speech is 2763 vs. 3083 for McCain's) but the analyzed part of McCain's performance (1765 words or 58% of the total) is much longer than the analyzed part of Obama's speech (857 words or 31% of the total). This is in part due to a second focus in Obama's talk, i.e. his family history and personal experience.

I will analyze the two texts for their content and the predominant verbal patterns. These textual features will be presented in sections 2.1 and 2.2, respectively, and then, in section 3, they will be analyzed and interpreted within the VT framework.

[6]That there is such a need can, among others, be deduced from VT's original rather confusing reference to vantages as *points of view* and a set of other phenomena as *viewpoints* (cf. e.g. MacLaury 1997: 278–290).

[7]In fact, only a small portion of the theory is used for immediate purposes here.

2.1 Speakers vis-à-vis Content

The central part of each speech will now be examined in terms of

- the number of issues mentioned;
- the kinds of issues mentioned;
- the degree of detail while discussing an issue.

Below I list the issues mentioned by each candidate. What counts as an issue is obviously debatable: in unclear cases I adopt a straightforward approach and follow the treatment of a given speaker. In some cases, two potentially separate issues are counted as one (e.g. retirement and social security in McCain's speech), others are naturally related but mentioned separately and therefore count as two (e.g. McCain's health and health care or the southern border and illegal immigrants).

Obama: taxation of companies, lower taxes for the less affluent, tax credits, retirement plans, minimum wage, fair credit card fees, bankruptcy laws, insurance, health care, lobbying, education for the less affluent (11 issues)

McCain: Iraq; Afghanistan – linked to terrorist threat in the US; nuclear security/danger: Russia, China, Iran, North Korea; Sudan–Darfur, NATO and U.N.; food in South America, Asia and Africa – linked to the US security; upgrading the military; veterans; independent energy sources; the southern US border; illegal immigrants; economy; simplified taxation; presidential veto; government spending reduction; jobs; education; health care; health – obesity of young people; insurance; retirement and social security; judiciary and the quality of judges; invigorated national and public service (21 issues)

Several differences between the two lists can be noticed. First, on a purely statistical level, McCain mentions nearly twice as many issues as Obama.[8]

Second, Obama deals with domestic issues only, whereas McCain brings up 5 to 7 international ones, depending on the count. Even when at a certain point the latter speaker zooms in on the United States and the country becomes the center of attention, it is also viewed sometimes in relation to what is happening overseas:

---

[8]Admittedly, the difference is pronounced only when calculated in absolute numbers. In relative terms, the "density" of the issues (in the central part of each speech) is slightly bigger for Obama, though comparable: on average, Obama mentions a new issue every 78 words, whereas McCain does so every 84 words.

(1) ... our southern border is now secure. Illegal immigrants who broke our laws after they came here have been arrested and deported. Illegal immigration has been finally brought under control ... (McCain)

Third, all the issues mentioned by Obama are related to the economy, either by their nature (taxation, bankruptcy laws) or because the speaker views them so (e.g., not education as such but educational problems of the less affluent). For McCain, the economy is merely one of the issues and not the most important one.

Fourth, and this goes beyond the mere listing of the issues, Obama is more specific as to *how* problems will be tackled. For example, he mentions four times the specific sums of money to be allocated to a given cause:

(2) This tax cut will be worth up to $1,000 for a working family. (Obama)

(3) And we're also going to give seniors a break by eliminating income taxes for any retiree making less than $50,000 a year ... (Obama)

(4) My plan does more to cut costs than any other plan in this race – up to $2,500 for a typical family. (Obama)

(5) And it means providing every American with a $4,000-a-year tax credit. (Obama)

The two speakers, then, operate within different purviews or fields of vision: Obama's is a more localized one, restricted to a certain aspect of life in the US, whereas McCain's has a global nature (although, which is only natural, the US is treated as the pivotal element in the world affairs). Obama's location is closer to the scene; the speaker is more engaged with the objects of conceptualization[9] and is exploring the American social reality "from within." The issues Obama mentions are treated selectively, but once mentioned, the speaker considers them with greater precision than McCain does. In contrast, McCain assumes a detached mental location so as to be able to project a wide, global purview. He zooms in onto the domestic issues but even then remains relatively distant: the speaker views a variety of problems and is not so precise with solutions as Obama.

[9]This impression is augmented by Obama's references to his family history.

2.2 Verb Forms

Another indication of viewpoint is the use of verb forms by the two candidates. Obama consistently uses the modal *will* with future reference (eighteen times), which indicates a promise or resolute intention:

(6) ... we'll stop giving tax breaks to companies who ship our jobs overseas... (Obama)

He also uses the *be going to* construction (once), which again expresses intention, though a premeditated one, or a plan:

(7) ... we're also going to give seniors a break by eliminating income taxes for any retiree making less than $50,000 a year ... (Obama)

The verb forms suggest that the speaker is moving along with the country; he is "here and now" and his presidency is portrayed as a matter of future for both the audience and the speaker himself.[10]

McCain, on the other hand, consistently uses the present perfect, present simple, and present progressive forms:

(8) The Iraq war has been won. (McCain)

(9) Congress has just passed ... a tax reform proposal ... (McCain)

(10) ... our southern border is now secure. (McCain)

(11) The Alternate Minimum Tax is being phased out ... (McCain)

Altogether there are about ninety occurrences of these forms in the crucial part of McCain's speech: a huge number. By using them, the speaker presents a list of accomplishments at the end of what he hopes to be his first term in office. In order to do that, he must assume a detached perspective, one that allows him to envisage not so much his own or others' *actions* as the *results* of those actions.[11]

---

[10]It is only natural to assume that the content of Obama's speech had been well prepared in advance, but his more frequent recourse to the "promising" modal *will* than to the *be going to* construction creates the impression of greater spontaneity and closer relationship with the audience.

[11]It has been called by one blogger as "McCain's Future Perfect Presidency" (www.perrspectives.com/blog/archives/001093.htm). For actions or events viewed as "past"

Figure 3 presents Obama's and McCain's mental positions vis-à-vis their respective object(s) of conceptualization, identifiable through the analysis of the content of their speeches and the use of verb forms.

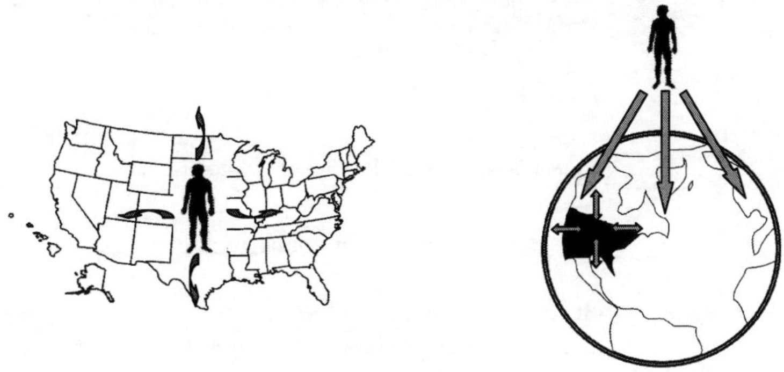

Obama McCain

Figure 3. Obama's and McCain's mental viewpoints

3 Vantage Theory Account

What light can be shed on these findings by Vantage Theory? VT seems to account for the findings very neatly, attributing the differences between the two speeches to different vantage constructions. These, in turn, consist of viewing modes which result from stronger attention to similarity or difference, in the manner spelled out above.

Obama occupies a location close to the setting (the US) and therefore operates within a narrow purview (no international affairs). He emphasizes similarity: distinctions disappear and the conceptualizer identifies issues of only one type (economic). The picture is homogeneous, which is characteristic of the non-discriminatory viewing mode. However, the issues identified within this picture are treated with a certain degree of precision (cf. the references to specific sums of money), which results from some attention to difference and weakly analytic viewing. In short, Obama's projection is a rather clear case of a dominant vantage (Figure 4).

---

from the end-of-term position a handful of simple past and past perfect forms are also used: these do not alter the overall impression in any significant way.

DOMINANT VANTAGE	**Entailments**
1. Sim Sim	*non-discrimination*: mental position close to object; engaged viewpoint; limited scope (domestic affairs only); homogeneous outlook
⇩	*zooming in*
2. Diff	*(weak) analysis*: issues few but tackled with (some) precision)

Figure 4. Obama: a dominant vantage

McCain's speech is a more complex case: it involves a succession of two recessive vantages, each being associated with a different mental viewpoint and a different purview. The speaker begins with a detached viewpoint and a broad purview, emphasizes difference and constructs a strongly analytic viewing mode: he mentions several countries and clearly separates the US from others. This is followed by somewhat stronger attention to similarity and synthetic–systemic viewing: the international problems are being related to the US, which plays a pivotal role in the system. Thus, strongly analytic and systemic viewing make up a recessive vantage. Then there is a change of scale: the viewpoint becomes more engaged and the purview is narrowed to domestic issues. Nevertheless, within that narrowed purview the viewpoint remains detached and another recessive vantage is constructed. Similarly to the broader purview, on the domestic front the speaker also mentions a variety of issues (attention to difference), some of which are being related to international ones. The projections are modeled in Figure 5.

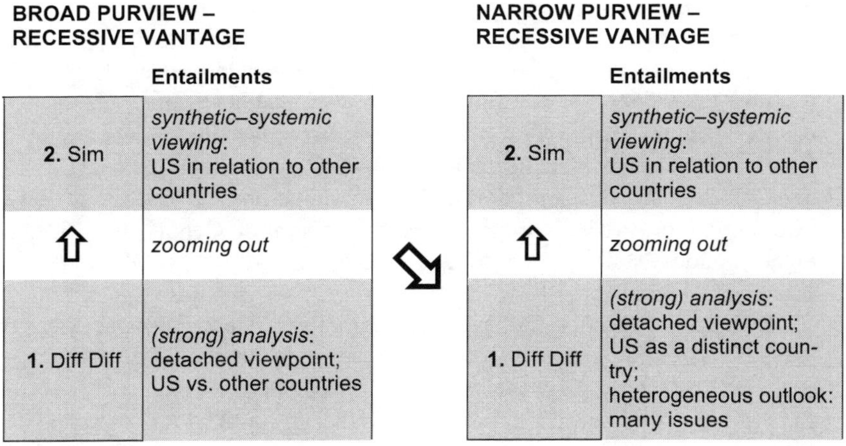

Figure 5. McCain: a change of purview and a succession of two recessive vantages

4 VT in Social Context

Although reliable data on the makeup of the two audiences are difficult to find, certain inferences can be made on the basis of available statistics. The two communities appear to be rather different at the level of state, county and city. I will now try to highlight some of the crucial differences.

Above all, the two communities differ in absolute population numbers: the state of Ohio (ca. 11,350,000 inhabitants) is about four times more populous than the state of Kansas (ca. 2,700,000[12]). The difference becomes more dramatic at the levels of county and city: there are over sixteen times more people in Franklin County (Ohio) than in Butler County (Kansas), and almost sixty times more in Columbus, OH than in El Dorado, KS (710,000 to 12,000). In other words, compared to Columbus' big-city character, El Dorado has a much more quiet, subdued, almost rural atmosphere.

Another kind of difference which becomes progressively more pronounced at lower levels concerns the ethnic makeup of the populace. Although the percentage of the white people in both states is the same (ca.

[12]All the data are approximations of the 2000 census figures available at http://factfinder.census.gov. Although almost a decade old, the data do shed light on the social context of the two speeches, especially when the differences are pronounced.

85%), the numbers at county level are 95% in Butler County, KS vs. 75% in Franklin County, OH, and at city level they are 94% (El Dorado) to 68% (Columbus). The differences in the proportion of the African American population are even more pronounced, especially at city level: 1.5% in El Dorado, KS vs. 24.5% in Columbus, OH (over sixteen times higher). At county level the disproportion is also huge (twelve times higher ratio in Ohio), while at the state level it is smaller but also significant (a twice higher ratio). The disproportion of Asian population is significant at lower levels: 0.5% in Butler County, KS vs. 3% in Franklin County, OH (6 times higher), and 0.2% in El Dorado, KS vs. 3.5% in Columbus, OH (over seventeen times higher).[13]

Clearly correlated with these numbers are the respective percentages of people who at home speak a language other than English. Although at the state level that percentage is somewhat lower in Ohio than in Kansas (6.1% vs. 8.7%), at the level of county or city the proportions are reversed: for Butler Country, KS vs. Franklin County, OH the numbers are 3.3% vs. 9% (almost three times higher), while for El Dorado, KS vs. Columbus, OH, they are 2% vs. 10% (five times higher).

Another difference potentially significant in the context of political campaigns is the level of education of the populace. Although the percentages of high school graduates in the two communities are comparable at all three levels (between 80% and 88%), and although the state of Kansas has a slightly higher proportion of bachelor degree holders (or higher) (ca. 26% vs. 20.5% in Ohio), the situation at county of city levels is reversed. The numbers for Butler County, KS vs. Franklin County, OH are 20% vs. 32%, and for El Dorado, KS vs. Columbus, OH they are 16% vs. 29%, respectively. The difference is pronounced especially at the lowest level: the ratio is almost twice as high.

Finally, a potentially important difference is the percentage of people at the age of 65 or higher: 18% in El Dorado, KS, which is twice as high a proportion as in Columbus, OH (9%).

In sum, then, a much smaller town of El Dorado, KS, compared to Columbus, OH, is also less diversified ethnically, with a smaller proportion of college graduates but a higher proportion of elderly citizens. This is of probable significance as to the content of the two speeches and the mental viewpoints adopted by the speakers. Obama's more down-to-earth, predominantly economic issues, as well as a vantage characterized by a smaller cognitive distance to his audience, is a probable attempt to target the immediate needs and concerns of his listeners. McCain, in turn, by adopting a

[13] Interestingly, the percentages of Hispanic population are significantly different only at state level and, in contrast to other minorities, are higher for Kansas (7%) than for Ohio (2%).

broader, more detached international perspective, might have hoped to relate to a more cosmopolitan character of his audience. Thus, vantage construction appears to constitute a response to contextual forces. However, the importance of the "local" factors in this case may not have been decisive, since in the media age the "real" audience of every speech of a presidential candidate is the whole nation. If so, the motivation behind constructing a particular vantage is as much a function of the immediate context as it is a projection of the speaker's outlook.

5 Final Comments

The two cases discussed here are relatively straightforward examples of the viewing modes and their arrangements. However, because a huge proportion of language data is "messy," a more complex VT formalism is required to accommodate the "messiness." Indeed, I have presented the framework in a rather skeletal form and omitted for reasons of space such notions as types of the dominant–recessive pattern, frames, coordinate stress, and many others (for details see MacLaury 1997). Besides, the model has had a history of adaptation and modification, various authors proposing such ideas as, among others, multidirectional vantage development (Preston 1993; Fabiszak forthcoming), a feeding relationship between vantages (Głaz 2006), or complex configurations of subvantages, tables and frames (Allan 2002).

While it is essential to spell out the details of a linguistics-adapted descriptive apparatus of Vantage Theory, it is perhaps more imperative for us at this stage to pinpoint what VT contributes to our understanding of perspective and point of view in discourse. I believe that the analysis above, sketchy as it is, sheds light on three areas.

First, a VT-based analysis provides tools for linking the content of discourse to perspectival projections of the speaker (called vantages) as complex arrangements of cognitions. This involves, as a component that is as vital as it is insufficient, an account of the speaker's mental point of view. It also links vantage construction to the social context of the speech event.

Second, it shows how the projections (vantages) are structured internally and how their components (viewing modes) arise through the dynamics of the similarity–difference cline. It shows how the mental operations involving non-discrimination, synthesis, and analysis coexist in a coherent manner.

Third, VT links categorization to linguistic behavior and the latter to our fundamental experience of spatiotemporal orientation. Thus, we are offered a framework which is multidisciplinary, cognitively grounded, and deeply embodied. The present analysis is an attempt to take a practical step by applying the framework to language.

Author Note

I would like to thank Liz Riddle (Ball State University, Muncie, IN) as well as two anonymous readers, for insightful suggestions and advice. Needless to say, full responsibility for any errors or inadequacies rests with me alone.

The author is affiliated with Maria Curie-Skłodowska University (UMCS) in Lublin, Poland.

References

Allan, K. 2002. Vantage Theory, VT2, and Number. *Language Sciences* 24, 5–6:679–703.

Einstein, A. 2000. *Relativity: The Special and General Theory*. Transl. Robert W. Lawson. New York: Henry Holt and Company.

Fabiszak, M. forthcoming. An Application of MacLaury's Vantage Theory to Abstract Categories: Identity and the Process of Categorisation. *Language Sciences*. Special issue on *Vantage Theory: Developments and Extensions*.

Głaz, A. 2006. Beyond Colour: Modelling Language in Colour-like Ways. *Progress in Colour Studies. Volume I. Language and Culture*, ed. C. P. Biggam & Ch. J. Kay, 73–87. Amsterdam/Philadelphia: John Benjamins.

Głaz, A. 2007. Vantage Theory: A Newcomer to the Cognitivist Scene? *Language and Meaning*, ed. M. Fabiszak, 91–112. Frankfurt am Main: Peter Lang.

Głaz, A. 2009. Cognition, Categorization and Language: Cognitive Grammar Meets Vantage Theory. *Rice Working Papers in Linguistics* 1:242–59. www.ruf.rice.edu/~rls/workingpapers.html

Głaz, A., Allan, K. forthcoming. Introduction. *Language Sciences*. Special issue on *Vantage Theory: Developments and Extensions*.

MacLaury, R. E. 1986. Color in Mesoamerica. Doctoral dissertation, University of California, Berkeley.

MacLaury, R. E. 1991. Social and Cognitive Motivations of Change: Measuring Variability in Color Semantics. *Language* 67–1: 34–62.

MacLaury, R. E. 1995. Vantage Theory. *Language and the Cognitive Construal of the World* (Trends in Linguistics. Studies and Monographs, 82.), ed. J. R. Taylor & R. E. MacLaury, 231–76. Berlin and New York: Mouton de Gruyter.

MacLaury, R. E. 1997. *Color and Cognition in Mesoamerica: Constructing Categories as Vantages*. Austin: University of Texas Press.

MacLaury, R. E. 2000. Linguistic Relativity and the Plasticity of Categorization. *Explorations in Linguistic Relativity* (Current Issues in Linguistic Theory, 199.), ed. M. Pütz & M. Verspoor, 251–93. Amsterdam/Philadelphia: John Benjamins.

MacLaury, R. E. 2002. Introducing Vantage Theory. *Language Sciences* 24, 5–6: 493–536.

MacLaury, R. E. 2003. Vantage Theory: Categorization as Spacetime Analogy. Ms.

Preston, D. 1993. The Uses of Folk Linguistics. *International Journal of Applied Linguistics* 3:159–259.

Rosch, E. 1978. Principles of Categorization. *Cognition and Categorization*, ed. E. Rosch and B. B. Lloyd, 27–48. Hillsdale, NJ: Erlbaum.

Zadeh, L. 1965. Fuzzy Sets. *Information and Control* 8:338–353.

Appendix

The analyzed fragments of speeches by Barack Obama and John McCain. The crucial features referred to in the analysis have been highlighted (the issues mentioned are in bold, the verb forms in italics).

Barack Obama[14]

...When I am President, *we'll* ***stop*** **giving tax breaks to companies** who ship our jobs overseas, and *I'll put* a middle-class tax cut into the pocket of working families. This **tax cut** *will be worth* up to $1000 for a working family. *We'll* provide struggling homeowners some relief by giving them a **tax credit** that would cover ten percent of a family's mortgage interest payment every year. And *we're also going to give* seniors a break by eliminating income taxes for any retiree making less than $50,000 a year, because every single American should be able to retire with dignity and respect.

That also means helping Americans save for retirement when they're still working. When I'm President, employers *will be required* to enroll every worker with a direct deposit **retirement** account that places a small percentage of each paycheck into savings. You can keep this account even if you change jobs, and the federal government *will match* the savings for lower-income, working families.

It's also time we had a President who won't wait another ten years to raise the **minimum wage**. *I will raise* it to keep pace every year so that workers don't fall behind. *I'll institute* a **Credit Card Bill of Rights** that *will ban* credit card companies from changing the agreement you signed up for, changing the interest on late fees. Americans should pay what they owe, but they should also pay what's fair, not what's profitable for some credit card company.

The same principle should apply to our **bankruptcy laws**. I opposed the credit card industry's bankruptcy bill that made it harder for working families to climb out of debt, and when I'm President, *I'll make sure* that CEOs can't dump your pension with one hand while they collect a bonus with the

[14] http:// www.barackobama.com/2008/01/29/remarks_of_senator_barack_obam_44.php

other. That's an outrage, and it's time we had a President who knows it's an outrage.

It's also time we had a President who stopped talking about the outrage of 47 million **uninsured Americans** and started doing something about it. When I hear that we can't come together and expand health care to the uninsured, I think back to how I was able to bring Democrats and Republicans together in Illinois to provide health insurance to 150,000 children and parents. And when I'm President, *we'll* finally *pass* a universal **health care plan** that *will make sure* every single American can get the same kind of health care that members of Congress get for themselves. My plan does more to cut costs than any other plan in this race – up to $2500 for a typical family. And *we won't pass* it twenty years from now, not ten years from now – *we'll pass* health care by the end of my first term in office.

When I hear that there's no way we can overcome to power of **lobbyists** and special interests, I think about how I was able to pass the first major ethics reform in Illinois twenty-five years. I think about how in Washington, I was able to bring Democrats and Republicans together to pass the strongest lobbying reform in a generation – we banned gifts from lobbyists, meals with lobbyists, subsidized travel on fancy jets, and for the first time in history, we forced lobbyists to tell the American public who they're raising money from and who in Congress they're funneling it to. Washington lobbyists haven't funded my campaign, *they won't run* my White House, and *they will not drown out* the voices of working Americans when I am President.

And when I hear that some of our kids just can't learn; that we can't do anything about crumbling schools and rising tuition, I think back to the chances that somebody, somewhere gave my family. The ticket my father got to come study in America. The opportunity my mother had to put herself through graduate school. The chance I had to go to the best schools in the country, even though we didn't have much.

It's time to give every child in American that kind of chance – no matter what they look like or where they come from. When I am President, *we will provide* all our children with a **world-class education**, from the day they're born until the day they graduate college. That means early childhood education to give them the best possible start. That means not just talking about how great teachers are, but rewarding them for their greatness, with better pay, and more support. And it means providing every American with a $4,000 a year tax credit that *will finally help* make a college education affordable and available for all.

John McCain[15]

So, what I want to do today is take a little time to describe what I would hope to have achieved at the end of my first term as President ...

....

By January 2013, America *has welcomed* home most of the servicemen and women who *have sacrificed* terribly so that America might be secure in her freedom. The **Iraq war** *has been won*. Iraq *is* a functioning democracy, although still *suffering* from the lingering effect of decades of tyranny and centuries of sectarian tension. Violence still *occurs*, but it *is* spasmodic and much reduced. Civil war *has been prevented*; militias *disbanded*; the Iraqi Security Force *is* professional and competent; al Qaeda in Iraq *has been defeated*; and the Government of Iraq *is* capable of imposing its authority in every province of Iraq and defending the integrity of its borders. The United States *maintains* a military presence there, but a much smaller one, and it *does not play* a direct combat role.

The threat from a resurgent Taliban in **Afghanistan** *has been* greatly *reduced* but not eliminated. U.S. and NATO forces *remain* there to help finish the job, and *continue* operations against the remnants of al Qaeda. The Government of Pakistan *has cooperated* with the U.S. in successfully adapting the counterinsurgency tactics that worked so well in Iraq and Afghanistan to its lawless tribal areas where al Qaeda fighters are based. The increase in actionable intelligence that the counterinsurgency produced led to the capture or death of Osama bin Laden, and his chief lieutenants. There *is* no longer any place in the world al Qaeda can consider a safe haven. Increased cooperation between the United States and its allies in the concerted use of military, diplomatic, and economic power and reforms in the intelligence capabilities of the United States *has disrupted* terrorist networks and exposed plots around the world. There still *has not been* a major terrorist attack in the United States since September 11, 2001.

The United States and its allies *have made* great progress in advancing **nuclear security**. Concerted action by the great democracies of the world *has persuaded* a reluctant **Russia** and **China** to cooperate in pressuring **Iran** to abandon its nuclear ambitions, and **North Korea** to discontinue its won. The single greatest threat facing the West – the prospect of nuclear materials in the hands of terrorists – *has been* vastly *diminished*.

The **size of the Army and Marine Corps** *has been* significantly *increased*, and *are* now better equipped and trained to defend us. Long overdue reforms to the way we acquire weapons programs, including fixed price

[15] http://www.johnmccain.com/Informing/News/Speeches/e8114732-e294-4a0d-b0b6-e5fa16857f61.htm

contracts, *have created* sufficient savings to pay for a larger military. A substantial increase in **veterans**' educational benefits and improvements in their health care *has aided* recruitment and retention. The strain on the National Guard and reserve forces *has been relieved*.

After efforts to pressure the Government in **Sudan** over **Darfur** failed again in the **U.N. Security Council**, the **United States**, acting in concert with a newly formed League of Democracies, applied stiff diplomatic and economic pressure that caused the government of Sudan to agree to a multinational peacekeeping force, with NATO countries providing logistical and air support, to stop the genocide that had made a mockery of the world's repeated declaration that we would "never again" tolerate such inhumanity. Encouraged by the success, the League *is* now occupied with using the economic power and prestige of its member states to end gross abuses of human rights such as the despicable crime of human trafficking.

The United States *has experienced* several years of **robust economic growth**, and Americans again *have* confidence in their economic future. A reduction in the corporate tax rate from the second highest in the world to one on a par with our trading partners; the low rate on capital gains; allowing business to deduct in a single year investments in equipment and technology, while eliminating tax loopholes and ending corporate welfare, *have spurred* innovation and productivity, and *encouraged* companies to keep their operations and jobs in the United States. The Alternate Minimum Tax *is being phased out*, with relief provided first to middle income families. Doubling the size of the child exemption *has put* more disposable income in the hands of taxpayers, further stimulating growth.

Congress *has just passed* a single up or down vote a **tax reform** proposal that *offers* Americans a choice of continuing to file under the rules of the current complicated and burdensome tax code or use a new, simpler, fairer and flatter tax, with two rates and a generous deduction. Millions of taxpayers *are expected* to file under that flat tax, and save billions in the cost of preparing their returns.

After exercising my **veto** several times in my first year in office, Congress *has not sent* me an appropriations bill containing earmarks for the last three years. A top to bottom review of every federal bureaucracy *has yielded* great **reductions in government spending** by identifying programs that serve no important purpose; and instigating far-reaching reforms of procurement and operating policies that have too long extravagantly wasted money for no better purpose than to increase federal payrolls.

New free trade agreements *have been ratified* and *led* to substantial increases in both exports and imports. The resulting growth in prosperity in countries from **South America** to **Asia** to **Africa** *has* greatly *strengthened* **America's security** and the global progress of our political ideals. U.S.

tariffs on agricultural imports *have been eliminated* and unneeded farm subsidies *are being phased out*. The world food crisis *has ended*, inflation *is* low, and the quality of life not only in our country, but in some of the most impoverished countries around the world *is* much improved.

Americans who through no fault of their own lost **jobs** in the global economy they once believed were theirs for life, *are assisted* by reformed unemployment insurance and worker retraining programs. Older workers who accept lower paying jobs while they acquire new skills *are provided assistance* to make up a good part of the income they have lost. Community colleges and technical schools all over the country *have developed* worker training programs suited to the specific economic opportunities available in their communities and *are helping* millions of workers who have lost a job that won't come back find a new one that won't go away.

Public **education** in the United States *is* much improved thanks to the competition provided by charter and private schools; the increase of quality teachers through incentives like merit pay and terrific programs that attract to the classroom enthusiastic and innovative teachers from many disciplines, like Teach for America and Troops to Teachers. Educational software and online teaching programs endorsed by qualified non-profits *are* much more widely in use, bringing to the smallest classrooms in America some of the greatest math, English, and science teachers in the country. This revolution in teaching methods *has* especially *benefited* rural America. Test scores and graduation rates *are rising* everywhere in the country.

Health care *has become* more accessible to more Americans than at any other time in history. Reforms of the insurance market; putting the choice of health care into the hands of American families rather than exclusively with the government of employers; walk-in clinics as alternatives to emergency room care; paying for outcome in the treatment of disease rather than individual procedures; and competition in the prescription drug market *have begun* to wring out the runway inflation once endemic in our health system. More small businesses *offer* their employees health plans. Schools *have* greatly *improved* their emphasis on physical education and nutritional content of meals offered in school cafeterias. **Obesity rates among the young** and the disease they engender *are stabilized* and *beginning* to decline. The federal government and states *have cooperated* in establishing backstop **insurance pools** that *provide* coverage to people hard pressed to find insurance elsewhere because of preexisting illness.

The reduction in the growth of health care costs *has begun* to relieve some of the pressure on Medicare; encouraging Congress to act in a bipartisan way to extend its solvency for twenty-five years without increasing taxes and raising premiums only for upper income seniors. Their success encouraged a group of congressional leaders from both parties to work with my administration to fix **Social Security** as well, without reducing benefits to those near **retirement**. The reforms *include* some form of personal retirement accounts in safe and reliable index funds, such as have been available to government employees since their retirement plans were made solvent a quarter century ago.

The United States *is* well on the way to **independence from foreign sources of oil**; progress that *has* not only *begun* to alleviate the environmental threat posed from climate change, but *has* greatly *improved* our security as well. A cap and trade system *has been implemented*, spurring great innovation in the development of green technologies and alternative energy sources. Clean coal technology *has advanced* considerably with federal assistance. Construction *has begun* on twenty new nuclear reactors thanks to improved incentives and streamlined regulatory process.

Scores of **judges** *have been confirmed* to the federal district and appellate courts, including the U.S. Supreme Court, who *understand* that they were not sent there to write our laws but to enforce them and make sure they are consistent with the Constitution. They *are* judges of exceptional character and quality, who *enforce* and do not make laws, and who *respect* the values of the people whose rights, laws and property they *are sworn* to defend.

Border state governors *have certified* and the American people *recognize* that after tremendous improvements to border security infrastructure and increases in the border patrol, and vigorous prosecution of companies that employ illegal aliens, our **southern border** *is* now secure. **Illegal immigrants** who broke our laws after they came here *have been arrested* and *deported*. Illegal immigration *has been* finally *brought* under control, and the American people accepted the practical necessity to institute a temporary worker program and deal humanely with the millions of immigrants who *have been* in this country illegally.

Voluntary national service *has grown* in popularity in part because of the educational benefits used as incentives, as well as frequent appeals from the bully pulpit of the White House, but mostly because the young Americans, no less than earlier generations, *understand* that true happiness is much greater than the pursuit of pleasure, and can only be found by serving causes greater than self-interest. Scores of accomplished private sector leaders *have joined* the ranks of administration for a dollar a year and *have instituted* some of the most innovative reforms of governmental programs ever known, often in partnership with willing private sector partners. A sense of community, a kinship of ideals, *has invigorated* **public service** again.

5

The Role of Semantic and Grammatical Context in Sentence Production

SVETLANA GOROKHOVA

1 Introduction

This paper approaches the controversial issue of the interference effects of semantic and grammatical context through an analysis of naturally occurring speech errors (slips of the tongue). Unlike the existing experimental studies that use picture-word interference paradigms to explore the effects of contextual variables on language production, evidence from Russian speech errors suggests that both semantic interference and grammatical feature interference are major effects implicit to language production mechanism.

1.1 Semantic context

Over the past decades, most models of lexical processing in language production have used spreading activation theories of semantic memory (Collins and Loftus 1975; Anderson 1983; Dell 1986; McNamara 1992). The theories suggest that lexical concepts are represented in a hierarchically structured semantic network. Concepts are linked through their shared features over a large number of nodes. Each node of the network accounts for a specific semantic microfeature and semantic relations between concepts are encoded in the microfeatures (Plaut 1995). Lexical retrieval is performed by spreading activation throughout the network, with each activated node (representing a linguistic unit) sending a proportion of its activation to all nodes

Meaning, Form & Body.
Fey Parrill, Vera Tobin, and Mark Turner (eds.).

linked to it. The existence and strength of these links are assumed to reflect learned semantic relationships between pairs of words. The semantic network is connected with the lexical network, where nodes are linked to each other on the basis of phonological and orthographic similarity (Collins & Loftus 1975).

Theories of semantic memory have largely been developed on the basis of semantic priming and semantic interference research.

The speed or accuracy of response to a target word or picture (e.g. *bread*) has been found to increase when it is preceded by a semantically related stimulus word, or prime (e.g. *cheese*), versus an unrelated word (e.g. *river*). The effect is referred to as semantic priming. In a spreading activation network, priming is caused by the activation that spreads from one concept node to another through nodes representing their shared features (Shelton & Martin 1992; Cree, McRae, & McNorgan 1999). In addition, because the network is hierarchically structured, activation may spread from the prime to the target through a shared superordinate category node (Lupker 1984).

Studies of semantic priming have shown the importance of distinguishing between semantic and associative relatedness (Hodgson 1991; Moss, Ostrin, Tyler, & Marslen-Wilson 1995). The commonly used definition of associatively related words is that if one word is produced in response to another in a word association task, they are related (Cree et al. 1999). It is clear, however, that many of the normatively associated items will also be semantically related (e.g. *bread – butter*). A number of researchers have suggested that associative relatedness should be defined in terms of cooccurrence frequency in speech or text, as measured by analyses of language corpora (McKoon & Ratcliff 1992; Williams 1996).

Frequently cooccurring words may become associated without being semantically related (e.g. *bread – bin*); semantically related words are not always associated (e.g. *bread – cake*) (Neely 1991; Prior & Geffet 2003; Silberman, Bentini, & Miikkulainen 2007). Prior and Geffet (2003) found that cooccurrence frequency and semantic similarity were significantly correlated with association strength for most English associates, but not for all types of Hebrew associates (semantic similarity appeared to reliably predict association strength only for antonyms). At the same time, Silberman et al. (2007) claim that semantically related words are associated more easily than unrelated words because each episode of cooccurrence adds associative strength to a word pair.

Analyzing various studies of semantic priming, Lucas (2000) concluded that there is evidence for an overall pure semantic priming effect in the absence of associative relationship. At the same time, she did not find any evidence of priming based purely on association. In contrast, Hutchison (2003), who analyzed the results of other studies of priming, claimed that there is strong evidence of automatic priming based purely on associative relationship whereas there is little evidence of automatic pure semantic priming.

A number of authors interpret semantic versus associative priming effects based on the distinction between semantic and lexical networks. On this view, semantically similar words are connected at the conceptual processing level, whereas associative priming is based on lexical cooccurrence of words and results from activation spread at the lexical level (Ferrand & New 2003; Hutchison 2003). Ferrand and New (2003) propose that such connections are built through repeated cooccurrence of two word forms and do not encode any information about the word' meanings. In Plaut (1995)'s model, semantic relatedness among words is encoded by the degree of feature overlap in their semantic representations, while associative relatedness is encoded by the frequency with which one word followed another during training.

It appears that a semantic relation between a target and a context stimulus (prime) facilitates language production in some paradigms, but hampers it in others (Bloem, van den Boogaard, & La Heij 2004). This effect is referred to as semantic interference. Most models of lexical access in language production (Glaser & Glaser 1989; Humphreys, Lloyd-Jones, & Fias 1995; Levelt, Roelofs, & Meyer 1999; Starreveld & La Heij 1996) localize the semantic interference effect obtained with context words at the lexical level of processing. They assume that the target concept spreads activation not only to its corresponding word at the lexical level, but also to semantically related words (Bloem et al. 2004 called it 'semantic cohort activation'). Consequently, the lexical representation of a semantically related context word begins to compete for selection with that of the target word, resulting in longer naming latencies. This inhibitory effect has been observed when the prime and the target were category coordinates (Kroll & Stewart 1994; Damian & Als 2005) or hierarchically related (Hantsch, Jescheniak, & Schriefers 2005). Damian and Als (2005) referred to the inhibition effect as 'semantic blocking effect' and proposed that it can be attributed to the lexical–semantic level. However, the semantic interference effect must be rather narrow since it is not observed when the distractor and the target belong to different semantic categories (Costa, Alario, & Caramazza 2005).

Finally, there is some evidence to suggest that the semantic context effect is different for semantically related and associatively related word pairs. By varying stimulus onset asynchrony in a picture naming task,

Alario, Segui, & Ferrand (2000) observed the inhibition effect for semantically related word pairs and the facilitation effect for associatively related pairs. They concluded that semantic inhibition is due to lexical selection by competition whereas associative facilitation can be accounted for by postulating the activation of a prime's associative links in the production lexicon. They interpreted their results as evidence for the existence, at an automatic level of processing, of 'dissociation' between semantic and associative relatedness.

To summarize, the models converge on the point that spreading activation between related items can prime conceptual access but also can hamper the retrieval of a target word. They claim that the interference effect of semantic context is observed when the distractor and the target belong to the same semantic category, leading to competition among the lexical nodes in the lexicon, and localize the effect at the lexical level of production. Conversely, other kinds of semantic relatedness between a distractor and a target lead to semantic facilitation and the locus of semantic facilitation is the conceptual level of production. The effect of associative relatedness between words also appears to be facilitatory. Associative priming is caused by activation spreading at the lexical level.

Recently, however, the hypothesis that lexical selection involves competition and that semantic interference effect reflects a lexical level process has been disputed (Finkbeiner & Caramazza 2006; Mahon et al. 2007; Mahon & Caramazza 2009). It was shown that the so-called semantic interference effect is a task-specific effect that does not reflect a general property of the lexical selection mechanism. Instead, a number of experiments (Mahon et al. 2007) revealed that semantic interference arises at a post-lexical locus. The authors proposed that the 'normal' effect of semantic context on correct lexical selection events should be facilitatory and that this effect arises as a consequence of activation spreading at the semantic level of sentence production (Mahon & Caramazza 2009).

While the studies discussed so far focused on the functioning of semantic memory, some experimental work has shown that semantic memory system interacts with episodic memory (memory for autobiographical episodes) (McKoon & Ratcliff 1986; Neely & Durgunoglu 1985; Shelton & Martin 1992), e.g. there is some evidence to indicate that the semantic priming effect on performance is bigger if the prime and the target are both semantically and episodically associated (Chiarello, Burgess, Richards, & Pollock 1990; McRae & Boisvert 1998; but see McKoon, Ratcliff, & Dell 1986 for a criticism of episodic-semantic distinction).

1.2 Grammatical context

Most experimental studies concerned with the processing of grammatical features used picture-word naming tasks to investigate the grammatical interference effect in sentence production. The experiments focused on the gender and number features of nouns. Schriefers (1993) used the picture–word interference paradigm to explore the processes involved in the selection of grammatical gender in German and discovered that the gender feature of a distractor word influenced the selection of the gender feature of the target word (determiner and/or adjective plus noun). The effect is referred to as the gender congruency effect. Schriefers concluded that the selection of the gender feature is a competitive process.

A contrary view was taken by Schiller & Caramazza (2002), who investigated the effect of the number feature of a distractor word on the production of a target noun phrase (determiner-noun), i.e. the number congruency effect, in German. Their results seem to indicate that the selection of the number diacritic in naming is a noncompetitive process. This led the authors to the more general conclusion that grammatical features in general are not selected by competition. They proposed that the so-called gender congruency effect observed in German and Dutch is in fact the 'determiner congruency effect' reflecting competition in the selection of gender determiner forms rather than in the selection of the gender feature. Costa, Kovacic, Fedorenko, & Caramazza (2003) made the same conclusion about the gender congruency effect in Croatian. Consequently, Caramazza and colleagues explained the fact that the gender congruency effect was not observed in any of Romance languages studied (French, Italian, Catalan and Spanish) by referring to some language-specific properties affecting determiner selection in these languages (Caramazza, Miozzo, Costa, Schiller, & Alario 2001). Unlike German and Dutch, where grammatical information is sufficient to select determiner forms, Romance languages are "late-selection" languages, where the forms of determiners cannot be selected until the phonological context is available. The authors argued that even though the selection of the gender feature in these languages might be competitive, any competition may have been resolved by the time phonological encoding is completed. Thus, the studies of Germanic and Romance languages left unresolved the question as to whether the gender congruency effect is universal across languages of different families.

Another question open for debate is the locus of the gender congruency effect. Schriefers (1993) attributed the effect to a level in sentence production where grammatical features of lexical nodes compete for selection, i.e. the grammatical encoding level. This suggestion implies that the retrieval of grammatical features is independent of lexical retrieval. Caramazza and colleagues claimed that the effect results from competition at the morphophonological encoding level; on this view, the competition is restricted to free-standing morphemes such as gender determiners whereas the selection of bound morphemes such as inflectional affixes is a non-competitive process (Schiller & Caramazza 2002; Costa et al. 2003). Contrary to their conclusion, the experimental studies of German and Dutch suggest that the competition is not restricted to free-standing items and that both types of gender-marked morphemes (determiners and inflectional affixes) are selected via the same basic processing mechanisms (Schriefers, Jescheniak, & Hantsch 2005; Lemhöfer, Schriefers, & Jescheniak 2006). Bordag and Pechmann (2008)'s results for Czech language indicate that bound morphemes are selected by competition; at the same time, the authors propose that it is more likely that the phonological forms, and not the abstract gender features, are involved in the competition.

In sum, most authors interpret their results as indicating that abstract grammatical features do not compete for selection and localize grammatical interference effect at a post-grammatical encoding level.

1.3 The present study

This paper reports a study of the effects of semantic and grammatical interference based on an analysis of naturally occurring Russian speech errors. The corpus of Russian speech errors, which comprises approximately 6,000 errors of different kinds, includes 306 examples relevant for the present study (152 examples demonstrating the semantic context effect and 154 examples demonstrating the effect of grammatical interference). The errors were collected by tape-recording and digitally recording everyday conversations, telephone conversations, and live TV and radio programs such as talk shows and interviews.

An analysis of naturally produced errors caused by semantic and grammatical contextual effects is expected to complement the results of the experimental studies and add a broader perspective to the discussion of how contextual variables affect the retrieval of words and the selection of their grammatical features. Cutler (1988:210) observed that whereas speech error research cannot replace laboratory experimentation, speech error studies have an advantage over laboratory studies of production because the latter

> tend either to lack validity (if the experimental situation is constrained to such an extent that the normal conditions of production cannot be guaranteed) or to be difficult to interpret (if the subjects' productions are relatively unconstrained).

The following section of the paper includes two parts. The first part addresses the issue of semantic context and discusses its effect on "lexical selection by activation" (Finkbeiner & Caramazza 2006) and the locus of this effect. It presents a study of speech errors which henceforth will be termed *contextual semantic substitutions*. These are production errors that occur when a word semantically related to a distractor word from the current sentence is substituted for the target word. The results of the study are then compared to word association norms and corpus data.

The second part contains an analysis of *contextual substitutions of a grammatical feature* resulting from the interference of a grammatical feature of a distractor word from the current sentence.

The results of both analyses are summarized in Conclusion.

2 Speech error analysis

2.1 Contextual semantic substitutions

152 examples of contextual semantic substitutions were analyzed to explore the interference effect of semantic context. Speech errors of this kind demonstrate the effect of lexical retrieval failure caused by the interference of a distractor word.

Although the present paper is not specifically concerned with classifying semantic relations between the distractor and the error, all the examples were grouped into the following subtypes: cohyponymy (the distractor and the error are category coordinates), hyponymy (the distractor is a hyponym of the error), holonymy (the error is a 'part' of the distractor), synonymy, antonymy, 'related' (semantic relations other than synonymy, antonymy, generic, and partitative), and 'episodic' (reflecting the speaker's personal life experience rather than semantic relations). Table 1 shows the distribution of the different types of relations across the total number of examples.

Table 1. Distribution of different types of distractor-error relations (per cent)

cohyponymy	hyponymy	holonymy	synonymy	antonymy	related	episodic
17.7	21	4	22.4	7.2	23.7	4

Below are sample examples that seem to be representative of the different types of relationships between the distractor and the error words involved in contextual semantic substitutions (the target and the error are in bold and the distractor, in bold italics).

In (1), the two words are **cohyponyms (category coordinates)**:

(1) Ne bog vest′ kakaja kapusta – raz v **nedelju** sxodit′ v ***teatr***

	Not much	dough – once in	**week**	go	to	***theater***
→	Ne bog vest' kakaja	kapusta – raz v	**kino**	sxodit'	v	***teatr***
	Not much	dough – once in	**cinema**	go	to	***theater***

Not much dough – going to the theater once a week

The word *kino* 'cinema' is selected instead of the target noun *nedelju* 'week' due to the interference of the distractor word *teatr* 'theater'. The error, 'cinema', and the distractor, 'theater', are coordinate category members – both are 'entertainments'.

The substitution can be accommodated in the framework of spreading activation models of lexical processing. When the concept THEATER is activated, the activation cascades down onto the lexical level, so that the related lexical representations of both 'theater' and 'cinema' are simultaneously activated. If the proportion of activation received by 'cinema' exceeds the proportion of activation received by 'week', 'cinema' can interfere, causing the selection of the lexeme *kino* instead of the target *nedelju*.

The distractor word either precedes or follows the target word. Thus, the context effect works both backward as in (1) and forward as in (2), which is another example of **cohyponymy** of the distractor and the error:

(2)	Ja	ètot	***džemper***	kupila	po	**slučaju**	s ruk
	I	this	***pullover***	bought	by	**chance**	privately
→	Ja	ètot	***džemper***	kupila	po	**sviteru**	s ruk
	I	this	***pullover***	bought	by	**sweater**	privately

I bought this pullover by chance, privately

In (2), the substitution of the word *sviteru* 'sweater' for the target *slučaju* 'chance' is caused by the interference of the distractor word *džemper* 'pullover', a cohyponym of 'sweater' (both belong to the category of 'knitted pieces of clothing', but *sviter* is a thicker woolen top).

The phonological similarity between the error and the target word in (2) is expectable given the account of contextual semantic substitutions proposed above. The tendency for the substitute word to be phonologically similar to the target is in line with the explanation of word substitution errors postulated by the spreading activation theory (Dell & Reich 1981). Since the lexicon is viewed as a network representation consisting of nodes representing linguistic units of different levels (semantic features, words, morphemes, phonemes, etc.), each activated node is assumed to send a proportion of its activation to all nodes connecting to it (e.g. semantic feature nodes connect to word nodes defining them, and word nodes connect to phoneme nodes). Thus, the error word that replaces the target will tend to show the phonological similarity effect because activation will spread to it via phoneme nodes shared with the target. Indeed, Fay and Cutler (1977) found that 75 per cent of target-error word pairs in semantic word substitutions had the same number of syllables, and 82 per cent had the same stress pattern. Dell and Reich (1981)'s study of word substitutions and word blends showed that the proportion of error words that were both semantically and phonologically similar to the intended words was statistically significant in their corpus of word substitution errors.

To account for (2), it seems plausible to suggest that the activated concept PULLOVER spreads activation to its lexical representation, *džemper* 'pullover', and to its semantically related lexical units, including *sviter* 'sweater'. At the same time, the concept CHANCE spreads activation to its lexical representation, *slučaj* 'chance'. The word *sviter* 'sweater' has an increased chance of being mistakenly selected instead of the target 'chance' because it receives activation both from the distractor word, *džemper* 'pullover' (sharing semantic nodes with it), and from the target *slučaj* 'chance' (with which it shares phonemic nodes). Besides the number of syllables and the location of stress, phonologically related target and substitute words have been shown to typically share word-initial segments. Thus, in (2), the error and the target, *sviter* and *slučaj*, are both two-syllable words with the first stressed syllable and both start with the phoneme *s*–.

Category members can spread activation to their semantic category name as in (3). The adjectives 'green' and 'red' activate their **hypernym**, 'color', which is substituted for the target 'size'.

(3) …	četyre	***zelënen'kix***	tarelki	i	tri	***krasnen'kix***	takogo že	**razmera**
	four	***green***	plates	and	three	***red*** [ones]	of the same	**size**
→…	četyre	***zelënen'kix***	tarelki	i	tri	***krasnen'kix***	takogo že	**cveta**
	four	***green***	plates	and	three	***red*** [ones]	of the same	**color**

[Give me] four green plates and three red ones of the same size

Similarly, (4) is another example of **hyponymy**, where the distractor, *treska* 'cod', activates its category name, *ryba* 'fish'.

(4)	Kakoj	bol'šoj	**rot**	u	***treski***!
	what	big:**M**.SG.NOM	**mouth**:**M**.SG.NOM	[has]	***cod***

*What a big **mouth** the cod has!*

→	Kakoj	bol'šoj	**ryb**	u	***treski!***
	what	big:**M**.SG.NOM	**fish**:**F→M**.SG.NOM	[has]	***cod***

*What a big **fish** the cod has!*

Interestingly, the error in (4) seems to result from **both semantic and grammatical context interference**. The effect of semantic context is backward: The interference of the word 'cod' causes the selection of its hypernym, 'fish', instead of the target 'mouth'. At the same time, the forward interference effect exerted by the masculine gender feature of the word *bol'šoj* 'big' entails the selection of the masculine gender feature for the word 'fish' instead of the target feminine feature (*ryba→ryb*) (see section 2.4 for the discussion of the effect of grammatical context). Not surprisingly, phonological similarity (the same number of syllables and initial consonant) seems to augment the semantic interference effect.

(5) is an example of **holonymy (whole-part relationship)**, when the distractor is the name of a whole activating the name of its part. The distractor word *nomer* 'number' spreads activation to the name of its meronym, *cifry* 'figures', which is substituted for the target *bukvy* 'letters':

(5) A čto označaet ***nomer*** u tebja na noskax?
And what is the meaning of the ***number*** *on your socks?*

	A,	èto	ne	***nomer*** –	e`to	kakie-to	**bukvy**	latinskie
	Ah	this	not	***number***	this	some	**letters**	Latin
→	A,	èto	ne	***nomer*** –	e`to	kakie-to	**cifry**	latinskie
	Ah	this	not	***number***	this	some	**figures**	Latin

Ah, this is not a number – these are some Latin letters

The famous phrase that 'A theater begins from its cloakroom' is attributed to Stanislavsky, a famous Russian director. In (6), the speaker quotes Stanislavsky, but the target *vešalki* 'cloakroom' is replaced with *zanavesa* 'curtain' (the slip is not due to the speaker's ignorance of the quotation as it was immediately corrected), even though the target expression is a fixed phrase. In fact, (6) can be regarded as another example of **holonymy** since the distractor word, *teatr* 'theater', is the 'whole' in relation to 'curtain'.

(6)	Kak	*teatr*	načinaetsja	s	**vešalki** ...
	Like a	*theater*	begins	from [its]	**cloakroom**
→	Kak	*teatr*	načinaetsja	s	**zanavesa** ...
	Like a	*theater*	begins	from [its]	**curtain**

In (7), the distractor and error are **synonymous** adjectives. The distractor adjective, *vsjakoj* 'any/every', activates is synonym, *ljuboj* 'any/every', which replaces the target adjective *drugoj* 'other'.

(7) Èto možno skazat' o ***vsjakoj*** **drugoj** strane

	This	can	be said	of	***any***	**other**	country
→	Èto	možno	skazat′	o	***vsjakoj***	**ljuboj**	strane
	This	can	be said	of	***any***	**every**	country

This can be said of any other country

(8) is another example of **synonymy** between the distractor and the target. It shows that even a formulaic expression with strong intra-phrase links can get decomposed due to the interference of a distractor word.

(8)	Dostojnoe	***ditja***	svoej	**materi**
	Worthy	***baby***	its:F.GEN	mother:F.GEN
→	Dostojnoe	***ditja***	svoego	**rebënka**
	Worthy	***baby***	its:M.GEN	child:M.GEN

Like mother, like daughter

The Russian phrase for 'Like mother, like daughter' is literally translated as 'a worthy baby of its mother'. The word *ditja* 'baby' activates its synonym, *rebënok* 'child', which is substituted for the target word *mat′* 'mother'. Unlike the target noun, which is feminine gender, the substitute is masculine, so the adjective pre-modifier, *svoego* 'its' takes the masculine gender feature, indicating that the error occurred at a level where the words' grammatical features are still unspecified. The phrase, although idiomatic, is equally possible with either one of the synonyms (it can start both with *dostojnoe ditja* and with *dostojnyj rebënok*) – a fact that may account for the simultaneous activation of both.

In (9), which is an example of backward interference, the distractor word and the error, *vspomnila* 'remembered' and *zabyvat′* 'forget', are **antonyms**. 'Forget' is substituted for the target 'fall asleep'. Here again, the target, *zasypat′* 'fall asleep', and the error, *zabyvat′* 'forget', share the number of syllables (three), the location of stress (the third syllable), and the word-initial phonemic segment (*za–*).

(9)	Ja	uže	načala	**zasypat′**,	a	potom	***vspomnila*** →
	I	just	was beginning	to **fall asleep**	and	then	*[I] remembered*
→	Ja	uže	načala	**zabyvat′**,	a	potom	***vspomnila***
	I	just	was beginning	to **forget**	and	then	*[I] remembered*

I was just beginning to fall asleep and then I remembered

In (10), another example of **antonymy,** the distractor predicative *možno* '(be) possible' activates its antonymous predicative *nel'zja* '(be) impossible', which is substituted for the target verb *ne snimat′* 'not to dismiss'.

(10)	Esli	***možno***	Krasovskuju	**ne snimat′**,	to	ne stoit
	If	***possible***	Krasovskaja	**not dismiss**	then	should not
→	Esli	***možno***	Krasovskuju	**nel′zja**,	to	ne stoit
	If	***possible***	Krasovskaja	**impossible**	then	should not

If Krasovskaya does not have to be dismissed, then we should not [do it]

The proportion of activation received by the antonym, *nel′zja* 'impossible', appears to be so high that even though it belongs to a different grammatical class than the target verb *ne snimat′* 'not to dismiss', it is substituted for the target, violating the well-known general rule of the preservation of the target word's grammatical class in word substitution errors (Fromkin 1971; Fay and Cutler 1977; Garrett 1980 etc.).

In (11), the distractor and the error words can be described as 'related words'. The relationship between them reflects the speaker's knowledge about a concept in the Fillmorean frame semantics sense (Fillmore 1982). The word *snega* 'snow' spreads activation to its related word, *zimoj* 'winter', which replaces the target *utrom* 'morning':

(11) *(a dialog in May)*

– Mne segodnja utrom mašinu prišlos′ otskrebat′ ot ***snega***!
I had to scrape ***snow*** *off my car this morning!*

– Kak – ot ***snega***?!
What do you mean – ***snow***?!

–	Nu,	tak –	ot	***snega***:	šël	**utrom**,	naverno,	snežok	nebol′šoj…
	Well	so	from	snow	was	**morning:INS**	probably	***snow***	light (adj)
→	Nu,	tak –	ot	***snega***:	šël	**zimoj**,	naverno,	snežok	nebol′šoj…
	Well	so	from	snow	was	**winter:INS**	probably	***snow***	light (adj)

Well, yes– snow: It must have been snowing lightly in the morning…

Interestingly, although the word *utrom* 'morning' is used in the conversation directly before the slip occurs, thus priming the correct selection of the target word, the word 'winter' appears to be so highly activated that it is still selected instead of the target 'morning'.

Likewise, in (12), the distractor word, *kassax* 'booking offices', and the error, *biletov* 'tickets', are 'related', and the activation of 'tickets' causes this word to replace the target *sigaret* 'cigarettes'.

(12)	V	teatral′nyx	***kassax***	**sigaret**	ne	prodajut
	in	theater	***booking offices***	**cigarettes**	not	sell
→	V	teatral′nyx	***kassax***	**biletov**	ne	prodajut
	in	theater	***booking offices***	**tickets**	not	sell

Theater booking offices don't sell cigarettes

The relationship between the distractor and the error can be **episodic**, reflecting the speaker's personal experience:

(13) Kuda-to zabrali ***knigu dlja sotrudnikov***, prišlos' **propusk** ostavit'
Somewhere removed ***staff register***, had to **pass** leave
→ … prišlos' **podpis'** ostavit'
had to **signature** leave

They'd removed the staff register somewhere, so I had to leave my [library] pass [as a deposit].

In (13), the speaker mentions the staff register book, in which members of the library staff have to sign their names when they borrow library books. The semantic frame activated by this word includes the speaker's knowledge about having to sign her name in it; as a result the concept STAFF REGISTER activates the concept SIGNATURE, which spreads activation to its lexical representation *podpis'* 'signature', causing it to replace the target *propusk* 'pass' (the target and the error share the same number of syllables, the stress pattern, and the word-initial phoneme).

2.2 Comparison with word association norms and corpus data

Assuming that the strength of associative links between a distractor and an error and their cooccurrence strength increase the likelihood that the error word might be selected during lexical retrieval, speech error data were analyzed both in terms of word association norms and in terms of cooccurrence frequency of the word pairs involved in contextual semantic substitutions.

To test the hypothesis that contextual semantic substitution errors and verbal associations represent the same kind of lexical relationship, the distractor-target and distractor-error pairs were compared to word association norms from Russian Word Association Thesaurus (2002).

Russian Word Association Thesaurus comprises about 7,000 stimulus words and 105,000 associative response words and phrases. The stimuli belong to various grammatical categories. To make the comparison with the speech error data, a distractor word was assumed to be a stimulus word and the target and the substitute words, to be its associative responses. Then each target word was compared to its substitute in terms of associative response frequency. The six episodically related distractor-error pairs such as (13) were not included in the analysis as such errors are assumed to be strongly biased by the speakers' professional experience or by their memory for autobiographical episodes and thus were not expected to find any parallels in the word association norms. Besides, one example of semantically related distractor-error word pairs was excluded from the list as it allowed ambiguous interpretation.

Since 15 distractor words from the speech error examples are not included in the thesaurus, a free association experiment was conducted using these words as stimuli. 102 undergraduate students of St Petersburg State University were presented with a list of the 15 stimulus words printed on sheets of paper and instructed to write an associated word next to each stimulus word. A total of 1,529 associate tokens were collected in addition to the thesaurus data.

Table 2 shows response frequencies for examples (1)–(12) of contextual semantic substitutions. As can be seen from Table 2, the frequencies tend to be higher for the error words. Interestingly, the tendency holds even for the cases when the target word is semantically related to the distractor word, e.g. *ditja* 'baby' – *mat'* 'mother', indicating that the proportion of activation received by the error word is so high that even a semantically related 'prime' ('baby') does not facilitate the retrieval of the target word ('mother') as would be expected in view of the experimental evidence discussed in the Introduction. One of the few exceptions is (6) ('theater' – 'cloakroom'), in which the response frequency of the target word is understandably higher than that of the error word (both the distractor and the target words are included in a famous quotation).

Table 2. Response frequencies for sample target and error words (distractor = stimulus, target/error = response)

Distractor word (stimulus)	Target word (response)	Response frequency (per cent)	Error word (response)	Response frequency (per cent)
teatr *theater*	nedelja *week*	0	kino *cinema*	6.2
džemper *pullover*	slučaj *chance*	0	sviter *sweater*	17.6
krasnen'kij *red*	razmer *size*	0	cvet *color*	7.7
treska *cod*	rot *mouth*	0	ryba *fish*	52
nomer *number*	bukva *letter*	0	cifra *figure*	1.1
teatr *theater*	vešalka *cloak room*	2.5	zanaves *curtain*	0.6
vsjakij *any/every*	drugoj *other*	1.7	ljuboj *any/every*	5.2

ditja *baby*	mat′ *mother*	3.3	rebënok *child*	9.8
vspominat′ *remember*	zasypat′ *fall asleep*	0	zabyvat′ *forget*	6.0
možno *possible*	ne snimat′ *not dismiss*	0	nel′zja *impossible*	15.7
sneg *snow*	utro *morning*	0	zima *winter*	41.1
kassa *booking office*	sigareta (-y) *cigarette(s)*	0	bilet(y) *ticket(s)*	2.9

Paired-samples t-tests comparing the response frequencies of the target and the substitute revealed that the frequency difference is statistically significant ($t\,(144) = 4.12,\ \ p < .001$).

The Russian National Corpus (http://ruscorpora.ru) was used to estimate the strength of cooccurrence of the words involved in contextual semantic substitutions. The corpus contains about 52,000 texts and transcripts totaling 150,000,000 tokens. The cooccurrence strength of each distractor-target word pair was compared to that of the corresponding distractor-error pair.

Table 3. MI and T-scores for sample distractor-target and distractor-error word pairs

Distractor-target	**MI**	**T**	**Distractor-error**	**MI**	**T**
teatr – nedelja *theater – week*	2.70	5.6	teatr – kino *theater – cinema*	12.7	24.8
džemper – slučaj *pullover– chance*	0	0	džemper – sviter *pullover - sweater*	7.7	1.4
krasnen'kij – razmer *red - size*	2.2	3.7	krasnen'kij – cvet *red – color*	6.1	35.6
treska – rot *cod – mouth*	0	0	treska – ryba *cod – fish*	8.9	4.7
nomer – bukva *number – letter*	3.7	5.6	nomer – cifra *number – figure*	6.2	10.5
teatr – vešalka *theater – cloakroom*	6.2	5.3	teatr – zanaves *theater – curtain*	6.4	6.8
vsjakij – drugoj *any/every – other*	2.9	40.6	vsjakij – ljuboj *any – any/every*	2.6	10.7
ditja – mat′ *baby – mother*	3.8	33.5	ditja – rebënok *baby – child*	2.7	16.2
vspominat′ – zasypat′ *remember – fall asleep*	5.7	6.4	vspominat′ – zabyvat′ *remember –forget*	6.8	18.7
možno – ne snimat′ *possible – not dismiss*	2.9	3.7	možno – nel′zja *possible – impossible*	3.4	27.2

sneg – utro *snow – morning*	2.6	10.5	sneg – zima *snow – winter*	5.9	21.1
kassa – sigareta *booking office - cigarette*	0	0	kassa – bilet *booking office - ticket*	8.6	12.9

Mutual information (MI) and T-test were used as measures of cooccurrence strength. MI compares the frequency of cooccurrence of two words with the frequency of their independent occurrence, whereas T takes into account mainly the absolute frequency of cooccurrence of two words. Since MI is known to overestimate low-frequency words, T-score was used in addition to MI because it highlights the word pairs whose cooccurrence frequency is high enough to be reliable. Church et al. (1994) suggest intersecting the two measures and considering pairs that have high scores in both measures. Thus, the MI test measures the strength of cooccurrence, whereas the T-test measures the confidence with which the cooccurrence frequency can be claimed to be reliable (Church & Hanks 1990). Two words were regarded as mutually informative (i.e. the occurrence of a word in a sentence increases the probability of occurrence of the other word of the pair) when both MI and T-scores exceeded their minimum acceptable values (MI ≥ 3 and T-score ≥ 2 – see Stubbs 1995; Hunston 2002). Importantly, both measures are nondirectional, so they can be used to compute cooccurrence frequency independent of the context direction. Both the right and the left contexts were included in the search as a distractor word can either precede or follow the target word.

MI and T-scores were computed for each distractor-target and distractor-error pair with a context window of ± 4 (the average distance between the distractor and the target in the speech error examples) by the following formulas (Church et al., 1991):

$$MI(n,c) = log_2\{[f(n,c) \times N] / f(n)f(c)\}$$

$$T = \{[f(n,c) / N] - [f(n)f(c) / N^2]\} / \{[\sqrt{f(n,c)}] / N\},$$

where n and c are the two cooccurring words (designated as ‘node’ and ‘collocate’, respectively), N is the size of the corpus (in word tokens), f(n) is the frequency of the first word of the pair (node), f(c) is the frequency of the second word (collocate), and f(n,c) is the cooccurrence frequency of the two words.

The MI and T-scores for a sample list of distractor-target and distractor-error word pairs are shown in Table 3.

As can be seen from Table 3, the MI and T-scores for distractor-error word pairs are generally higher than the scores for the respective distractor-target word pairs. This tendency holds for 74.4 per cent of the contextual semantic substitutions. The exceptions include mostly cases when the distractor and error are synonyms (19.7 per cent of the total number of contextual semantic substitutions) and when the distractor and target belong to fixed expressions such as quotations. Thus, in (7) and in (8), where the distractor and error pairs, 'any' – 'any/every' and 'baby' – 'child', respectively, are synonyms, the MI scores for the distractor-target pairs are higher compared to those for the distractor-error pairs. The result is not surprising considering that two synonyms do not often cooccur in the same sentence. In (6), which is a famous quotation, the MI scores for the distractor-target and distractor-error pairs are almost equal. Again, the result is expectable since both the target and the distractor belong to a fixed phrase.

2.3 Discussion

Contextual semantic substitutions result from the interference of a distractor word from the current sentence, causing a malfunction of the lexical selection mechanism. The effect can be captured by spreading activation models of lexical processing. The distractor word spreads activation to related lexical nodes, and if a related node receives a higher proportion of activation compared to the target word, it can be selected instead of the target word.

The point that needs to be clarified is the type of relationship involved in contextual semantic substitutions. The examples of speech errors cited in Section 2.1 are very diverse. Many of the distractor-error pairs are semantically related. The types of semantic relations involved include co-hyponymy, holonymy, synonymy, antonymy etc. Such examples would seem prima facie cases demonstrating the psychological reality of formal semantic relations in the production lexicon. On the other hand, some of the examples in Section 2.1 represent associative rather than formal semantic relationships. Does this mean that the effect involves both semantic and associative relations?

The comparison with the word association norms indicates that even when the distractor and error are semantically related, they are also associatively related. Thus, so far it would be premature to claim that the interference effect reflects semantic relations between words; rather, we should hypothesize that the links between the distractor and the error activated during natural language production are associative.

Fromkin (1988) was the first to report the occurrence of word substitutions such as *The Mafia moved into* ***Boston*** → *The Mafia moved into* ***Italy.*** She observed that such examples suggest that semantic features or properties may be anticipated or persevere just as segments, syllables and words, e.g. the substitution of the word *Italy* for *Boston* may be due to the perseveration of the [+Italian] element in the semantic representation of *Mafia*. Indeed, similar examples such as (11) or (12) cited in Section 2.1 can be interpreted as the perseveration of the [+winter] element in the semantic representation of *snow* and the perseveration of the [+tickets] element in the semantic representation of *booking office*, respectively. It could well be, however, that *Italy* is also associatively related to *Mafia* and that the selection of the word *Mafia* activated *Italy* as its associate.

As concerns the locus of the effect, it does not seem plausible that associative links encode no information about the words' meanings and are formed only between the phonological and orthographic representations of words (Ferrand & New 2003). In some of the cited examples, e.g. in (8), the error word has to change its grammatical features to replace the target word without disrupting the syntactic structure of the sentence. This means that it had to be retrieved at a pre-phonological production level. In view of the data showing that there is a statistically significant correlation between semantic similarity and associative strength both for syntagmatic and for paradigmatic English associates (Prior and Geffet 2003) and that semantic and associative memory systems interact (Silberman et al. 2007), the effect is more likely to arise at the lexical-semantic level of production.

The comparison with the corpus data suggests that distractor-error cooccurrence frequency affects the likelihood that an error word might be selected instead of the target word. There is also a certain correlation between cooccurrence strength data and associative norms. This is in line with the results of Plaut (1995) and Prior and Geffet (2003) suggesting that associative links between words may be encoded based on their cooccurrence frequency. However, there seem to exist some exceptions to this tendency. In Prior and Geffet (2003)'s study, Mutual Information and association strength for Hebrew associates were significantly correlated in only four categories: part-whole, category coordinates, functional relations and idiomatic relations. Although the present study did not specifically aim to explore the correlation between cooccurrence measures and association strength, one more exception from the correlation tendency is clearly revealed by the speech error data: Not surprisingly, when the distractor and error are synonyms, their cooccurrence frequency does not significantly exceed that of the distractor-target pair. Consequently, evidence from speech errors is in line with Prior and Geffet's proposal that associative connections between words are not necessarily formed on the basis of their cooccurrence frequency but appear to involve semantic networks as well. In particular, speech error data suggest that synonymy is a major kind of associative relationship between lexical items activated during sentence production. Within the framework of spreading activation theories of semantic memory, the synonym that receives a higher proportion of activation is more likely to be selected.

The interference effect reflected by contextual semantic substitutions appears to be fairly strong. It can even cause fixed expressions such as quotations (6) and idioms (8) to decompose, suggesting that the interfering effect of semantic context plays an important role in the lexical retrieval process.

Caramazza et al. (2009) propose that the semantic interference effect observed in picture naming studies does not reflect a general property of the lexical retrieval mechanism. It is possible that the effect that they refer to and the effect reflected by speech errors represent two different linguistic phenomena. Unlike the semantic interference effect observed in experimental studies, the effect reflected by speech errors is not confined to category coordinates; instead, the distractor and the target are commonly unrelated to each other. The effect reflects associative relations between words and can be well described as "lexical selection by activation". To distinguish it from the phenomenon observed in experimental studies, it might be appropriate to refer to it as the *semantic context effect*. Thus, we propose that unlike the effect described by Caramazza and colleagues, the semantic context effect *does* reflect a general property of lexical retrieval mechanism in natural language production.

To summarize, the comparison with the rates of cooccurrence and with word association norms suggests that contextual semantic substitutions reflect associative relationships between words. Even when the distractor and the error are semantically related, they are also associatively related and (with the likely exception of synonyms) tend to cooccur frequently in speech and texts. It seems, however, that the information encoded by these associative relations is not confined to phonological and orthographic information; rather, the links between lexical items activated during sentence production involve both lexical and semantic networks.

2.4 Contextual substitutions of a grammatical feature

Once the lexical node is selected, there is another process responsible for the selection of the word's grammatical features. An analysis of 154 contextual substitutions of a grammatical feature such as case, number, gender and person, resulting from the interference of a grammatical feature of an "interloper" (a distractor word form from the current sentence, either preceding or following the target word), reveals that a word's grammatical feature can be overwritten by the similar feature of a distractor word within the current utterance. Below are some representative examples of substitutions of the different grammatical features (the target and error features are in bold and the distractor feature in bold italics).

In (14), the genitive **case** form of the pronoun *ego* 'he' is substituted for the target dative case form *emu* due to the backward interference of the genitive case feature of the following noun *begemotika* 'hippo':

(14)	Miška	segodnja	vesëlyj.		
	Mishka	today	cheerful		
	Èto	potomu čto	**emu**	***begemotik-a***	podarili?
	This	because	he:**DAT**	hippo-SG.M.***GEN***	gave
		→ …	**ego**	***begemotik-a***	podarili?
			he:**GEN**	hippo-SG.M.***GEN***	gave

Mishka is cheerful today. Is that because he was given a [toy] hippo?

Conversely, in (15), the target genitive **case** form of the pronoun *menja* 'I' is replaced by the dative case form *mne* owing to the forward interference of the dative case form *im* of the preceding pronoun 'they':

(15)	***Im***	by	**menja**	v	pomošč
	they:***DAT***		I:**GEN**	in	help
→	***Im***	by	**mne**	v	pomošč
	they:***DAT***		I:**DAT**	in	help

I wish I were there to help them

The interference effect exerted by the plural **number** feature of the noun *klassax* 'classes' in (16) leads to the selection of the plural form of the ordinal numeral *tret'ix* 'third' instead of the target singular form:

(16)	… v perv-om,	vtor-om	i	**tret'-em**	***klass-ax***
	first-SG.M.LOC	second-SG.M.LOC		third-**SG**.M.LOC	class-***PL***.LOC
	… v perv-om,	vtor-om	i	**tret'-ix**	***klass-ax***
	first-SG.M.LOC	second-SG.M.LOC		third-**PL**.LOC	class-***PL***.LOC

…in the first, second and third classes [=years] at school

Likewise, in (17), the interference of the plural **number** feature of the preceding noun *geroi* 'heroes' causes the selection of the plural form of the following noun *skazok* 'fairy tales' and its adjective pre-modifier *ljubimyx* 'favorite' instead of the target singular form:

(17)	… ***vyxod-jat***	***gero-i***	**ljubim-oj**	**skazk-i**
	come out-PRS.***PL***	hero-***PL***.NOM	favorite-**SG**.F.GEN	tale-**SG**.F.GEN
→	***vyxod-jat***	***gero-i***	**ljubim-yx**	**skazok**
	come out-PRS.***PL***	hero-***PL***.NOM	favorite-**PL**.GEN	tale:**PL**.F.GEN

... the heroes of [our] favorite fairy tales come out [on the stage]

In (18), the speaker (a woman) is talking to a man. However, the interference of the feminine **gender** feature of the verb *xotela* 'wanted' (which she uses to refer to herself) results in the selection of the feminine form of the verb *udivilas'* 'be surprised' which, because it refers to a man, has to take the masculine form:

(18)	Nu,	ja že	***xotel-a***,	čtob ty	**udivil-sja**
	Well	I	want-PST.SG.***F***	that 2SG	be surprised-PST.**M**
→	Nu,	ja že	***xotel-a***,	čtob ty	**udivil-as'**
	Well	I	want-PST.SG.***F***	that 2SG	be surprised-PST.**F**

Well, I wanted to surprise you

(19) is another case of misselection of a **gender** feature. The gender feature of the adjectival pronoun pre-modifier, *v drugoj* 'in the other', has to agree with the feminine gender feature of the noun *ruke* 'hand'; however, the interference of the masculine gender feature of the preceding noun, *čemodan* 'case', causes the substitution of the masculine gender feature for the target feminine feature:

(19) v odnoj	ruke	***čemodan***,	v **drug-oj**	sumka
in one:**F**.SG.LOC	hand:**F**.SG.LOC	case:**M**.SG.NOM	in other–**F**.SG.LOC	bag:**F**.SG.NOM
→ v odnoj	ruke	***čemodan***,	v **drug-om**	sumka
in one:**F**.SG.LOC	hand:**F**.SG.LOC	case:**M**.SG.NOM	in other–**M**.SG.LOC	bag:**F**.SG.NOM

...a case in one hand and a bag in the other

In (20), the interference of the 2SG pronoun *ty* 'you' causes the selection of a wrong **person** feature (2SG instead of 3SG) of the verb *zanjat'* 'take', which has to agree with the pronoun *e`to* 'it':

(20)	***Ty***	skazala,	čto	<u>èto</u>	**zaim-ët**	čas
	*2*SG	said	that	it:**3**SG	take-**3**SG.FUT	hour
→	***Ty***	skazala,	čto	<u>èto</u>	**zaim-ëš'**	čas
	*2*SG	said	that	it:**3**SG	take-**2**SG.FUT	hour

You said that it would take an hour

(21) is another case of **person** feature substitution, this time resulting from backward interference. Although the verb *ujdët* 'leave' has to agree with the pronoun *ona* 'she' and thus has to take 3SG form, the interference of the 2SG feature of the following verb *dozvoniš'sja* 'reach [by phone]' results in the substitution of the 2SG form of 'leave' for the target 3SG:

(21)	A to ved'	utrom	ona	v zal	**ujd-ët**,	i	ne	***dozvon-iš'sja***
	Or else	in the morning	she	in room	go-**3**SG.FUT	and	not	reach-*2*SG.FUT
→	A to ved'	utrom	ona	v zal	**ujd-ëš'**,	I	ne	***dozvon-iš'sja***
	Or else	in the morning	she	in room	go-**2**SG.FUT	and	not	reach-*2*SG.FUT

...Or else she will go to the [reading] room in the morning, and you won't be able to reach her

In (22), the future form of the verb 'tell', *skažu*, is substituted for the target past form *skazal* due to the interference of the future **tense feature** of the following verbs *odenus'* 'will get dressed' and *pridu* 'will come':

(22)	Ja	tebe	**skaz-al**,	čto ja sejčas	***oden-us'***	i	***prid-u***
	I	2SG.DAT	tell-SG.**PST**	that I now	get dressed-1SG.***FUT***	and	come-1SG.***FUT***
→	Ja	tebe	**skaž-u**,	čto ja sejčas	***oden-us'***	i	***prid-u***
	I	2SG.DAT	tell-SG.**FUT**	that I now	get dressed-1SG.***FUT***	and	come-1SG.***FUT***

I told you I'll get dressed and come right now

Conversely, in (23), it is the future **tense feature** of the preceding verb *vytru* 'will wipe' that interferes with the target past form of the verb 'forget', *zabyla*, replacing it with the future form *zabudu*:

(23)	Ja	rešila,	čto	ja	vsë	***vytr-u***,	i	**zaby-la**
	I	decide-SG.PST	that	I	everything	wipe-1SG.***FUT***	and	forget-1SG.**PST**
→	Ja	rešila,	čto	ja	vsë	***vytr-u***,	i	**zabu-du**
	I	decide-SG.PST	that	I	everything	wipe-1SG.***FUT***	and	forget-1SG.**FUT**

I decided that I'd wipe everything dry, and forgot

2.5 Discussion

Speech error data suggest that the selection of grammatical features is generally a competitive process and that grammatical features, like lexical nodes, can spread activation to other words within the current sentence.

This conclusion runs counter to most theories of lexical retrieval, which claim that although the selection of lexical nodes may be competitive, the selection of their grammatical properties is an automatic consequence of lexical selection (Caramazza et al. 2001; Schiller & Caramazza 2002; Costa et al. 2003). Contrary to this view and in line with Schriefers (1993), evidence from Russian speech errors points to competitive nature of grammatical feature selection. Moreover, unlike picture-word interference studies which focus on the interference effect exerted by the gender or number feature of a distractor word, contextual grammatical feature substitutions show that the list of interfering grammatical features is not confined to gender and number. Other features such as case, tense, and aspect also appear to be involved. Thus, the interfering effect of grammatical context seems to reflect a general property of the language production mechanism.

The difference between Russian speech error data and the results of the picture-word interference studies might be due to language specific properties such as the degree of inflectionality and the interaction of the gender feature with other grammatical features. Bordag and Pechmann (2009) have recently proposed that the occurrence of the congruency effect might depend on whether a given grammatical feature is indispensable or dispensable for further encoding. On this view, internal features like gender that become available only after the word has been marked for its grammatical category can be bypassed by the encoding process if the information about external features like number and case is available earlier and is sufficient for the determination of the word's inflectional variant. Clearly more experimental research is needed to investigate the effect of grammatical context on the selection of grammatical features other than gender and number in other languages.

Another question to be resolved concerns the locus of the interference effect. Speech error evidence shows that the effect should emerge at a level where a word's grammatical features are specified because the irrelevant feature surfaces as its respective inflection suffixed to the stem of the target word. Thus, contextual grammatical feature substitutions suggest the existence of a distinct grammatical encoding level of sentence production, where abstract grammatical features may compete for selection. A grammatical feature of an interfering distractor word can overwrite the similar feature of the target word. This view is consistent with Schriefer (1993)'s theory but it contradicts the view that it is only at a level of morphophonological transformations that the competition takes place (Schiller & Caramazza 2002; Costa et al. 2003; Bordag & Pechmann 2008).

3 Conclusions

The effects of contextual variables on language production have mostly been explored using picture-word interference studies.

The effect referred to as semantic interference seems to be confined to category coordinates and has been shown to be irrelevant to the general property of lexical retrieval mechanism.

Experimental studies of grammatical priming have led most authors to conclude that grammatical features of a distractor word such as gender and number have no inhibitory effect on the selection of the grammatical features of a target word. Consequently, grammatical interference is not regarded as a major effect implicit to grammatical encoding mechanism.

Unlike the experimental studies of semantic and grammatical priming, Russian speech error data demonstrate pervasive within-speaker interference of both word meanings and grammatical features throughout the sentence production process. The interference effects during natural language production can be accounted for by suggesting that alongside its associative field, a word form activates a field of its grammatical features, spreading activation to other words within the current sentence.

Evidence from contextual substitution speech errors and its comparison to related data suggest that the locus of the semantic context effect is the lexical-semantic level of production. In all likelihood, the interference occurs before the specification of words' grammatical features. The locus of the grammatical context effect is the grammatical encoding level, where words' grammatical features are specified.

Author note

Svetlana Gorokhova, St. Petersburg State University, Russia.

References

Alario, F.-X., Segui, J., & Ferrand, L. 2000. Semantic and associative priming in picture naming. *The Quarterly Journal of Experimental Psychology* 53A(3): 741–64.

Anderson, J. R. 1983. A spreading activation theory of memory. *Journal of Verbal Learning and Verbal Behavior* 22(3): 261–95.

Bloem, I., van den Boogaard, S., & La Heij, W. 2004. Semantic facilitation and semantic interference in language production: Further evidence for the conceptual selection model of lexical access. *Journal of Memory and Language* 51: 307–23.

Bordag, D., & Pechmann, T. 2008. Grammatical gender in speech production: Evidence from Czech. *Journal of Psycholinguistic Research* 37: 69–85.

Bordag, D., & Pechmann, T. 2009. Externality, internality, and (in)dispensability of grammatical features in speech production: Evidence from Czech declension and conjugation. *Journal of Experimental Psychology: Learning, Memory, and Cognition*, 35: 446-465.

Caramazza, A., Miozzo, M., Costa, A., Schiller, N., & Alario, F. X. 2001. A crosslinguistic investigation of determiner production. *Language, Brain, and Cognitive Development: Essays in Honor of Jacques Mehler*, ed. E. Dupoux, 209–26. Cambridge, MA: MIT Press.

Chiarello, C., Burgess, C., Richards, L., & Pollock, A. 1990. Semantic and associative priming in the cerebral hemispheres: Some words do, some words don't ... sometimes, some places. *Brain and Language* 38: 75–104.

Church, K. & Hanks, P. 1990. Word Association Norms, Mutual Information, and Lexicography. *Computational Linguistics* 16(1): 22–29.

Church, K., Gale, W., Hanks, P., & Hindle, D. 1991. Using statistics in lexical analysis. *Lexical Acquisition*, ed. U. Zernik, 115-64. Englewood Cliff, NJ: Erlbaum.

Church, K., Hanks, P., Hindle, D., Gale, W., & Moon, R. 1994. Lexical substitutability. *Computational Approaches to the Lexicon*, eds. B.T.S. Atkins and A. Zampolli, 153–80. Oxford: Oxford University Press.

Collins, A. M., & Loftus, E. F. 1975. A spreading-activation theory of semantic processing. *Psychological Review* 82: 407–28.

Costa, A., Kovacic, D., Fedorenko, E., & Caramazza, A. 2003. The gender congruency effect and the selection of freestanding and bound morphemes: Evidence from Croatian. *Journal of Experimental Psychology: Learning, Memory, and Cognition* 29: 1270–82.

Costa, A., Alario, F.-X., & Caramazza, A. 2005. On the categorical nature of the semantic interference effect in the picture–word interference paradigm. *Psychonomic Bulletin & Review* 12(1): 125–31.

Cree, G. S., McRae, K., & McNorgan, C. 1999. An Attractor Model of Lexical Conceptual Processing: Simulating Semantic Priming. *Cognitive Science* 23(3): 371–414.

Cutler, A. The perfect speech error. 1988. *Language, Speech and Mind: Studies in Honour of Victoria A. Fromkin*, ed. L.M. Hyman & C.N. Li, 209-223. London & New York: Routledge.

Damian, M. F., & Als, L. C. 2005. Long-Lasting Semantic Context Effects in the Spoken Production of Object Names. *Journal of Experimental Psychology: Learning, Memory, and Cognition* 31: 1372–84.

Dell, G. S. 1986. A spreading-activation theory of retrieval in sentence production. *Psychological Review* 93(3): 283–321.

Dell, G.S., & Reich, P.A. 1981. Stages in sentence production: An analysis of speech-error data. *Journal of Verbal Learning and Verbal Behavior* 20: 611-29.

Fay, D., & Cutler, A. 1977. Malaprorisms and the structure of the mental lexicon. *Linguistic Inquiry* 8(3): 505-20.

Ferrand, L., & New, B. 2003. Semantic and associative priming in the mental lexicon. *Mental Lexicon: Some words to talk about words*, ed. P. Bonin, 25–43. Hauppauge, NY: Nova Science Publisher.

Finkbeiner, M., & Caramazza, A. 2006. Lexical selection is not a competitive process: A reply to La Heij et al. *Cortex* 42: 1032–35.

Fillmore, C. J. 1982. Frame semantics. *Linguistics in the Morning Calm*, eds. the Linguistic Society of Korea, 111-37. Seoul: Hanshin Publishing Co.

Fromkin, V.A. 1971. The non-anomalous nature of anomalous utterances. *Language* 47: 27-53.

Fromkin, V. A. 1988. Grammatical aspects of speech errors. *Linguistic Theory: Extensions and Implications*, ed. F. J. Newmeyer, 117–38. Cambridge etc.: Cambridge University Press.

Garrett, M. 1980. Levels of processing in sentence production. *Language Production. Vol. 1. Speech and Talk*, ed. B. Butterworth, 177-220. New York: Academic Press.

Glaser, W. R., & Glaser, M. O. 1989. Context effects on Stroop-like word and picture processing. *Journal of Experimental Psychology: General* 118: 13–42.

Hantsch, A., Jescheniak, J. D., & Schriefers, H. 2005. *Memory and Cognition* 33(6): 984–1000.

Hodgson, J. M. 1991. Informational constraints on pre-lexical priming. *Language and Cognitive Processes* 6: 169–264.

Humphreys, G. W., Lloyd-Jones, T. J., & Fias, W. 1995. Semantic interference effects on naming using a postcue procedure: Tapping the links between semantics and phonology with pictures and words. *Journal of Experimental Psychology: Learning, Memory, and Cognition* 21: 961–80.

Hunston, S. 2002. *Corpora in Applied Linguistics*. Cambridge: Cambridge University Press.

Hutchison, K. A. 2003. Is semantic priming due to association strength or feature overlap? A *micro*analytic review. *Psychonomic Bulletin and Review* 10(4): 785–813.

Kroll, J. F., Stewart, E. 1994. Category interference in translation and picture naming: Evidence for asymmetric connections between bilingual memory representations. *Journal of Memory and Language* 33: 149–74.

Lemhöfer, K., Schriefers, H., & Jescheniak, J. 2006. The processing of free and bound gender-marked morphemes in speech production: Evidence from Dutch. *Journal of Experimental Psychology: Learning, Memory, and Cognition* 32: 437–42.

Levelt, W. J. M., Roelofs, A., & Meyer, A. S. 1999. A theory of lexical access in speech production. *Behavioral and Brain Sciences* 22: 1–75.

Lucas, M. 2000. Semantic priming without association: A meta-analytic review. *Psychonomic Bulletin & Review* 7: 618–30.

Lupker, S. J. 1984. Semantic priming without association: A second look. *Journal of Verbal Learning and Verbal Behavior* 23: 709–33.

Mahon, B. Z., & Caramazza, A. 2009. Why does lexical selection have to be so hard? Comment on Abdel Rahman and Melinger's swinging lexical network proposal. *Language and Cognitive Processes* 24 (5): 735-48.

Mahon, B. Z., Costa, A., Peterson, R., Vargas, K. A., & Caramazza, A. 2007. Lexical selection is not by competition: A reinterpretation of semantic interference and facilitation effects in the picture–word interference paradigm. *Journal of Experimental Psychology: Learning, Memory, and Cognition* 33(3): 503–35.

McKoon, G., & Ratcliff, R. 1986. Automatic activation of episodic information in a semantic memory task. *Journal of Experimental Psychology: Learning, Memory, and Cognition* 12: 108–15.

McKoon, G., & Ratcliff, R. 1992. Spreading activation versus compound cue accounts of priming: Mediated priming revisited. *Journal of Experimental Psychology: Learning, Memory, and Cognition* 18: 1155–72.

McKoon, G., Ratcliff, R., & Dell, G. 1986. A critical evaluation of the semantic-episodic distinction. *Journal of Experimental Psychology: Learning, Memory, and Cognition* 12(2): 295-306.

McNamara, T. P. 1992. Theories of priming: I. Associative distance and lag. *Journal of Experimental Psychology: Learning, Memory, & Cognition* 18: 1173–90.

McRae, K. & Boisvert, S. 1998. Automatic semantic similarity priming. *Journal of Experimental Psychology: Learning, Memory and Cognition* 24: 558–72.

Moss, H. E., Ostrin, R. K., Tyler, L. K., & Marslen-Wilson, W. D. 1995. Accessing different types of lexical semantic information: Evidence from priming. *Journal of Experimental Psychology: Learning, Memory and Cognition* 21: 863–83.

Neely, J. H. 1991. Semantic priming effects in visual word recognition: A selective view of current findings and theories. *Basic processes in reading: Visual word recognition*, ed. D. Besner & G. Humphreys, 264–336. Hillsdale, NJ: Erlbaum.

Neely, J. H., & Durgunoglu, A. 1985. Dissociative episodic and semantic priming effects in episodic recognition and lexical decision tasks. *Journal of Memory and Language* 24: 466–89.

Plaut, D. C. 1995. Semantic and associative priming in a distributed attractor network. *Proceedings of the Seventeenth Annual Conference of the Cognitive Science Society* 17: 37–42. Hillsdale, NJ: Lawrence Erlbaum Associates.

Prior, A., & Geffet, M. 2003. Mutual information and semantic similarity as predictors of word association strength: Modulation by association type and semantic relation. *Proceedings of the 1st European Cognitive Science Conference 2003*, ed. F. Schmalhofer, R. Young, & G. Katz. Mahwah, NJ: Lawrence Erlbaum Associates.

Russian National Corpus (http://ruscorpora.ru)

Russian Word Association Thesaurus/Русский Ассоциативный Словарь. 2002. Ред. Ю. Н. Караулов, Г. А. Черкасова, Н. В. Уфимцева, Ю. А. Сорокин, Е.Ф.Тарасов. Москва: Астрель.

Schiller, N. O., & Caramazza, A. 2002. The selection of grammatical features in word production: The case of plural nouns in German. *Brain and Language* 81: 342–57.

Schriefers, H. 1993. Syntactic processes in the production of noun phrases. *Journal of Experimental Psychology: Learning, Memory, and Cognition* 19: 841–50.

Schriefers, H., Jescheniak, J. D., & Hantsch, A. 2005. Selection of gender-marked morphemes in speech production. *Journal of Experimental Psychology: Learning, Memory and Cognition* 31: 159–68.

Shelton, J. R., & Martin, R. C. 1992. How semantic is automatic semantic priming? *Journal of Experimental Psychology: Learning, Memory and Cognition* 18: 1191–210.

Silberman, Y., Bentini, S., & Miikkulainen, R. 2007. Semantic boost on episodic associations: An empirically-based computational model. *Cognitive Science* 31: 645–71.

Starreveld, P. A., & La Heij, W. 1996. Time-course analysis of semantic and orthographic context effects in picture naming. *Journal of Experimental Psychology: Learning, Memory, and Cognition* 22: 896–918.

Stubbs, M. 1995. Collocations and semantic profiles: on the cause of the trouble with quantitative studies. *Functions of Language* 2, 1: 23–55.

Williams, J. N. 1996. Is automatic priming semantic? *European Journal of Cognitive Psychology* 8: 113–61.

6

Conceptualizing Change as Deictic Abstract Motion: Metaphorical and Grammatical Uses of 'Come' and 'Go' in Finnish

TUOMAS HUUMO & JARI SIVONEN

1 Introduction

Languages often extend the use of deictic motion verbs for many kinds of metaphorical and grammatical purposes. Deictic motion verbs are verbs that indicate motion with respect to the deictic center, which is canonically the position of the speech act participants but may also be shifted into another location where the viewpoint of the conceptualizer is situated. Langacker (1987: 126) defines deictic elements as elements that include some reference to a ground element within their scope of predication (the term *ground* indicating the speech act event, its participants and its setting). Canonical deictic motion verbs indicate meanings like 'come' and 'go', and Langacker (1987: 127) points out that the deictic construal is primary for them though it can sometimes be overridden by context. Canonically, according to Langacker, these verbs presuppose a reference point that is equated with some facet of the ground (e.g. the position of the speaker) unless there is an indication to the contrary. Such verbs often develop into more abstract functions, such as the expression of future or abstract change (for an overview, see Wilkins and Hill 1995). Typical English examples include (1) (from

Meaning, Form, and Body.
Fey Parrill, Vera Tobin & Mark Turner (eds.)

Traugott and Dasher 2005: 84), (2) (from Radden 1995: 445), and (3) (from Langacker 1990: 155–156).

(1) Do you think it's going to rain?
(2) The water is coming to a boil.
(3) The milk is about to go sour.

Such developments can be argued to reflect the nature of grammatical structure as determined by the choices and viewpoints of a human conceptualizer. As has been repeatedly demonstrated in cognitive linguistic literature, such extensions are not random but semantically/conceptually motivated. In the present paper, we analyze metaphorical and grammatical uses of two Finnish deictic motion verbs, *tulla* 'come' and *mennä* 'go', and show how their development into more abstract functions follows certain conceptual metaphors but also other kinds of cognitive operations where a viewing strategy is imposed upon a situation. These factors include, for instance, the windowing of attention over the situation (in terms of Talmy 2000: 257–310) and the selection of a static vs. a dynamic point of view. We start by introducing the basic spatial usage of the two verbs and then proceed to consider their more abstract uses and the conceptualization strategies that motivate them.

When indicating objective motion, *mennä* 'go' expresses motion away from the deictic center and *tulla* 'come' profiles motion towards it. Since the deictic center is usually identified with the location of the speech act participants, *mennä* 'go' thus typically indicates motion away from the speaker and *tulla* 'come' motion towards the speaker. However, it is also quite common to represent events from different vantage points by using deictic elements, and the conceptualizer may select a viewpoint other than his/her own location, for instance by associating the viewpoint with one participant of the designated relationship (Larjavaara 1990: 259–260). In terms of Cognitive Grammar, such transfers of the conceptualizer's vantage point represent instances of *shifted deictic center* (Langacker 1991: 266–267). For example, in (4), the viewpoint is situated in the speaker's (initial) location, whereas in (5), the viewpoint is situated in the location of the kitchen (for the glosses, see Appendix 1).

(4) Minä men-i-n keittiö-ön.
I go-PST-1SG kitchen-ILLAT
'I went to the kitchen.'

(5) Minä tul-i-n keittiö-ön.
I come-PST-1SG kitchen-ILLAT

'I came to the kitchen.'

In addition to designating motion with respect to the deictic center, the verbs *tulla* 'come' and *mennä* 'go' also display other oppositions. One kind of opposition that is relevant for our point of view concerns the windowing of attention over the situation: when the viewpoint of the conceptualizer is dynamic and follows the motion of the mover, the verb *tulla* 'come' can be used to indicate a punctual arrival into a location (6). In the same context, *mennä* 'go' profiles a more extensive motion that takes place on the path leading towards the goal (7) (for windowing of attention in general, see Talmy 2000: Chapter 4).

(6) Tule-n juuri Turku-un.
come-PRES.3SG just name-ILLAT
'I'm just coming / getting to / arriving in Turku'.

(7) Mene-n juuri Turku-un.
go-PRES.1SG just name-ILLAT
'I'm going to Turku right now'.

Example (6) allows different readings that vary in accordance with the selection of the conceptualizer's viewpoint. If the viewpoint is static, then (6) is appropriate in a context where the addressee is already in Turku, and the selection of the verb 'come' reflects the positioning of the deictic center in the goal location. In another reading, the viewpoint is dynamic and follows the motion of the mover in space and time; in that context the addressee does not need to be in Turku for the verb 'come' to be appropriate. In this reading, the selection of the verb reflects a narrow windowing of attention: the mover (the speaker) is just arriving in Turku, and the example only profiles this punctual event and the final portion of the path traversed. In contrast, example (7) with the verb 'go' indicates a more canonical, wider windowing over the path traversed – this is in part due to the fact that (7) is the neutral way of expressing motion into a location where the deictic center is not situated. Such usages thus represent a deviation from the canonical, deictic usage of these verbs.

The verbs *mennä* and *tulla* have various metaphorical and grammaticalized functions that can be explained as extensions of their basic spatial meanings. In this paper we analyze such functions by using a cognitive linguistic approach. Though our general assumption is that the semantic extensions of *mennä* and *tulla* have developed from the objective senses of these verbs, our present approach is synchronic. Nevertheless, it should be mentioned that many of the metaphorical usages of these verbs already occur in the earliest written documents of the Finnish language. For example, the expression *tulla hulluksi* 'go crazy ' (see example 13) is pervasive in 16th century Finnish as it is found in Mikael Agricola's texts (the earliest literary materials available, including the first Finnish translation of the New Testament) among others. Since there is no older data available, it is not easy to pinpoint the exact time when the semantic developments from the concrete to the abstract senses took place.

Our paper is divided into four sections. After this introduction, we discuss the general pattern of the metaphorical uses of these verbs in Section 2. Both verbs have the function of indicating abstract, non-spatial changes, and it will be shown that *mennä* 'go' is usually associated with changes conceptualized as negative, whereas *tulla* 'come' indicates a positive change. In Section 3, we analyze a more grammaticalized use of the two verbs: the constructions *men-nä kerto-ma-an* [go-1INF tell-3INF-ILLAT][1] and *tul-la sano-ma-an* [come-1INF say-3INF-ILLAT], which do not profile motion but an aspectual and simultaneously affective meaning. In the first case, the conceptualizer considers the indicated speech act as involving the revealing of information that should not be revealed, and the latter type indicates an aggressive way of speaking, possibly involving picking a quarrel with the person spoken to. In such readings no actual motion needs to be involved: the verbs profile the inchoative aspect together with the speaker's subjective evaluation of the event. Our analysis shows that these non-motional and affective meanings of the verbs *mennä* and *tulla* are semantically motivated, and that they can be seen as instances of abstract motion away from or towards the dominion of control of the conceptualizer or of a participant in the situation. In the final chapter, we sum up the results and conclusions of the study.

2 General Pattern of the Metaphorical Uses

A cross-linguistically common metaphorical use of verbs meaning 'come' and 'go' are expressions of a change-of-state where an entity enters or leaves an internal state. Some English examples have already been discussed above (examples 2 and 3). Huumo (1996), working with the Mental Spaces framework (e.g., Fauconnier 1985, 1997), calls internal states *bound spaces*, since they are conceptually dependent on (= "bound to") the entity that is metaphorically situated in the space. He shows with Finnish data how

[1] The *1st infinitive* and the *3rd infinitive* are classical terms used for different infinitival forms. The 1st infinitive is the "basic" infinitive, roughly corresponding to the English *to* infinitive, and it is used in syntactic core roles (subject and object) whereas the 3rd infinitive is used adverbially and indicates locative-aspectual functions; cf. Footnote 2.

this dependence affects the scope relations between locatives indicating a bound space and other locatives in the sentence.

When indicating a change with respect to a bound space, such as an internal state or condition, Finnish uses its deictic motion verbs that, in addition to the change itself, indicate the viewpoint of the conceptualizer. In the expressions to be studied in this section, the state itself is referred to by a locative phrase (in a locative case), implementing the cross-linguistically common STATES ARE LOCATIONS metaphor (e.g. Lakoff and Turner, 1989: 97). In the metaphor, the entity undergoing a change is represented as moving into (or sometimes out of) a state. In addition, deictic motion verbs relate the event to the viewpoint of the conceptualizer, which can be situated either outside the metaphorical space (when the verb 'go' is used) or inside it (when the verb 'come' is used). Both verbs thus designate the mover's motion into the metaphorical space, but relate the space and the viewpoint of the conceptualizer differently. The selection of the viewpoint is subjective, since the speaker is not actually situated in the metaphorical space. This subjectivity distinguishes the metaphorical expressions from deictic expressions of actual motion which typically (though not always) relate the direction of the motion to the speaker's actual position.

In the Finnish expressions following this metaphor, a general tendency is that *mennä* 'go' indicates a negative change, such as a change from normal to abnormal in (8) and (10), whereas *tulla* 'come' indicates a positive change like the one from abnormal to normal in (9) and (11) (Onikki-Rantajääskö 2001: 207). In this respect, the Finnish verbs resemble their English counterparts. In many cases, the English *come* denotes entry into a normal state (*He came round very slowly*) whereas *go* implies change into something abnormal (*He went out of his mind*) (Radden 1995: 432).

(8) Potilas mene-e kooma-an.
patient go-PRES.3SG coma-ILLAT
'The patient is going into a coma'.

(9) Potilas tule-e taju-i-hin-sa
patient come-PRES.3SG consciousness-PL-ILLAT-3PX
'The patient is becoming conscious'.

(10) Kone men-i rikki.
machine go-PST.3SG broken
'The machine broke'.

(11) Kone tul-i kunto-on.
machine come-PST.3SG condition-ILLAT
'The machine was repaired' [lit.: came into condition].

In (8) and (9), there are many factors that motivate the selection of the deictic motion verbs. First, the event of going into a coma is negative, whereas becoming conscious is positive. Furthermore, a patient who goes into a coma becomes inaccessible to other people and communication, whereas a patient who gains his/her consciousness becomes accessible to others. Examples (10) and (11) designate a change undergone by an inanimate entity but utilize the same metaphor: (10) shows that when the entity enters a non-canonical, nonfunctional state, the verb 'go' is used, whereas entering a canonical state or a state of functionality is expressed by 'come' (11).

What these examples show, then, is that the position of the conceptualizer's viewpoint determines the selection of the deictic center and varies between the inside and the outside of the metaphorical space. The conceptualizer tends to set the viewpoint into spaces like NORMALITY, ACCESSIBILITY and FUNCTIONALITY instead of their opposites, and prefers to observe the (abstract) motion from within such spaces. Therefore, when entering a space conceptualized as positive, the mover is metaphorically approaching the deictic center, where the conceptualizer is already situated. When entering a negative space, the mover is moving away from the deictic centre and also from the conceptualizer. The general conceptual metaphor motivating this kind of a viewpoint selection is thus GOOD IS HERE.

However, in Finnish, matters are more complicated than this just like they are with the English *come* and *go* (see Radden 1995: 432–433). The following examples show that the tendency to use the GOOD IS HERE metaphor is not without exceptions. In (12) and (13), the internal states entered by the mover are 'drunkenness' and 'madness', respectively, and it would be awkward to consider them positive or canonical. In spite of this, the verb *tulla* 'come' is used. In (14), on the other hand, 'getting married' is certainly a positive change (in any normal context), and therefore it may be surprising that the verb *mennä* 'go' is used.

(12) Pekka tul-i humala-an.
name come-PST.3SG intoxication-ILLAT
'Pekka got drunk'.

(13) Potilas tule-e hullu-ksi.
Patient come-PRES.3SG crazy-TRANSL
'The patient is going crazy'.

(14) Mene-n naimis-i-in.
go-PRES.1SG marriage-PL-ILLAT
'I'm getting married'.

If we try to switch the verbs in these examples, we see, first, that *mennä* 'go' would also be possible in (12) and (13), though it would not be the canonical way of expressing such relations. It would assume an external point of view, saying that when getting drunk or going crazy, the person is becoming inaccessible to the conceptualizer, in a way similar to the 'coma' example (8). However, we would not like to argue that by using the verb 'come' in (12) and (13) the conceptualizer is placing his/her viewpoint in the mental space of drunkenness or madness, but rather that here the conceptualizer's point of view moves together with the entity undergoing the change, and follows the change from the viewpoint of that entity. In other words, the viewpoint is not static but dynamic. Thus, relevant objective motion counterparts of (12) and (13) would not be actual-motion expressions like (4) and (5), where the conceptualizer observes the motion from a static point of view anchored into one location only, but rather expressions like (6), where 'coming' indicates a narrow profiling over a punctual arrival at a location.

Note, too, that what distinguishes (12) and (13) from (8) is that in the situations they designate, the animate mover remains conscious all the time, and is thus a participant with whom the conceptualizer can identify. In the metaphor motivating (8), on the other hand, the person entering the 'coma' space loses his or her consciousness, and thus metaphorically "vanishes into" the 'coma' space and becomes inaccessible to the conceptualizer (cf. also Huumo 2006: 58–63 where a similar explanation is given to the use of directional cases in expressions that indicate the cessation of an entity's existence). In (14), on the other hand, 'getting married' is not profiled as a punctual event of entering a metaphorical space but as a more extensive process that involves numerous component events that take time. This wide windowing, in our view, motivates the use of the verb 'go' in example (14) (in the same way as in (7)).

In addition to the uses discussed above, *tulla* 'come' is also used in referring to a situation where an entity or a matter is brought up in discourse, revealed, or otherwise enters the *cognitive dominion* of the conceptualizer. A dominion, in general, is defined by Langacker (1999: 173–174) as "the conceptual region (or the set of entities) to which a particular reference point affords direct access" (cf. also Langacker 1993: 6). A canonical example is the possessive construction (e.g. *Sara's book*), where the possessor (*Sara*) functions as a reference point for the possessee (*book*), which is thus situated within the (possessive) dominion surrounding the reference point.

A cognitive dominion is similar to a possessive dominion but it is based on a cognitive relationship between the (animate, sentient) reference point and the entity to be located. A cognitive dominion includes all entities the reference point has a cognitive relationship with (e.g., by knowing, perceiving, being aware of or remembering them; Huumo 2006: 41). In one of its abstract uses, the verb 'come' indicates a change in a cognitive relationship: an entity enters the cognitive dominion of a reference point, which can be either explicitly indicated by another element of the clause, or implicit. This usage is obviously related to the 'accessibility' meaning of the verb 'come' discussed above with examples (8) and (9), where it was pointed out that when the mover enters a metaphorical space where it remains accessible to the conceptualizer, the verb 'come' is often used. In (15) and (16) it is the entrance into the abstract space of 'publicity' that makes the mover accessible.

(15) Asia tul-i julki.
matter come-PST.3SG public
'The matter was disclosed'.

(16) Ongelma tul-i ilmi.
problem come-PST.3SG "overt"
'The problem was noticed/revealed'.

In yet another type of usage, the verb 'come' implies agentivity, i.e. that the change is intentionally brought about by an implicit agent, which is not overtly referred to in the sentence. In the same context, 'go' indicates lack of agentivity and thus an automative (anticausative) meaning:

(17) Tul-i-ko ovi lukko-on?
come-PST.3SG-QUEST door lock-ILLAT
'Did the door get locked [= did you/we lock it]?'
[lit.: "Did the door come into lock?"].

(18) Men-i-kö ovi lukko-on?
go-PST.3SG-QUEST door lock-ILLAT
'Did the door get locked ["by itself"]?'
[lit.: "Did the door go into lock?"]

(19) Tankki tul-i tyhjä-ksi.
tank come-PST.3SG empty-TRANSL
'The tank got empty [was emptied].'

(20) Tankki men-i tyhjä-ksi.
tank go-PST.3SG empty-TRANSL
'The tank went empty'.

Example (17) is appropriate in a context where the speaker wants to make sure that the door has been locked, whereas (18) designates an unintentional change that has taken place without the involvement of an active agent. The same opposition distinguishes (19) from (20): the selection of the verb reflects the choice between a meaning where the tank is emptied on purpose ('come') and one where the tank becomes empty without such purposefulness (as in a car running out of fuel; 'go'). Such oppositions of course have a close association with the other opposition types discussed above: an agent normally works to achieve a goal that s/he considers positive or worth striving for, whereas events that occur without such an intention may more naturally be considered negative.

To summarize the observations made in this section, we have seen that the general-level conceptual metaphor motivating the uses of the two verbs is GOOD IS HERE, where the quality 'good' may be understood as consisting of or co-occurring with other, more specific (positive) concepts such as 'available', 'conscious', 'accessible', 'canonical' or 'brought about intentionally by an agent'. In all these uses, the conceptualizer prefers to select a viewpoint situated inside a metaphorical space that is conceptualized as positive, and an external viewpoint to changes that involve the entering of a metaphorical space conceptualized as negative. The only exception to this tendency is the usage represented by examples (12)–(14) where it is not the nature of the metaphorical space but the selected windowing over the event that determine the choice of the deictic motion verb.

3 Expressing affectivity: from spatial motion to revelation of information and quarrel picking

Perhaps the farthest grammaticalized use of the verbs *mennä* 'go' and *tulla* 'come' is the one where they take an infinitival complement marked with the illative ('into') case and indicate affectivity (disapproval by the speaker) together with an inchoative aspectual meaning. With locative case-marked infinitives, the motion indicated by the deictic motion verbs is thus further abstracted and grammaticalized into the meaning of inception of an activity (conceivable as metaphorical motion into the activity space). In such instances, the motion verbs form a conventional unit together with the infinitive, a conventional construction in the sense of Goldberg (2006). In addition to the inception of the activity, such expressions also indicate an affective meaning: the speaker's disapproval of the situation. This development is an instance of *subjectification* in the sense of Traugott and Dasher (2005: 30; see also Hopper and Tragott 1993) – “the semasiological process whereby [speakers/writers] come, over time, to develop meanings for [lexemes] that encode or externalize their perspectives and attitudes as constrained by the communicative world of the speech event, rather than by the so-called ‘real-world’ characteristics of the event or situation referred to”.

In this section, we analyze two constructions where *mennä* ‘go’ and *tulla* ‘come’ are followed by a speech act verb in the so-called 3rd infinitive illative form. Examples include *men-nä kerto-ma-an* [go-1INF tell-3INF-ILL] (lit. ‘go to tell’, abstractly meaning ‘tell against the speaker's will’) and *tul-la sano-ma-an* [come-1INF say-3INF-ILL] (lit. ‘come to say’, abstractly indicating ‘saying’ in an aggressive or belligerent manner, e.g. in a situation involving quarrel picking). As can be seen, the marker of the 3rd infinitive is the affix *-mA*, which occurs together with a locative case ending.[2] In constructions where the 3rd infinitive illative is used as a complement of the deictic motion verbs, the infinitive can thus be seen as indicating an abstract goal which the trajector enters. In such constructions, the deictic motion verbs indicate a concrete or a metaphorical transition of the trajector into the activity space. In the concrete meaning, this transition involves actual motion in space (the trajector moves to a certain location to perform the activity), whereas the abstract meaning lacks the sense of motion and merely indicates the inception of the activity (for the grammaticalization phenomena involved, see e.g. Heine et al. 1991). In addition, both constructions indicate affective meanings, which we now set out to explain. To achieve this, we need to consider the direction of the abstract motion and its relationship with the conceptualizer's viewpoint. It also needs to be pointed out that the constructions are not quite symmetric, since the one involving the verb *mennä* ‘go’ has a wider distribution and allows many kinds of verbs as its infinitival complement, whereas the one involving *tulla* ‘come’ (in the relevant abstract meaning) seems to be restricted to speech act verbs only. In this paper, we only consider instances where the infinitival complement is a speech act verb.

---

[2] The Finnish locative case system consists of three series of local cases (internal vs. external vs. general), where each series has one lative (‘into’, ‘to-at’), one locative (‘in’ / ‘at’) and one separative (‘out of’ / ‘from’) case (for an overview, see e.g. Huumo and Ojutkangas 2006). The 3rd infinitive is inflected in the internal local cases, which are the illative (general meaning: ‘into’), the inessive (‘in’) and the elative (‘out of’), and these case forms of the infinitive indicate an inceptive, a progressive and a cessative meaning, respectively. The general function of the 3rd infinitive illative is thus to indicate the inception of an activity, but it has slightly different functions in different constructions.

Consider first examples (21) and (22), which can be interpreted in two ways, depending on whether the motion verbs *mennä* 'go' and *tulla* 'come' are understood as indicating spatial or abstract motion.

(21) Liisa men-i kerto-ma-an
name go-PST.3SG tell-3INF-ILLAT
asia-n Heiki-lle.
matter-GEN name-ALLAT
'Liisa went to tell the matter to Heikki.'
'Liisa revealed the matter to Heikki (the speaker disapproves this).'

(22) Liisa tul-i sano-ma-an
name go-PST.3SG say-3INF-ILLAT
(asia-n) Heiki-lle.
(matter-GEN) name-ALLAT
'Liisa came to say (the matter) to Heikki.'
'Liisa said (the matter) to Heikki in a belligerent manner.' ~ 'Liisa was picking a quarrel with Heikki.'

As stated above, examples (21) and (22) are semantically ambiguous since in addition to the idiomatic meaning they can also be understood as indicating objective, physical motion. In this reading, (21) means that Liisa goes to Heikki to perform the speech act. In the abstract-motion interpretation, no spatial motion needs to be involved, and it is possible that Liisa is already in the same location with Heikki when the speech act takes place. With such a reading, the deictic motion verb does not refer to motion in space but indicates only abstract motion (inception of the activity) together with the speaker's affective judgment. Correspondingly, example (22) has a reading with actual motion where Liisa comes to Heikki to perform the speech act, and the abstract meaning where, again, no spatial motion is involved. Remarkably, this abstract meaning also implies that Liisa is behaving aggressively and picking a quarrel with Heikki. The affective meanings of these constructions seem to be due to the deictic motion verbs: if only the speech act verbs were used (as finite forms), the affective meaning would vanish.

In cross-linguistic terms it is not at all extraordinary that constructions involving a (deictic) motion verb that is followed by another verb profile affective evaluations. Such structures have been found in many languages. In linguistic analyses, such multi-verb expressions are classified under a variety of categories, such as *hendiadic expressions*, *pseudo-coordinative structures*, *simple juxtaposition* and *zero strategy* (see Payne 1997, Stefanowitsch 1999, Hopper 2001). Constructions containing motion verbs have often been observed to express affective meanings, such as bitterness, frustration, annoyance, disappointment, and disapproval (Stefanowitsch 1999: 127).[3] As far as Finnish is concerned, it has also been pointed out by some scholars that when a deictic motion verb (such as *mennä* or *tulla*) is followed by another verb, the sentence often has a particular meaning which differs from the sense of motion (Kiuru 1977: 263). Furthermore, the recent Finnish reference grammar acknowledges that constructions where the verb *mennä* 'go' is followed by another verb in the 3rd infinitive illative case express 'undesirable activity' (ISK 2004: 463). However, the earlier studies have not explained this phenomenon and the reasons for using deictic motion verbs to convey such extra meanings.

A basic tenet of cognitive semantics is that grammatical structures are semantically motivated to a great extent. As Langacker points out, in language, "virtually everything is motivated" (Langacker 2008: 88). Following this argument, we find it reasonable to search for an explanation to the lexical composition the *mennä kertomaan* 'go to tell' and *tulla sanomaan* 'come to say' types: why is it that deictic motion verbs specialize in this kind of a function, and how (and why) does the affective meaning emerge? We now provide an explanation based on the concepts of *control* and *cognitive dominions*.

The affective meaning indicated by these constructions begins to make sense when they are considered as examples of abstract motion towards or away from a dominion of control of a human participant that occupies the deictic center of the directional motion. The dominion of control is yet another kind of dominion that surrounds an animate, sentient reference point (cf. Section 2 and the discussion on dominions there). A dominion of control includes entities and relationships that are controlled (in one sense or another) by the sentient reference point. Entities that exit the dominion of control thus escape the control of the reference point. Since human beings canonically wish to control situations and events where they participate, it is not surprising that an expression indicating motion out of a dominion of control may undergo subjectification and begin to indicate a negative affective meaning, such as disapproval of the speaker. Lakoff and Johnson (1980: 117–118) propose that control is one of the basic domains of experience and thus one type of a natural experience. Following this view, we assume control to be a relevant factor motivating the representation of an

[3] It is crucial to point out that in addition to the Conceptualizer's evaluative judgment, the *mennä kertomaan* and *tulla sanomaan* types refer to another person's speech act (indicated by the infinitive verb) and may therefore be called polyphonic. Especially in the last-mentioned type, the disapproval of the verbal action designated by the infinitive may be due to the conceptualizer's own judgments but also to the judgment of the person spoken to.

entity's relation with a dominion of control. Control also affects the motion of entities with respect to (= into or out of) dominions of control: such motion may be in keeping with the intentions of the animate reference point, or in conflict with them.

In the infinitival expressions considered here, there are thus three factors that may be reflected by the directionality of the (abstract) motion involved: 1) motion with respect to the activity itself (= into the activity space), 2) motion with respect to other participants of the situation and 3) motion with respect to the conceptualizer's viewpoint location (the deictic center). As far as the first type is concerned, according to Lakoff and Johnson, it is a common phenomenon that activities are metaphorically conceived of as substances (Lakoff–Johnson 1980: 30–32). Therefore they can also be conceptualized as CONTAINERS which have a capacity to "take in" other entities. In the conceptualization of the *mennä kertomaan* ('go to tell') construction, the entity occupying the shifted deictic center (i.e. the trajector of the verb *mennä* 'go') is conceived of as abstractly moving into the CONTAINER of the activity – which is expressed by the 3rd infinitive verb form – and at the same time it is metaphorically moving away from its original position, which has some kind of a relationship with the cognitive dominion of the person spoken to, and also with the conceptualizer's viewpoint. This motion is clearly indicated by the illative case of the infinitival form. At the same time, however, the deictic motion verb 'go' means that the trajector moves *out of* the dominion of control of the conceptualizer. In our view, it is this latter kind of abstract motion that motivates the use of the verb *mennä* 'go'. In other words, this construction can be seen as an elaboration of a metaphor where the revelation of information against the conceptualizer's will involves motion out of the control dominion. This analysis is supported by observations of certain other Finnish expressions with the verb *mennä* (discussed in Section 2), which have a strong tendency to relate to negative states or actions in general, i.e. situations that are out of control. Larjavaara (1990: 261) also points out that certain metaphorical uses of the verb *mennä*, such as the meaning 'become shamefaced' *men-nä nolo-ksi* [go-1INF shamefaced-TRANS], profile a change away from something "primary" or "normal".

In the *tulla sanomaan* 'come to say' construction the deictic motion verb *tulla* is used, and as argued in Section 2, the abstract uses of this verb tend to be conceptualized as positive. However, the meaning of the *tulla sanomaan* type is not positive (as in examples 9 and 11), but negative. We thus need to explain why a meaning like 'speak aggressively' is expressed by the verb 'come' – in fact, the analysis given above for 'going' as motion out of control would lead one to expect that the 'go' verb be used here as well. However, there is one relevant difference in the conceptualization of these situations that needs to be taken into account: because *tulla* profiles motion towards the deictic center, it is now the landmark (the person to whom something is said) who occupies the shifted deictic center. The trajector (the person speaking aggressively) is another human participant, abstractly penetrating the cognitive dominion of the landmark participant against his or her will. In our account, this is the reason for associating the abstract motion with a threat to the landmark. In contrast to the expressions including *mennä* 'go', the dominion involved in the *tulla sanomaan* type is not one of control, since by entering it the person who is speaking aggressively does not submit her/himself to the control of the landmark participant but in fact poses a threat to the landmark. This is also the reason why the use of the 'come' verb together with the speech act verb creates a meaning of rudeness even though neither the deictic motion verb nor the speech act verb by itself expresses such a meaning (cf. KS 2004 s.v. *sanoa*)[4].

To sum up, we conclude that the Finnish *mennä kertomaan* and *tulla sanomaan* constructions are motivated by abstract deictic meaning of the motion verbs. This explanation can be seen through an image-schematic pattern or a deictic metaphorical conceptualization (see also Stefanowitsch 1999: 125, 128). These constructions exhibit metaphorical motion away from or towards the cognitive dominion of control experienced by the conceptualizer or the landmark. Thus, the role of the dominion of control is highly important since it links together the image-schema of directional motion associated with the deictic verbs *mennä* and *tulla* and the affective meanings of the *mennä kertomaan* 'go to tell' and *tulla sanomaan* 'come to say' constructions.

4 Conclusions

Above we have discussed the abstract-motion uses of the Finnish deictic motion verbs *tulla* 'come' and *mennä* 'go', showing how the deictic meaning of the motion they indicate in the spatial domain may give rise to different kinds of abstract (metaphorical) extensions in the abstract domains. The general starting point for the abstract uses is the conceptual metaphor GOOD IS HERE, which can be seen as motivating (more or less directly) most of the abstract uses of the verbs discussed in Section 2. Below we give a summary of the general oppositions at work between the two verbs in the domain of abstract motion.

[4] However, in particular idiomatic infinitive forms *sanoa* has similar semantic ability and it profiles meanings 'remark' *ol-la sano-ma-ssa* [be-1INF say-3INF-INESS] and ' cause criticisms ' *tul-la sanomis-ta* [come-1INF saying-PART].

'come':	'go':
positive change	negative change
narrow windowing	wide windowing
becoming conscious	becoming unconscious
entering awareness of the Conceptualizer	leaving awareness of the Conceptualizer
caused by agent	automative
entering dominion of Control	exiting dominion of Control

As this list of oppositions shows, the GOOD IS HERE metaphor alone is not sufficient to explain all uses. In addition, our study has shown that we need to take into account factors related to control and cognitive dominions, as well as the windowing of attention over the event, both of which are not just abstract but also grammaticalized extensions of the basic uses.

Appendix – Gloss conventions

1 = first person
3 = third person
ADESS = adessive
ALLAT = allative
CL = clitic
COND = conditional
GEN = genitive
ILLAT = illative
INESS = inessive
INF = infinitive
NEG = negation verb
NOM = nominative
PART = partitive
PL = plural
PRES = present (tense)
PST = past tense = imperfect
PX = possessive suffix
QUEST = question particle
SG = singular
TRANSL = translative

Author note

Tuomas Huumo
University of Tartu
Department Finno-ugric languages
Ülikooli 18
50090 Tartu, Estonia
e-mail: thuumo@ut.ee

Jari Sivonen
ELTE University of Budapest
Department of Finno-ugric languages
Budapest, VIII. Múzeum krt. 4/i
Hungary
e-mail: jari.sivonen@oulu.fi

Tuomas Huumo's contribution to this research was funded by the Estonian Science Foundation (Eesti Teadusfond, grant 7552).

References

Fauconnier, G. 1985. *Mental spaces*. Cambridge, Mass. MIT Press.

Fauconnier, G. 1997. *Mappings in thought and language*. Cambridge: Cambridge University Press.

Goldberg, A. 2006. *Constructions at work. The nature of generalization in language*. Oxford: Oxford University Press.

Heine, B., U. Claudi & F. Hünnemeyer. 1991. *Grammaticalization: A conceptual framework*. Chicago: The University of Chicago Press.

Hopper, P. 2001. Hendiadys and auxiliation in English. *Complex Sentences in Grammar and Discourse. Essays in honor of Sandra A. Thomson*, ed. J. L. Bybee, 145–73. Amsterdam: John Benjamins Publishing Company.

Hopper, P. & E. C. Traugott 1993. *Grammaticalization*. Cambridge: Cambridge University Press.

Huumo, T. 1996. Bound Spaces and the semantic interpretation of existentials. *Linguistics 41(3)*: 461–493.

Huumo, T. 2006. 'I woke up from the sofa' Subjective directionality in Finnish expressions of a spatio-cognitive transfer. *Grammar from the human perspective. Case, space and person in Finnish*, eds. M.-L. Helasvuo & L. Campbell, 41–65. Amsterdam: John Benjamins Publishing Company.

Huumo, T. & K. Ojutkangas. 2006. An introduction to Finnish spatial relations: Local cases and adpositions. *Grammar from the human perspective. Case, space and person in Finnish*, eds. M.-L. Helasvuo & L. Campbell, 41–65. Amsterdam: John Benjamins Publishing Company.

ISK 2004. *Iso suomen kielioppi*, eds. A. Hakulinen et al. Helsinki: Suomalaisen Kirjallisuuden Seura.

Kielitoimiston sanakirja 2004. *Kielitoimiston sanakirja*. Helsinki: Kotimaisten kielten tutkimuskeskus ja Kielikone Oy.

Kiuru, S. 1977. *Suomen kielen kieltohakuiset verbit*. Helsinki: Suomalaisen Kirjallisuuden Seura.

KS = Kielitoimiston sanakirja.

Lakoff, G. & M. Johnson 1980. *Metaphors We Live By*. Chicago: The University of Chicago Press.

Lakoff, G. & M. Turner 1989. *More than cool reason: A field guide to poetic metaphor*. Chicago: The University of Chicago Press.

Langacker, R. W. 1987. *Foundations of Cognitive Grammar. Volume I. Theoretical prerequisites*. Stanford: Stanford University Press.

Langacker, R. W. 1990. *Concept, Image, and Symbol. The Cognitive Basis of Grammar*. Berlin: Mouton de Gruyter.

Langacker, R. W. 1991. *Foundations of Cognitive Grammar. Volume II. Descriptive Application*. Standford: Standford University Press.

Langacker, R. W. 1993. Reference-point constructions. *Cognitive Linguistics 4–1*: 1–38.

Langacker, R. W. 1999. *Grammar and conceptualization. Cognitive linguistics research 14*. Berlin: Mouton de Gruyter.

Langacker, R. W. 2008. *Cognitive Grammar. A Basic Introduction*. Oxford: Oxford University Press.

Larjavaara, M. 1990. *Suomen deiksis*. Helsinki: Suomalaisen Kirjallisuuden Seura.

Onikki-Rantajääskö, T. 2001. *Sarjoja. Nykysuomen paikallissijaiset olotilanilmaukset kielen analogisuuden ilmentäjinä*. Helsinki: Suomalaisen Kirjallisuuden Seura.

Payne, T. E. 1997. *Describing Morphosyntax*. Cambridge: Cambridge University Press.

Radden, G. 1995. Motion metaphorized: The case of *coming* and *going*. *Cognitive Linguistics in the Redwoods*, ed. E. H. Casad, 423–458. Berlin: Mouton de Gruyter.

Stefanowitsch, A. 1999. The Go-and-verb construction in a Cross-Linguistic Perspective: Image-Schema Blending and the Construal of Events. *Proceedings of the Second Annual High Desert Linguistics Society Conference,* eds. D. Nordquist & C. Berkenfield, 123–34. Albuquerque, NM: High Desert Linguistics Society.

Talmy, L. 2000. *Toward a Cognitive Semantics. Volume I: Concept Structuring Systems*. Cambridge: The MIT Press.

Traugott, E. C. & R. B. Dasher 2005. *Regularity in semantic change*. Cambridge Studies in Linguistics 97. Cambridge: Cambridge University Press.

Wilkins, D. P. & D. Hill 1995. When "go" means "come": Questioning the basicness of basic motion verbs. *Cognitive Linguistics 6-2/3*: 209–59.

7

A Cognitive Approach to Nominative / Genitive Conversion in Japanese

TAKESHI KOGUMA

1 Introduction

Modern Japanese exhibits a case-particle alternation phenomenon commonly referred to as *ga/no* conversion (or nominative/genitive conversion) in embedded clauses with a nominal head such as relative clauses and nominal complements to the formal noun *koto,* as shown below:[1]

(1) *kore-wa* [*Taro-{ga/no}* *kat-ta*] *hon* *desu.*
This-TOP Taro-NOM/GEN buy-PAST book be
'This is the book that Taro bought.' (relative clause)

(2) [*Taro-{ga/no}* *nai-ta*] *riyuu-wa* *wakar-anai.*
Taro-NOM/GEN cry-PAST reason-TOP know-NEG
'(I) don't know why Taro cried.' (relative clause)

(3) [*Taro-{ga/no}* *nai-ta*] *koto-o* *sitte* *odoroi-ta.*
Taro-NOM/GEN cry-PAST NML-ACC know:GER became surprised
'(I) was surprised to know that Taro had cried.' (complement clause)

[1] The abbreviations used in the glosses are as follows: ACC=Accusative, ADN=Adnominal, COMP=Complementizer, COP=Copula, DAT=Dative, GEN=Genitive, GER=Gerund, NEG=Negative, NML=Nominalizer, NOM=Nominative, OBL=Oblique, PAST=Past tense, PRES=Present tense, PROG=Progressive, TOP=Topic.

Meaning, Form & Body.
Fey Parrill, Vera Tobin, and Mark Turner (eds.).

Square brackets in each example mark off the adnominal clause. Example (1) involves a relative clause predicated by the transitive verb *katta* 'bought,' which modifies the following head noun *hon* 'book,' which is characterized as being in a grammatical relation (i.e. object) to the predicate of the relative clause. Example (2) involves a relative clause predicated by the intransitive verb *naita* 'cried,' which modifies the following head noun which has no grammatical relation to the predicate of the relative clause. Example (3) involves a complement clause predicated by the intransitive verb *naita* 'cried.'

It is worth noting that the nominative-case-marker alternates with the genitive-case-marker optionally, and the semantic contrast between the corresponding expressions appears to be indiscernible in practical terms. This characteristic poses numerous descriptive and theoretical challenges particularly to the semantic approaches. On the other hand, this linguistic phenomenon has drawn great attention from generative grammarians and the so-called *ga/no* conversion has been intensively investigated in the framework of generative grammar (Harada 1971, 1976, Shibatani 1975, Nakai 1980, Miyagawa 1989, 1993, Watanabe 1994, 1996, 2005, Hiraiwa 2001, 2002, Saito 2004, among many others).

The aim of this paper is to offer a natural semantic account of this case-particle alternation phenomenon from the standpoint of cognitive grammar (Langacker 1987, 1990, 1991, 1999, 2000), rejecting the generative approaches, which regard the case particles as purely grammatical meaningless elements. In this paper, I will limit the discussion to the relative clause constructions.

We must note that although the genitive-marked subject, which displays limited distribution, is a marked expression in Modern Japanese, this does not give us justification for analyzing the genitive-marked subject as derived from the nominative-marked subject.

2 Characteristics of *ga/no* Conversion

Ga/no conversion exhibits no semantic contrast. Syntactically, however, the two particles display different behavior. The occurrence of the genitive-particle *no* in place of the nominative particle *ga* is basically limited in the construction as in (4). The genitive particle *no*, as illustrated in (5) and (6), cannot mark subject in independent clauses.

(4) [NP1-*no* PREDICATE] NP2

(5) *Taro-{ga/*no}* *hon-o* *kat-ta.*
Taro-NOM/*GEN book-ACC buy-PAST
'Taro bought a/the book.' (independent clause)

(6) *Taro-{ga/*no}* *nai-ta.*
Taro-NOM/*GEN cry-PAST
'Taro cried.' (independent clause)

2.1 Transitivity Restriction

It is also well known that even in adnominal clauses the genitive-particle *no* cannot mark subject nominals as freely as the nominative-particle *ga*. It has been pointed out that embedded clauses that have an accusative-marked nominal do not allow the genitive-marked subject, regardless of syntactic position (Watanabe 1994, 1996). Let us consider examples (7) through (9). The intervention of a postpositional phrase does not prevent the genitive-particle from marking the subject nominal, as observed in (7), while the presence of an accusative-marked nominal excludes the genitive-marked subject, regardless of its syntactic position, as illustrated in (8) and (9). This alleged syntactic constraint is generally called 'transitivity restriction' (Watanabe 1994, 1996, 2005).

(7) [*Taro-{ga/no}* *Amerika-e* *it-ta*] *hi*
Taro-NOM/GEN America-to go-PAST day
'the day on which Taro went to the United States of America'

(8) [*Taro-{ga/*no}* *hon-o* *kat-ta*] *mise*
Taro-NOM/*GEN book-ACC buy-PAST shop
'the shop where Taro bought the book'

(9) [*hon-o* *Taro-{ga/*no}* *kat-ta*] *mise*
book-ACC Taro-NOM/*GEN buy-PAST shop
'the shop where Taro bought the book'

2.2 Historical Changes of Subject Marking

In Modern written Japanese, subjects are obligatorily marked by postpositional particles (i.e. discourse particle *wa* or nominative particle *ga*), whereas in Old Japanese subjects are usually unmarked (i.e. NP-zero).

In the previous literature, it has been analyzed that the nominative function of both particles was derived from their original associative function, based on the fact that the original function of both *no* and *ga* was genitive, which linked two NPs, as illustrated in (10) and (11):

(10) *hito-no* *kokoro*
People-GEN mind
'people's mind' (*Genji Monogatari*)

(11) *wa-ga* *mi*
I-GEN body
'my body / myself' (*ibid.*)

It is also well known that it was in adnominal clauses with a nominal head, not in independent clauses that the particle *ga* and *no* began to occur on subjects. This means that it was the presence of a nominal head that allowed the emergence of *ga* and *no* on subjects. This suggests that the development of subject-marking in Japanese should be best characterized with reference to the genitive use.

Adjectives are common predicates that exhibit *ga/no* conversion in Modern Japanese. It has been reported that the subject nominal of an adnominal clause predicated by an adjective was not marked by *ga*, while an adnominal clause predicated by a verb allowed either *ga* or *no* to mark the subject, as illustrated in (12) (Ono 1977:11).

(12) a. [NP1-{**ga/no*} ADJECTVE (adnominal form)] NP2
 b. [NP1-{ *ga/no* } VERB (adnominal form)] NP2

This historical note casts much light on the development of the subject-marking in adnominal constructions. The historical observation that *no*-adnominal expressions predicated by an adjective were established prior to the corresponding *ga*-adnominal expressions strongly suggests that the *no*-adnominal construction predicated by a verb was also established prior to the corresponding *ga*-adnominal construction (Koguma 2006:341, 2007: 22).[2] This prediction is congruent with the observation of Fujii (1991, 1992) examining the first 400 clauses of *Genji Monogatari* (The Tale of Genji).[3]

3 Previous Studies and their Empirical Problems

Harada (1971) first points out that Japanese exhibits case-particle alternation under the same intended interpretation. In addition to the static aspect of the case alternation phenomenon, he also points out a diachronic change in subject-case-marking.

(13) Japanese has a syntactic rule which optionally converts the particle *ga* into the particle *no* in certain types of embedded sentences, typically in relative clauses. (Harada 1971:26)

---

[2] Yamauchi (2003:190) also points out that historically the establishment of *no*-adnominal construction preceded that of *ga*-adnominal construction.

[3] She states that the frequency of *ga* as a subject-marker is extremely low, reporting that there are only three instances (only once in a relative clause, and twice in subordinate clauses), against a total of twenty-four instances of *no* functioning as subject-marker in either relative clauses or subordinate clauses (Fujii 1992:268).

He hypothesizes the derivational direction (i.e. *ga* into *no*) based on the fact that the nominative particle *ga* is unmarked, displaying broader distribution. This theoretical position, however, cannot capture the historical changes of the subject-marking in Japanese.

In the subsequent literature, there have been two major syntactic approaches to the *ga/no* conversion, namely DP-spec Analysis (Miyagawa 1993, among many others) and Wh-agreement Analysis (Watanabe 1994, 1996, 2005). The former proposal claims that the genitive case is assigned by raising a subject nominal to an external relative head (i.e. DP-spec). The latter proposal claims that the genitive-marked subject is a disguised form of nominative case, remaining within VP in overt syntax.

Let us now discuss two notable problems we encounter with DP-spec analysis. DP-spec analysis claims that the genitive-marked subject is derived from an unmarked nominative-marked subject of the underlying structure. It would be overhasty, however, to conclude that historically the genitive-marked subject has been developed from the nominative-marked subject. The theoretical position that the nominative-marked subject optionally converts to the genitive-marked subject cannot capture the diachronic findings in previous studies (Ono 1977, Fujii 1991, 1992).

Watanabe (1996) points out that DP-spec analysis fails to account for the grammaticality of the genitive-marked subject in a comparative construction. Since DP-spec hypothesis inevitably requires an external nominal head where the genitive case is to be assigned, it predicts incorrectly that the genitive-marked subject is not allowed in constructions lacking an external nominal head, which is contrary to fact. The genitive-marked subject does occur in headless relative clause constructions, which lack a nominal head, as illustrated in (14) and (15):

(14) *John-wa [Mary-{ga/no} yon-da] yori takusan no*
John-TOP Mary-NOM/GEN read-PAST than many-GEN
hon-o yon-da.
book-ACC read-PAST
'John read more books than Mary did.' (Watanabe 1996:394)

(15) [*kyaku-{ga/no} kuru*] *yori nimotsu-ga*
guest-NOM/GEN come than luggage-NOM
sakini tsui-ta.
in advance arrive-PAST
'Their luggage arrived earlier than the guests.' (Kikuta 2002:76)

He claims that case-marking on the subject is a realization of wh-agreement. He argues that it is the presence of the accusative nominal that prevents the genitive-particle *no* from marking the subject (Watanabe 1994:343), illustrating the fact that the scrambling of the accusative nominal does not save the example, as shown in (9). He argues that the grammaticality of the genitive-marked subject in (14) is also attributed to wh-agreement, assuming that the accusative nominal *hon* 'book,' which is in grammatical relation (i.e. object) to the predicate *yonda* 'read,' undergoes the process of 'wh-extraction' and 'deletion.' This approach, however, cannot provide a straightforward explanation for the *ga/no* conversion observed in (3). He argues that the *koto*-complement clause also involves wh-agreement, assuming that the formal noun *koto* is a subjunctive complementizer which heads subjunctive clauses. However, this argument seems unconvincing and untenable, as pointed out in Kikuta (2002, 2003). Furthermore, this approach cannot accommodate the *ga/no* conversion observed in the following example (16a). The predicate *kogeru* 'scorch,' is an intransitive verb as illustrated in (16b). The modified head noun *nioi* 'smell' in (16a) is not in a grammatical relation to the predicate. This conclusively shows that the relative clause (16a) does not involve wh-extraction at all.

(16) a. [*nanika-{ga/no}* *kogeru*] *nioi*
something-NOM/GEN scorch smell
'the smell of something burning'
b. *nanika-ga* *kogete-iru*.
something-NOM scorch:GER-PROG
'Something is burning.'

Hiraiwa (2001) argues that genitive-marked subjects are licensed sentence-internally by the special verbal inflection (i.e. adnominal form) on the ground that the so-called *ga/no* conversion is only available in structures with predicates in adnominal form.

Verbs and adjectives in Modern Japanese have lost their morphological distinction between adnominal form and conclusive form. Nominal adjectives and copulas, however, still retain the distinction. It is well known that the occurrence of genitive-particle marking NP1 is limited to the environment in which the predicate is in adnominal form in Old Japanese. Therefore, the predicates of adnominal clauses in Modern Japanese have also been analyzed as being in adnominal form despite the fact that they are morphologically identical to those in conclusive form. His claim theoretically accommodates the *ga/no* conversion in headless relative clauses. He proposes that the spelling out of morphological accusative case triggers checking of the nominative case, resulting in a nominative-marked subject (i.e. transitivity restriction).

His discussion with reference to Old Japanese and genitive-marked subjects in other languages seems attractive and persuasive. However, his approach gives us no straightforward explanation for the linguistic fact that adjective-predicates in Old Japanese disallowed the nominative-marked subject. Moreover, it is not always the case that a predicate in adnominal form allows the genitive-marked subject, as illustrated in (17) (Hiraiwa 2002).[4]

(17) *John-{ga/*no}* *genkina*
John-NOM/*GEN healthy:ADN
no-da / *no-de* / *no-ni*
COMP-COP / COMP-OBL / COMP-DAT
'John is healthy/ since John is healthy/ although John is healthy'

4 Symbolic View of Grammar

Cognitive grammar is fundamentally distinct from the generative linguistic theories in its symbolic view of the grammar. In this theory, grammar is claimed to be reduced to the structuring and symbolization of conceptual content. A symbol is defined as the paring of a semantic structure (some kind of conceptualization) and a phonological structure, such that one is able to evoke the other (Langacker 1987, 2000). The symbolic view of grammar—that language consists of semantic structure, phonological structure, and symbolic links between the two—leads to the position that lexicon, morphology, and syntax are all symbolic structures and thus form a continuum. Thus all the grammatical elements posited in grammatical description, including what are claimed to be meaningless in the generative framework, are also claimed to have some kind of semantic import (often highly schematic). Furthermore, we must note that 'meaning' is not identified with 'concept' but with 'conceptualization,' which resides in cognitive processing (Langacker 1987, 2000). Our apprehension of the world is active, dynamic, and constructive in nature. Cognitive grammar presupposes a conceptualist semantics that accommodates our various cognitive abilities to construe a given scene in alternate ways. The same conceived situation can result in alternate meanings since linguistic meaning consists of conceptual content and a particular way of construing that content (e.g. level of specificity, perspective, profiling, trajector/landmark alignment, and so forth).

[4] Hiraiwa (2002) states that the apparent counterexamples are not real problems for his generalization itself, but that rather their ungrammaticality is closely related to a process of grammaticalization.

4.1 Reference Point Model

Langacker (1993, 1999:Ch.6) demonstrates that we have the fundamental and ubiquitous scanning ability that allows us to invoke the conception of one entity with a certain degree of cognitive salience either inherently or contextually for purposes of establishing MENTAL CONTACT with another, and introduces a REFERENCE-POINT MODEL that represents this aspect of our conceptualization. The entity evoked in order to access the intended referent, which is referred to as a TARGET, is called a REFERENCE POINT. The set of potential targets of a particular reference point is termed a DOMINION. The essential aspects of the REFERENCE-POINT ABILITY are summarized in the reference-point model sketched in Figure 1.

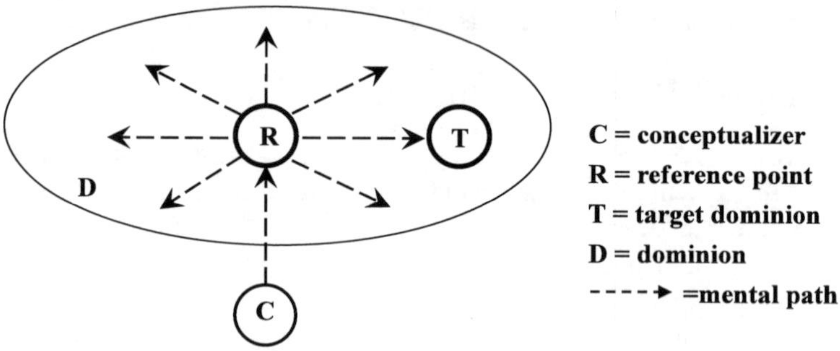

Figure 1: Reference-point Model

The model illustrates that the conceptualizer (abbreviated as 'C') accesses the target (abbreviated as 'T') via the reference point (abbreviated as 'R'). The dashed arrows represent the mental path the conceptualizer follows in accessing the target. The ellipse labeled 'D' indicates the dominion, which is defined as the class of potential targets of the reference point.

4.2 Trajector/ Landmark Alignment

TRAJECTOR/LANDMARK ALIGNMENT reflects the packaging of experience in one particular way for specific expressive purposes. Expressions profiling a relationship between two participants typically involve a prominence asymmetry. When a relationship is profiled, its participants receive varying degrees of prominence. The most prominent participant, which is conceived as the primary figure within the profiled relationship, is construed as being located, evaluated, or described. This focal participant is termed the trajector (abbreviated as 'tr'). The other secondary prominent focal participant is called the landmark (abbreviated as 'lm'). Prominence is a conceptual phenomenon, inhering in our apprehension of the world, not in the outside world per se. It is of great importance to note that prominence asymmetry, namely trajector/landmark alignment, is imposed by a conceptualizer.

5 Proposed Analysis

Since the particles *ga* and *no* are grammatical elements, they are characterized as profiling not so much semantic contents as the way we conceptualize. As we have seen, we can safely posit that historically the emergence of the genitive-marked subject preceded that of the nominative-marked subject. This diachronic change of subject-marking in Japanese leads us to explore the so-called *ga/no* conversion with a reference to the genitive use of *no*.

It is well known that the Japanese possessive *no* serves as a polyfunctional element, namely as a genitive marker, a pronominal, and a nominalizer. Nomura (2000:65-69) suggests that most if not all uses of the Japanese genitive particle *no* may be best characterized as designating a reference-point relationship, listing the following representative uses of *no*:

(18) (a) ownership; (b) body part; (c) kinship; (d) holder of attributes;
(e) agent/experiencer (subjective genitive);
(f) patient (objective genitive); (g) partitive; (h) origin; (i) cause;
(j) constituent material; (k) attributive/descriptive; (l) property;
(m) reference point; (n) time; (o) place; (p) organization;
(q) appositive

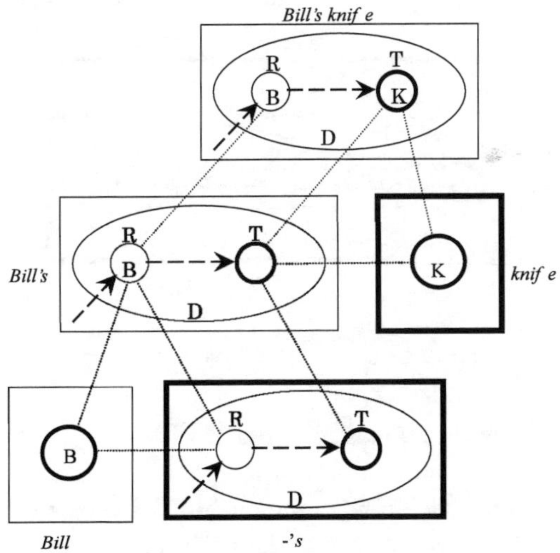

Figure 2: Nominal Possessive Construction of English

Let us first look at the compositional paths through which an English nominal possessive construction (e.g. *Bill's knife*) is being integrated. The successive assembling of the component structures is sketched in Figure 2 (Kumashiro and Langacker 2003:11). The box in bold indicates that the enclosed component structure is a PROFILE DETERMINANT, from which the composite structure inherits the profile. The correspondences between the substructures of the component structures are represented by dotted lines.

At the most schematic level, *-'s* profiles no more than the reference-point relationship. The profile of noun *Bill* (whose semantic specifications are abbreviated 'B') spells out the schematic reference point of the reference-point relationship at the first composition, and then the resulting composite structure has its target elaborated by the profile of the noun *knife* (abbreviated as 'K') at the next composition.

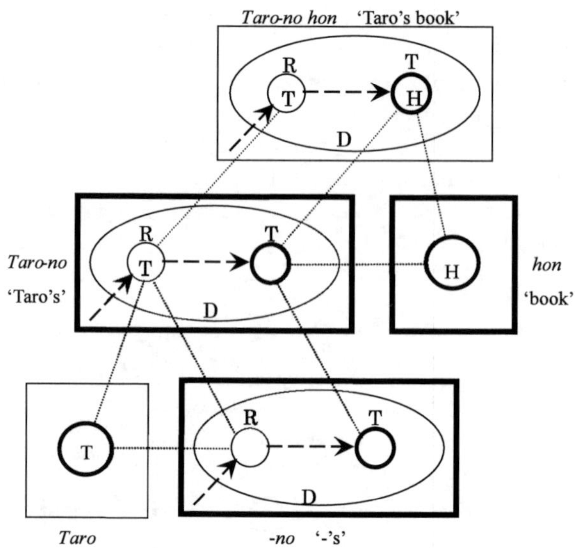

Figure 3: Nominal Possessive Construction of Japanese

Let us now turn to Japanese simple possessive construction. The most entrenched and conventional use of the genitive particle *no* is characterized as profiling a reference-point relationship between two 'things.' We can observe the possessor-possessed relationship in prototypical examples such as *Taro no hon* 'Taro's book.' As a maximally schematic description, a possessor is characterized as a reference point, and the possessed as its target. Figure 3 shows the compositional paths through which *Taro no hon* 'Taro's book' is being semantically integrated. At the most schematic level, the genitive particle *no* profiles no more than the reference-point relationship. The profile of noun *Taro* (whose semantic specifications are abbreviated as 'T') spells out the schematic reference point of the reference-point relationship at the first composition, and then the resulting composite structure has its target elaborated by the profile of the noun *hon* 'book' (abbreviated as 'H') at the next composition.

The semantic structure proposed here as shown in Figure 3 is slightly different from the schematic description in Figure 2 in that both of the component structures at the second level are regarded as profile determinants. The composite structure *Taro-no* 'Taro's' is also defined as its profile determinant, since the semantic structure of the schematic reference-point construction itself has a nominal profile, retaining its target unelaborated. It is well known that the Japanese possessive particle *no* serves as a polyfunctional element, including a pronominal use as shown below:

(19) a. *Hanako-no* *e-wa* <u>*Taro-no*</u> *yori* *ii.*
Hanako-GEN picture-TOP Taro-GEN than good
'Hanako's picture is better than Taro's.'

b. *Taro-no-o* *kari-ta.*
Taro-GEN-ACC borrow-PAST
'(I) borrowed Taro's.'

In comparative expression (19a), though the second possessive expression *Taro-no* 'Taro's' (which is underscored) is not followed by a nominal (i.e. possessed), it nevertheless has a nominal profile (i.e. its implicit target *e* '(Taro's) picture'). In (19b), the nominal profile of the expression *Taro-no* is evidenced by the accusative particle *o* attached to it. We thus contend that the composite semantic component *Taro-no*, where the target is unspecified, has a nominal profile. This characterization is particularly important for the foregoing discussion on the headless relative clause constructions.

Let us now turn to *no*-adnominal construction. We have observed in examples (14) and (15) that some constructions without a nominal head, such as a comparative construction, also allow the genitive-marked subject. However, it is worth noting that both *ga* and *no* historically first appeared as subject-case-markers in embedded structures with a nominal head, as schematically illustrated in (20):

(20) [NP1-GEN PREDICATE:ADN] NP2

The diachronic finding in the previous literature that the nominative function of the particles has developed from the genitive function associating two 'things,' leads us to contend that the particle *no* appearing after the initial NP (i.e. subject) in adnominal clauses should also be best characterized in the reference-point model.

(21) *Taro-no* *hon*
Taro-GEN book
'Taro's book' (a/the book that has something to do with Taro)

(22) [*Taro-no* *kat-ta*] *hon*
Taro-GEN buy-PAST book
'a/the book that Taro bought' (relative clause)

The referent of the simple possessive expression (21) is identical to that of the adnominal expression (22). In (21), *Taro* is evoked as a reference point in order to establish mental contact with *hon* 'book,' whereas in (22) the adnominal clause *Taro no katta* 'Taro bought' is evoked for the purpose of establishing mental contact with *hon* 'book.' The unmarked reading of (21) is 'a/the book that belongs to Taro.' This expression is, however, highly schematic in terms of the relation between the profile of the initial NP (i.e. *Taro*) and the profile of the modified NP (i.e. *hon* 'book'). There are also various possible readings such as 'the book that Taro read,' 'the book that Taro wrote,' and so on. The same conceived situation thus can be profiled by either (21) or (22). This observation strongly suggests that the *no*-adnominal construction should be analyzed in the reference-point model.

The following independent sentence (23) corresponds to the *no*-adnominal expression (22). The subject *Taro*, as the conceptual starting point and the most prominent participant in the process profiled by the transitive verb *katta* 'bought,' is therefore the most natural reference point for the rest of the profile, including the other salient participant *hon* 'book.'

(23) *Taro-ga* *hon-o* *kat-ta*
Taro-NOM book-ACC buy-PAST
'Taro bought a/the book.'

We can, therefore, posit that the corresponding participant *Taro* in (22) is also a natural reference point for the rest of the profile, including the profile of the modified head noun (i.e. *hon* 'book'). On the ground that the simple possessive construction NP1-*no* NP2, which is characterized in the reference-point model, is one of the most basic noun-modifying constructions, we can assume that the composite semantic structure of *no*-adnominal construction contains the reference-point model as its component structure. Furthermore, it is reasonable to assume that an unspecified schematic relation between the reference point and the target of a simple possessive expression is elaborated by the semantic specification of a predicate in adnominal form. Figure 4 depicts the schematic semantic structure of (21) and Figure 5 the structure of (22). The labeled circle (T) represents *Taro* and the labeled circle (H) in bold face stands for *hon* 'book,' which is the overall profile of the expression. The double arrow in Figure 5 indicates an energy transmission (i.e. *Taro* ACT ON *hon* 'book'). It is assumed that a predicate in adnominal form, which is one of the semantic components, serves to introduce a conceived scene in which salient participants interact in a specific way.

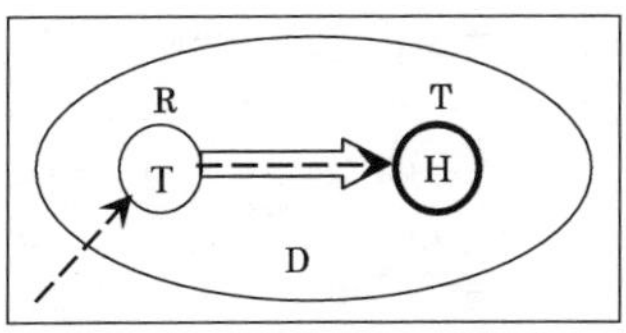

Taro-no katta hon 'the book that Taro bought'

Figure 4: Nominal Possessive Construction

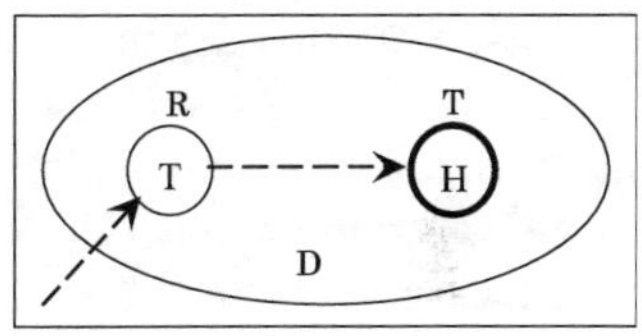

Taro- no hon 'Taro's book'

Figure 5: *no*-Adnominal Construction

Figure 6 illustrates the successive semantic assembling of the component structures, which amounts to the *no*-adnominal expression (23).

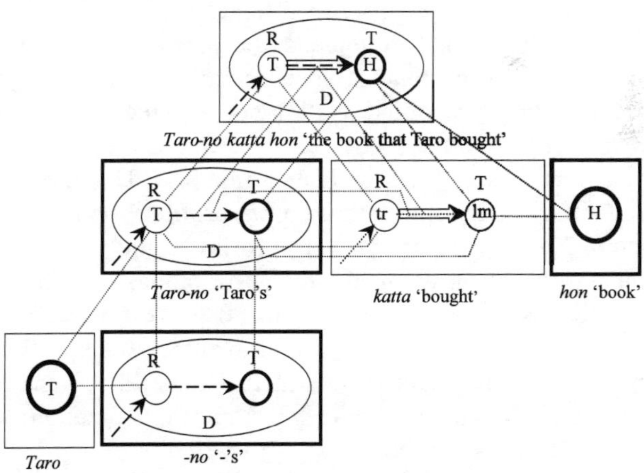

Figure 6: Semantic Integration of *no*-Adnominal Construction

The lower-level construction represents the regular possessive construction, where the profile of the noun *Taro* elaborates the schematic reference-point participant. The heavy-line box indicates that the semantic component imposes its profile onto the resulting composite structure (i.e. profile determinant). At a higher level of organization, this composite structure *Taro no* 'Taro's X' in turn functions as a component structure integrated with the other component structures to form the overall expression. Note again that this composite structure has a nominal profile. The intermediate-level component depicted in the middle stands for the semantic structure of the predicate in adnominal form (i.e. *katta* 'bought'). The fine dotted arrow between the schematic trajector and landmark represents the immanent reference-point/target relationship (cf. the trajector functions as a 'starting point' or initial point of access in conceptualizing the relationship profiled by the predicate). Depicted on the right is the noun *hon* 'book.' At this level of semantic assembling, the lines of integration connect the three component structures. Note that the three participants, namely the unspecified target of the semantic structure shown on the left, the schematic landmark of the relational component in the middle, and the profile of the third component on the right, all correspond. These three components are integrated by correspondences connecting the shared participants.[5] The overall composite structure of this expression *Taro no katta hon* 'the book that Taro bought' inherits its nominal profile from both of the component structures depicted on the left and right at the intermediate-level composition. In this respect, this semantic integration is parallel to that of the nominal possessive construction (shown in Figure 3). We can observe complete overlap of the participants of these two component structures in the intermediate level, namely *Taro* and the schematic trajector of the predicate in adnominal form *katta* on one hand, the unspecified target and the schematic landmark of the predicate on the other. The semantic specification of *katta* 'bought' elaborates the corresponding unspecified relation between the reference point and the target accordingly. In other words, an implicit substructure of the reference-point relationship serves as the elaboration-site. The resulting overall composite semantic structure has the nominal profile. The composite component structure *Taro no* contributes its profile to the overall composite structure, whereas the predicate in adnominal form does not. This goes right to the heart of the issue we are dealing with. It is the component structure manifesting our reference-point ability that functions as the profile determinant. The resulting overall composite structure thus reflects the reference-point/target conceptualization (henceforth R/T conceptualization).

[5] The presence of at least one correspondence is perhaps the only invariant feature of valence relations (Langacker 1991:181-182).

Before proceeding to a discussion of the semantic structure of the *ga*-adnominal construction, it will be helpful to look at the following English possessive expressions (24a) and (24b), which can profile precisely the same conceived situation.

(24) a. Taro's brother
 b. Taro has a brother.

The two expressions above differ in the manner of the conceptualization. Example (24a) reflects solely R/T conceptualization, whereas example (24b) employs a conceptualization based on trajector/landmark alignment (henceforth tr/lm conceptualization), backgrounding the inherent and immanent R/T conceptualization entertained by a conceptualizer. We must note that the R/T conceptualization and the tr/lm conceptualization pertain to very different levels of organization (Langacker 1999:181-182). The simple determiner expression (24a) is the most abstract description, profiling minimal conceptual content and manifesting our fundamental cognitive ability to conceptualize the conceived entities. On the other hand, expression (24b) is yielded by applying the tr/lm conceptualization to the given scene at another level of conceptual organization.

We have already seen that the R/T conceptualization provides the conceptual platform that enables a conceptualizer to entertain the tr/lm conceptualization at the higher level of organization by examining English possessive expressions in (24). In the same fashion, the *no*-adnominal construction, which is a manifestation of R/T conceptualization, provides a conceptual platform for tr/lm conceptualization pertaining to another conceptual organization. This is the same as saying that the resulting composite structure of the *no*-adnominal clause would readily employ tr/lm conceptualization. This is the mechanism of the optionality of the so-called *ga/no* conversion. Their overall composite semantic structures are sketched in Figure 7 and Figure 8 respectively.

Taro-no katta hon
'the book that Taro bought'

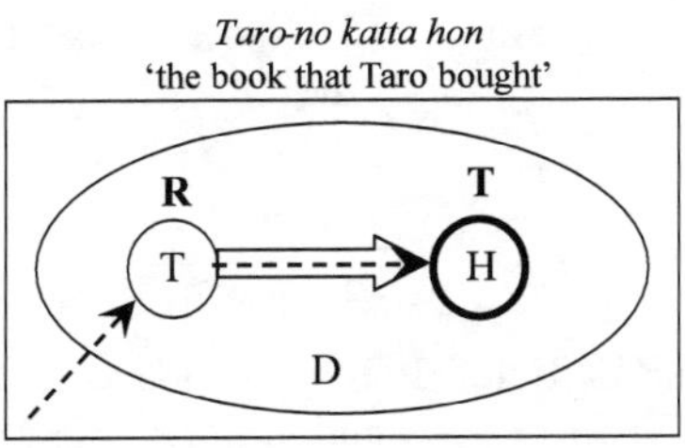

Figure 7: R/T Conceptualization

Taro-ga katta hon
'the book that Taro bought'

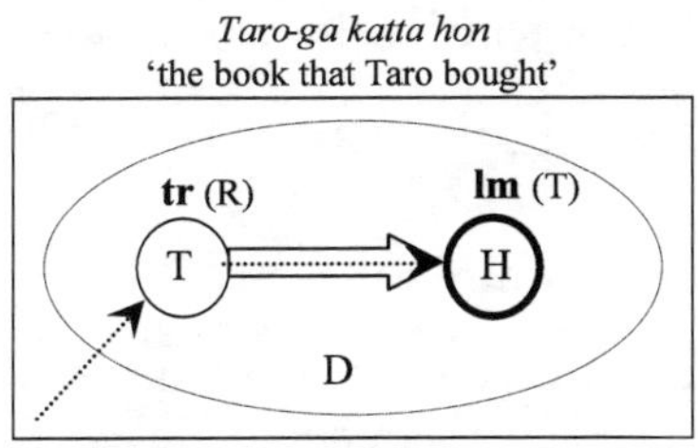

Figure 8: tr/lm Conceptualization

Not only their overall composite semantic structures but also their compositional paths are identical. This is the reason why they exhibit little semantic contrast and thus defy clear semantic distinction. It is worth emphasizing that the distinction between *no*-adnominal and *ga*-adnominal constructions resides solely in the manner of conceptualization, namely R/T conceptualization vs. tr/lm conceptualization.

The syntactic constraint called 'transitivity restriction' as observed in (8) and (9) is naturally and straightforwardly explained in the proposed analysis within the theoretical framework of cognitive grammar. The profile of an accusative marked nominal is defined as a landmark of a relation. A landmark is characterized as the second most prominent participant in a profiled relation; therefore, it inevitably presupposes the presence of the most prominent participant, namely a trajector. In other words, the presence of a landmark indicates that a conceptualizer entertains the tr/lm conceptualization to profile the relation.[6] The newly introduced accusative-marked participant in the overall composite structure cannot be conceptualized without resorting to the tr/lm conceptualization. The other participant (i.e. subject) involved in the process profiled by the predicate serves as the trajector and thus appears with nominative-particle *ga*.

The genitive-marked subject in a headless environment such as a comparative construction is not problematic at all under the proposed analysis. Since the proposed analysis posits that (i) the component structure of the reference-point model has a nominal profile on its own account and (ii) this semantic component continues to serve as a profile determinant all the way through successive semantic assembling up to the overall semantic composite structure. This means that its target entity continues to be the profile irrespective of whether it is elaborated or not. In this regard, the headless adnominal expression is captured in a natural and principled manner. Those expressions are characterized as a special case where the schematic target entity remains unelaborated.

It is worth noting that the presence of the so-called pragmatic relative clause construction provides strong support for the proposed analysis. The preposition *of* in the English translation of example (16) suggests that this type of relative clause construction would be best analyzed in the reference-point model.

6 Conclusion

In this paper, I have examined the case-particle alternation phenomenon commonly referred to as *ga/no* conversion from the standpoint of cognitive

[6] p.c. Nakamura (2003)

grammar, demonstrating that the relative clause construction in Japanese is best characterized in the reference-point model. *No*-adnominal construction reflects solely R/T conceptualization, whereas *ga*-adnominal construction reflects tr/lm conceptualization. Applying another conceptual manipulation based on trajector/landmark alignment to the overall composite semantic structure of a genitive-marked subject expression amounts to the corresponding nominative-marked subject expression, backgrounding the inherent and immanent R/T conceptualization entertained by a conceptualizer. The semantic structure of *no*-adnominal construction, which is a manifestation of R/T conceptualization, would readily employ tr/lm conceptualization. This is the mechanism of the optionality of the so-called *ga/no* conversion. The semantic distinction between the two corresponding adnominal expressions resides in the manner of conceptualization, not in their overall composite semantic structures or the compositional paths in which their semantic components are successively integrated. This is the reason the two different case-particles can alternate without causing a semantic contrast.

The proposed analysis differs from those in the previous studies in that it offers a natural and straightforward account of (a) the historical changes of subject-marking in Japanese, (b) the nature of the so-called transitivity restriction, (c) the genitive-marked subject in a headless environment, and (d) the so-called pragmatic relative construction.

Author Note

Ishikawa National College of Technology

I would like to thank two anonymous reviewers for their valuable comments and suggestions. Remaining inadequacies are of course my own.

This research was partially supported by the Ministry of Education, Science, Sports and Culture, Grant-in-Aid for Scientific Research (C), 19520381, 2007.

References

Fujii, N. 1991. *Historical Discourse Analysis: Grammatical Subject in Japanese.* (*Discourse perspectives on grammar* 3). Berlin; New York: Mouton de Gruyter.

Fujii, N.1992. Changes in Subject Marking in Japanese. *Internal and external factors in syntactic change* (*Trends in linguistics; Studies and monographs* 61), eds. Marinel Gerritsen, Dieter Stein, 257-293Berlin; New York: Mouton de Gruyter.

Harada,S.I. 1971. Ga-No Conversion and Idiolectal Variations in Japanese. *Gengo-Kenkyu* 60: 25-38.

Harada, S.I. 1976. Ga-No Conversion Revisited: A Reply to Shibatani. *Gengo Kenkyu* 70, 23-38.

Hiraiwa, K. 2001. On Nominative-Genitive Conversion. *A Few from Building* 39, *MIT Working Papers in Linguistics* 39: 65-123.

Hiraiwa, K. 2002. Nominative-Genitive Conversion Revisited. *Japanese/Korean Linguistics* 10: 546-559.

Keenan, E.L. 1985. Relative Clauses. *Language Typology and Syntactic Description*, vol.2, *Complex Constructions,* ed. T.Shopen, 141-170. Cambridge: Cambridge University Press.

Kikuta, C. 2002. Ga/No Kootai Genshoo ni Hasei wa Hitsuyoo-ka?: HPSG de Meishisei to Jutsugosei o Tsunagu [Ga-No Conversion without Derivation: A Mixed Category Analysis]. *Conference Handbook of English Linguistic Society of Japan* 20: 73-84.

Kikuta, C. 2003. Ga/No Kootai Genshoo ni Hasei wa Hitsuyoo-ka: [Derivation is not Necessary to Account for Ga/No Conversion]. *JELS* 20: 61-70.

Koguma, T. 2006. Keiyoshi o Jutsubu to-suru 'GA/NO' Kotai ni kansuru Ninchiteki Kosatsu [A Cognitive Approach to the Nominative/Genitive Conversion in the Adnominal Clauses Predicated by an Adjective]. *JCLA* 6: 341-350.

Koguma, T. 2007. Nominative-Genitive Conversion in Japanese: A Cognitive Grammar Approach. Doctoral dissertation, Kanazawa University.

Kumashiro, T. & R.W.Langacker. 2003. Double-subject and Complex-predicate Constructions. *Cognitive Linguistics* 14-1; 1-45.

Langacker, R.W. 1987. *Foundations of Cognitive Grammar vol.1: Theoretical Prerequisites*. Berlin; New York: Mouton de Gruyter.

Langacker, R.W. 1990. *Concept, Image, and Symbol: The Cognitive Basis of Grammar*. Berlin; New York: Mouton de Gruyter.

Langacker, R.W. 1991. *Foundations of Cognitive Grammar vol.2: Descriptive Application*. Berlin; New York: Mouton de Gruyter.

Langacker, R.W. 1993. Reference-Point Constructions. *Cognitive Linguistics* 4:1-38.

Langacker, R.W. 1999. Grammar and Conceptualization. Berlin and New York: Mouton de Gruyter.

Langacker, R.W.2000. A Course in Cognitive Grammar, ms., UCSD.

Miyagawa, S. 1993. LF Case-checking and Minimal Link Condition. *Papers on Case and Agreement II, MIT Working Papers in Linguistics* 19: 213-254.

Nakai, S.1980. A Reconsideration of Ga-No Conversion in Japanese. *Papers in Linguistics* 13: 279-320.

Nakamura, Y. 1998. Ninchi-Ruikeiron no Kokoromi: Kiwadachi vs. Sanshoten [Toward a Cognitive Typology: Prominence vs. Reference point]. *KLS* 18:252-62.

Nambu, S. 2005. Corpus-based Study of the Change in GA/NO Conversion. MA thesis, Graduate School of Kobe Shoin University.

Nomura, M. 2000. The Internally-Headed Relative Clause Construction in Japanese: A Cognitive Grammar Approach. Doctoral dissertation, UCSD.

Ono, S. 1977. Shukaku-joshi *ga* no Seiritsu: joo [Emergence of the nominative particle *ga*, no.1]. *Bungaku* 43.9, Sept., 1-16.

Saito, M. 2004. Genitive Subject in Japanese: Implication for the theory of null objects. *Non-nominative Subject*, vol.2, eds. Bhaskararao, P. and K.V. Subbarao, 103-118. Amsterdam; Philadelphia: John Benjamin.

Shibatani, M. 1975. Perceptual Strategies and the Phenomena of Particle Conversion in Japanese. *Papers from the Parasession on Functionalism*, 469-480. Chicago Linguistic Society, University of Chicago.

Shibatani, M. 1990. *The Languages of Japan*. New York: Cambridge University Press.

Ura, H. 1993. L-relatedness and its Parametric Variation. *Papers on Case and Agreement, MIT Working Papers in Linguistics* 19: 377-399.

Ura, H. 2000. *Checking Theory and Grammatical Functions in Universal Grammar*. Oxford: Oxford University Press.

Watanabe, A. 1994. A Cross-linguistic Perspective on Japanese Nominative-Genitive Conversion and its Implications for Japanese Syntax. *Current topics in English and Japanese*. ed. M.Nakamura, 341-369. Tokyo: Hitsuji Shoboo.

Watanabe, A. 1996. Nominative-Genitive Conversion and Agreement in Japanese: A Cross-linguistic Perspective. *Journal of East Asian Linguistics* 5: 373-410.

Watanabe, A. 2005. *Minimarisuto Puroguramu Josestu: Seisei-bumpo no Aratanaru Chosen [Introduction to Minimalist Program]*. Tokyo: Taishukan.

Yamauchi, Y. 2003. *Katsuyo to Katsuyo-kei no Tsuuji-teki Kenkyu [Diachronical Study on Inflections and Inflectional forms]*. Osaka: Seibundoshuppan.

8

Day After Day After Day

RONALD W. LANGACKER

The construction exemplified by my title is descriptively challenging and theoretically significant. I myself have used it to argue that "classical" constituency is inadequate for grammatical description (Langacker 1997). More recently, Jackendoff (2008) has taken it as showing the need for a construction-based approach, observing that its syntax and "the way it maps to semantics are sufficiently distant from canonical structures that it appears hopeless to find a classical derivation" (p. 27). Here I will sketch an analysis from the standpoint of Cognitive Grammar (Langacker 1987, 1991, 2008a). Requiring no special apparatus, it offers a unified account of the construction's form and meaning.

As noted by Jackendoff, *day after day* belongs to a large network of constructions with the basic form N P N (e.g. *house by house*, *dollar for dollar*, *bumper to bumper*, *book upon book*), exhibiting varied meanings and degrees of productivity. Within this network I will limit my attention to *day after day* and parallel expressions with other temporal nouns: *hour after hour*, *week after week*, *year after year*, etc. I will however consider them in relation to a substantial range of other constructions, both "canonical" and otherwise.

1 Temporal Adverbs

Let us first consider them in relation to other temporal adverbs. One issue that arises is whether they actually are adverbial, given that an adverb is characterized in Cognitive Grammar (CG) as profiling a (non-processual) relationship whose trajector is also a relationship. Thus adverbial expres-

Meaning, Form & Body.
Fey Parrill, Vera Tobin, and Mark Turner (eds.).

sions are often headed by clearly relational elements such as *after* and *in*. On the other hand, *day after day* appears to be headed by a noun, hence is nominal in form, and I do indeed analyze such expressions as profiling things rather than relationships. Of course, these are not the only nominal expressions that seemingly function as temporal adverbials. So do various others, like *the whole month* and *every morning*.

(1)(a) *It rained {after sunset / day after day / the whole month}.*
(b) *{In the morning / Week after week / Every morning} it rained.*

Whether we describe such expressions as nominal or adverbial depends on whether we consider their internal form and meaning or their function in a clause. I have in the past been guilty of assuming that only relational expressions could function analogously to *after sunset* or *in the morning* in (1). For this reason I posited relational variants of nouns like *yesterday* to accommodate their adverbial uses. In Figure 1(a), this variant is shown as profiling a relationship of temporal inclusion between its trajector (tr), some kind of process, and its landmark (lm), characterized as the day (d) prior to the ground (G) defined by the speech event. The two component structures, *it rained* and *yesterday*, are then integrated by a correspondence equating the former with the relational trajector. The clausal component is enclosed in a heavy-line box to indicate that the composite expression (*It rained yesterday*) inherits its processual profile.

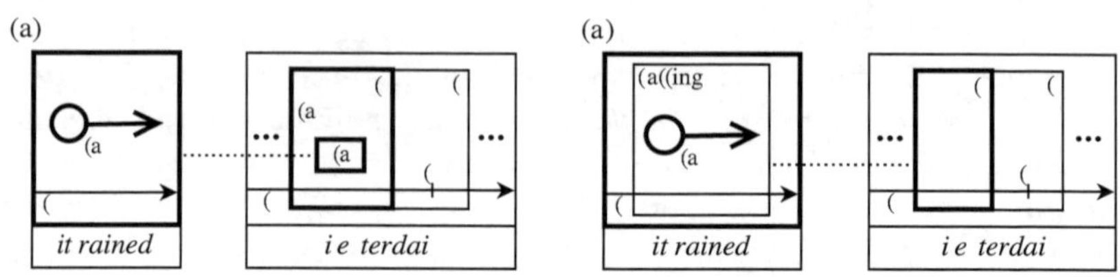

Figure 1: Alternate descriptions of *yesterday*

On this account, *It rained yesterday* was precisely analogous to *It rained in the morning*. I eventually realized, however, that the apparent need to posit a relational variant of *yesterday* reflected the lingering influence of predicate-argument descriptions and classical constituency. In CG, owing to the greater flexibility afforded by encyclopedic semantics and symbolic assemblies, we also have the option in Figure 1(b). Here *yesterday* is simply a noun: it profiles an abstract thing, the day prior to the ground (G). As part of its encyclopedic meaning, a verb like *rain* includes the notion that the profiled event occurs in a spatial and temporal setting. The component structures can thus be integrated by means of a correspondence identifying this implicit temporal setting with the time span profiled by *yesterday*. In other words, the **relationship** between event and time span need not be introduced as the profile of a separate morphological element—it can simply be established by the **construction** (Goldberg 1995; Langacker 2002). Note that this does not imply any "mismatch" between syntax and semantics. The syntax includes the construction employed, which specifies the temporal relationship as an aspect of **constructional meaning**.

The next matter to consider is the **kind** of temporal specification made by phrases like *day after day*. Expressions like *after sunset*, *in the morning*, and *yesterday* specify the temporal **location** of an occurrence. This is shown in Figure 2(a), where a heavy bar represents the profiled process unfolding through time. Clearly, though, *day after day* does not specify a simple location of this sort. To grasp its import we need to examine various other kinds of temporal specification, each of which it resembles in some respect.

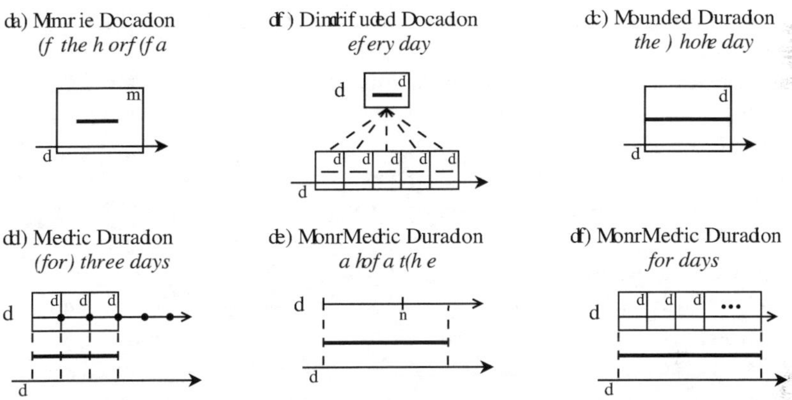

Figure 2: Expressions of the form *It rained X*

First, *day after day* resembles *every day* by invoking multiple days in each of which the profiled process occurs. As shown in 2(b), I analyze *every day* as designating a **fictive** or **virtual** instance of *day* construed as being **representative** of a contextually identified set of actual instances. This representative instance (labeled V to indicate its virtual nature) hosts the profiled event *it rained*, which is likewise a fictive entity, being representative of a set of actual occurrences. Hence the composite expression *It rained every day*, while it profiles just a single (fictive) event, projects to a number of actual ones distributed over a number of days. Comparing it now with *It* *rained day after day*, we find that they share the properties of invoking multiple days and requiring that in each day some rain must fall.

Still, the latter expression is rather different, for it emphasizes **duration** rather than location, with the default interpretation that the rain in question constitutes a single, more or less continuous episode. In this respect it is comparable to expressions like *It rained the whole day*, in 2(c). Here, though, the duration is specified in terms of a single, discretely bounded unit of time: a particular day evident from the context. By contrast, *day after day* indicates a succession of days, without however defining any specific duration or tying the event to any particular temporal location.

This last property, that of indicating duration not tied to any particular location, is shared by adverbial expressions formed on indefinites, like those in 2(d)-(f). Like *every day*, these expressions invoke a virtual entity, in this case an abstract scale of comparison, indicated by an arrow. But instead of hosting the profiled occurrence, here this entity is merely used to measure it: *It rained (for) three days* profiles a single, actual occurrence that unfolds during a particular (albeit unspecified) span of time. The profiled event is also mapped onto a metric scale in which days function as the units of measurement. As such, the days explicitly referred to are themselves virtual entities which can correspond to any actual sequence of days. The scale employed can also be non-metric, as in *It rained a long time*, which specifies only that the time span surpasses a norm (n). The adverbial expression *for days* represents an intermediate case, in that days are still invoked as units of measurement, but with no specific indication of their number.

Day after day comes closest to this last adverbial construction. It too expresses duration in terms of multiple days without indicating any specific number. Of course, the two constructions are not equivalent. In the case of *for days*, the preposition directly symbolizes the relationship between the clausal process and its temporal duration, collectively indicated by a plural noun. With *day after day*, on the other hand, the relation between event and duration is not individually symbolized but emerges as an aspect of constructional meaning (as with *yesterday* in Figure 1(b)). And rather than collectively, the duration is expressed by partial enumeration of temporal units representing it. These differences in what is individually symbolized constitute a difference in linguistic meaning even if the expressions describe the same objective situation.

The formal differences are indicative of a further semantic contrast. Iconically, through repetition of the temporal unit, the *day after day* construction effects a **mental simulation** of the experience associated with the profiled occurrence. It does not just **describe** the event's long duration, but to some extent—in the partial and attenuated manner of simulations—recreates the extended experience of time passing and the monotony thus engendered. This is a conventional aspect of its meaning, naturally more evident in longer sequences: *day after day after day after day after day….* As part of a simulation, the days enumerated are virtual entities; although they **represent** the actual days involved, they cannot be **identified** with them. Observe that the days explicitly mentioned are generally fewer than those comprising the actual time span. The sentence *It rained day after day* tells us that the rain lasted at least two days, but we would normally conclude that it lasted considerably longer.

2 Serial Constructions

Mental simulation is now widely accepted as being a fundamental component of conceptualization and linguistic meaning. Presumably it figures to some extent in the meaning of all the durational adverbs. What is special about the *day after day* construction is that the simulation of passing time is iconically reinforced at the level of grammatical organization, where it is more evident owing to the larger time scale of formal expression. This iconicity is in fact the key to the construction's grammatical analysis. If its structure seems problematic, this is mainly due to the standard assumption that constituency is the universal basis for grammatical description. One might propose, based on the usual sort of constituency hierarchy, that the construction has the organization in (2)(a). However, there is no evidence of any kind—semantic, grammatical, or intonational—for this hierarchical arrangement. On the face of it, what we have instead is the linear arrangement in (2)(b), a chain-like succession of grammatically parallel intonational units. The succession of units thus mirrors the succession of days.

(2)(a) *(day (after (day (after (day (after (day (after (day)))))))))*
(b) *((day) (after day) (after day) (after day) (after day))*

Instead of rigid constituency hierarchies, CG posits flexible **assemblies** consisting of **conceptual groupings**, **phonological groupings**, and **symbolic links** between them (Langacker 1997). Within such assemblies, grammatical constituency of the "classical" sort represents a special case. It involves an arrangement of **symbolic** structures, where—at multiple levels of organization—a certain kind of conceptual grouping happens to be symbolized by a certain kind of phonological grouping: at each level the conceptual grouping is based on correspondences between component elements, giving rise to a composite conception with a single overall profile, while the phonological grouping is based on temporal adjacency. However, constituency does not invariably emerge, nor is a single hierarchy ever exhaustive of the groupings relevant to semantic and grammatical description.

In particular, numerous constructions are most straightforwardly analyzed as having a basically linear organization, comprising a chain-like succession of roughly similar symbolic structures. These structures are indeed linked by correspondences to form a symbolic assembly, which may, as a whole, serve some higher-level function. But internally the connections are mainly local, consisting in correspondences between elements of adjacent structures in the chain. Owing to their adjacency and conceptual integration, each pair of structures may well give rise to a composite symbolic structure, thereby defining a grammatical constituent. But any hierarchical arrangement that emerges in this manner is local rather than global: instead of nesting to form a single, well-behaved, multilevel hierarchy, locally-defined constituents intersect in pairwise fashion.

Consider a chain of complement clauses, as in (3). It is generally assumed to have the constituency shown by the bracketing in (3)(a). The clauses are all incorporated in a single hierarchy, so that the expression as a whole designates the "main-clause" act of saying. However, intonation suggests the "flat" structure shown in (3)(b), where slashes (/) indicate pauses.

(3)(a) *[Amy says [Bob thinks [Chris knows [Doris left.]]]]*
(b) *Amy says / Bob thinks / Chris knows / Doris left.*

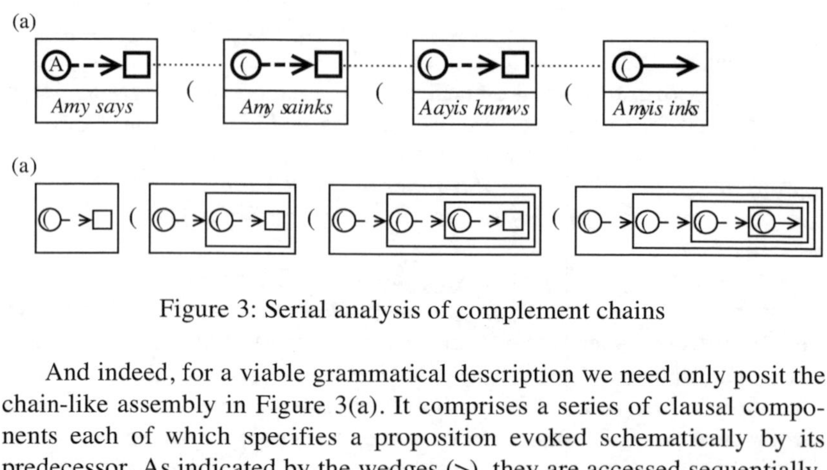

Figure 3: Serial analysis of complement chains

And indeed, for a viable grammatical description we need only posit the chain-like assembly in Figure 3(a). It comprises a series of clausal components each of which specifies a proposition evoked schematically by its predecessor. As indicated by the wedges (>), they are accessed sequentially, each representing an **intonational grouping** as well as a **window of attention** in which a single element—the clausal process—is focused as the profile (Langacker 2001a, 2001b). There is thus a succession of profiles, each in its own window, rather than a single overall profile. On this account the hierarchical arrangement in (3)(a) is an aspect of **semantic** structure: the successive embedding of **mental spaces** (Fauconnier 1985). Through the correspondences indicated, the grammar does provide instructions for building this layered conception, which proceeds step by step as shown in Figure 3(b). But there is no evident basis for positing **grammatical** constituents larger than clauses or presuming that the sentence as a whole profiles the act of saying (Langacker 2008b).

In (4) I give a sample of the varied expressions that lend themselves to this type of analysis. They are based on different kinds of constructions (predicate nominative, relative clause, path preposition, *of*-phrase, coordination) and are not claimed to be parallel in all respects. They do however share a number of properties suggesting that they all instantiate a general pattern. They all follow the same intonational scheme, in which a series of equally prominent prosodic groupings are separated by slight pauses but connected by suspended (as opposed to falling) intonation. The series can be of any length and consists of elements that are either identical or structurally analogous. In all these expressions iconicity is a salient factor. Here there are two basic patterns. In some cases the series of elements corresponds to a natural path of mental access: a path that leads through space, time, successively embedded mental spaces, a chain of connected individuals, or a hierarchy of whole/part relationships. In other cases the length of the series is used iconically for conveying magnitude. And in some examples both are involved. Not only do the successive elements in (4)(e)-(f) correspond to successive occurrences, but the number of repetitions gives a sense of their overall length.

(4)(a) *A lie / is a lie / is a lie / is a lie / is a lie.*
(b) *I have a friend / who has a friend / who knows Barack Obama.*
(c) *She flew from San Diego / to Dallas / to Chicago / to Cleveland.*
(d) *The sculpture is just a line / of groups / of rows / of stacks / of plates.*
(e) *He ran / and ran / and ran / and ran / and ran / and ran / and ran.*
(f) *It happened again / and again / and again / and again / and again.*
(g) *I want an iMac / and an iPod / and an iPhone / and a new Mercedes.*

Within a series, the connections are mainly local: each element is primarily associated with the one that immediately precedes. Even in (4)(g), where the items mentioned are all directly linked to *want* as specifications of its landmark, one can argue that each successive item bears a special relation to its predecessor, replacing it as the potentially final member of an exhaustive enumeration. This basically linear arrangement does not, of course, imply the total absence of hierarchical organization. Internally, each element in a series exhibits constituency. The entire series may, as a whole, serve a higher-level function (e.g. in (4)(c) it specifies the path of motion).

And locally, constituents may emerge when the connected elements are integrated in the manner specified by the construction employed. In (4)(a), for example, we can reasonably posit the clausal constituents shown in Figure 4, in each of which a subject and predicate combine to form a composite symbolic structure that profiles an identity relation. This hierarchical arrangement is only local, however. In global terms, the clauses relate to one another by intersection rather than inclusion, a clear violation of classical constituency (cf. Lambrecht 1988).

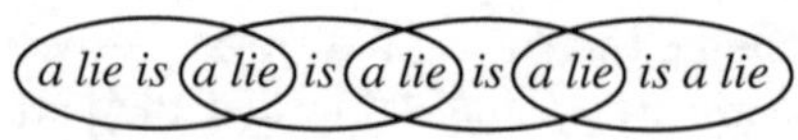

Figure 4: Intersecting constituents

3 Coordination

It is no accident that coordinate structures participate in this pattern. The essential feature of coordination is that the conjuncts are equal in status and parallel in terms of their semantic and grammatical function (Langacker 1991: §11.2). This breaks down into several, more specific properties with analogs in the other serial constructions. The first pertains to the role of the conjuncts within a larger structure: together (either individually or collectively) the conjuncts serve a function that is typically served by a single element. This is shown abstractly in Figure 5, where Q is the encompassing structure, and R is a particular role within it (e.g. the role of clausal object). In the case of coordination the role is filled by a number of elements—r_1, r_2, and r_3—rather than just one.

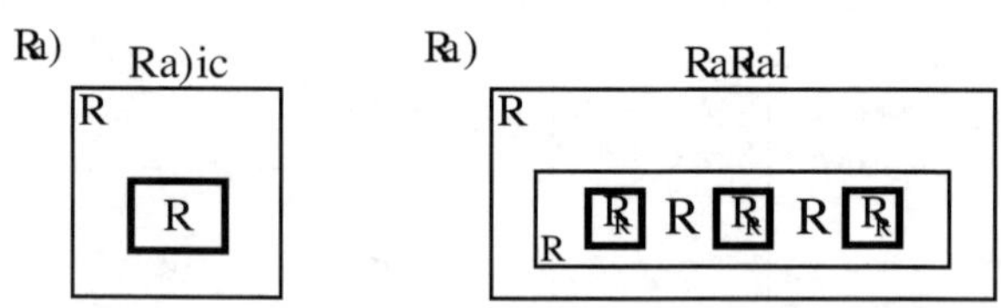

Figure 5: Abstract description of coordination

A second property, a matter of the conjuncts being equal in status, is that a conjoined structure has multiple, coexisting profiles rather than a single overall profile. This is represented by the heavy-line boxes enclosing r_1, r_2, and r_3. Finally, the conjuncts are necessarily accessed in sequence, despite their common function and equal prominence. This is especially so when *and* occurs before every non-initial conjunct; it explicitly indicates that they are being viewed in successive windows of attention. I am using wedges (>) as a notational device for showing this.

Though details vary, the non-coordinate constructions in (4) show comparable properties. In (4)(c), for example, the path of motion is specified by a number of prepositional phrases rather than just one, they would seem to be equal in status, and they are accessed in iconic sequence. These various constructions might indeed be considered coordinate, as broadly defined above. They differ from "true" coordination mainly in that adjacent elements in the series bear specific semantic relationships to one another, above and beyond their common role (R) in a larger structure (Q). Conversely, coordinate expressions approximate the other serial constructions to the extent that they incorporate additional semantic relationships between the conjuncts. An obvious case is the iconic temporal sequencing in (4)(e)-(f), where events follow one another in the order of their description.

In Figure 6(a) I show the basic analysis for coordinate expressions of the form *X and Y and Z*. The construction involves a series of conjuncts (in this case three) accessed sequentially (>) in successive windows of attention. The conjuncts are alike in that each profiles a thing. In all but the first, *and* has been incorporated at a lower level of organization (not shown). The semantic contribution of *and* is simply to portray the profiled thing as one of two such entities, each of which fulfills the same role in a larger structure (given as a rectangle). In the case of Y, the other entity is identified as X; in the case of Z, it is identified as Y. Through these correspondences the conjuncts are thus connected in chain-like fashion.

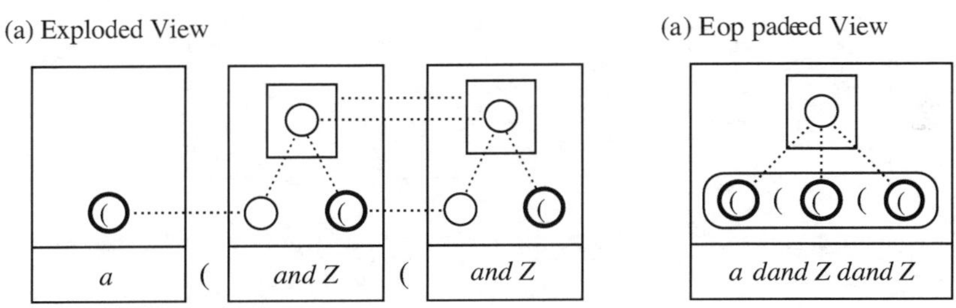

Figure 6: A serial coordinate construction

These linked structures constitute a symbolic assembly which, as a whole, can function as one component in a larger assembly. It is thus a kind of constituent. But it is not a **classical** constituent, for it does not include a composite conception in which the content of all the conjuncts is accessed simultaneously and construed as having single, overall profile. The key to this construction is precisely its linear, chain-like nature and the sequential access it affords to component elements. Still, since the conjuncts do function as a group for higher-level purposes, it is convenient to have a notation which reflects this. I thus adopt Figure 6(b) as a notational variant of 6(a). The semantic pole is obtained by merging corresponding entities, so as to directly show their identity. I have also added a box to represent the fact that X, Y, and Z—despite being accessed sequentially—implicitly form a group just by virtue of their common role in a larger structure. At the phonological pole, I have indicated that sequential access is manifested (at least potentially) by pauses (/).

Let us next consider how the symbolic assembly in Figure 6 is integrated into the larger structure it evokes schematically. Shown in Figure 7 is the formation of a clause like (4)(g): *I want X and Y and Z*. In diagram (a) *I want* is taken to be a constituent, which combines as a whole with the coordinate structure; this constituency is not essential, since the key factors in determining the composite conception are profiling and correspondences. Note that correspondences identify the landmark of *I want* as being the role filled by all the conjuncts (a **functional** identification), and also equate it with the group comprising X, Y, and Z (a **referential** identification). The composite result, shown in diagram (b), is that multiple referents are viewed successively as serving the landmark function.

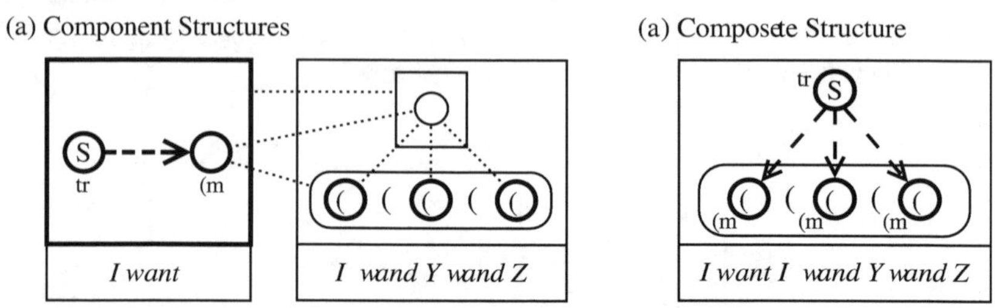

Figure 7: A coordinate structure as part of a larger symbolic assembly

4 Temporal Iconicity

We must now add temporal iconicity to this picture. In the simplest case, exemplified in (5)(a), the conjuncts profile events which are understood as occurring in the order of their description. This is sketched in Figure 8(a). It is just a matter of sequential access through processing time (>) correlating with the relative position of events in conceived time (t). This type of iconicity amounts to a mental simulation of the sequentiality inherent in the complex occurrence.

(5)(a) *She heard a noise / and turned around / and saw a bear.*
(b) *He complained / and complained / and complained.*
(c) *All morning he complained.*
(d) *Every five minutes he complained.*

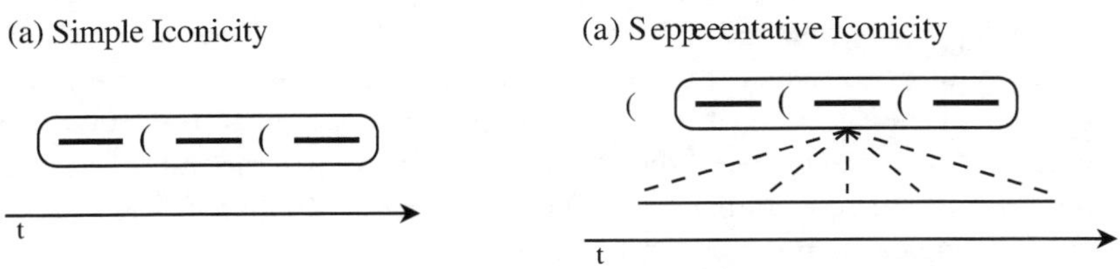

Figure 8: Kinds of temporal iconicity

The iconicity in (5)(b) is more complex. The sentence does imply that there were multiple, sequenced instances of complaining. It does not however mean that there were exactly three such instances, nor can the profiled events be identified with any particular ones. The import is rather that an excessive amount of complaining went on, with too many instances for exhaustive enumeration. Note that (5)(c) is perfectly natural as a continuation of (5)(b) and a summary of what transpired. The events designated by the conjuncts are thus interpreted as being representative of what happened, not as specific actual occurrences. As such they are virtual (V) entities, invoked in order to convey, through a partial simulation, the extended and repetitive nature of the actual experience. The dashed lines in Figure 8(b) are meant to indicate that this virtual series of events projects to any portion of the overall episode; it thereby effects a **conceptual compression** (Fauconnier and Turner 2002) in which the fictive profiled sequence serves to characterize the entire actual sequence. This is not dissimilar to the representativeness achieved by *every*, as shown in Figure 2(b). And indeed, a continuation employing *every*, like (5)(d), is also quite natural.

5 The Analysis

We are now in a position to analyze the *day after day* construction: *It rained day after day after day*. As should be evident, it belongs to the family of serial constructions exemplified in (4). In particular, it is straightforwardly analyzed as a case of representative temporal iconicity, like (4)(e) and (5)(b), except that the conjuncts are nouns (rather than verbs) with adverbial function in the clause. I noted previously that the days mentioned are generally fewer than those of the actual span of time involved and cannot be identified with any specific sequence within it. Rather, they are evoked by way of mentally simulating an extended experience of passing time.

Like others in (4), the *day after day* construction involves a chain of what appear to be prepositional phrases. And in fact, *after*-phrases do participate in chaining, as in (6)(a). There are however some crucial differences between the expressions in (6)(a) and (6)(b). The *day after day* construction uses simple (ungrounded) nouns rather than full (grounded) nominals (i.e. "noun phrases"). Also, the same noun is repeated throughout. These properties reflect the function of the overall expression, which is to simulate long duration (rather than specifying a particular event or temporal location). A further difference pertains to temporal sequence. In (6)(a), the order of events—indicated by subscripts—runs counter to the order of description (e.g. the wedding comes first but is mentioned last). On the other hand, the days in (6)(b) are mentioned in iconic sequence, each extending the period of time already described.

(6)(a) *the fight*$_4$ / *after the party*$_3$ / *after the reception*$_2$ / *after his wedding*$_1$
(b) *day*$_1$ / *after day*$_2$ / *after day*$_3$ / *after day*$_4$

I analyze both expressions as serial constructions based on local connections. They differ in the specific constructions employed to form each element and to make the local connections. In the case of (6)(a), the successive elements are formed by means of the regular prepositional phrase construction, and connections are established via the regular construction for using prepositional phrases to modify nouns. By contrast, (6)(b) employs special constructions suitable for achieving temporal iconicity.

The regular constructions are exemplified in Figure 9. At the first level of organization, the preposition combines with a nominal to form a prepositional phrase. Specifically, the nominal profile corresponds to the landmark of the preposition, which functions as constructional head by imposing its relational profile on the composite expression, in this case *after the party*. At the second level of organization, this composite structure functions in turn as one of the two component structures, where it modifies the nominal head. Their integration, effected by a correspondence between the nominal profile and relational trajector, results in the overall composite structure shown in diagram (c). At the phonological pole, this modifying construction specifies that the modifier follows the head. So in terms of word order, the head comes first, even though—at the semantic pole—the event it designates comes later (being the trajector of *after*). Hence the counter-iconic order in (6)(a).

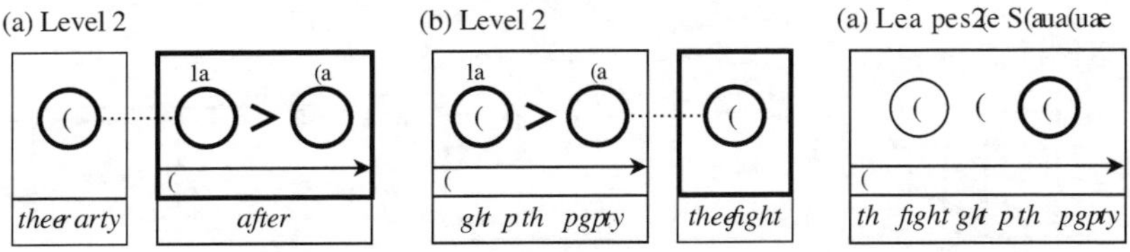

Figure 9: Regular prepositional phrase constructions

In (6)(b), on the other hand, I analyze each element as profiling a thing, in the manner of Figure 6(a), rather than a relationship. Accordingly I posit the construction in Figure 10, where *day* functions as profile determinant (head) and serves to specify the trajector of the preposition. It is thus a modifying construction, in which the nominal referent is characterized as being temporally subsequent to another entity. In terms of word order, *after* precedes the head (as non-complex modifiers generally do in English). We thus have temporal iconicity, since *day* is the second word in the sequence and designates the second participant in a relationship of temporal succession.

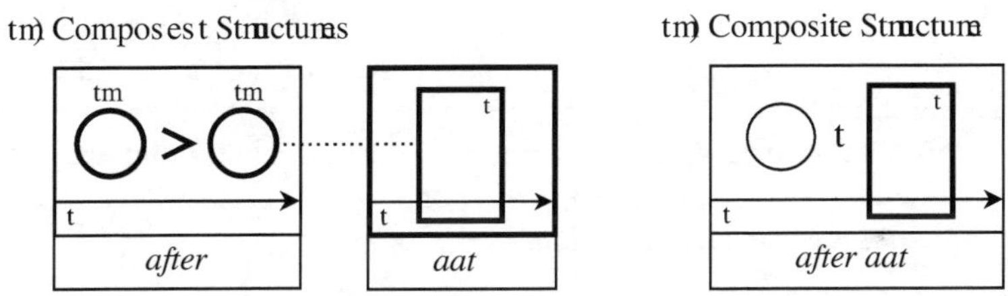

Figure 10: Special construction with *after*

Instances of the composite expression in diagram (b) function as component elements at the next level of organization, where local connections effect their chaining. This is shown in Figure 11, which is precisely analgous to Figure 6—for the coordinate structure *X and Y and Z*—except that *after* is semantically more specific (and less abstract) than *and*. Establishing the local connections are correspondences that identify the day profiled by one element with the temporally prior entity invoked by the next. As before, the chained elements are accessed sequentially (>), in separate windows, so while they form a kind of constituent, it is not a classical constituent (where all the content is viewed in a single window with a single overall profile). Also as before, it is convenient to adopt a compacted notation obtained by merging corresponding entities.

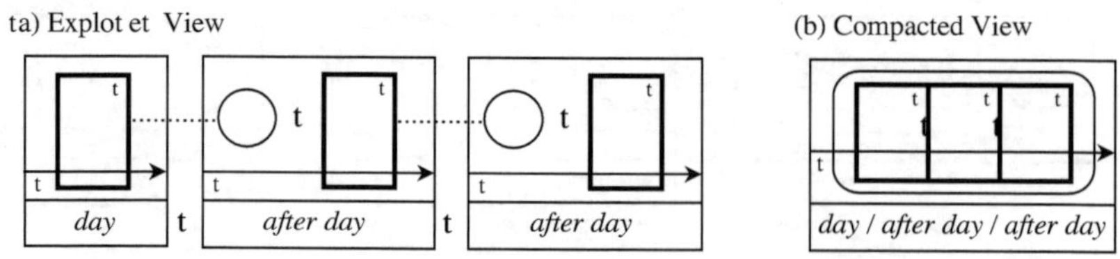

Figure 11: Serial construction with *after*-phrases

All that remains is to show how *day after day* combines with a clause to indicate the duration of the clausal process. I have already argued it to be a case of representative temporal iconicity, hence comparable to (5)(b)—*He complained / and complained / and complained*—except that the chained elements are nouns rather than verbs. Since the days mentioned are only representative, the time span they collectively define is only virtual (V). It is therefore shown in Figure 12(a) as projecting to any portion of some actual span of time, given as a rectangle. Integration with the clausal process is then straightforward. The clausal component *it rained* profiles an occurrence that occupies some span of time prior to the speech event (G). A correspondence identifies this actual span of time with the one evoked by *day after day after day*. The composite expression thus indicates that the simulated durational experience is characteristic of the profiled event, being associated with arbitrary portions of it. And despite its nominal character (as determined by its complex profile), *day after day after day* serves a function traditionally regarded as "adverbial".

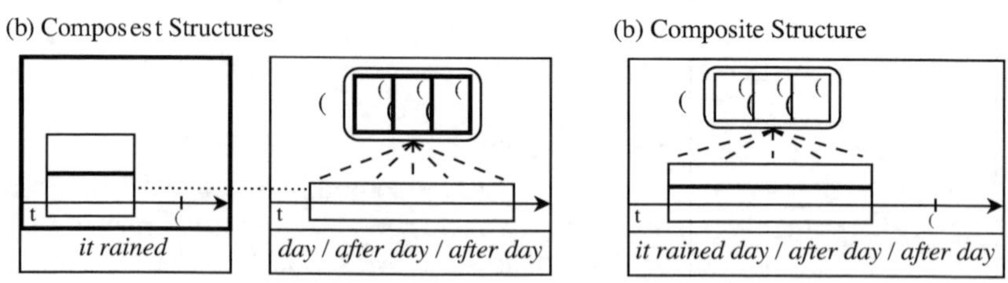

Figure 12: Clausal integration of the serial construction

6 Conclusion

I have tried to show that the *day after day* construction, though it may not be "canonical", conforms to more general patterns of English grammar. Moreover, I disagree with the contention that the "best hope" for describing it "lies in a theory of grammar that ... recognizes the autonomy of syntax from semantics and vice versa" (Jackendoff 2008: 8). I have in fact described it—with some success, I believe—in terms of a theory that explicitly rejects the autonomy thesis, positing only semantic structures, phonological structures, and symbolic links between the two. The key to the analysis lies in recognizing that "canonical" structures are quite limited relative to the varied forms that symbolic assemblies can assume.

Author Note

The author is Research Professor in Linguistics at the University of California, San Diego.

References

Fauconnier, G. 1985. *Mental Spaces: Aspects of Meaning Construction in Natural Language*. Cambridge, MA and London: MIT Press.

Fauconnier, G. and Turner, M. 2002. *The Way We Think: Conceptual Blending and the Mind's Hidden Complexities*. New York: Basic Books.

Goldberg, A. E. 1995. *Constructions: A Construction Grammar Approach to Argument Structure*. Chicago and London: University of Chicago Press.

Jackendoff, R. 2008. *Construction after construction* and its theoretical challenges. *Language* 84:8-28.

Lambrecht, K. 1988. There was a farmer had a dog: Syntactic amalgams revisited. *Proceedings of the Annual Meeting of the Berkeley Linguistics Society* 14:319-339.

Langacker, R. W. 1987. *Foundations of Cognitive Grammar*, vol. 1, *Theoretical Prerequisites*. Stanford: Stanford University Press.

-----. 1991. *Foundations of Cognitive Grammar*, vol. 2, *Descriptive Application*. Stanford: Stanford University Press.

-----. 1997. Constituency, dependency, and conceptual grouping. *Cognitive Linguistics* 8:1-32.

-----. 2001a. Discourse in cognitive grammar. *Cognitive Linguistics* 12:143-188.

-----. 2001b. Dynamicity in grammar. *Axiomathes* 12:7-33.

-----. 2002. A study in unified diversity: English and Mixtec locatives. *Ethnosyntax: Explorations in Grammar and Culture*, ed. N. J. Enfield, 138-161. Oxford and London: Oxford University Press.

-----. 2005. Dynamicity, fictivity, and scanning: The imaginative basis of logic and linguistic meaning. *Grounding Cognition: The Role of Perception and Action in Memory, Language and Thinking*, ed. D. Pecher and R. A. Zwaan, 164-197. Cambridge: Cambridge University Press.

-----. 2008a. *Cognitive Grammar: A Basic Introduction*. New York: Oxford University Press.

-----. 2008b. Subordination in cognitive grammar. *Asymmetric Events*, ed. B. Lewandowska-Tomaszczyk, 137-149. (Converging Evidence in Language and Communication Research 11.) Amsterdam and Philadelphia: John Benjamins.

9

Conceptual Modeling and Sense Construction: The Example of the French Adjective 'Curieux'

HÉLÈNE MAZALEYRAT & AUDREY RUDEL

This paper presents a semantic cognitive analysis of the French adjective 'curieux'. Our choice to study this adjective has a twofold motivation. On the one hand, 'curieux' can have different meanings when it is combined with a noun. On the other hand, it is well known that in French, adjectives can be anteposed or postposed. Taking into account its various meanings, our purpose is firstly to propose a conceptual modeling which representing the semantic content of 'curieux'. Secondly, we aim to examine sense construction in expressions containing such an adjective, and attempt to search for regularities.

1 Conceptual modeling of the French adjective 'curieux'

1.1 Postulate

To elaborate the conceptual modeling of linguistic expressions, we postulate that lexical items are associated with organized conceptual structures composed of numerous pieces of information, which are stored into the mental lexicon of speakers-hearers. In other words, we consider that the various aspects of words (phonetic, orthographical, morphological, syntactic, semantic and so on) are integrated in a multidimensional system of knowledge recorded in speakers-hearers' memory (cf. Lecocq & Segui 1989: 8).

Meaning, Form & Body.
Fey Parrill, Vera Tobin, and Mark Turner (eds.).

This paper is devoted more particularly to the study of the semantic content of the French adjective 'curieux'. As it has multiple meanings, we first need to determine if it is a homonym or a polysem before defining which semantic pieces of information are conveyed by its different senses and finally how they may be organized within its conceptual structure.

1.2. Semantic analysis: homonymy or polysemy?

According to French dictionaries, the two meanings of 'curieux' can be paraphrased by the following expressions:

- 'eager to learn'
- 'odd, strange'

They are so different that we must wonder if 'curieux' is homonymic or polysemic. Indeed, does 'curieux' correspond to two different words that have the same spelling and pronunciation but different meanings (homonymy) or is it a single word with multiple and related meanings (polysemy)? To conclude that an item is polysemic, Recanati (1997) affirms that its meanings must be both genetically and semantically joined up. In others words, they must have the same etymon and at the same time speakers-hearers must be able to detect a link between them, even if they are no longer conscious of the etymological origin of the present meanings. If one of these conditions is not fulfilled, the item is considered to be homonymic.

So what about 'curieux'? A priori, there is no etymological link between its two meanings. Only a diachronic analysis will reveal if they are genetically connected or not.

1.2.1 Diachrony and genetic connection

We learn in French etymological dictionaries, such as the *Dictionnaire Historique de la Langue Française* (1992) and the *Trésor de la Langue Française* (1985), that 'curieux' is from the Latin 'curiosus' which was akin to 'cura' (care).

'Cura' had two meanings. On the one hand, it meant 'concern, worry, anxiety' and on the other hand it signified 'office, task, responsibility'. We can see that these two meanings are closely linked (if you are concerned, worried or anxious about something, you may want to take care of it). The adjectives 'curiosus' and its antonym 'incuriosus' (careless, negligent, indifferent), the noun 'incuria' (negligence, unconcern, apathy, indifference), the verb 'curare' (arrange, see, attend to; undertake; procure; regard), etc. derived from these meanings. 'Cura' led to many Modern French words such as 'cure' (course of treatment) – from 'curatus' originally meaning 'well looked after; carefully prepared; anxious' and which is a derivation of 'curare' – and many other words of the medical vocabulary: 'curable, curateur, curative, curetage, curette, curie', etc. (curable, guardian, curative, curettage, curette, curie, etc.). 'Cura' is also the etymon of the noun 'curé' (parish priest) - 'curatus' took progressively the meaning 'in charge of souls' (Medieval Latine). 'Cura' and its derivation 'procurare' (to minister , to take care) are also the etymons of the verb 'procurer' (to procure) which first meant 'to take care' at the end of the 12th century, then 'to make somebody obtain something' (end of the 13th century), and finally 'to obtain by care or effort' (from the 17th century up today). Another example of Modern French word etymologically linked to 'cura' is the noun 'sinécure' (sinecure) which means 'profitable or prestigious position requiring little or no work'.

To go back more specifically to the etymology of the adjective 'curieux', let us underline that somebody being 'curiosus' was so careful that he was nearly indiscreet. From 'curiosus', the word 'curios (us, ous)'[1] was used up to the 12th century in Old and Middle French. It also meant 'careful'. But this sense no longer exists since 'curieux' started to develop simultaneously toward two other distinct semantic poles from the 12th century.

From the 16th century to the present day (i.e. in Classical and Modern French), it has meant 'eager to learn, to see, to know'. Its synonyms were 'burrowing, inquisitive, etc.'. Today, the meaning of the adjective is not necessarily pejorative as it was in the past so that someone being 'curieux' only refers to somebody showing interest in somebody or something. It corresponds to the lexicographic paraphrase 'eager to learn'.

Again from the 16th century onwards, 'curieux' has also been used to qualify something or somebody that excited attention or speculation through being inexplicable or highly unusual. Its synonyms were 'original, extraordinary, etc.'. Nowadays, being 'curieux' still means 'arousing interest'. This meaning is noted by the paraphrases 'odd, strange' in the dictionaries.

Let us notice that 'curios' in Old and Middle French gave birth to the English adjective 'curious', whose earliest known usage dates from the 14th

---

[1] Progressively, 'curios' changed into 'curieus' (see Lorris (1237) *Le Roman de la Rose*, completed by Meung (1275-1280), line 1040 "*Ce sunt cil qui sunt* curieus *De desprisier et de blasmer Tous ceus qui font miex*" and line 4056 "*Las ! J'en doi bien avoir paor, Quant je voi que losengeor, Et traïtor, et enveus, sont de moi nuire* curieus") because of the declension system inherited from the Antiquity. Thus, all the adjectives descended from Latine adjectives ending by '-us, -a, -um' such as 'curiosus' took a '-s' when it was masculine, and an '-e' when it was feminine in Old and Middle French. Finally, the adjective became 'curieux' when the declension system disappeared around the 15th century.

century (see *The American Heritage Dictionary of the English Language*, 2000). It is worth noticing that the meaning of 'curious' manifests the same main bifurcation. In 1340, it only meant 'eager to know' (often in a pejorative sense). The other sense 'exciting interest' was only attested in 1715. In consequence, the adjective 'curious' has today the same meanings as 'curieux' in French.

Following Pottier's works (1985), the figure below represents the diachronic evolution of the semantic content of the adjective 'curieux':

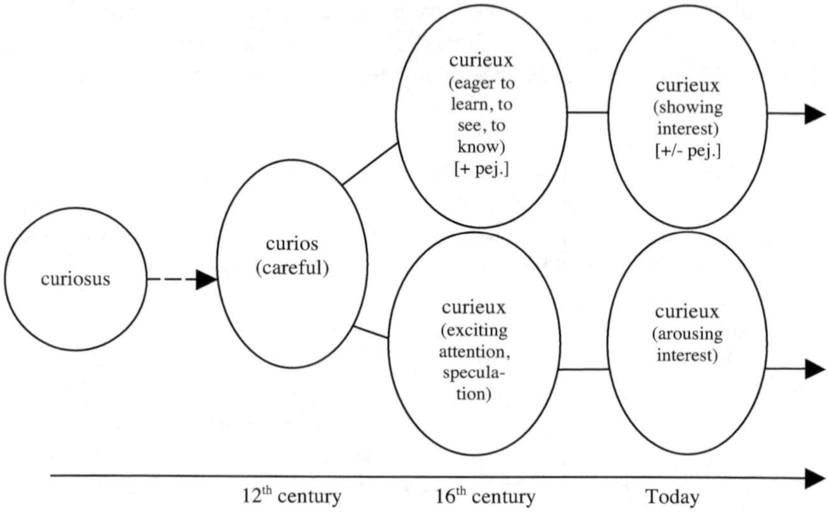

Figure 1. Diachronic evolution of the adjective 'curieux'

To sum up, the current meanings of the adjective 'curieux' result from a bidirectional evolution of its semantics through time. The diachronic analysis reveals that they have the same etymon 'curiosus', so that we may conclude that they are genetically linked. We must determine now if its meanings are also semantically connected to decide whether 'curieux' is polysemic.

1.2.2 Synchrony and semantic connection

The adjective 'curieux' has already been studied by linguists such as François, Manguin & Victorri (2003) and Bat-Zeev Shildkrot (1997). In accordance with our diachronic analysis and lexicographic sources, they also consider that today 'curieux' has two different meanings.

On the one hand, 'curieux' can mean 'showing interest'. Its synonyms are 'chercheur, intéressé, fouineur, indiscret, etc.' (inquiring, interested, nosey, indiscreet, etc.)[2]. In this case, it qualifies a psychological attitude, a natural temperament. For example, 'un garçon curieux' (a boy who is eager to learn) is a boy who has an inquiring mind. He may be curious about everything or especially interested in a particular domain (mathematics, history, etc.). Then being 'curieux' refers to a particular behavior, which is the physical manifestation of that mental disposition.

On the other hand, 'curieux' can mean 'arousing interest'. Its synonyms are 'bizarre, étonnant, étrange, intéressant, drôle, singulier, etc.' (odd, surprising, strange, interesting, funny, singular, etc.)[3]. In this case, it qualifies somebody or something (an object, a situation, an event) you cannot fail to notice. Using 'curieux' with this sense amounts to making implicit reference to a norm. For example, 'une maison curieuse' (an odd house) does not look like a traditional house, maybe because of its architecture, its form or its building materials. Likewise, you may say 'une curieuse situation', 'un détail curieux', 'une question curieuse' (a strange situation/detail/question) if you think they are quite extraordinary. Besides you may think that somebody is 'curieux' because of his physical aspect, his behavior or his personality.

In our opinion, there is a common element between the two meanings of 'curieux'. Taking into account the synonyms 'interested' for the sense 'showing interest' and 'interesting' for the sense 'arousing interest', we can assume that the notion of 'interest' is in the heart of the semantics of 'curieux'. This concept would be the semantic link joining together the two meanings of the adjective.

In a nutshell, if the diachronic study of 'curieux' shows that its two senses were genetically related, the synchronic analysis reveals that they are also semantically linked. Therefore, it is now possible to conclude that 'curieux' is a polysemic adjective.

To elaborate its conceptual modeling, we must determine now which semantic pieces of information are specifically associated with that adjective.

2. Conceptual representation: a cognitive approach

According to the *Trésor de la langue française*, 'showing interest' is the active meaning of 'curieux'. In this case, the referent of the noun combined

---

2 (See François, Manguin & Victorri 2003).

3 Ibid.

with 'curieux' makes the action. In other words, the referent being eager to learn shows interest, is interested. 'Arousing interest' corresponds to the passive meaning of the adjective. Here, the thing or the person being 'curieux' is the target of someone's interest. The referent of the noun qualified by the adjective undergoes the action because it arouses interest, it is interesting.

Thus, the polarity between the active sense and the passive one of the adjective 'curieux' suggests a kind of Subject-Object schema[4], which would be the following:

Subject interested in interesting Object

We postulate that these two meanings are respectively associated with numerous semantic pieces of information. For each of them, we propose to distinguish one main semantic piece of information from all the others. We note it [INTERESTED] for the active meaning, and [INTERESTING] for the passive meaning. When 'curieux' is combined with a noun, it has either the active sense or the passive sense. It depends on which piece of information is activated during the process of sense construction. When [INTERESTED] is selected and activated, 'curieux' has the active sense and means 'showing interest'. When [INTERESTING] is selected and activated, it has the passive sense and means 'arousing interest'.

How can we represent the semantic content of 'curieux', taking into account its polysemy i.e. its two different meanings with their specific semantic pieces of information and the link between them? According to many psycholinguists, each meaning of a polysemic item has to be represented into the mental lexicon of speakers-hearers (Frazier & Rayner 1990, Pickering & Frisson 2001, Klepousniostou 2002). Thus, the semantic conceptual structure of polysems would be organized in function of their different meanings and therefore would present as many substructures as they have polysemic senses. In addition, we believe that the link relating the different meanings of the item have to be represented as well.

We propose to organize the conceptual content of 'curieux' into two substructures : one for its active meaning containing [INTERESTED] as main semantic piece of information, the other for its passive meaning conveying [INTERESTING] as main semantic piece of information. Moreover,

[4] Let us notice that such an observation has already been pointed out, more particularly as far as the semantics of verbs is concerned. Indeed, using Subject-object schemas seems to be a general tendency in the cognitive semantics of perception verbs in many languages (Object smells and Subject smells Object; Object looks nice and Subject looks at Object, etc.). See Pottier (2000).

as the notion of interest seems to be at the core of the semantics of 'curieux', we consider the concept [INTEREST] as the common element between the two substructures. In other words, both of them share the concept piece of information [INTEREST].

Following Langacker's terminology (1987) also used by Tuggy (1993), we call 'schema' the conceptual structure composed of the common elements of the conceptual structures representing the different meanings of a polysemic item. It subsumes them, which are 'elaborations' of the schematic sense.

> A schema [...] is an abstract characterization that is fully compatible with all the members of the category it defines[5]. [...] It is an integrated structure that embodies the commonality of its members, which are conceptions of greater specificity and detail that elaborate the schema in contrasting ways (Langacker 1987: 371)

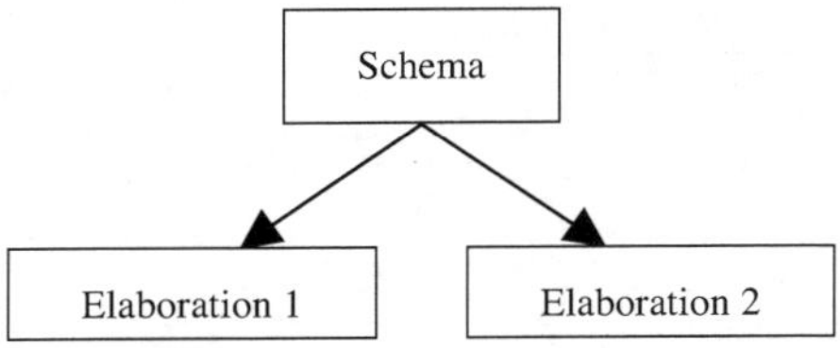

Figure 2. Schema and elaborations

Considering that the concept [INTEREST] is in the heart of the semantics of the adjective 'curieux', we consider that it belongs to its schematic meaning (among other pieces of information). When the adjective is used to qualify a noun, its schematic meaning would be elaborated so that either 'curieux' presents its active meaning or it presents its passive meaning.

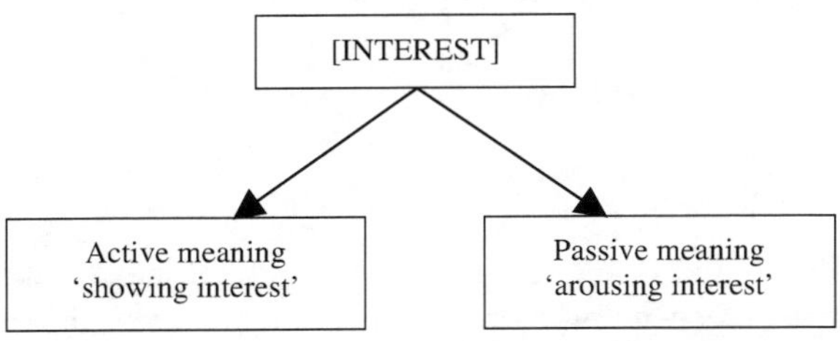

Figure 3. Architecture of the conceptual modeling of 'curieux'

5 In Langacker's Cognitive Grammar, lexical items constitute complex linguistic categories whose members are 'established values' such as 'interrelated senses' and 'conventionally sanctioned usages' (1987: 370).

As far as 'curieux' is concerned, speakers-hearers can only have access to its two meanings: 'showing interest' and 'arousing interest', which are more salient than the schematic sense of the adjective. This one can only be accessible through its elaborations. That is why we chose to represent it with a dotted line and the two salient meanings with a bold line.

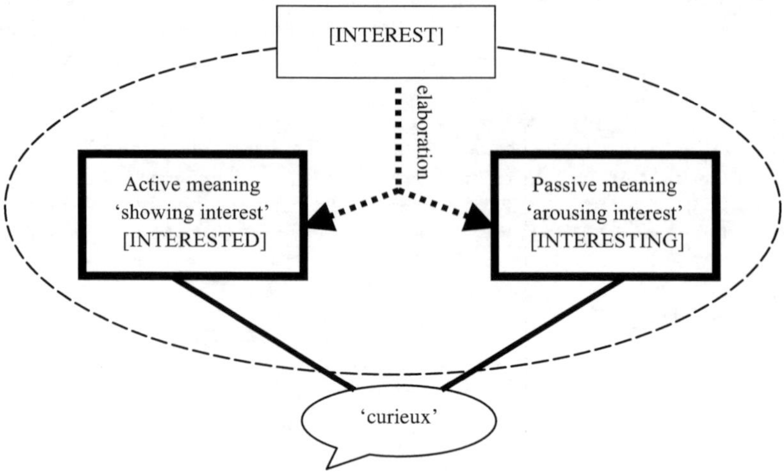

Figure 4. Conceptual structure associated with the adjective 'curieux'

After determining the semantic content of 'curieux', we are now able to examine the sense construction of complex expressions containing that adjective and a noun. The section below is devoted to the selective activation of semantic pieces of information associated with 'curieux' when it is combined with a noun. Various parameters coming into play during the process of sense construction will be highlighted.

3. Sense construction

3.1 Sense activation

Sense construction of expressions containing 'curieux' and a substantive is very complex. Depending on which semantic pieces of information are activated within the conceptual content of the adjective, 'curieux' can present either its active meaning or its passive meaning. The brief study of some examples will help us to underline this phenomenon.

So, let us examine first of all the expression 'une voiture curieuse' (an odd car) which denotes a car which arouses interest because of its strangeness. Various pieces of information associated with 'voiture' and 'curieux' are activated. Concerning 'voiture' (car), they can be linked to the physical aspect of the referent and more exactly to the constituent of the car that is the body. They can also be relative to the motorization (for example, a car with a specific engine). As far as 'curieux' is concerned, the main activated piece of information is [INTERESTING].

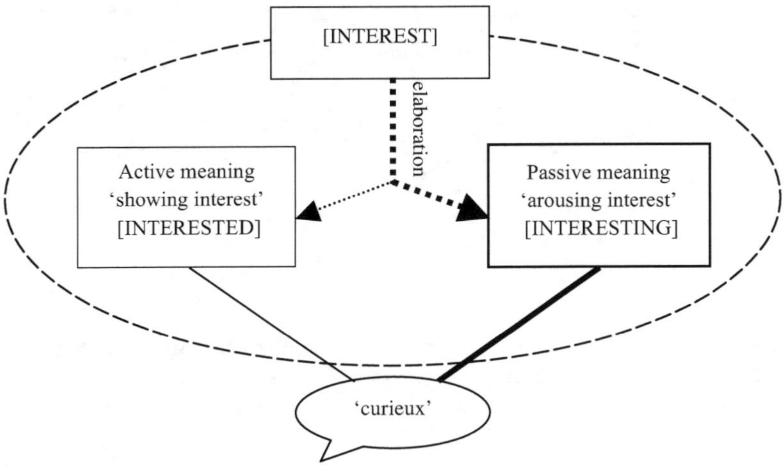

Figure 5. Activation of the passive meaning into the conceptual content of 'curieux' in the expression 'une voiture curieuse' (an odd car)

Let us now consider the expression 'une personne curieuse'. It can make reference to somebody who is eager to learn or to somebody who is strange (a person who is eager to learn/an odd person). Thus, in this expression, both pieces of information, [INTERESTED] and [INTERESTING] can be activated into the conceptual content of 'curieux' and can apply to the noun 'personne'.

When [INTERESTED] is activated (Figure 6a), 'curieux' has its active meaning and 'une personne curieuse' means 'somebody who is eager to learn'. Otherwise, when [INTERESTING] is activated (Figure 6b), 'curieux' has its passive meaning so that the person in question will be considered outside a kind of standard either by the physical aspect, or by the psychological one.

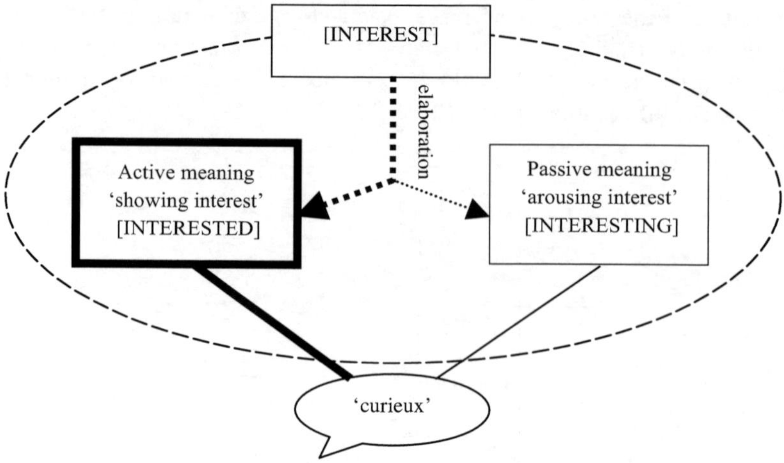

Figure 6a. Activation of the active meaning into the conceptual content of 'curieux' in the expression 'une personne curieuse' (somebody being eager to learn)

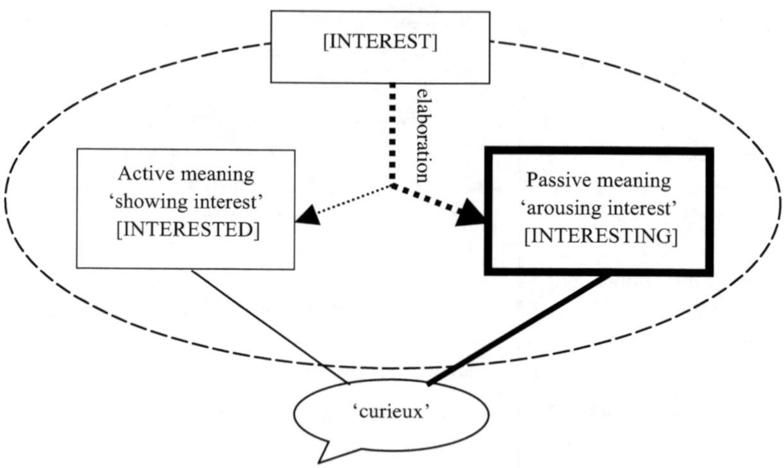

Figure 6b. Activation of the passive meaning into the conceptual content of 'curieux' in the expression 'une personne curieuse' (somebody being strange, odd)

So Figures 5 and 6b illustrate the activation of the passive sense – with the activation of the semantic piece of information [INTERESTING] – whereas figure 6a represents the activation of the active sense – when the main semantic piece of information, namely [INTERESTED], is activated.

These examples suggest that the combinatorial processes seem to be different according to nouns and that the interactions between the adjective and the noun are multiple. The interpretation of expressions containing 'curieux' thus results from complex mechanisms depending on the pieces of information which are present and activated into the conceptual structure of the adjective **and** also into the conceptual structure of the noun. Both items influence each other as far as the activation of information is concerned.

The sub-section below is dedicated to the analysis of the adjective 'curieux' in a reduced context, namely the context of the noun phrase (with a brief extension to the structure be-'curieux').

Considering the combination of this polysemic adjective with a noun, it seems possible to detect regularities in the process of sense construction, according to the position of the adjective (anteposition or postposition) and also according to the semantics of the noun which it qualifies.

3.2 In search of regularities

In order to look for semantic regularities, we will use the minimal pairs below which are examples of combinations of 'curieux' with different nouns: 'voiture' (car), 'roi' (king), 'personne' (person), 'idée' (idea), 'maison' (house) and 'enfant' (child).

(1) une curieuse voiture (odd) –une voiture curieuse (odd)
(2) un curieux roi (odd) – un roi curieux (odd /eager to learn)
(3) une curieuse personne (odd) – une personne curieuse (odd/eager to learn ?)
(4) une curieuse idée (odd) – une idée curieuse (odd)
(5) une curieuse maison (odd) – une maison curieuse (odd)
(6) un curieux enfant (odd) – un enfant curieux (odd /eager to learn ?)

3.2.1 Position and function of the adjective

This part concentrates on the relationship between position and meaning, since the activated pieces of information for the adjective 'curieux' can be different depending on its anteposition or postposition.

Some of the minimal pairs stated above ((1), (4) and (5)) do not show different meanings between anteposition and postposition. In such cases, the activated piece of information into the conceptual content of 'curieux' is

[INTERESTING] and the meaning is 'arousing interest' (passive meaning). In these noun phrases, 'curieux' presents the same meaning for the anteposition and the postposition.

However, there may be strong semantic variations in the others pairs: (2), (3) and (6). Indeed, in such expressions, when 'curieux' is anteposed, [INTERESTING] is activated and the adjective takes its passive meaning. But when 'curieux' is postposted, the active and passive meanings are both possible because both pieces of information are co-present without excluding each other. In such a restricted context, we face with an actual ambiguity and consequently an interpretative vagueness.

Considering these semantic variations, we can already assert that the pieces of information associated with 'curieux' which will be activated in combination are partially determined by the position of the adjective[6]. Indeed, the passive meaning – with [INTERESTING] activated – is always expressed when 'curieux' is anteposed. Nevertheless, it seems impossible (for the moment) to detect regularities as far as postposition is concerned.

In order to study the semantics of 'curieux' as a predicative adjective, we use examples corresponding to the previous minimal pairs.

(1') cette voiture est curieuse	(this car is odd)
(2') ce roi est curieux	(this king is odd / eager to learn?)
(3') cette personne est curieuse	(this person is odd / eager to learn?)
(4') cette idée est curieuse	(this idea is odd)
(5') cette maison est curieuse	(this house is odd)
(6') cet enfant est curieux	(this child is odd / eager to learn?)

When 'curieux' is used as a predicative adjective, we notice that in (1'), (4') and (5'), the piece of information [INTERESTING] is activated within its conceptual content.

As far as sense activation is concerned, we note a parallel between (1'), (4'), (5') and (1), (4), (5), since the same semantic piece of information is activated in such cases. Indeed, when 'curieux' is a predicative adjective or

[6] Let us notice that in French anteposed adjectives often have a stylistic, affective, subjective or even intensive value. Many linguists such as Blinkenberg (1933), Goes (1999), Hutchinson (1969), etc. consider that anteposition can express affectivity, appreciation or a moral nuance. On the contrary, postposed adjectives are considered as non-emotional, concrete, determinative, logic or technical. Thus, according to Hutchinson (1969), postposed adjectives are objective, impersonal, or factual. This comment concerning anteposition and postposition has to do with the semantics of word order in noun phrases containing an adjective in French. Indeed, the position of the adjective within the noun phrase has an impact on the value of the adjective.

when it is used as an attributive one (whether it is ante or postposed), [INTERESTING] is activated into its conceptual content.

Moreover, for the expressions (2'), (3') and (6'), the two pieces of information [INTERESTING] and [INTERESTED] are possibly activable when 'curieux' is predicative. We face here the same semantic phenomenon as in (2), (3) and (6) when 'curieux' is postposed – since the two meanings of this lexical item are probable – semantic pieces of information being co-present and not excluding each other. Consequently, this limited context can also lead to interpretative vagueness. We can conclude that the activated pieces of information for 'curieux' as a predicative adjective are identical to the activated ones when it is used in postposition as an attributive adjective with the nouns 'roi', 'personne' and 'enfant'.

The semantic variations are related to the potential meanings of the adjective (before any activation of information). What is more, our analysis displays that the semantic variations are also linked to its position and to its function.

As we consider 'curieux' in the reduced context of the noun phrase, it also seems obvious to wonder about the impact of the substantive itself. Consequently, we will bring to the fore its influence in sense construction and we will especially pay attention to the regularities linked to its semantics.

3.2.2 Inanimate and animate nouns

According to the minimal pairs seen above ((1) to (6) and (1') to (6')), we note that the place of 'curieux' does not involve variations of meaning when it is employed with inanimate nouns such as 'voiture', 'idée' and 'maison' (car, idea, house):

(1) une curieuse voiture – une voiture curieuse
(1') cette voiture est curieuse
(4) une curieuse idée – une idée curieuse
(4') cette idée est curieuse
(5) une curieuse maison – une maison curieuse
(5') cette maison est curieuse

On the contrary, 'curieux' shows a potential difference of meaning between ante and postposition when it is combined with substantives of the category /animate/: 'roi', 'personne', 'enfant' (king, person, child).

(2) un curieux roi – un roi curieux
(2') ce roi est curieux

(3) une curieuse personne – une personne curieuse
(3') cette personne est curieuse
(6) un curieux enfant – un enfant curieux
(6') cet enfant est curieux

So, 'curieux' can present a different meaning according to the substantive with which it is employed. Therefore, 'curieux' is sensitive to the class of the noun in combination.

The active sense 'eager to learn' can only be activated when 'curieux' is combined with a noun belonging to the /animate/ category, since such a category is a virtual agent of mental activity. /Animate/ includes animals. Nevertheless, the active sense 'eager to learn' can only be activated if a context enhances the mental activity aspect of the noun sense. Thus, when 'curieux' qualifies nouns denoting an animal, the adjective takes its active sense only if there is a kind a personification of the animal. In such a case, the extra-linguistic context – such as the situation of statement – may have an influence on the semantic activation. For example, somebody would say "Voici un chien curieux!" ("This is a curious dog!") speaking about a dog who is on the lookout for everything. The linguistic context can also plays a role, as the presence of a prepositional complement. For example, the active sense is activated in the expression 'mon chien curieux de tout' (my dog is interested in everything).

To conclude, even if sense construction is a complex phenomenon, it is possible to detect regularities which make it possible to predict which meaning will be activated for the adjective 'curieux'.

When it combines with an /inanimate/ noun, the piece of information [INTERESTING] is activated and the passive meaning is expressed.

On the contrary, in combination with an /animate/ noun, it is more difficult to predict its meaning. If 'curieux' is anteposed, the piece of information [INTERESTING] is activated and thus the passive meaning emerges. In the opposite case, it is not possible to envisage which piece of information – and then which meaning – will be activated when 'curieux' (as an attributive adjective) is placed after an /animate/ noun or when it is a predicative adjective employed with such a noun. In fact, the active and passive meanings are both possible and the listener is facing interpretative vagueness noted as 'indet.' in the table below. Only the recourse to a broader context makes it possible to dispel ambiguity, and thus determine which is the activated meaning.

The following table is a summary of the various possible meanings of 'curieux' according to its position, its function and the class of nouns with which it is combined.

Table 1. Semantic regularities of the adjective 'curieux'

<table>
<tr><td colspan="2" rowspan="3"></td><td colspan="3">Function of the adjective 'curieux'</td></tr>
<tr><td colspan="2">Attributive adjective</td><td rowspan="2">Predicative</td></tr>
<tr><td>Anteposition</td><td>Postposition</td></tr>
<tr><td rowspan="2">Noun class</td><td>Inanimate noun</td><td>[INTERESTING] Passive meaning</td><td>[INTERESTING] Passive meaning</td><td>[INTERESTING] Passive meaning</td></tr>
<tr><td>Animate noun</td><td>[INTERESTING] Passive meaning</td><td>Indet.</td><td>Indet.</td></tr>
</table>

4 Conclusion

The French polysemic adjective has two different meanings: 'showing interest' (active meaning) and 'arousing interest' (passive meaning). In the framework of R.W. Langacker's Cognitive Grammar, we propose to consider them as elaborations of the schematic sense of this adjective.

So, the conceptual modeling we proposed to represent the semantic content of 'curieux' contains two substructures, corresponding to the two meanings of the adjective. By hypothesis, each of them is associated with semantic pieces of information. The main ones are [INTERESTED] for the active meaning, and [INTERESTING] for the passive meaning. The two substructures are subsumed by the schematic sense of 'curieux', which conveys the semantic piece of information [INTEREST], which is therefore the link between them.

In context, 'curieux' presents either its active meaning or its passive one. It depends on which main semantic piece of information is selected and activated according to various parameters, namely the position of the adjective towards the substantive (ante or postposition) and the noun class (/animate/ or /inanimate/). In combination with a noun, there are regularities in sense construction which allow to predict which meaning of 'curieux' will be activated.

Author note

Hélène Mazaleyrat, Université Blaise Pascal – Clermont II, France; IUT SRC Saint-Raphael, France. Audrey Rudel, Université Blaise Pascal (Clermont-Ferrand II), France.

References

Bat-Zeev Shildkrot, H. 1997. Synonymie et polysémie : le cas de *curieux* comme parcours sémantique d'un mot. *Langue française* 128:113-125.

Blinkenberg, A. 1933. *L'ordre des mots en français moderne*, vol.2, Kobenhavn: Levin & Munksgaard.

Dictionnaire du moyen français (1300-1350). http://www.atilf.fr/dmf/

François, J., Manguin, J.L. & Victorri, B. 2003. La réduction de la polysémie adjectivale en cotexte nominal : une méthode de sémantique combinatoire. *Cahiers du CRISCO* 14, Caen: Presses universitaires de Caen.

Frazier, L. et Rayner, K. 1990. Taking on semantic commitments: Processing multiple meanings vs multiple senses. Constraint satisfaction as a theory of sentence processing. *Journal of Memory and Language* 29:181-200.

Godefroy, F. 1892. *Dictionnaire de l'ancienne langue française et de tous ses dialectes*. Paris: F. Vieweg.

Goes, J. 1999. *L'adjectif: entre nom et verbe*, Paris-Brussels: De Boeck-Larcier.

Hutchinson, J.A. 1969. Le désordre des mots. La place de l'adjectif. *Le français dans le monde* 62:15-23.

Klepousniotou, E. 2002. The processing of lexical ambiguity: Homonymy and polysemy in the mental lexicon. *Brain and Language* 81:205-223.

Langacker, R.W. 1987. *Foundations of Cognitive Grammar*, vol. 1, Stanford: Stanford University Press.

Lecocq, P. & Segui, J. 1989. L'accès lexical. *Lexique* 8:1-9.

Lorris de G. 1237, Meung de J. 1275-80. Reedited in 1997, *Le Roman de la Rose*. Paris: Lgf Editions.

Pickering, M.J. et Frisson, S. 2001. Processing ambiguous verbs: Evidence from eye

Movements. *Journal of Experimental Psychology: Learning, Memory and Cognition* 27(2):556-573.

Pottier, B. 1985. *Linguistique générale. Théorie et description*, Paris: Klincksieck.

Pottier, B. 2001. *Représentations mentales et catégorisations linguistiques*. Paris-Louvain: Editions Peeters.

Récanati, F. 1997. La polysémie contre le fixisme. *Langue française* 113:107-123.

The American Heritage Dictionary of the English Language 4th edition 2000. Boston, Mass.: Houghton Mifflin Company.

Tuggy, D. 1993. Ambiguity, polysemy and vagueness. *Cognitive Linguistics* 4-3:273-290.

10

Sign-Gesture Symbiosis in Brazilian Sign Language Narrative

LELAND MCCLEARY & EVANI VIOTTI

While the relation of gesture to speech has now been of interest to oral language linguists for several decades, the same cannot be said of sign linguists. To the contrary, these same decades have been devoted to demonstrating the nongestural nature of signed languages (SLs) in order to establish them firmly as natural languages. The success of this effort can be seen by the placement of SLs at the extreme linguistic end of McNeill's presentation of what he calls the Kendon Continuum (1992: 3), as it reflects the presence of linguistic properties:

Gesticulation → Pantomime → Emblems → Sign Language

In this array, gesticulation and pantomime are understood to be devoid of linguistic properties, while emblems are thought to have some linguistic properties, and SLs to be totally linguistic. By compacting SLs at the nongestural end of the gesture continuum, students of gesture have isolated them from anything that approaches gesticulation.

Meanwhile, on the oral language side, research piles up in support of the proposals of Kendon (1980, 2004) and McNeill (1992) that gesture and speech form, in the words of McNeill, 'a single integrated process of utterance formation in which there is a synthesis of opposite modes of thought—global-synthetic and instantaneous imagery with linear-segmented temporally extended verbalization' (1992: 35). Most work advancing this single integrated process hypothesis has been done on cospeech gesture, that is, gesture accompanying the speech of users of oral languages. These

Meaning, Form, and Body.
Fey Parrill, Vera Tobin, & Mark Turner (eds.).

studies focus on the gesticulation end of the gesture continuum, at which speech is a necessary prerequisite for the occurrence of gesture. In terms of co-occurrence of speech, as opposed to the presence of linguistic properties, the order of the Kendon Continuum shifts: Gesticulation is followed by emblems, with which speech is optional, then by pantomime and sign language, both of which are only produced in the obligatory *absence* of speech (McNeill 1992: 2). The result of this analysis is that SLs appear to be self-contained systems, co-occurring with neither speech nor gesture.[1]

Ironically, it has been partly the success of gesture studies in showing the universality of cospeech gesture that has created an environment in which SL linguists can begin to break with the taboo against describing SLs in anything but strictly linguistic terms. If the co-occurrence of what is considered linguistic (discrete, categorical, combinatorial, linear, conventional, hierarchically organized) with what is gestural (analogical, continuous, noncombinatorial, spatial, idiosyncratic, nonhierarchical) is found to be universal among spoken languages, why should it not also be so among SLs? (Duncan 2003).

1 The Search for Gesture in Gestural Languages

Fortunately, several recent studies of gesture and sign have begun to shed new light on the gesture-sign continuum. Before mentioning these works, however, it will be useful to break open the monolithic box of sign language at the extreme linguistic end of the continuum and, similarly, observe the variety of distinct types of gesture that inhabit the category of gesticulation at the other end. For McNeill (1992: 12–25), gesticulation can appear in any of the following forms: iconics, metaphorics, beats, cohesives, and deictics.

By the same token, SLs are not composed of a single stuff. If there are several gesture types, there are at least as many signing types compressed into the sign language category at the other end of the spectrum which are apparently used universally in the world's SLs. SLs use a variety of resources, some of which are quite unlike any that are found in oral languages. These resources can be arrayed from the most discrete, conventionalized and arbitrary of manual signs to what is essentially mime. In order of unruliness, from most well behaved to least, these resources are: conventional lexical signs (from highly iconic to totally arbitrary); deictic signs (pronouns and indicating verbs, which point at referents in discourse);

[1] In practice, of course, the coarticulation of speech and sign is massively attested. At one extreme is what could be called cospeech sign, in which hearing bilinguals attempt to speak and sign simultaneously for deaf or deaf and hearing audiences. At the other extreme is cosign speech in which deaf SL users articulate words in the oral language as they sign, particularly to nonproficient hearing interlocutors.

polycomponential signs, which combine conventional handshapes with iconic movements and paths; nonmanual signs, notably facial expressions and eye gaze, which have been described as serving grammatical or prosodic functions, but which may also be deictics, iconics or expressive of emotion or attitude; and pantomime, as found in constructed action, a phenomenon in which part of the signer's body moves in such a way as to iconically represent the body of a human character or other participant in a narrative.[2] All of these have been attested in a great number of SLs and appear to be common and favored resources used by native and proficient signers. As can be seen, they overlap to some extent with McNeill's gesture types, and are themselves composed of varying degrees and mixes of linguistic and gestural features, which will become clearer in the course of our analysis.

When viewed in this way, the approximation of gesture to sign begins to look not only more feasible but even quite compelling. The descriptions of iconics, metaphorics, cohesives and deictics immediately bring to mind equivalent resources used in SLs. Some of these (notably iconics, cohesives and deictics) will not necessarily be produced by the hands and arms, however, but with other parts of the body, suggesting that a study of gesture in SLs will require a broad understanding of gesture to include any 'visible bodily activity' that contributes to the communicative import of an utterance (Kendon 2004: 110)—with the qualification that it must not be linguistic in nature. If, however, it should turn out that all visible bodily activity in SLs proves to be linguistically structured, then it would appear that there is a constraint against coverbal gesture operating in SLs that does not hold for oral languages, a fact that would require explanation.[3] Nonetheless, that is not the direction in which the evidence appears to be falling.

As mentioned, a small but growing body of research is beginning to call into question the purely linguistic analyses given for certain of these signing resources, considering their idiosyncratic, analogical and otherwise gestural manifestations in continuous discourse, particularly in narrative, the object of this study. For example, to account for what he considered to be the undeniable presence of gesture in discourse, Liddell (1995, 2000, 2003a, b)

---

[2] Indicating verb is the term introduced by Liddell to refer to what are called directional verbs or agreement verbs in the literature (see Liddell 2003). Polycomponential verb is the term introduced by Schembri (2003) to refer to what are traditionally known in SL linguistics as classifiers, and for which we adopt the more general term polycomponential sign. We are also adopting the term constructed action, preferred by Winston (1991), Metzger (1995), Liddell and others to refer to what has been called in other analyses 'referential shift' or 'role shifting' (see Quinto-Pozos 2007).

[3] We will use 'coverbal' as generic for oral and signed linguistic systems, as distinguished from 'cospeech' which will refer only to oral language.

breaks new ground by proposing a series of reanalyses of signing phenomena, applying blending theory to explain the behavior of indicating verbs (blends of conventional signs with deictics); depictive verbs, his term for polycomponential signs (blends of conventional handshapes with gestural paths, positions and manners), and constructed action ('surrogate blends' of 'real space' with 'event space').[4] Schembri (2003) has investigated the dual nature of polycomponential signs as made up of more conventional and less conventional components and Schembri et al. (2005) have demonstrated the partially gestural nature of these signs by showing their similarity to gestures made by nonsigners. The fact that these gestures are shown to come from a common storehouse of communicative resources means that they may be assigned privileged status as signs or grammar in SLs only with care. Sandler (2009) shows that in Israeli Sign Language, iconic mouth gestures accompany conventional manual signs. With the gestural component in the mouth and the verbal component in the hands, the situation is exactly the reverse of what is found in the case of iconic manual gestures that accompany speech in oral languages. Finally, Quinto-Pozos (2007) demonstrates the obligatory nature of constructed action under some conditions, showing that the pantomime that seems to be an ever present feature of narrative in SLs is not felt to be something extra or optional, but an integral part of signing. That would mean that this most gestural feature of signing that has not yet received a fully satisfactory linguistic analysis is still felt to be an integral part of the language.[5]

Part of the unease, perhaps, in allowing gesture to cohabit the same utterances as sign, lies in a lack of clarity about what might regulate this marriage. If it is true (and it does seem to be true) that not only the more conventionally linguistic, but also the clearly gestural resources of sign are used to heightened effect by native and highly proficient signers, *and* that when thus used, they seem to be more tightly controlled and carefully articulated (Costello et al. 2008), it does seem that some regularization of their use has taken place. Does this result from the operation of linguistic processes alone? Or might other types of regularization be in play?

Certainly linguistic processes account for a good part of the domestication of gesture that is found in SLs. The migration from gesture to sign has been known to be a primary source of lexicon since Klima & Bellugi (1979). Wilcox, a pioneer in and leading advocate for the study of gesture as a source for meaningful, embodied signs in all language, signed and oral, has studied the processes of both lexicalization and gramaticization of

[4] These concepts will be further explained and illustrated as part of our analysis.

[5] For one attempt at fitting constructed action into a generative analysis, see Lillo-Martin (1995). For other analyses, see Poulin & Miller (1995) and Engberg-Pedersen (2005).

gesture. Wilcox and colleagues have carefully documented the movement across the 'gesture-language interface' that gives rise, for example, to modality, and have shown that this movement can take the familiar path of lexicalization or an alternative route through prosody (Armstrong, Stokoe & Wilcox 1995; Armstrong & Wilcox 2007; Wilcox & Wilcox 1995; Wilcox 2004a, 2004b, 2008; Wilcox & Shaffer 2006). While they claim that 'At no point in this process do we detect a categorical break between where gestures disappear and linguistic units take their place', the focus of their work has been on the processes through which gestures 'finally become complex, grammatically organized utterances' (Armstrong & Wilcox 2007: 104). Work like that of Wilcox and colleagues explains the copresence of the gestural and the verbal as different stages in a neverending movement. What remains to be worked out is how these copresent resources, from the prototypically gestural to the prototypically verbal, all of which are meaning bearing, work together systematically to produce a tightly woven fabric of discourse.

One place to look for understanding how gesture might be said to be 'well formed' without being 'linguistic' may be in the semiotics of visual and spatial communicative practices. As early as 1978, no less a linguist than Charles Hockett was proposing an investigation into what he called 'syntactic dimensionality' to account for the use of spatial and gestural resources by deaf signers (Hockett 1978: 274). Hockett's contemporary William Stokoe, father of SL linguistics, suggested that SLs might well be described using cinematic concepts (Stokoe 1979). This challenge has recently been taken up by Bauman (2003) to describe American Sign Language poetry. The idea is that, if there is a 'grammar of cinema', such a grammar is a reasonable candidate for accounting for some of the regularity to be found in what appears to be gesture in SLs.

In our research on Brazilian Sign Language narrative, we have been persuaded that much of what is going on can be elegantly described in the terminology of cinematography. In narrative, signers use techniques strikingly analogous to such cinematic standbys as 'establishing shot', 'close up', 'shot/reverse shot', and so on. We are not claiming, however, that cinematography supplies the missing link to understanding the gestural regularity of sign. The differences between signing and film are too great to be ignored: Film makes use of information rich photographic (or animated) images collected or produced specifically for the edited final product; it conveys action, but in a two-dimensional frame; typically, the narrator/director/editor of the film does not bodily appear to the audience; it is not produced for simultaneous consumption in real time. These differences suggest that there might also be other reasonable sources from which to derive visual-gestural grammar. Live theater is a candidate, as is puppet theater. There we have human bodies (or surrogates) performing in sight of an audience, with limited visual resources that require manipulation. Another possibility is live television editing, which uses techniques from cinema, but must apply them in real time to content not necessarily under the director's or editor's control.

In our research, we have been able to juxtapose an input for the narrative that is purely cinematic with an output that is purely signed. In this way, we are able to compare the story information available and its manner of presentation (its 'utterances') with the information presented in the signed rendition. The film chosen was Wallace Chafe's the Pear Film, a film without words produced in the 1970s explicitly for the crosslinguistic elicitation of narrative (Chafe 1980).[6] In doing this, we have unwittingly followed the recommendation of Sarapik (2009), who discusses methods of examining the relationship between image and text. After suggesting two other possibilities—comparing distinct art fields to find features held in common, and studying unequivocal and distinctive hybrid forms that are neither one nor the other (in her case comic strips, caricatures, illustrations, and advertisements)—she settles on a third, which is 'functional and comparative: to focus on artifacts where word and image exist together, and compare them with similar phenomena that mainly rely on one means of expression, analyzing their different and similar functions in the communication process' (p. 280). That is what we have done, by comparing a mixed product of verbal (sign) and gestural elements with an analogous version which is wholly visual, without any verbal complement whatever, spoken or signed. Thus we should be able to find clues as to what elements in the filmic version are reproduced visually and gesturally in the signed version, and what elements are verbalized; further, what precise functions the verbal and nonverbal elements exercise within the context of a spatialized recounting.

In the next section, we will describe the data we are using, both the original film and the signed retelling. In the third section we will present a detailed analysis of the verbal and gestural components of the signed version.

2 The Data

To illustrate the nature of the functional integration of prototypical verbal elements (lexical signs) within the contextualizing mimetic performance of

[6]The film has now been made available for viewing on YouTube at <http://www.youtube.com/watch?v=bRNSTxTpG7U>. It can also be downloaded from Wallace Chafe's homepage at <http://www.linguistics.ucsb.edu/faculty/chafe/pearfilm.htm>.

the body-in-space, we will analyze parts of a retelling of the Pear Film story signed by a fluent deaf adult. The data were collected in 2002, according to procedures described in Chafe (1980).[7] For convenience, we will refer to the signed version of the story as the 'signed pear story', to distinguish it from the story as shown in the film. Our analysis will focus on a single sequence of the film, comparing the story as it appears in the film with the story as retold. First, we will describe the film as a whole, then the selected episode in more detail.

The opening sequence of the film begins with an establishing shot of a rural setting and then introduces the protagonist as pear picker, with his ladder, apron, scarf and hat, and his three baskets being filled with pears. This scene is followed by a second (side) sequence in which another farmer passes below the tree leading a goat. In the third sequence, one of the baskets of pears is stolen. This episode will be described in detail below.

The fourth sequence begins with the boy riding his bike along a dirt road with the stolen pears. He passes a girl coming in the opposite direction on a bike, gets distracted, runs into a large rock and tumbles to the ground with his basket of pears. Three friends appear at the scene, help the boy collect the pears and set the basket back on the bike, and then, after a short interlude in which one of the boys returns the bike boy's fallen hat, walk off in the direction from which the boy came, each carrying a pear. This complex sequence is followed by a cut to the tree and the pear picker. The pear picker descends the ladder and notices that one of his baskets is missing. As he ponders the missing basket, perplexed, the three boys walk by eating their pears.

Our retelling of the story closely follows the filmic demarcations of the scenes and sequences. These demarcations, however, would surely not have appeared as clearly to our untrained eyes had it not been for our narrator's signed rendition, in which the filmic transitions are given gestural and postural markings: The opening scene ends with the narrator returning to rest position; the following goat man scene ends with the narrator gesturing that he is wiping the slate clean, and returning once again to rest position; the theft episode also ends with the narrator returning to rest position. At this point, the narrator looks down and scratches his head before taking up the scene in which the accident will occur. This extra planning may reflect the major shift of setting from pear tree to open field as well as the com-

[7] The volunteer storyteller was thirty years old at the time, had been deaf since the age of three, and was a user of sign from the age of nine. He is an instructor of Brazilian Sign Language in a school for deaf children in his city and a leader in the deaf community. He viewed the Pear Film once before videotaping his retelling of the story to one of the authors and another researcher fluent in Brazilian Sign Language.

plexity of the ensuing sequence. After the accident proper, the transition to the appearance of the threesome of boys is marked only by a rapid narrator glance at the interlocutor, without any discontinuity of action, as is the whole of the episode of the return of the hat. The transition from the boys walking away with their pears to the scene of the pear man and his tree does not even merit the typical instantaneous narrator glance at the interlocutor; it is as abrupt as it is in the film. We see in this brief account how the narrator has faithfully conveyed the structure of the story as found in the film. In our more detailed description of the pear stealing sequence below, and in our analysis, we will show how gesture becomes a central element in recreating the film's cinematic effect.

The sequence in focus, in which a basket of pears is stolen from under a tree, in broad daylight, by a boy passing by on a bicycle while the farmer is distracted overhead with his pear picking, is part of the complicating action (such as there is) of the story.

The filmed sequence of pear theft is made up of three scenes. The first re-establishes the farmer on his ladder in the tree engaged in carefully picking pears and placing them in the pocket of his apron; the second shows a boy on his bicycle winding toward the tree along a path; and the third and longest shows the boy and his bicycle under the tree as he calculates his risks and then loads a basket of pears onto his bike and rides away. Each of the scenes is composed of several shots, edited in such a way as to establish a tension between the pear picker in the tree and the boy immediately below plotting to relieve him of the fruits of his labor.

The first scene is composed of four shots, all of which emphasize the deliberate care with which the farmer is picking his pears within an enveloping canopy of leaves which darkens and obscures our view of his face and movements. The only clear pictures of the man are two insert shots, one of his hand grasping a pear against a solid backdrop of leaves and another of his face in an expression of total concentration. The second scene, also composed of four shots, begins with a shift of focus from foreground (farmer in the tree) to background (the sunny meadow behind the tree) to reveal a boy riding his bicycle along a path. The scene cuts back to the farmer in the tree and then returns to two more shots of the boy winding toward the tree as seen through the ladder. The final and longest scene is composed of seven shots. All but two of them are medium long shots from roughly the same viewpoint showing the boy, his bike (when it is standing), the ladder, and (in the widest of them) the tops of the baskets of pears. In these shots, the boy is stopping, laying down his bike, inspecting the pears in the baskets (he puts his hand on one of the pears), checking on the man in the tree, and then moving an entire basket, picking up his bike, lifting the basket onto his bike, and riding off. The remaining two shots, the fourth and last in the series, are cutaway shots showing a boy's-eye view of the distracted farmer. The first is inserted between two shots showing the boy looking up into the tree, and the last confirms that the boy has ridden off without being noticed.

This is the episode that our storyteller will have to narrate, relating not only the sequence of events, but also capturing the effect of the farmer's distraction and the excitement of the boy's risktaking as he decides to cart off a basket of pears. All this the storyteller accomplishes with twenty-nine lexical sign tokens, using twenty-one unique signs, as follows:

> MAN CLIMB NOT-SEE ANOTHER MAN CHILD YOUNG RIDE-BIKE SEE PEAR TASTY DESIRE TAKE LOOK MAN NOT-SEE MAN PICK-PUT NOT-LOOK NOT-SEE PICK-PUT THERE MAN BIKE THINK I GRASP RIDE-BIKE DISAPPEAR-INTO-THE-DISTANCE

Obviously, much is missing from the lexical account. Yet, the story as enacted by the storyteller is remarkably—even eerily—similar to the filmic account. Any running interpretation of the retelling (or careful translation) would require scores of words. How is this accomplished?

While it is clear that the gestural component in sign language narrative is doing much of the work, it is equally clear that this is not just acting out. It is not just mime. There are crucial ways in which the reduced verbal component contributes to the interpretation of what is going on gesturally. The two components mutually contextualize one another.

3 Analysis

As mentioned above, there have been several recent attempts to describe the function and grammar of a massively recurrent phenomenon in SLs called constructed action. Constructed action is not a direct copy of a certain character's action; it is that action as constructed by the narrator.

Liddell (2003a) has provided an elegant account of constructed action in terms of mental space blends (Fauconnier & Turner 2002) in which a shift of the body or facial expression may create a real-space blend he calls surrogate space. In Liddell's work, real space is the term used to refer to the mental space built from our immediate sensory-perceptual experience of our current situation, plus our knowledge of the world. It is a conceptualization of the enunciative setting, including conceptualizations of the people, objects and empty space around us.

Surrogate spaces, or surrogate blends, result from the integration of real space with an event space, a space which contains a conceptualization of the 'world of the story' (Oakley 1998: 329), with its participants, objects, actions and settings. From real space, surrogate blends inherit the signer's body, parts of which conceptually integrate with the participants in the event space, to represent their actions, thoughts, or speech. Thus, through blending, the signer's body becomes a surrogate of some character or some object from the event space. Surrogates may be present visibly (as manifest in the signer's body), or invisibly, as evidenced by the fact that signs may be directed toward them. As surrogate, the narrator can use facial expressions and gestural and mimetic demonstrations to enact an event.

As Liddell points out, surrogate blends are not foreign to oral language discourse. When describing the location of objects, for example, speakers often create spatialized representations in real space in order to then use a combination of language and gesture to give a detailed description of the object's location. These blends may include objects in real space, such as cups and pens, or imaginary lines drawn on table tops. Liddell observes that the use of such blends in oral language discourse, and the combination of language and gesture used in relation to the blend, is very efficient. When blends of this kind are not created, and when language alone is used, the linguistic effort required to express target locations and spatial relationships is substantially greater (Liddell 2003a: 150).

In SLs, as we will see, surrogate blends are not only a useful resource for spatial representation per se, but are fundamental both for the construction of content meaning and for the organization of discourse proper. At the same time that they provide a (partial) visual demonstration of the events being described, they help in the structuring of the signing space, thus preparing a topology that can be used to establish grammatical and discourse relations, such as discourse cohesion and coherence, coreference, shifts of attention frames, temporal and cause-effect relations, and narrative voices and viewpoints.

It might seem (and this would be in accord with Liddell's analyses of surrogates), that the signed pear story must be a blend of the real space of the signer and the event space created by the film version of the story, which the signer has conceptualized as a result of having viewed it.

For our purposes, it is necessary to alter this arrangement. It is clear that, in narrating the story, the signer assumes a role of narrator. This can be seen at the beginning of the narration by comparing the relaxed body of the signer, as the camera is being readied, to the upright, tensed body of the narrator, as he prepares to begin. From this point on, the signer is signaling that his utterances are to be understood not as coming from his voice, but from the voice of the narrator. We will consider this shift to narrator as being also the result of a real space blend, which we will call 'narrator space'. At the end of the narration, the signer will undo the narrator blend and return to his role simply as signer/collaborator/friend, indicated by his relaxed body posture and facial expression. In the narrator blend, the signer's body (or parts of it) will stand in as surrogate for the narrator, as distinct from the signer, who is also able to sign or gesture from outside his role as |narrator|.[8]

We have said that narrator space is a real space blend, such that one of its inputs is real space. But what is the second input? We propose that the narrator space is a simplex network in which one of the inputs is a narration frame containing the roles of narrator, narratee, story, and accompanying cultural expectations (Fauconnier & Turner 2002: 120–122). In the blend, the signer is projected from the enunciation space as the value of the narrator role.[9]

The story space created by the signed narration can be best understood as a multiple blend whose inputs are the narrator space and the event space that originates with the viewing of the Pear Film. From the event space, the signed pear story space inherits a broad setting (a pear orchard and its surroundings), a narrow setting (the space around a pear tree), several characters (the pear man, the bike boy, the goat man, the girl, the threesome),[10] some objects (three bushel baskets, pears, a ladder, a bicycle, etc.), and the actions performed by the characters.

The pear stealing episode is organized around the activities of two characters (the pear man and the bike boy) and the |narrator|. The |narrator| is free to function either as the |narrator| himself, or as a blend with one of the characters in the story. He may even lend part of his body to function as the surrogate of a thing, as we will see below.

In the segment of the narrative under analysis, the signing space is organized as follows: The |narrator| is conceptualized in what is called the neutral signing space, that is, the space immediately in front of the signer's body. Mimicking the film itself, the |pear man| is constructed above and to the right of the signer's body (since the |pear man| is conceptualized as having climbed a ladder to pick pears), and the |bike boy| is conceptualized to be below, on ground level and to the left, where the |bushel baskets| had been conceptually placed in a previous segment of the narrative.

The |pear man|, the |pear tree|, and the pear man's paraphernalia, blends which had been created at the beginning of the narrative, are reactivated at the outset of this sequence by the narrator's initial utterance, thus becoming readily accessible for use in this segment. The utterance includes three signs, MAN CLIMB NOT-SEE, and a gesture that symbolizes a tree. This one utterance illustrates the gray area between sign and gesture. Of the three signs, the only simple conventional sign is MAN. The two verbs, CLIMB

[8] Following Liddell, we will use the symbols | | to refer to surrogates.

[9] The narration frame appears to be what Oakley (1998: 329) has called 'storytelling space'.

[10] These labels are standard names given to these characters in Du Bois (1980: 207).

and NOT-SEE, both involve a gestural and a linguistic component.[11] The gesture that symbolizes a tree in this utterance is part of the sign TREE, in Brazilian Sign Language. Prototypically, TREE is signed with both forearms, one in vertical position, with an open hand initially oriented to the front, the other in horizontal position, with the palm of the hand facing down. The elbow of the arm in vertical position lightly touches the back of the hand in horizontal position. The vertical forearm rotates, so that the palm ends up facing the signer. What is used in the utterance that starts the pear stealing sequence is just one forearm in vertical position, with the palm oriented to the side. This gesture, which out of context would be meaningless, in context clearly stands for the surrogate |pear tree|. The sign CLIMB is directed toward this surrogate, conceptualizing an event of *climbing a tree*.

The |narrator| then creates the |bike boy| with the utterance of four signs, ANOTHER MAN CHILD YOUNG,[12] and a hybrid expression, RIDE-BIKE, which combines sign and gesture. In Brazilian Sign Language, RIDE-BIKE is an iconic sign that represents the two hands holding a bicycle's handlebars, with the arms making pedaling movements. In the story, while signing RIDE-BIKE, the |narrator| moves his body rhythmically from side to side, accompanying the circular motion of his pedaling arms to mimic the characteristic movement of bike riding. As the |narrator| is signing RIDE-BIKE in this manner, his eye gaze and facial expression shifts from the neutrality of narrator to a joyful expression of someone taking in the landscape. In this way, the surrogate |bike boy| is created as not only a character in the story, but as a presence in the story space. This is a typical example of how a sign can be incremented by constructed action to create surrogates and to add expressive content.

In the next action of the |bike boy|, the |narrator| makes use of the surrogate that has just been created, producing a pantomime that enacts the |bike boy| stopping his bike. As the |bike boy| approaches the action of stopping the bike, the |narrator| uncrosses his legs, and then 'stops the bike' by lifting both heels off the floor and clicking them down sharply. At this point, the |narrator|'s body has fully become a surrogate for the boy, and his downward gaze symbolizes the |bike boy| eyeing the |bushel baskets| that had been conceptually placed in the space below the tree in previous scenes. Only now does the |narrator| utter the signs SEE PEAR TASTY DESIRE

---

[11] NOT-SEE, an indicating verb, will be described later. CLIMB is an example of a polycomponential sign. For descriptions of polycomponential signs, see TAKE and PICK-PUT below.

[12] The sign for MAN is used as a generic to mean 'male', in this case referring to the boy, described here on first mention with the attributes of 'child' and 'young'.

TAKE. The signs SEE PEAR confirm the interpretation that had been construed up to now on the basis of nonverbal cues alone.

TAKE is a polycomponential sign. These signs are intrinsically iconic and seem to be formed by more than one meaningful component. In the case of TAKE, for example, the hand configuration represents the shape of the object taken, and the movement of the hand represents the direction and the manner of motion. The status of these meaningful components as morphemes is a matter which has generated much debate, basically because these components are not meaningful per se: They acquire meaning when they are put together, and when they are used in a particular context.

While this sequence of words is being signed, the |bike boy|, with his eyes still looking down, adopts a facial expression that shows he is up to no good. The |narrator| has partitioned his body: His right hand is signing to express the narrator's voice; his left hand keeps the iconic shape of a hand holding the handlebars of the bike; and his eyes and facial expression represent the boy. Body partitioning is a concept introduced by Liddell (2003a: 153–154), who observed that signers are only partially mapped onto characters in surrogate blends.[13] If this were not the case, we would interpret the utterance SEE PEAR TASTY DESIRE TAKE as being signed by the |bike boy|, and not the |narrator|. This is clearly not the case. The boy is looking at the pears and feeling a desire to taste them. He is not *saying* that. Here we see a type of constructed action we will call 'constructed thought'. Within the surrogate blend, the |narrator| is not only able to represent the surrogate's state of mind with gestures and facial expression; he is also able to articulate in sign what the surrogate is thinking: TASTY DESIRE TAKE.[14]

From this brief description, we can already see many of the intricate relationships that hold between the verbal and nonverbal elements that make up SL discourse. They work jointly to construct both meaningful content and grammatical relations. The introduction and reactivation of surrogates in the discourse space rely on:

- the use of lexical signs (ANOTHER MAN CHILD YOUNG);
- manual gestures (the iconic gesture that reactivated |the pear tree|);

[13] The functioning of body partitioning is further elaborated by Dudis (2004). A phenomenon which is a common accompaniment of body partitioning is what we will call 'sign partitioning', as exemplified here by the single, static hand representing the sign BIKE. By maintaining only part of a sign to stand in for that sign, the signer frees a hand or arm to simultaneously produce other gestures or signs. See also the description of the partitioning of the sign TREE, mentioned earlier.

[14] We suspect that this form of constructed thought is akin to free indirect discourse in oral languages.

- eye gaze shifts (when the |narrator| looks down at the |bushel baskets|);
- pantomime (when the |narrator| mimics the action of stopping the |bike|); and
- facial expressions (when the |narrator| adopts a mischievous look that mimics the look of the boy in the original film).

Things, relations, and attributes are also expressed by both verbal and nonverbal elements. We find signs expressing things (MAN, CHILD, PEAR, DESIRE); relations (NOT-SEE, SEE); and attributes (YOUNG, TASTY). At the same time, we also find gestures (including body posture and facial expressions) expressing things (the gesture that symbolizes the |pear tree|); relations (the pantomime that represents the stopping of the bike, the |narrator| looking down at the |bushel baskets|, the side to side body movement that is part of RIDE-BIKE, the iconic handshapes and movement that constitute CLIMB and TAKE); and attributes (the mischievous boy).

In terms of sentence grammar, the same conspiracy between the verbal and the nonverbal occurs. In an utterance like MAN CLIMB NOT-SEE, the sign MAN clearly elaborates the trajector of the verbs CLIMB and NOT-SEE. However, in an utterance like SEE PEAR TASTY DESIRE TAKE, the trajector of the verbs SEE and TAKE can only be interpreted as being the |bike boy|, a surrogate that is not codified by any manual sign, but which was created and placed in the signed pear story space by gestures and facial expressions. Furthermore, if we consider how the pantomime of stopping the bike would be expressed in any oral language (as a sentence such as *He stopped his bike*), we see that, in Brazilian Sign Language, pantomime can stand for entire propositions which are essential to the conceptualization of the story.

Returning to the unfolding narration of the pear stealing episode, the |bike boy|, still with the same mischievous expression on his face, and holding the |pear| he had taken from the |basket|, turns his head to the right and upward, to look at the |pear man|. At this point, the |narrator| signs LOOK MAN NOT-SEE, corroborating the meaning that has already been built by body posture and facial expression. Verbal and nonverbal elements together cooperate to reactivate discourse referents and to construct meaning. Once again, the signer's body has been partitioned: The right hand is signing to express the |narrator|'s voice; the body posture and facial expression are representing the |bike boy|. The trajector of the verb LOOK is interpreted as being the |bike boy|, a surrogate that is present in the signed pear story space but which is not codified by any verbal element.

The next segment shows a complex narration technique that opens another window of attention, profiling new characters and activities, while leaving the information associated with previous actions in the base. With his head still turned to the right and upward, the |narrator| closes his eyes and signs MAN, indicating that he is no longer going to lend his body to the |bike boy|. From that moment on, his body will be mapped onto the |pear man|. He turns his torso to the right, changes his facial expression to show that he is now the |pear man|, oblivious to what is going on by the |bushel baskets|. He repeats the gesture that symbolizes the |pear tree|, and signs PICK-PUT NOT-LOOK NOT-SEE PICK-PUT.[15] Once again, the |narrator|'s body has been partitioned: His body and facial expression symbolize the |pear man|; his hands sign as the |narrator|.

This sequence of signs is particularly interesting in that it shows how much the organization of discourse in SLs relies on gestures and on the organization of the signing space.

NOT-LOOK is an indicating verb. These verbs can be meaningfully directed in the signing space to point at places, objects, and people or their surrogates. They are hybrid signs: They have a fixed semantic meaning, but the mapping of their trajectors and/or landmarks varies according to the discourse situation and to the organization of the signing space. In the case of the signed pear story, the sign NOT-LOOK is directed downward to where the |bike boy| and the |bushel baskets| have been conceptualized. The |narrator| does not need to elaborate the landmark of the verb NOT-LOOK by means of any verbal element. The directionality of the verb movement takes care of that.

The sign NOT-SEE is also an indicating verb. It is usually made by an up-and-down movement of the palm in front of the signer's eyes. In the pear stealing sequence of the signed pear story, it is signed on the left side of the |pear man|'s face to show that what he cannot see is not what is conceptualized as being in front of him (the |pear tree|), but what is on his left (the |bike boy|).

At the same time that the signed utterance MAN PICK-PUT NOT-LOOK NOT-SEE PICK-PUT describes the activities of the |pear man|, the |narrator|'s body posture, facial expression and gestures reinforce and

[15] The signs PICK and PUT are both polycomponential signs that have been used since the beginning of the story. When they were first employed, the context of use was made explicit by constructing the scene of the |pear man| in the |tree|, picking |pears|, with pears identified by a lexical sign. Even under these conditions, the motion of picking pears and putting them in the |pear man|'s |apron pocket| was clearly a gesture meaningful only in that setting. At the current point in the story, PICK-PUT has become reduced to a mere suggestion of motion that retains very little of the iconic gesture.

complement that description, adding information regarding the position and attitude of total concentration of the |pear man|.

Immediately after this utterance, the |narrator| relaxes his posture, turns to the front and directs his eye gaze toward his interlocutor, showing that his body no longer symbolizes the |pear man|: Now he is simply the |narrator|. He signs THERE MAN BIKE THINK. By signing THERE, he proposes that we shift our attention back to the |bike boy|. THERE is a deictic pronoun that is realized as a pointing gesture. The |narrator| points down, toward the place where the |bike boy| is located in the blend. Still looking down, he signs MAN. His facial expression is already changing to take on again the |bike boy|'s mischievous smile. When he signs BIKE, he looks up toward the |pear man|. From this moment on, he is clearly the |bike boy|. To reactivate the |bike boy|, the |narrator| uses gestures (he points at the conceptual space associated with the |bike boy|), signs (MAN BIKE), and body posture and facial expressions (he takes on the facial expression and body posture the |bike boy| had earlier). These shifts from the activities of the |bike boy| to those of the |pear man| and back to the |bike boy| establish a temporal relation between them; that is, while the |pear man| is up in the tree working, the |bike boy| is thinking about stealing his |pears|. This alternation of shots from |bike boy| to |pear man| and back to |bike boy| precisely mimics the cinematic technique of cutaway shots found in the input.

THINK is signed by the |narrator| while the |bike boy| assumes a facial expression of someone who has just had a great idea. THINK and the facial expression of having an idea work together as space triggers: The |narrator| indicates that a new mental space, that of the |bike boy|'s thought, is being built. The next utterance is I GRASP. This is the only time we see the voice of a character: It is the |bike boy|'s constructed thought. The pronoun I is a pointing gesture, directed toward the enunciator's body. We know that I refers to the |bike boy| because it is being uttered from the mental space of the |bike boy|'s thought, by someone who has the facial expression and body posture of the |bike boy|. GRASP is another example of a polycomponential sign. It iconically represents the action of someone picking up something. We know that it is one of the |bushel baskets| that is being picked up because of both the discourse context and the organization of the signing space. The |bike boy| is looking down to the place where the |bushel baskets| had been conceptualized.[16]

[16] During the signing of THINK, I, and GRASP, the |narrator|'s left hand holds the same shape and position it had when BIKE was signed. This sign-partitioning gesture is one more way of showing that the focus of attention is on the |bike boy|.

The next frames show a series of gestures and pantomime that describe the actions of the |bike boy| grasping one of the |bushel baskets|, picking it up and putting it on his |bike|. As he lifts the |basket|, the |bike boy|'s tongue appears, showing his effort in lifting the heavy |basket| full of |pears| over the |handlebars| of his |bike|. The climax of the pear stealing segment is all gestural, made possible by the availability of an elaborate surrogate blend.

The next shot shows the |bike boy| with a happy expression on his face while the |narrator| signs RIDE-BIKE. And, finally, the |narrator| looks at his interlocutors, his left hand still positioned as if holding a handlebar, and makes a gesture-sign with his right hand that we have glossed as DISAPPEAR-INTO-THE-DISTANCE. This sign, used in identical pear story contexts by three different signers, is the kind of imaginative and graphic gesture that is typical of the iconic creativity found in sign language discourse, in this case literally cinematic. The signer holds his thumb and index finger apart in an L handshape, indicating the height of a certain object. As he extends his arm away from his body, his thumb and index finger are brought closer together until they touch, illustrating the object getting smaller and smaller until it disappears.

4 Conclusion

In recent years, researchers in usage based and cognitive linguistics have become increasingly involved in the growing interdisciplinary area of gesture studies. It might seem that the study of gesture would be of special interest to SL linguists, but this has not proven to be the case. Historically, SL linguists have been concerned with establishing SLs as natural languages, by hypothesizing arbitrary, segmental characteristics believed to be the hallmark of language. This is the legacy of mainstream linguistics.[17] Studies of oral languages have focused on arbitrariness, possibly a design feature, as Hockett suggested, imposed by the need to channel information through a one-dimensional linear medium (1978: 275). In SLs, by contrast, the medium itself is gestural, multidimensional, and it is out of this medium that SL linguists have managed, against odds, to extract the arbitrary and segmental features that have put SLs on the linguistic map. Allowing the introduction of the analogical, iconic nature of gestuality into the discussion of discourse phenomena might seem to threaten the integrity of the very core of what has been painstakingly established to be linguistic.

---

[17] There have been voices, of course, which have warned against the excesses of this legacy, notably Bolinger, who has repeatedly pointed out the iconicity and gradience of oral languages (e.g. 1961).

In the last decade this situation has begun to change. In the light of advances in gesture studies and cognitive linguistics, some SL linguists have ventured to investigate the copresence of gestuality in SLs. There is still a step to take, as Hockett so perceptively pointed out forty years ago: to begin to see the gestuality of SLs as a virtue. According to Hockett, SLs have no structural requirement to be limited by the constraints of oral languages, and do well to exploit their pluridimensionality:

> Indeed, the dimensionality of signing is that of life itself, and it would be stupid not to resort to picturing, pantomiming, or pointing whenever convenient (Hockett: 1978: 274–275).

Our study has aimed to contribute to this new trend in SL linguistics by highlighting the complex array of integrated resources that signers make use of in producing richly informative, grammatically cohesive, and artful texts. By analyzing a scene in a signed narrative, we have shown how gestures and verbal elements of varying degrees of conventionality work tightly together to mutually catalize their expressive potentials. Neither gesture alone nor lexical signs alone would be able to produce the kind of discourse sophistication that we have seen. In addition, we have suggested that we can find grammar in the very gestuality that seemed to be such a threat, if by grammar we understand patternings like those found in other visual and spatial semiotic systems. SL linguistics could benefit from the study of these systems to learn how they contribute to conceptualization, making possible the formation of a symbiotic ecology in which both gesture and sign are equal partners.

Author Note

Leland McCleary and Evani Viotti are members, respectively, of the Modern Languages and Linguistics Departments of the University of São Paulo, Brasil. We wish to thank our deaf collaborator, Alex Melendez, for his patience and assistance, and to thank Scott Liddell and Sherman Wilcox for their inspiration and encouragement. Acknowledgement is due to the National Research Council and to the Dean of Postgraduate Studies of the University of São Paulo for grants that have aided this work. Thanks are also due to the Research Nucleus 'School of the Future', University of São Paulo, for their continuing support.

References

Armstrong, D. F., W. C. Stokoe, & S. Wilcox. 1995. *Gesture and the Nature of Language*. Cambridge University Press.

Armstrong, D. F. & S. Wilcox. 2007. *The Gestural Origin of Language*. Oxford University Press.

Bauman, H-D. L. 2003. Rede*signing* Literature: The Cinematic Poetics of American Sign Language poetry. *Sign Language Studies* 4(1):34–47.

Bolinger, D. L. 1961. *Generality, Gradience, and the All-or-none*. Gravenhage: Mouton & Co.

Chafe, W. L. 1980. *The Pear Stories: Cognitive, Cultural and Linguistic Aspects of Narrative Production*. (Advances in Discourse Processes, 3.) Norwood, NJ: Ablex.

Costello, B., J. Fernández, & A. Landa. 2008. The Non-(Existent) Native Signer: Sign language Research in a Small Deaf Population. *TISLR9. Sign Languages: Spinning and Unraveling the Past, Present and Future*, ed. R. M. de Quadros. Petrópolis, RJ: Editora Arara Azul, Brazil. Available at <http://www.editora-arara-azul.com.br/ebooks/catalogo/complete.pdf>.

Du Bois, J. W. 1980. Beyond Definiteness: The Trace of Identity in Discourse. *The Pear Stories*, ed. W. L. Chafe, 203–274. Norwood, NJ: Ablex.

Dudis, P.G. (2004). Body Partitioning and Real-Space Blends. *Cognitive Linguistics*, 15(2): 223–238.

Duncan, S. 2003. Gesture in Language: Issues for Sign Language Research. *Perspectives on Classifier Constructions in Sign Language*, ed. K. Emmorey, 259–268. Mahwah, NJ: Lawrence Earlbaum Associates.

Engberg-Pedersen, E. 1995. Point of View Expressed through Shifters. *Language, Gesture, and Space*, ed. K. Emmorey & J. Reilly, 133–154. Mawah, NJ: Lawrence Erlbaum Associates.

Fauconnier, G. & M. Turner. 2002. *The Way we Think: Conceptual Blending and the Mind's Hidden Complexities*. New York: Basic Books.

Hockett, C. F. 1978. In Search of Jove's Brow. *American Speech* 53(4): 243–313.

Kendon, A. 1980. Gesticulation and Speech: Two Aspects of the Process of Utterance. *The Relationship of Verbal and Nonverbal Communication,* ed. M. R. Key, 207–227. The Hague: Mouton.

Kendon, A. 2004. *Gesture: Visible Action as Utterance*. Cambridge: Cambridge University Press.

Klima, E. & Bellugi, U. 1979. *The Signs of Language*. Harvard University Press.

Liddell, S. K. 1995. Real, Surrogate, and Token Space: Grammatical Consequences in ASL. *Language, Gesture, and Space*, ed. K. Emmorey & J. Reilly, 19–41. Mawah, NJ: Lawrence Erlbaum Associates.

Liddell, S. K. 2000. Blended Spaces and Deixis in Sign Language Discourse. *Language and Gesture*, ed. D. McNeill, 331-357. Cambridge: Cambridge University Press.

Liddell, S. K. 2003a. *Grammar, Gesture, and Meaning in American Sign Language*. Cambridge: Cambridge University Press.

Liddell, S. K. 2003b. Sources of Meaning in ASL Classifier Predicates. *Perspectives on Classifier Constructions in Sign Language*, ed. K. Emmorey, 199–220. Mahwah, NJ: Lawrence Erlbaum Associates.

Lillo-Martin, D. 1995. The Point of View Predicate in American Sign Language. *Language, Gesture, and Space*, ed. K. Emmorey & J. Reilly, 155–170. Mawah, NJ: Lawrence Erlbaum Associates.

McNeill, D. 1992. *Hand and Mind: What Gestures Reveal about Thought*. Chicago and London: The University of Chicago Press.

Metzger, M. 1995. Constructed Dialogue and Constructed Action in American Sign Language. *Sociolinguistics in Deaf Communities*, ed. C. Lucas, 255–271. Washington, DC: Gallaudet University Press.

Oakley, T. V. 1998. Conceptual Blending, Narrative Discourse, and Rhetoric. *Cognitive Linguistics* 9(4): 321–360.

Poulin, C. & C. Miller. 1995. On Narrative Discourse and Point of View in Quebec Sign Language. *Language, Gesture, and Space*, ed. K. Emmorey & J. Reilly, 117–131. Mawah, NJ: Lawrence Erlbaum Associates.

Quinto-Pozos, D. 2007. Can Constructed Action be Considered Obligatory? *Lingua* 117: 1285–1314.

Sandler, W. 2009. Symbiotic Symbolization by Hand and Mouth in Sign Language. *Semiotica* 174: 241–275.

Sarapik, Virve. 2009. Picture, Text, and Imagetext: Textual Polygoly. *Semiotica* 174: 277–308.

Schembri, A. 2003. Rethinking 'Classifiers' in Signed Languages. *Perspectives on Classifier Constructions in Sign Language*, ed. K. Emmorey, 3–34. Mahwah, NJ: Lawrence Earlbaum Associates.

Schembri, A., C. Jones, & D. Burnham. 2005. Comparing Action Gestures and Classifier Verbs of Motion: Evidence from Australian Sign Language, Taiwan Sign Language, and Nonsigners' Gestures without Speech. *Journal of Deaf Studies and Deaf Education* 10(3): 272–290.

Stokoe, W. C. 1979. Syntactic Dimensionality: Language in Four Dimensions. Paper presented to the New York Academy of Sciences.

Wilcox, S. 2004a. Cognitive Iconicity: Conceptual Spaces, Meaning, and Gesture in Signed Language. *Cognitive Linguistics* 15(2): 119–148.

Wilcox, S. 2004b. Gesture and Language: Cross-Linguistic and Historical Data from Signed Languages. *Gesture* 4: 43-73.

Wilcox, S. 2008. Sign and Gesture: Towards a New Paradigm. *Metaphor and Gesture*, ed. A. J. Cienki & C. Müller, 273–275. Amsterdam: John Benjamins.

Wilcox, S. & P. P. Wilcox. 1995. The Gestural Expression of Modality in ASL. *Modality in Grammar and Discourse*, ed. J. Bybee & S. Fleischman, 135–162. Amsterdam: John Benjamins.

Wilcox, S. & Shaffer, B. 2006. Modality in ASL. *The Expression of Modality*, ed. W. Frawley, 207–237. Berlin: Mouton de Gruyter.

Winston, E. 1991. Spatial Referencing and Cohesion in an American Sign Language text. *Sign Language Studies* 73: 397–410.

11

Form, Discourse, & Construction: American English *like* NP

CAROL LYNN MODER

This study examines American English expressions using *like* to introduce noun phrases in naturally-occurring discourse contexts within the framework of grammatical construction theory (Fillmore, Kay & O'Connor 1988; Goldberg 1995, 2006; Croft 2001; Tomasello 2003). The study takes a usage-based approach (Langacker 2000, Barlow & Kemmer 2000, Bybee 2007) which considers the frequency and function of the expression in specific constructions in discourse contexts.

1 *Like* in Cognitive Linguistics

In cognitive linguistics, *like* has been mainly studied in its use in metaphorical expressions of the sort that have been referred to traditionally as similes. However, because of its focus on the conceptual aspects of metaphor, cognitive metaphor theory has focused little attention on the relation of a specific form to discourse function (cf. Lakoff & Johnson 1980, 1999). In a more broad-ranging cognitive linguistic study of simile, Israel, Harding and Tobin (2004) highlight the contribution of grammatical form to a number of comparative constructions. Their study takes as its guiding feature the domain of comparison and examines a variety of expressions that are used to realize this function, without focusing specifically on any of the individual forms or constructions involved.

More attention to the contribution of form is inherent in the Blended Spaces Theory of Fauconnier and Turner (2002). While not specifically discussing either similes or the expression *like*, Fauconnier and Turner do

Meaning, Form & Body.
Fey Parrill, Vera Tobin, and Mark Turner (eds.).

suggest that grammatical variations in expressions function as cues to the listener to construct a blend. This analysis builds on the insight from Mental Spaces Theory that linguistic expressions, including comparatives, function as 'spacebuilders,' which establish mental spaces, elements within the spaces, and relations among elements (Fauconnier 1994). Thus, one might expect within this framework that the function of *like* would be to explicitly cue the construction of the relevant mental spaces in order to establish a blend. A major tenet of Blending Theory is that the blending process cued by a specific space building form in non-metaphorical integrations is identical to that cued in metaphorical expressions (Fauconnier & Turner 2002: 154). Thus, in the context of this approach, one would assume that *like* used in similes would draw on the same blending processes cued by *like* in non-metaphorical expressions.

The assumption that all uses of a form or a construction may be relevant to the formation of grammatical schemas is also common to usage-based approaches to form-function relations (Bybee 1985, 2007; Barlow & Kemmer 2000, Langacker 2000). Those studies which examine examples from naturally-occurring data also suggest the importance of considering the frequency with which forms and related patterns occur (Bybee 1995, 2007; Tomasello 2003; Goldberg 2006).[1] Bybee and Thompson (1997) and Bybee (2007) have suggested that the token frequency, or the overall frequency of occurrence of a word, phrase, or construction, will contribute to the form's entrenchment. Entrenchment makes the form more autonomous and more readily processed. Bybee and Thompson have further stipulated that the productivity of a construction is closely related to its type frequency, or the number of different lexical items that can occur in a given slot in the pattern. The more forms with which a given pattern co-occurs, the more productive the pattern will be. Research on the acquisition of constructions has suggested that some general linguistic patterns may be acquired more easily based on semantically general forms that occur with great frequency in the pattern (Tomasello 2003, Goldberg 2006). However, Bybee (2007) and Bybee and Thompson (1997) note the possibility that more general collocates of very high frequency may be lexically autonomous, resisting categorization with other items in a construction. For

[1] In corpus-based research, Stefanowitsch and Gries (2003) and Stefanowitsch (2008) have suggested that the strength of the association of a pattern with particular forms may also be relevant. However, their proposed formulas for collexeme and collostructional analysis require a count of relevant competing constructions, which may not be appropriate for open or highly schematic structures. Their analysis also does not account for the possible autonomy of high frequency forms. Furthermore, it requires a large corpus of examples.

example, they note that pronouns, which are higher in token frequency than full NPs, often tend to retain older conservative syntactic structure.

The present study takes a usage-based approach to the form *like*, focusing on instances in which it precedes an NP. Because of the importance of discourse context in assessing both the use of the lexical expression and the functions of related constructions, this study relies exclusively on the examination of naturally occurring examples in context. Furthermore, following the hypotheses of Bybee (2007) it will also examine frequency data in order to better understand these constructions.

2 *Like* NP in Discourse

Much of the research on *like* in similes and other constructions has assumed that the main function of the lexical expression is to introduce a comparison or similarity. However, in a discourse-based corpus study, Moder (2008) found that the expression *like* preceding an NP was polysemous and occurred in multiple discourse functions. The first of these functions, the widely-acknowledged comparative function, is illustrated in example (1).[2] Here *like* introduces a relational similarity between the radio commentator and 20 million AOL users, many of whom have teenage children.

(1) *Like* in comparison

But surprisingly no one else has yet put together a package that is as clean and clear and simple as AOL. I think what it has now is 20 million users who don't want to change their e-mail addresses. **Many of them**, **like myself**, have teen-age kids who are online chatting with their friends in chat rooms, they're sending instant messages all afternoon, who will not let their parents go to another online service. (ATC 1/10/00)

On the other hand, the examples in (2) use *like* to fulfill a second distinctive discourse function. Here *like* does not introduce a similarity, but rather it serves to introduce an exemplar of the category named by the preceding noun phrase. Time Warner is provided as an example of the category 'traditional media companies,' and AOL is introduced as an example of 'Internet startups.'

[2] All examples are taken from naturally occurring discourse from the corpus under study. Examples are transcribed using orthographic conventions to facilitate reading. Here the abbreviation ATC 1/10/00 indicates that the example came from the National Public Radio program All Things Considered broadcast on January 10, 2000. Similar abbreviations are used for all examples. ME in later examples refers to the program Morning Edition. The expression under discussion is presented in bold face.

(2) *Like* in categorization

Rather than buying into the new media revolution when they had the chance, **traditional media companies, like Time Warner,** stood by and smirked while **Internet start-ups, like AOL**, went from being an acquisition target to merger prospect to an acquirer itself. (ATC 1/11/00)

The polysemy of *like* suggests that it would be productive to further investigate *like* NP expressions in terms of the ways in which the form cues the discourse relations between speakers and hearers (see also Cameron & Deignan 2003, Dancygier & Sweetser 2005).

In addition to the examples cited above, in which the *like* phrase follows the NP it modifies, a number of expressions occurred in the corpus studied in Moder (2008) in which the *like* phrase preceded the NP. An example of such an initial *like* phrase is given in (3).

(3) Initial *like* NP

Republican Whit Ayers agrees with that and says Gore runs the risk of sounding condescending or appearing too much like an attack dog. And **like many partisans who are handicapping tonight's debate, Ayers** is eager to stress just how effective a debater Gore is, raising expectations for the vice president while lowering them for the Texas governor. (ATC 10/3/00)

This initial use of *like* NP may appear to share some elements of the comparative function since the commentator relates Ayers to the 'many partisans.' However, the expression is not instantiating a comparison *per se*. It serves to establish Ayers as representative of a broader category of individuals. The listener is thus meant to take his opinion to be more than just the view of an isolated individual. The initial *like* NP phrase also appears to have a discourse organizing function (cf. Thompson 1985). It serves to position Ayers as the next speaker and to provide a context against which his comments are to be viewed. The differences in the discourse meanings of the initial *like* phrase and the *like* phrase that follows the NP suggest the possibility that *like* may be participating in different constructions.

Previous discourse-based studies have proposed similarly distinctive discourse functions for initial and final adverbial clauses. Thompson (1985) found that in written discourse initial and final adverbial clauses behaved in such radically different ways that they should be considered different constructions. The findings of Thompson (1985) have been confirmed and extended to spoken English in later studies (Ford 1993, Diessel 2005). These studies describe initial adverbial clauses as having more than one subsequent clause in their scope and as providing a general framework or background for the following discourse. In contrast, final adverbial clauses are said to be more local in scope, typically encompassing and delimiting the semantics of the main clause to which they relate. These researchers also observe different discourse behaviors for different types of adverbial clauses, based on their semantic domains.

Given these findings, the present study undertakes a further investigation of the discourse functions of the two types of *like* phrases, those in which *like* NP precedes an NP in the main clause and those in which it follows the NP. These expressions will be examined within the framework of grammatical construction theory (Goldberg1995, 2006; Croft 2001; Tomasello 2003). Grammatical constructions, in the frameworks of these researchers, are form-meaning pairings which may be fully or partially schematic. Because of their differences in form and their posited differences in discourse function, NP *like* NP and *like* NP NP will be analyzed as distinct constructions.

3 Examining *like* Constructions in Discourse

The primary purpose of the present study was to investigate the grammatical constructions using *like* to connect two NPs in their naturally-occurring American English discourse contexts. A secondary purpose was to examine a third *like* construction that relates two NPs, the *It be*-TNS *like* NP,[3] which occurs in both non-metaphorical and metaphorical uses.

Examples of the three constructions examined are provided in (4), (5) and (6) below.

(4) NP *like* NP

Traditional media companies, like Time Warner, stood by and smirked while Internet start-ups, like AOL, went from being an acquisition target to merger prospect to an acquirer itself.

(5) *like* NP, NP

Like others who apply, the potential workers here…

(6) *It be*-TNS *like* NP

It's like two corks bobbing on the ocean.

It was like a presentation.

The corpus used for the study was a researcher-collected set of American English spoken data taken from two American public radio news programs, *All Things Considered* and *Morning Edition*. Both programs are

[3] We represent the construction as *It be*-TNS *like* NP to allow for both the present and past tense forms *It's* and *It was*. However, the *It's like* NP construction may be distinct in its uses.

broadcast across the United States five days a week for two hours and comprise a variety of news, arts, science, and human-interest stories. The programs include edited excerpts of spontaneous discourse interspersed with scripted introductions, transitions, and closing comments delivered by the reporter or commentator. The total number of words in the spoken corpus was 584,515 words.

The corpus was first examined for all exemplars of *like*. These exemplars were then sorted into patterns based on the grammatical form in which *like* appeared and the kind of phrase it modified.

Table 1: Frequency of all uses of *like*

Use		*f*	*f*/1000 words	% *like*
Prepositional *like NP*	*Traditional media companies, like Time Warner…..* *Like others who apply, the potential workers here…*	406	.69	34
Adverbial *be*-TNS *like* V *like*	*It's like two corks bobbing…* *It was like a presentation.* *It looks like something you'd see at the North Pole.*	406	.69	34
Verb	*I like Bill.* *A lot of people would like to see it.*	238	.41	20
Discourse particle	*so you could, like, show us the bird?* *That was back in, like, 1962.*	94	.16	7
Conjunction *like* S	*I can't run like she can.* *The consumer may not see the charge directly like they do now…*	56	.09	5
Noun *the like*	*genetics and genetic engineering, biotechnology and the like.*	1	.001	--
Adjectival	*just take an area like search.*	1	.001	--
TOTAL		**1202**		**100**

Table 1 provides examples of each of these patterns of use, along with the token frequency and frequency per hundred words of all exemplars appearing in each pattern. The final column gives the percentage of all uses of *like* in the corpus that each pattern comprises. The corpus included 1202 exemplars in which *like* appeared. The most frequently occurring patterns were the prepositional uses of *like* preceding one NP and modifying a second NP and the adverbial uses of *like* preceding an NP and modifying either a verb or an entire clause. These patterns each accounted for 406 tokens in the corpus. The next most frequent pattern was the use of *like* as a verb at 238 tokens. The various discourse particle uses of *like,* all subsumed under one category, accounted for 94 tokens. The conjunction pattern in which *like* precedes a full clause, once widely denigrated as 'ungrammatical,' accounted for 56 tokens. The use of *like* as a noun and as an adjectival each accounted for only a single token.

The main focus of this study is on the prepositional uses of *like,* which constitute one of the most commonly occurring constructions in the corpus. As discussed above, we will be examining the prepositional uses separately based on the position of the *like* NP phrase. Table 2 presents the token frequency in the corpus of the prepositional uses of *like* NP that we will investigate in detail, along with the frequency per 1000 words.

Table 2: Frequency of prepositional constructions

Construction		***f***	***f*/1000 words**	**% *Like* NP**
NP *like* NP	*Traditional media companies, like Time Warner.....*	368	.63	91
like NP NP	*Like others who apply, the potential workers here...*	38	.06	9
TOTAL		**406**	**.69**	**100**

As Table 2 indicates, NP *like* NP is overwhelmingly the more frequent of the two constructional patterns, with a token frequency of 368, constituting 91 percent of these prepositional uses. The *like* NP NP construction has a token frequency of only 38, constituting 9 percent of the prepositional uses in the corpus. Thus, the NP *like* NP pattern is much more widely used than the *like* NP NP construction in this corpus.

We will also briefly consider adverbial uses in the form *It be*-TNS *like* NP. Table 3 provides the frequency of *It* be-TNS *like* NP separated from the other adverbial uses of *like*. As Table 3 shows, the *It be*-TNS *like* NP construction constitutes only 37 tokens of *like*, accounting for only 9% of the adverbial uses of *like* in the corpus. Of these occurrences, 29 tokens occurred in the form *It's like* NP and 8 occurred in the form *It was like* NP.

Table 3: Frequency of Adverbial uses of *like*

Use		*f*	*f*/1000 words	% Adverbial *like*
be-TNS *like*	*It's like two corks…, It was like a presentation*	37	.06	9
V *like*	*It looks like something you'd see at the North Pole.*	369	.63	91
TOTAL		**406**	**.69**	**100**

We will now turn to an examination of each of these constructions in their discourse contexts.

3.1 NP *like* NP

As discussed above in the context of Example (2), the NP like NP construction is often used in discourse to introduce exemplars of the category named in the first NP. Example (7) further illustrates this pattern. The radio segment in which the example occurs concerns investigations into smuggling from the port of Xiamen. At the beginning of the excerpt, the reporter, Rob Gifford, introduces the city of Xiamen, describing why it is well situated for smuggling activities. The host of the program, Linda Wertheimer, then asks him 'what kind of thing' goes through the port. It is in response to this request to elaborate the category of the kinds of things that move through the port that Gifford uses the NP like NP construction. He first names some of these things and then designates two categories of things, 'simple things' and 'basic things.' He elaborates each of these rather general categories by providing examples in NP like NP constructions, 'simple things like cigarettes' and 'basic things like building materials and machinery and stuff that has very high tariffs.'

(7) GIFFORD: Xiamen is on the southeastern coast of China, just opposite the island of Taiwan. And it's really a bustling city port. And its proximity to Taiwan, I think, is one of the things that makes it such a center for smuggling now, as we go into the 21st century.
WERTHEIMER: What kind of thing is moving through that port?
GIFFORD: Well, it's cars and guns and **simple things, like cigarettes**. But it's also **basic things, like building materials and machinery, and stuff that** has **very high tariffs on it if you import it officially**. And people want to skip the tariffs, obviously, and get it in on the quiet. (ATC 1/21/00)

The generality of the first NPs in this example provides a clear motivation for the speaker to elaborate through the use of examples. The need for examples is particularly great here since the categories are created spontaneously by the speaker and would remain vague without the elaboration the *like* NP phrase provides.

Although the NP *like* NP construction occurred with a large number of NP types in both the first and the second NP slot, it is noteworthy that the frequency of occurrence of general NPs in the first NP slot is very high. Table 4 illustrates this point. It lists the most frequent first NPs that occurred in the corpus in the NP *like* NP construction.

Table 4: Frequent first NPs in NP *like* NP Constructions

First NP	*f*
things	33
people	15
states/state	13
places/place	12
issues	9
stuff	5
songs, groups	4
programs, cities, companies, voters, advocates, pictures	3 (each)

As Table 4 shows, the most frequent first NPs include very general nouns, *things, people, places* and *stuff*.[4] The other frequent first NPs are categories that occur often based on the particular content of the reports. The corpus includes coverage of presidential elections in the United States,

[4] We also find indefinite general nouns like *something* and *anything* as the first NP in what appear structurally to be NP *like* NP patterns. However, these patterns are different in use from those discussed here. First, the indefinite general nouns occur almost always in the expressions *something like that* or *anything like that*. Second, they typically occur at the end of an utterance elaborating a context, as in 'So put a helmet on, just the same as a parent would put a helmet on their child if they went bicycling **or something like that**'(ATC 1/20/00). Here the expression has a generalizing function, referring vaguely to other possible exemplars of a category of actions already named. In the corpus these expressions extend actions, entities, or statements previously named. The demonstrative pronoun *that* also appears as the second NP following NP *like* in other cases. As with the examples following the indefinite NPs, the *like that* phrase usually follows a list of items, as in 'if I write prescriptions for insulin and I write prescriptions for statins for their cholesterol and blood pressure medications and **things like that'** (ME 6-15-04). It is also worth noting that the *something like that* and *anything like that* phrases are typically articulated in one intonation unit, whereas the other NP *like* NP phrases are often divided across intonation units. Following Bybee 2007, these differences suggest that the *something like that/ anything like that* patterns are autonomous.

which made frequent mention of *states, cities, programs, issues*, and *voters*. The radio programs also include featured segments on music and art which mention *songs* and *pictures*. The other general nouns, *companies, groups*, and *advocates*, are regular subjects for issues reported in the programs. The second NP in the NP *like* NP construction varies widely. Few noun types appear more than once, and many proper noun types appear in this slot. This wide variety of noun types supports the proposed analysis that the construction serves to introduce discourse relevant specific exemplars in the second NP slot.

In the context of these radio programs, the use of the NP *like* NP construction often does more than just explicate a general category by providing examples. In nominating a general category and then providing an exemplar of that category, the construction also invites the listener to consider the individual case as representative of the larger category. Example (8) illustrates this function. This segment was broadcast on the day that Nelson Mandela and the African National Congress first assumed power in South Africa. The excerpt comes as part of a report on the mood of those in the anti-apartheid movement as the new government took office. Reporter Ann Cooper describes the scene, focusing on 'people who a few years ago were considered public enemies.' She names two examples, introducing each with 'people like.'

> (8) I must say it was stunning to see people walking into this parliament building who just a few years ago were considered public enemies here. They were exiled, they were imprisoned, their families were persecuted. **People like Moses Miakesa**, who's now a member of parliament. In the 1980s, he was a firebrand leader of township rebellions in Alexandra outside Johannesburg...Some of the happiest people I saw today were the handful of whites who were involved in the anti-apartheid movement, **people like Joe Slovo**, whose wife, Ruth, first was also involved in the movement, was killed in Mozambique by South African agents. Today, Joe Slovo is in parliament. He's probably going to be a member of the new cabinet.
>
> (ME 5/9/994)

In example (8), the categories are already well delineated prior to the introduction of the two individuals. The introduction of Miakesa and Slovo is not needed to clarify the nature of the category. Each of these 'people,' their pasts, and their likely futures are described to illustrate the change in the status of anti-apartheid activists. The use of the NP *like* NP construction introduces them as representative exemplars. This discourse function was very typical for NP *like* NP constructions in this corpus.

The NP *like* NP construction shows all the evidence of a productive pattern. It has a high overall token frequency, created largely by its application to a large number of NP types in both slots. The first NP slot is characterized by the occurrence of general nouns that collocate with the construction with low to moderate frequency. The higher frequency of general nouns, like *things* and *people*, may well contribute to the salience of the pattern, but here their use is inextricably linked to the discourse function of the construction. The second NP slot was filled with a wide variety of NP types that occurred in the construction with very low token frequencies.

We now turn to an examination of the second *like* NP construction.

3.2 *Like* NP NP

As discussed previously, the *like* NP NP construction was much less frequent in the corpus than the NP *like* NP construction and appears to have a primarily discourse organizing function. Example (9) illustrates this function.

(9) LIFSON: The Bohots are in their 50s. **Like most Germans their age, they**'ve been counting on a generous government-operated pension system. But the government has acknowledged it won't be able to keep paying the average German pension of about 70 percent of average salary. **Like many Germans, the Bohots haven't saved much for their old age;** Mrs. Bohot says they counted on the government and expected to maintain their comfortable lifestyle into retirement. (ATC 1/10/00)

The segment begins with an introduction of cutbacks to pension and health benefits proposed by the German government in response to economic problems. The program host then segues to the reporter, Edward Lifson. Lifson begins his report by describing in detail the home setting, background, and comfortable economic position of a German couple, the Bohots. The excerpt quoted in the example continues this description and introduces the pension expectations of the couple. Lifson uses the first *like* NP NP phrase, situating the Bohots' pension expectations in relation to the broader contextualizing phrase 'like most German their age.' He continues with a contrast to these expectations that makes reference to the general situation of the German government.[5] The second *like* NP phrase serves as a bridge between the general description of Germany's economic situation and the specific ramifications it will have on the Bohots. In these two examples, the Bohots are contextualized as typical of 'most Germans their

[5] Note that this contrasting discourse segment is introduced with *but*. The use of this discourse marker is discussed further in example (11).

age' and 'many Germans.' The listener is thus invited to consider them a representative examplar. Following these examples, we get a quote from Bohot and then the segment continues with a focus on the historical economic background and other issues related to the proposal.

This use of the *like* NP NP construction to signal a shift in discourse focus by reinstating a previously mentioned discourse entity as a representative case illustrating a broader issue is common to most of the examples of this construction.

An examination of the lexical items that occur in this construction provides further evidence for the discourse-based differences we have predicated. The first nouns in the *like* NP NP construction vary widely according to the discourse context. Many noun types occur in the first NP slot and few nouns occur more than once. This is consistent with the context-specific nature of the discourse topics and themes that are structured by the *like* NP NP construction. Of interest is that the NPs in the *like* NP phrase of the construction are often modified by quantifiers like *most*, *many* or *a lot*. Such modifiers occurred in the *like* NP phrase in 16 out of the 38 tokens of this construction. The frequent occurrence of these generalizing quantifiers is consistent with the use of the *like* NP phrase in this construction to provide a broader category as background for generalizing the specific example presented in the subsequent NP. The second NP slot in this construction was a third person pronoun in 12 of the 38 tokens (*he* 4 tokens, *she* 2 tokens, *it* 3 tokens, and *they* 3 tokens). The remaining second slot NPs were almost entirely definite NPs or proper nouns, and all occurred only once. The occurrence of these forms in this slot is consistent with the proposed function of the construction, since they code the entity in the second NP slot as one that has been in focus in the discourse.

Another lexical co-occurrence pattern that is consistent with the discourse organizing function of the *like* NP NP construction is the frequent appearance of the discourse markers *and* or *but* at the beginning of the *like* NP phrase.

Example (10) illustrates the *and like* NP NP pattern. The example comes from a segment concerning the widespread problem of obesity in the United States, which features the campaign of Arkansas Governor Mick Huckabee to promote lifestyle changes in his state in order to reduce obesity-related diseases. The segment begins by introducing the problem of obesity and related diseases. It then describes the lifestyle changes that helped Huckabee to lose 105 pounds. The reporter, Patricia Neighmond, next introduces Dr. Philip Kern from the Weight Control Program at the University of Arkansas as the man who helped Huckabee lose weight.

(10) NEIGHMOND: Today he talks to a patient about his progress. Kern doesn't use the word `diet.' He wants patients to change how they view food: from fast food to fresh, from fried to grilled or barbecued, and from fatty to lean. Kern says that was the first step for the governor.
KERN: He loves to barbecue and so I managed to convince him that a barbecue doesn't need to be, you know, high fat beef and chicken and something. He can barbecue--you know, zucchini and squash do very well on the barbie.
NEIGHMOND: **And like many successful people,** Kern says once **the governor** set his mind to something, he did it extremely well. (ME 6/15/04)

In the excerpt shown in example (10), Neighmond describes Kern's general approach to helping patients with weight loss and then transitions to his explanation of the specific approach he took with Huckabee. Neighmond uses the *like* NP NP construction to highlight the broader category of 'successful people' to which the governor belongs – a discourse shift that highlights the move from the specific instance to the more general applicability of the approach to weight loss. This use is similar to that we saw in example (9), but in this case the discourse shift between the general issue of obesity and the specific case of Huckabee has already been prominently highlighted by the introduction to the segment. More importantly, the shift recurs repeatedly in the radio segment. Beginning such a use with *and* is consistent with prior findings concerning *and* as a discourse marker. *And* typically signals a unit of discourse that serves a joint purpose or that continues previous actions (Schiffrin 1987). The use of the *and like* NP phrase in example (10) marks a unit of discourse by prefacing the main shift in the focus of the commentary to typical patients and the programs that help them to overcome obesity, but it also marks a continuation of previous actions since both themes have previously occurred in the discourse. The use of *and* highlights the segmentation as continuation, while the *like* NP NP construction signals the theme of contextualizing the example within a broader category as part of the discourse organization.

Example (11) shows the use of the discourse marker *but* in the *like* NP NP construction. As a discourse marker, initial *but* typically signals a shift in discourse focus, introducing a counter-claim, or a contrast with the prior discourse (Schiffrin 1987). It appeared frequently before an initial *like* NP phrase when the phrase signaled a shift to a contrasting discourse theme.

The segment in which example (11) occurred discusses John Rocker, a pitcher for the baseball team, the Atlanta Braves, who was ordered to undergo a psychological evaluation following aggressive actions and inflammatory comments to the media about groups that form the diverse population of New York City. The segment begins with a brief description of John Rocker's rise to prominence as a relief pitcher. Then, as seen in example (11), the sports commentator Stefan Fatsis, describes the conflict between Rocker and the fans of the New York team, the Mets, which led to his negative statements in the press.

(11) FATSIS: Rocker did not exactly endear himself with fans around the country, particularly in New York, partly because of his actions, partly because of the way Mets fans responded to him late in the season and then again in the playoffs. He was ridden mercilessly by fans at Shea Stadium. Rocker fought back in the media. It was a big to-do at the end of the season.
ADAMS: And Rocker sort of says the Mets started this fight.
FATSIS: He does, indeed. He says fans threw batteries at him, tried to pour beer on him. **But like a lot of young athletes, he** couldn't walk away from the confrontation. Part of the bargain in pro sports is that you're paid millions of dollars, you gotta take it a little bit. (ATC 1/7/00)

The program host, Noah Adams, then asks Fatsis about Rocker's statement that the Mets and their fans started the fight. Fatsis responds to this question, and then uses the *but like* NP NP phrase to introduce a broader discourse theme, categorizing Rocker as representative of the larger group of young athletes. His subsequent comments and the remaining segments of the discourse focus on the responsibilities of athletes in professional sports. Fatsis concludes the segment by saying that 'the larger issue' is the responsibility that professional athletes have to be positive role models because of the forum they are given to express themselves and the disproportionate value their opinions have for the public. His use of *but like* NP NP highlights the contrastive shift in the discourse theme from the particular case of John Rocker to the implications for professional athletes in general. Unlike in examples (9) and (10), the discourse shift in example (11) was not previously highlighted in the discourse.

The *like* NP NP construction has a much lower overall token frequency than the previous construction discussed, but it also allows a wide range of NP types as collocates. The construction is clearly productive within its particular discourse. Its lower token frequency may well be related to its use in a less common, more restricted discourse context.

3.3 *It be*-TNS *like* NP

We will now briefly consider the *It be*-TNS *like* NP construction. This construction appears to share the generalizing discourse function of other *like* NP constructions, but it does not signal a shift in discourse focus or theme. In fact, it typically introduces a mapping that provides evidence or summation for the ongoing discourse topic.

The segment in which example (12) occurs concerns high impact fees added to the sale price of new homes in the State of Florida to pay for the costs of building new schools. After the introduction of this topic by the host, the reporter presents the specific case of a young family who had just purchased a home, followed by statements from a school board member. The next view presented is that of a spokesperson for the building industry, which filed a lawsuit alleging that the impact fee is a regressive tax. Dr. James Browder, the Lee County School Superintendent, is introduced to present the opposing view.

(12) BROWDER: I think growth should be paid for by growth. Those 3,000 new kids come from families that move to our community. **It's like any kind of infrastructure cost.** It ought to be paid by the people that are creating the need. (ME 6/1/04)

Browder's statement relates the impact fee to 'any kind of infrastructure cost.' Like example (2) above, example (12) appears at first to be a comparison, and yet it also invites categorization. The listener is encouraged not just to compare the impact to an infrastructure cost, but to categorize it as such a cost. This categorization then provides support for the statement that follows, that the cost should be paid by those that create the need. Both the X *is* Y form of the utterance and the constructionally-derived meaning of the *like* NP phrase encourage a categorization construal.

We see similar categorization construals in more metaphorical utterances, as shown in example (13).

(13) WERTHEIMER: Gentlemen, first of all, let's talk about the standing of the candidates in the polls. As far as I can tell, in overnight tracking with my imperfect vision, the two lines seem to be so close together, that it's very hard for me to tell who's on first. How did this race suddenly become so close?
BROOKS: It's sort of formless. It's like not lines. **It's like two corks bobbing on the ocean**. First, Bush is up, then Gore is up, then suddenly Bush has come back. The most striking poll to me has Bush actually leading by a slight margin in Gore's home state of Tennessee. Now why has this happened? Is it because Bush was funny on 'Oprah' or because he went on 'Regis Philbin'? I'm not really sure. I think it's an incredibly formless election. (ATC 10/2/00)

The segment from which example (13) comes deals with the standing of two candidates for U.S. presidency in the 2000 election. The host, Linda Wertheimer, is joined by two regular commentators to discuss the trends. She frames the discussion by describing the polls in terms of two trend lines. One of the commentators, David Brooks, responds by rejecting the term ‘lines.’ He proposes an alternative categorization in the form of a simile, ‘It’s like two corks bobbing on the ocean.’ He then goes on to explain the mapping of this simile, which provides support for his contention that the election is ‘formless.’

In the corpus, the present tense form *It’s like* introduced non-metaphorical NPs in 19 expressions and metaphorical NPs in 10 expressions. On the other hand, the past tense form *It was like* introduced non-metaphorical NPs all 8 times in which it occurred. This tendency for the past tense pattern not to be extended to metaphorical contexts may relate to the discourse contexts in which it appears. As example (14) shows, the past tense pattern *It was like* NP usually has a very specific discourse situation as its antecedent.

(14) HEATH: From the first time I recall him coming to the town of Bow, which was one of his first stops in the state, he had this huge entourage and it was a big splash. That's a long way from coming to--walking into a Rotary Club and making some remarks and mixing it up with people. **It was like a presentation**. Boom, you're gone. So it hasn't left a good taste with me.
(ATC 1/5/00)

In this example, Richard Heath, a voter from New Hampshire, was asked his opinion about then candidate-for-President George Bush. He indicates that if he had had an opportunity to interact with Bush more personally, as he had with other candidates, he might have formed a more favorable view. At the beginning of the excerpt, he specifically describes an event in which Bush appeared and then sums that event up with the statement ‘It was like a presentation.’ In this example, the pronoun *it* refers clearly to the antecedent event described. By comparision, the antecedent of *it* in example (13) is much less clear, especially given the two uses of *it* in the utterances immediately preceding ‘It’s like two corks.’ The antecedent could be the lines on the graph of the opinion polls; it could be the election; it could be a more general situational *it*.[6] The general tendency for the phrase *it’s* to frame a generic or vague reference may contribute more readily to the use of *It’s like* NP in metaphorical contexts. However, this speculation would require more extensive investigation to be fully justified.

Both the metaphorical and non-metaphorical examples of *It be*-TNS *like* NP appear to draw elements of categorization from the *like* NP phrase, but

[6] See example (7) for additional expressions in which it’s appears with generic or vague reference.

they do not instantiate the same discourse organizing properties of the *like* NP NP construction. Nor do they show the representative exemplar function of the NP *like* NP constructions. The *It be*-TNS *like* NP construction, whether present or past, metaphorical or non-metaphorical, shows a distinctive discourse function. It typically occurs as part of an ongoing discourse topic, providing a compressed mapping of relations and supporting inferences from the prior discourse that are then briefly elaborated in the immediately following discourse (see Oakley & Coulson 2008, Moder 2008).

4 Conclusions

This analysis of the occurrence of *like* preceding NPs in English has demonstrated that the phrase *like* NP performs distinctive functions depending on the constructions in which it occurs. Based on this analysis, the lexical item *like* may function as a spacebuilder, opening spaces for relational links between two discourse entities, but the relationship mapped may be more likely to entail categorization than comparison, depending on the construction in which the lexical item appears.[7]

From a usage-based perspective, one might assume that the recurrence of the expression *like* before a wide variety of NP types might lead speakers to chunk this phrase as a productive schematic unit. However, the discourse examination of the contexts in which the *like* NP phrase occurs suggests very distinctive semantic and pragmatic functions for the phrase in different constructions.

Table 5 provides a summary of the three constructions examined and their discourse functions. In the most frequently occurring construction in this corpus, the NP *like* NP construction, the first NP is often a general category. The NP following *like* typically provides an example of the category, which in the discourse will then be discussed as a representative of the category.

[7] The constructions we have examined occur in this discourse genre primarily in a categorization function. However, some of the constructions listed in Table 1, especially the adverbial uses, appear to have clear comparison functions. In addition, there may be genre variation in the discourse functions of particular constructions. This would be a topic for further exploration.

Table 5: *like* NP constructions and their discourse functions

Construction	Discourse Function
NP_1 *like* NP_2 NP_1 = category NP_2= exemplar	Introduces representative exemplar of category
like NP_1 NP_2 NP_1 = broader category NP_2= discourse entity	Signals discourse shift; Contextualizes discourse entity for broader implications
It be-TNS *like* NP *It*= discourse topic NP= new category	Introduces new entity; Relational mappings provide elaboration of or summation for ongoing discourse topic

The second construction, the *like* NP NP construction, was considerably less frequent in the corpus and served a discourse organizing function, signaling shifts in the discourse topic or theme. In this construction, the first NP is typically a broad category and the second NP is the entity that is in focus in the discourse. This construction often co-occurred with the discourse marker *and* to signal a recurring discourse shift. It co-occurred with the discourse marker *but* to introduce a new or contrastive discourse shift.

The third construction *It be*-TNS *like* NP was also of relatively low frequency. It shared the categorization meaning with the other two constructions but served a distinctive discourse function, providing a categorization that licensed support of an ongoing discourse purpose. In this construction, the pronoun *it* typically represented a situation or entity in focus in the discourse and the NP introduced a new category, which would serve as the basis for a relational mapping.

Goldberg (2005) has suggested that the variety of constructions in a given language is motivated by their importance in allowing speakers to effectively structure information. This study confirms the critical importance of lexical form and grammatical construction in cueing particular discourse-based functions. It further suggests that a detailed examination of the discourse use of particular patterns, together with a consideration of type and token frequency, may be essential to a complete understanding of constructions and their interrelations. The distinctive form-meaning correspondences of related constructions are only made accessible through a detailed study of language in use.

Author Note

Carol Lynn Moder (carol.moder@okstate.edu) is an Associate Professor of Linguistics in the Department of English at Oklahoma State University.

References

Barlow, M. & S. Kemmer. 2000. *Usage-based Models of Grammar*. Stanford: CSLI Publications.

Bybee, J. L. 1985. *Morphology: A Study of the Relation between Meaning and Form*. Philadelphia: John Benjamins.

Bybee, J. L. 2007. *Frequency of Use and the Organization of Language*. Oxford: Oxford University Press.

Bybee, J. L. & S.A. Thompson. 1997. Three Frequency Effects in Syntax. *Proceedings of the Berkeley Linguistics Society* 23: 65-85. [Reprinted in Bybee 2007].

Cameron, L. & A. Deignan. 2003. Combining Large and Small Corpora to Investigate Tuning Devices Around Metaphor in Spoken Discourse. *Metaphor and Symbol* 18: 149-160.

Croft, W. 2001. *Radical Construction Grammar: Syntactic Theory in Typological Perspective*. Oxford: Oxford University Press.

Dancygier, B. & E. Sweetser. 2005. *Mental Spaces in Grammar: Conditional Constructions*. Cambridge: Cambridge University Press.

Diessel, H. 2005. Competing Motivations for the Ordering of Main and Adverbial Clauses. *Linguistics* 43: 449-470.

Fauconnier, G. 1994. *Mental Spaces: Aspects of Meaning Construction in Natural Language*. Cambridge: Cambridge University Press.

Fauconnier, G. & M.Turner. 2002. *The Way We Think*. New York: Basic Books.

Fillmore, C.J., P. Kay & M. K. O'Connor. 1988. Regularity and Idiomaticity in Grammatical Constructions: The Case of *let alone*. *Language* 64: 501-538.

Ford, C.F. 1993. *Grammar in Interaction: Adverbial Clauses in American English Conversations*. Cambridge: Cambridge University Press.

Goldberg, A. 1995. *Constructions: A Construction Grammar Approach to Argument Structure*. Chicago: University of Chicago Press.

Goldberg, A.. 2006. *Constructions at Work: The Nature of Generalization in Language*. Oxford: Oxford University Press.

Israel, M., J.R. Harding, & V. Tobin. 2004. On Simile. *Language, Culture and Mind*, eds. M. Achard & S. Kemmer, 123-135. CSLI Publications.

Lakoff, G. & M. Johnson. 1980. *Metaphors We Live By*. Chicago: University of Chicago Press.

Lakoff, G. & M. Johnson. 1999. *Philosophy in the Flesh*. New York: Basic Books.

Langacker, R. W. 2000. *Grammar and Conceptualization*. Berlin: Mouton de Gruyter.

Moder, C. L. 2008. *It's like making a soup*: Metaphors and Similes in Spoken News Discourse. *Language in the Context of Use: Cognitive Approaches to Language and Language Learning*, eds. A..Tyler, Y. Kim, & M. Takada, 301-320. Berlin: Mouton de Gruyter.

Oakley, T. & S. Coulson. 2008. Connecting the Dots: Mental Spaces and Metaphoric Language in Discourse. *Mental Spaces in Discourse and Interactions*, eds. T. Oakley & A. Hougaard, 27-50. Amsterdam: John Benjamins.

Schiffrin, D. 1987. *Discourse Markers*. Cambridge: Cambridge University Press.

Stefanowitsch, A. 2008. Negative Entrenchment: A Usage-based Approach to Negative Evidence. *Cognitive Linguistics* 19: 513-531.

Stefanowitsch, A. & S. T. Gries. 2003. Collostructions: Investigating the Interaction of Words and Constructions. *International Journal of Corpus Linguistics* 8: 209-243.

Thompson, S.A. 1985. Grammar and Written Discourse: Initial vs. Final Purpose Clauses in English. *Text* 5:55-84.

Tomasello, M. 2003. *Constructing a Language: A Usage-based Theory of Language Acquisition*. Cambridge, MA: Harvard University Press.

12

The Discourse-Organizing Function of the *aside* Constructions: From a Cognitive and Discourse-Functional Perspective

NAOKI OTANI

1 Introduction

There are two reasons why cognitive linguistic research should be usage-based. First, linguistic units are inseparable from their usage in discourse. They have not only local and semantic functions, but also global and pragmatic functions in discourse. The latter function can never be discussed with elicited data that is independent of discourse. Second, grammar is not a static, closed, or self-contained system; it is susceptible to change and affected by language use (Bybee 2003: 145). To capture this dynamic nature of language, linguistic research must focus on discourse because linguistic units are modified, shifted and established by discourse pressure.

In fact, more and more recent works in cognitive linguistics have been presented based on the usage-based model (hereafter, UBM). These studies have found not only established patterns in discourse but also clarified that these patterns are dynamic in nature. Since UBM is a model that is suitable to capture the dynamic change of language, it is often applied to the study of language change in areas such as grammaticalization, lexicalization and meaning shift. At the same time, the usage-based orientation is also shared by other empirically-oriented linguistic research trends such as discourse-

Meaning, Form & Body.
Fey Parrill, Vera Tobin, and Mark Turner (eds.).

functional grammar (Bybee 1985, Hopper and Bybee 2001) which regards the frequency of linguistic units as the primary factor of the cause of linguistic change.

The development of UBM has been supported by the evolution of the data and methods of corpus linguistics. Specifically, more and more corpora which are composed for both specific and general purposes are now available, and various statistical models have been applied to linguistic research. Due to these developments, many researches now exploit the data from corpora to test the legitimacy of their hypotheses and have succeeded in finding previously undiscovered discourse patterns (i.e. constructions).

Another crucial advantage of UBM is that it reveals a close relation between discourse and cognitive bases of language. The distribution in discourse of linguistic units and their conceptual structure are two sides of the same coin in the sense that the surface distributions of language are reflection of conceptual structures and that conceptual structures are likewise motivated by discourse pressure. Cognitive and discourse functional analyses are therefore complementary.

1.1 The *aside* constructions

From these two perspectives, the present paper discusses the discourse-organizing function of two types of 'the *aside* constructions.' These constructions have discourse-organizing functions and include the particle *aside* in dependent clauses and phrases, respectively. Some examples are as follows:

(1) a. Leaving aside this particular controversy, there is a great deal of interest in the topic.
  b. Setting this show and its problems aside, what we need generally is some fresh thinking and some fresh air.

(2) a. Politics aside, the Vietnam industry is a profitable one.
  b. Prejudice aside, the Republic have shown the best form in the group so far.[1]

As shown in (1), the first *aside* construction is a clausal type that includes a present participle. Hereafter, I call this type of *aside* construction AC1. In contrast, the second *aside* construction is a phrasal type as shown in (2). This construction does not include a present participle and *aside* only appears after a noun phrase. Hereafter, I call this type of *aside* construction AC2. Both constructions are dependent structures that are combined with

---

[1] All examples in this paper are extracted from British National Corpus (hereafter, BNC).

the associated main clause.[2] Their locations relative to the main clauses are flexible. They may precede or follow the associated main clause, or they may sometimes be located inside the main clause.

These two constructions share three fundamental characteristics. First, they both exhibit a discourse-organizing function (or global function) as in the examples in (1) and (2) above. They exclude one aspect or topic and introduce a new topic in the associated main clause. This function is opposed to the local function of *aside* exemplified in (3) and (4).

(3) a. He pushed the pad aside and began to type again.
b. She had stepped aside, so that her face was in shadow.

(4) a. Pushing temptation aside, he left the casino and ....
b. Seeing her wince, Mike lifted her, brushing her objections aside.

Aside in (3) and (4) illustrates the spatial and metaphorical path of TR, respectively. What is important here is that *aside* in (3) and (4) functions at the semantic or local level, i.e., the meaning of *aside* expresses a part of a proposition. Second, AC1 and AC2 are used in limited contexts. Specifically, they never appear in the main clause but are used only in dependent clauses and phrases. In contrast, the spatial or metaphorical use of *aside* can be used both in main and dependent clauses. Third, the *aside* constructions are grammatically fixed or syntactically irregular. For example, AC1 is an instance of a dangling participle where the subject of the main clause and semantic subject of the present participle clause do not correspond. The non-correspondence of the subjects between the two clauses is commonly judged to be ungrammatical in English (see 2.1 for more discussion). Similarly, AC2 includes the postpositional use of the particle *aside*. Conventionalized postpositions are very rare in English (*ago* is one such example). Though the particle *aside* is not a prototypical postposition,[3] the contrast in (5) illustrates *aside*'s status as a postposition.

(5) a. Politics aside, the Vietnam industry is a profitable one. (=(2a))
b. *Politics, the Vietnam industry is a profitable one.
c. *Aside politics, the Vietnam industry is a profitable one.

The clause in (5a) is wholly grammatical. However, the clause is judged to be ungrammatical without *aside* as shown in (5b). In addition, (5c) shows

[2] In AmE, the complex preposition *aside from* is often used. However, BNC does not include the examples where *aside from* appears in the dependent structures.

[3] The postpositional use of the particle *aside* differs from prototypical postpositions as follows: First, it can appear only in the dependent structures. Second, it does not show case relation but has functions at the discourse level.

that the prepositional use of the particle *aside* is ungrammatical in a dependent phrase. These facts suggest that *aside* has a postpositional status here and that the NP *politics* seems the argument of the particle *aside* since it can only be sanctioned with the particle *aside*.

Interestingly, these three characteristics together suggest that AC1 and AC2 function as phrasal discourse markers.

1.2 Hypotheses

A mass of evidence suggests that constructions emerge in discourse contexts, and various frequency effects motivate the establishment of the constructions. Grammaticalization (i.e. the emergence of new grammatical units from content units) is no exception. Grammatical units emerge in discourse contexts as a result of frequent repetition (Bybee 1985, Langacker 1988).

The present paper raises two hypotheses concerning the *aside* constructions AC1 and AC2 on the basis of this dynamic view of language. The first hypothesis is the following:

(6) Hypothesis 1: AC1 and AC2 show an on-going process of grammaticalization toward becoming discourse markers.

The *aside* constructions AC1 and AC2 are best described in terms of the ongoing process of grammaticalization: as they acquire a discourse-organizing function, they are reanalyzed and behave like other discourse markers in general.

The second hypothesis is related to the different discourse functions of AC1 and AC2. Though they are synonymous, they differ as to function in discourse.

(6) Hypothesis 2: AC1 and AC2 have different functions in discourse. AC1 has more global function in the sense that it is more closely related to the previous context.

To test these two hypotheses from a usage-based perspective, I have done two case studies by using data from BNC. The hypothesis 1 and 2 will be discussed in the section 4 and 5, respectively.

2 Constructions in discourse contexts

Researchers have long argued that constructions should be discussed from a discourse perspective, because constructions are established as a result of linguistic changes such as grammaticalization and lexicalization. However, few studies deal with the emergence of constructions in terms of the interaction between constructions and discourse in actual usage.

The *aside* constructions are constructions that have the discourse-organizing functions. Therefore, the present study discusses the *aside* construction in terms of the grammaticalization toward discourse markers. Traugott (1995) clarifies the role of subjectification[4] in grammaticalization and provides various dimensions in which subjectification operates.

(8) a. Propositional function ---→ Discourse markers
b. Objective meaning ---→ Subjective meaning
c. Non-epistemic modality ---→ Epistemic modality
d. Non-syntactic subject ---→ Syntactic subject
e. Syntactic subject ---→ Speaking subject
f. Full, free form ---→ Bonded form

These dimensions are convenient for discussing the characteristics of AC1 and AC2. The various characteristics observed in AC1 and AC2 altogether show an on-going process toward discourse markers. For example, the representative examples of ACs behave in a manner characteristic of discourse markers. Their meanings are subjective; their form is bonded; and they are speaker-based expressions.

In what follows, I will introduce three crucial notions and phenomena that are necessary to discuss AC1 and AC2 from a discourse perspective. They are dangling participles, discourse motivations for word orders and discourse markers.

2.1 Dangling participles

The first phenomenon related to AC1 and AC2 is dangling participles. Huddleston and Pullum (2002: 611) define dangling participle as a dependent clause for which '[n]o subject for the ... verb is recoverable from the matrix clause.' Generally, English speakers will consider dangling participles ungrammatical, but speakers may consider them acceptable under various circumstances, as discussed in previous studies (Quirk et al. 1985). For example, when the semantic subject of the participle clauses is presumably *I* and when its semantic role is a perceiver or cognizer as in (9), the acceptability of the clauses increases.

(9) a. Looking up, there were two boys standing there.
b. Seeing there are just three people, it would make sense if I helped them.

[4] Traugott (1995: 31) defines Subjectification as a pragmatic-semantic process whereby 'meanings become increasingly based in the speaker's subjective belief state/attitude toward a proposition.'

Dangling participle constructions are highly subjective expressions in that the unexpressed speaker of the utterance is embedded in the speech ground. The semantic subject of the participle clause is not complemented by the syntactic subject in the associated main clause but by the ground information of the present discourse.

Some dangling participles such as *strictly speaking*, *taking everything into account* and *supposing*, are conventionalized to some extent. These highly conventionalized constructions are used frequently and have discourse-organizing functions. In each case, the semantic subjects of the dangling participles are the first person as well.[5]

As mentioned above, one of the prominent characteristics of AC1 is that the semantic subject of the present participle does not correspond to the subject of the main clause. AC1 can be thought as partially conventionalized dangling participles.

2.2 Discourse motivations for word order

One of the central tenets of both cognitive and construction grammars is that word order conveys schematic meanings (Langacker 1987; Goldberg 2006). This is applicable not only to the core parts of grammar such as argument structure but also to the peripheral parts of grammar such as the position of adverbs. For example, Dixon (2005) argues that the polysemous senses of the adverb *once* are disambiguated by the position of the word.

(10) a. He ***once*** didn't come.
b. He didn't ***once*** come. (Dixon 2005: 442)

(10a) and (10b) illustrate different situations. (10a) describes a situation where he came on every occasion but one; while (10b) describes one where he never came. In these cases, the positions of the adverb *once* directly indicate the situation described.

As such, the position of adverbial phrases has varying function in discourse. Thompson (1985) focuses on the initial and end position of the purpose clause in English.

(11) a. ***To cool***, place the loaf on a wire rack.
b. Place the loaf on a wire rack ***to cool***. (Thompson 1985)

Thompson explains that '[t]he initial purpose clause functions to state a 'problem' within the context of expectations raised by **the preceding discourse**, to which the following material (often many clauses) provides a

[5] In the extreme case of conventionalized dangling participles, there are deverbal prepositions such as *given*, *granted*, *providing* and *seeing*. They only have grammatical functions and can be classified as one type of grammaticalization from verbs to prepositions.

solution, while the final purpose clause plays the much more **local** role of stating the purpose for which the action named in the immediately preceding clause is performed' (ibid. 55). A similar phenomenon is observed in other dependent structures such as the epistemic *I think* (Thompson and Mulac 1991) and If-conditionals (Ford 1997). In these cases, the initial position has a more global function than the end position does.

As such, how AC1 and AC2 are related to the previous contexts is a crucial issue because they are constructions that have discourse functions.

2.3 Discourse markers

Although discourse markers were once treated as a grammar trash box, various studies in conversational analysis, discourse-functional grammar and sociolinguistics clarify that they function not just to fill up gaps in utterances. Instead, the use of discourse markers is highly systematic because the discourse markers reflect the mental attitude of the speaker and the speaker's unconscious conversation strategy.

In cognitive and discourse-functional grammar, discourse markers are often discussed in terms of grammaticalization. This is partly because discourse markers do not constitute a distinct grammatical class. They are derived from other grammatical classes. Fraser (1999) argues that '[t]here are three sources of DMs [discourse markers]– conjunction, adverbs, and prepositional phrases – as well as a few idioms like *still and all* and *all things considered*' (ibid. 943). The particle *aside* is usually classified as an adverbial particle, which is one of primary sources of discourse markers. Though its prototypical meaning indicates spatial location, it develops the discourse-organizing function when used in dependent structures.

There is no precise definition of discourse markers. However, after Zwicky (1985), most researchers agreed that discourse markers share at least the four following criteria.

(12) a. It has to be syntactically detachable from a sentence.
b. It has to be commonly used in initial position of an utterance.
c. It has to have a range of prosodic contours.
d. It has to be able to operate at both local and global levels of discourse.

It is obvious that the prototypical meaning of the particle *aside* does not meet these four criteria. So, if the *aside* constructions meet them, it can be concluded that the *aside* constructions are in the ongoing process of grammaticalization toward discourse markers.

3 Data and methods

This study discusses two types of constructions including the particle *aside* in dependent clauses and phrases. To collect a large number of examples of *aside* from actual usage, this study uses the data from the British National Corpus (Hereafter, *BNC*) that consist of over 100 million words of written and spoken British English. The data is composed by approximately ninety percent written and ten percent spoken data.

All examples are collected in the following way. First, I extracted all examples of the particle *aside*. There are 3447 examples of the particle *aside* in the *BNC*. Second, I selected all examples of the particle *aside* in dependent clauses and phrases manually. There are 588 examples of *aside* that are used in dependent clauses and phrases. This study deals with these 588 examples.

In the *BNC*, there are thirty nine verbs which co-occur with *aside* in dependent clauses. (13) lists these verbs.

(13) *bat, beat, brush, cast, drag, draw, elbow, flick, fling, force, glance, hurl, kick, knock, lay, leave, lie, lift, move, nose, NP aside, nudge, order, pull, push, put, say, set, shoulder, shove, stand, step, swing, take, throw, thrust, toss, turn, twist, wave*

It should be noted that only a few verbs are used with high frequency, others occurring in low frequency. Seventeen out of thirty-nine verbs are used only once. More than 75 percent of all verbs (thirty verbs) are used less than 5 times. The following is the token frequency of the top six sub-constructions in AC1 and AC2: *leaving aside* (182), NP *aside* (176), *setting aside* (48), *pushing aside* (38), *putting aside* (32) and *brushing aside* (20). The token frequencies of other constructions are less than ten. About 80 percent of the examples are used in the top six sub-constructions. Moreover, among the high frequency constructions, the two constructions, the frequencies of the *leaving aside* construction and the NP *aside* construction (=AC2), are extremely high.

To examine the discourse-organizing function of AC1 and AC2, all examples are annotated for linguistic features. Table 1 shows the list of all features.

Table 1 Variables

(a)	function of *aside*
	(1) global or pragmatic (2) local or semantic
(b)	types of NP in the dependent structures
	(1) definite (2) non-specific (3) pronoun

(c)	location of the dependent structure relative to the main clause
	(1) initial (2) middle (3) end
(d)	word order within the present participle clause
	(1) sequential type (V-*aside*-NP) (2) insertion type (V-NP-*aside*)
(e)	weight of NP
	the number of words in NP
(f)	registers
	(1) spoken (2) written

Usually semantic features are hard to classify, as opposed to grammatical features. Especially difficult in the case of *aside* is the classification of the feature (a), the function of *aside*. To annotate this factor, the present study focuses on the relation between the subjects of the main and dependent clause. In sentences where the subject of the main clause and semantic subject of the dependent clause do not correspond, *aside* is considered to have a discourse organizing function as in (14).

(14) But there are changes in what readers know automatically, even ***leaving aside*** questions of education, social background, gender, ethnicity or age.

4 Case Study 1: Grammaticalization of AC1 and AC2

This section deals with the various characteristics observed in AC1 and AC2 in terms of grammaticalization toward discourse markers. The hypothesis tested here is as follows:

(15) Hypothesis 1: AC1 and AC2 show an on-going process of grammaticalization toward becoming discourse markers.

If the hypothesis 1 is correct, that is, if AC1 and AC2 are undergoing grammaticalization toward becoming discourse markers, they should show similar behavior to general discourse markers (see four criteria in (12)).

4.1 Result

To test hypothesis 1, this study first compares the frequency of globally and locally functional instances of *aside*. Table 2 summarizes these results.

Table 2 Distribution of functions relative to each *aside* construction

	GLOBAL	LOCAL	total
leave	**181** (99%)	1 (1%)[6]	182
NP *aside*	**176** (100%)	0 (0%)	176
set	**40** (83%)	8 (17%)	48
push	0 (0%)	**38** (100%)	38
put	16 (50%)	16 (50%)	32
brush	3 (15%)	17 (85%)	20
other verbs	5 (5%)	**87** (95%)	92
total	421 (72%)	167 (28%)	588

The data in Table 2 shows an interesting correlation between frequency and function. The two highest frequency constructions, *leaving aside* and NP *aside*, exclusively have the global function. In contrast, the lower the frequency of the sub-construction becomes, the greater the tendency becomes for the sub-construction to have a local function. In fact, in low frequency verbs, eighty-seven out of ninety-two examples have a local function. Other than the *pushing aside* sub-construction, the ratio of the local function to overall frequency is inversely related.

Table 3 demonstrates the distribution of three positions--initial, middle and final--in the functions of *aside*.

Table 3 Distribution of functions to three positions

	GLOBAL	LOCAL	total
initial	**351** (87%)	53 (13%)	404
middle	52 (66%)	27 (34%)	79
final	18 (17%)	**87** (83%)	105
total	421 (72%)	167 (28%)	588

Table 3 shows a correlation between the function and position of the relevant *aside* construction. Eighty-seven percent of *aside* clauses and phrases

[6] The example of the *leaving aside* construction with non-discourse organizing function is:

(i) ***leaving*** that ***aside*** for a moment, he tried to make some sense of Steen's behaviour.

In the sentence, the subjects between the main/dependent clauses correspond.

that appear before the main clause have a global function. In contrast, in the final position, the majority of *aside* clauses and phrases (83%) have a local function. Another crucial finding revealed by Table 3 is that *aside* constructions with global function have a strong tendency to be located before the main clause. In contrast, only less than five percent of these examples are located after the main clause.

Table 4 presents the distribution of the two types of word order among sub-constructions of AC1. The word order of the NP, particle, and verb has been one of the central interests in previous study of verb-particle constructions and has been studied in the terms of 'particle placement,' 'heavy NP shift,' and 'particle movement.' Previous studies have revealed that not only the phonological and grammatical nature but also its semantic and discourse nature motivate the particle placement (Cheng 1976).

Table 4 Distribution of word order among subtypes of AC1

	GLOBAL	LOCAL	total
AC1(V + *aside* + NP)	196 (73%)	74 (27%)	270
AC1(V + NP + *aside*)	48 (39%)	<u>75</u> (61%)	123
AC1(no overt object NP)	2 (10%)	18 (90%)	20
total	246 (72%)	167 (28%)	413[7]

Table 4 shows that the instances of the verb-particle sequential type (270 instances) are more than twice as many as that of the object insertion type (123 instances). It also demonstrates the interesting correlation between function and word order. That is, the *aside* constructions with global function tend to be located in the verb-particle sequence as in (16a), while, in the *aside* constructions with local function, the object NP tends to be located between the verb and *aside* as in (16b).

(16) a. Leaving aside this particular controversy, there is a great deal of interest in the topic.

b. Putting the handout aside, he continued his presentation.

To sum up, case study 1 clarifies the following three crucial characteristics of the *aside* constructions. First, the three most frequent types of the *aside* constructions (*leaving aside*, NP *aside* and *setting aside*) tend to have a global function, while the *aside* constructions with low frequency verbs tend to have a local function. Second, global use of the *aside* constructions

[7] Observe that the total frequency is 413 in the table. I excluded AC2 from Table 4, because it does not include verbs in dependent structures, and, in addition, its function is always global.

tends to be located before the main clause, while local use is more likely to appear after the main clause. Third, in global use, a verb and *aside* tend to be used in sequence, while the NP tends to be located between a verb and *aside* in local use.

4.2 Grammaticalization of the *aside* constructions toward discourse marker

These three characteristics collectively suggest that AC1 and AC2 are under the process of grammaticalization toward discourse markers. These characteristics are also general characteristics that are found in linguistic units under grammaticalization.

From the results of case study 1, it can be concluded that the *leaving aside* construction is most grammaticalized within AC1 in the sense that (1) it has an exclusively global function; (2) it tends to be located before the main clause; (3) *leaving* and *aside* are used in sequence; and (4) usage frequency is high. Characteristics (1) and (2) are generally found in linguistic units that undergo grammaticalization toward becoming discourse markers. Characteristic (3) shows semantic fusion within the construction, which also occurs with the progress of grammaticalization. Finally, the frequency of functional words are much higher than that of content words in general. These four characteristics of the *leaving aside* sub-construction are also prominent in AC2.

In fact, these four characteristics are general characteristics of discourse markers as well.[8] The *leaving aside* construction and AC2 meet the criteria of discourse markers that were listed in (12). For example, Table 3 shows that the *aside* constructions with a global function have a strong tendency to be located before the main clause, as opposed to the *aside* constructions with a local function. This result meets the criterion (12b).

Finally, it should be noted that two types of change in status, pragmatization and subjectification, are observed, accompanied by a shift in grammatical status. The first change is pragmatization. Prototypically, the particle *aside* shows spatial location, but it tends to have a discourse-organizing function in AC1 and AC2. This shift from semantic to pragmatic function, pragmatization, can be described in the following manner.

(17) semantic > less semantic > pragmatic (global, rhetorical)

The grammaticalization and pragmatization of the *aside* construction develops at the same time and, therefore, impossible to discuss separately.

---

[8] However, it can be said that the *aside* constructions are not prototypical discourse markers in that they have open slots in the NP position.

The second change is subjectification. Traugott (1995) discusses the role of subjectification in grammaticalization. What is important here is the role of subjectification as a trigger of grammaticalization. Traugott notes the role of subjectification in grammaticalization as follows: ‘forms and constructions that at first express primarily concrete, lexical, and objective meanings come through repeated use in local syntactic contexts to serve increasingly abstract, pragmatic, interpersonal, and speaker-based functions’ (ibid. 32).

The close relation between grammaticalization and subjectification are obvious from the examples in (18), where the examples (18a) through (18d) can be captured in the gradience of subjectification.

(18) a. Putting this pad aside, he continued his presentation.
b. Putting the bad image aside, he continued his presentation.
c. Putting the bad image aside, let’s talk about this good one.
d. Putting this aside, there are some good points in the project.

The participle clause in (18a) is a very objective expression. It describes the propositional state and spatial movement of the NP *this pad*. In contrast, the participle clause in (18b) describes a metaphorical movement, although it still indicates a propositional state. The participle clause in (18c) has a global function. Therefore, it is more subjective than (18a) and (18b). In contrast to (18c), (18d) is a speaker-based expression. The participle clause in (18d) is the most subjective in the four examples. It not only has the pragmatic function but also is a speaker oriented expression. The subjects of the main/dependent clauses do not corresponded. The semantic subject of the present participle clause is complemented by the speaker who exists in the speech ground. These examples show that as grammaticalization goes on, the commitment of the speaker to the content of the utterance increases.[9]

Table 5 summarizes grammaticalization of AC1 and AC2 toward becoming discourse markers.

[9] A reviewer has suggested the possibility of force dynamic aspects in the sub-constructions. He/she focuses on the fact that the force-dynamic examples of AC1, such as pushing and brushing, are less frequent than its more neutral counterparts in leaving and setting, and he/she furthermore argues the possibility that a “high force dynamic may prevent ACs from subjectification, because force dynamics tends to place two entities on stage, so if the one entity is the speaker/discourse participant(s), then it is harder to ‘subjectivize.’”

Though further discussion is needed, this is an interesting idea. It seems natural that each sub-construction of AC1 has not only common but also its own semantic motivations.

Table 5. Summary of grammaticalization in the *aside* constructions

prototypical use	the *aside* constructions	level of components
local (semantic)	global (pragmatic)	semantic level
subject-oriented	speaker-oriented	
low frequency	high frequency	grammatical level
low fusion	high fusion	
	initial position	

---------------unidirectionality-------------->

The data in Table 5 implies that grammaticalization, subjectification and pragmatization are different aspects of one dynamic change of language. These three phenomena share a fundamental characteristic, i.e. unidirectionality. Seen from a different perspective, the dynamic shift of the grammatical status of AC1 and AC2 is motivated by its cognitive basis, subjectification and pragmatization. That is, as the speaker's role increases, the grammatical status of AC1 and AC2 changes.

5 Case study 2: The discourse functions of AC1 and AC2

In case study 1, I argued that the *aside* constructions are in the process of grammaticalization toward becoming discourse markers. The next question which immediately occurs is whether or not AC1 and AC2 are functionally different. It seems, at first, that the postpositional *aside* construction AC2, is derived from the present participle construction AC1. However, although it is likely that these two constructions have the same historical origin, in present day English, they are quite different constructions, which differ in their discourse functions. To analyze different discourse functions, this section discusses the hypothesis 2.

(19) Hypothesis 2: AC1 and AC2 have different functions in discourse. AC1 has more global function in the sense that it is more closely related to the previous context.

To test the legitimacy of hypothesis 2, this section deals only with the *aside* constructions with a global function. The total frequency of these constructions is 421. The following is the token frequency of each sub-construction: *leaving aside* (181), NP *aside* (176), *setting aside* (40), *putting aside* (16) and *brushing aside* (3), *laying aside* (1), *shouldering aside* (1), *taking aside* (1), *turning aside* (1) and *waving aside* (1). Among sub-constructions, the frequencies of the *leaving aside* construction and AC2 stand out.

5.1 Result

To discuss different discourse functions, I first focus on the definiteness of the noun phrase within the *aside* clauses and phrases. Table 6 classifies the type of nouns.

Table 6 Distribution of definiteness to each *aside* construction

	definite	non-specific	pronoun	total
leave	**132**	43	6	181
NP *aside*	44	**103**	**29**	176
set	**24**	**15**	1	40
put	**11**	2	2	15(+1)[10]
others	4	3	1	8
total	215	166	40	420(+1)

Table 6 shows an interesting contrast between the two highest frequency constructions. The *leaving aside* construction tends to take a definite noun as its object, while AC2 has a strong tendency to take a non-specific noun phrase. Other constructions in AC1 tend to take a definite NP as well as the *leaving aside* construction. Another finding is that the distribution of the pronoun objects such as *this* and *that*. They tend to appear in the AC2.

This overall result becomes much clearer when it is rearranged with respect to AC1 and AC2, as in Table 7.

Table 7. Distribution of definiteness to AC1 and AC2

	definite	non-specific	pronoun	total
AC1	**171 (70%)**	63 (26%)	10 (4%)	244 (100%)
AC2	44 (25%)	**103 (59%)**	**29 (16%)**	176 (100%)
total	215 (51%)	166 (40%)	39 (9%)	420 (100%)

There are two interesting points in Table 7. First, the ratios of the definite to non-specific NP in AC1 and AC2 are inversely related. AC1 tends to take a definite NP, while AC2 tends to take a non-specific NP. Seventy percent of AC1 take a definite NP, while more than half of examples (59%) of AC2 have a non-specific NP, e.g. an indefinite article and 'bare noun.' Second,

[10] There is no expressed NP in this example.

though total frequency of pronoun objects is rather low, they tend to appear in AC2.

I now count the average word number within the NPs in AC1 and AC2.

Table 8 The average word count in NP

AC2	AC1(V-*aside*-NP)	AC1(V-NP-*aside*)
1.97	**8.71**	2.33

The average word count in NPs is lowest with AC2, where the average is less than two. AC2 constructions tend to take only a pronoun, or one noun with an article. Within AC1, the *verb*-NP-*aside* pattern shows a similar tendency to AC2. In contrast, the sequential pattern of AC1 shows rather different characteristics. The average word count of the NPs is 8.71. This result matches with previous studies of heavy NP shift. That is, when the word length of NP is heavy, it tends to appear in a position to the right of their canonical position.

5.2 The Discourse motivation of AC1 and AC2

The result of case study 2 provided evidence that AC1 and AC2 have different functions in discourse. For example, the results of Table 7 shows that AC1 tends to take a definite NP while AC2 tends to take a non-specific NP. This strongly suggests that AC1 is more closely related to the previous contexts when compared to AC2, because definite NPs imply that they have already been referred to in their previous context. Based on these results, this section gives the definition of the different discourse functions of AC1 and AC2.

Now, I start the discussion with AC1. The following are representative examples of AC1.

(20) However, the fact that fewer people in low ***income*** groups use credit at all means that, of those who do, a higher proportion are likely to be heavy credit users. ***Leaving income aside***, the people with the heaviest credit commitment tend to be young.

(21) Comte (Martineau 1853) proposed a hierarchy of positive sciences [...] The hierarchy begins with ***mathematics***, and then moves up through astronomy, physics, chemistry and biology to sociology at the top. ***Setting aside mathematics*** for the moment, the different levels can be seen in terms of scale [...], in terms of envelopes [...] or perhaps best in terms of levels of organization [...].

In (20) and (21), the nouns *income* and *mathematics* are respectively referred to in the previous context. (20) is taken out of a larger conversation where the participants are discussing the relation between income and heavy credit users. Here, the function of the AC1 is to exclude the old topic income and introduce the new topic age. Similarly, in (21), the function of AC1 is to exclude the old topic mathematics and introduce the various new topics.

From these observations, the discourse function of AC1 can be defined as follows:

(22) The discourse function of AC1 is to exclude an old topic (=NP), which was mentioned in the previous context, and introduce a new topic in the associated main clause.

Since the function of AC1 is to exclude an old topic, the NP in AC1 tends to be mentioned in the previous contexts and, therefore, take a definite NP.

In contrast, AC2 clauses have quite different functions in discourse. The following are representative examples of the AC2.

(23) Hence, one could conclude, for instance, Middlesbrough's success in Heseltine's City Challenge scheme; a part of which will, if the council's full bid is passed, see a £50m housing investment programme for hard-hit outlying areas. ***Politics aside***, however, there are growing doubts about the validity of all main party housing policies.

(24) Date: Mon, 18 Oct 1993 14:03:29 Subject: The Referee's a German Hello, Contrary to Stu's reports , I wasn't deported from the Netherlands for looking like E. Cantona! I actually had a happy week's holiday (***Black Wednesday aside***) free from the clutches of the Dutch police dragnet. I came back of my own free will on Friday, and went to the game yesterday.

In (23), the NP *politics* is not mentioned in the previous context. In fact, politics is a crucial part of a new topic introduced in the associated main clause. The speaker attempts to exclude politics in advance from the new topic. Likewise, in (24), the NP *Black Wednesday* is never mentioned in the previous context. Though it is a crucial component of the new topic *a happy week*, the speaker excludes *Black Wednesday* from a happy week's holiday to avoid anticipated criticisms.

From these observations, the discourse function of AC2 can be defined as follows:

(25) The discourse function of AC2 is to exclude one crucial but unfavorable aspect of a new topic in advance for the specific purpose of avoiding anticipated criticisms.

What is important here is that the different grammatical structures of AC1 and AC2 (i.e. clause and phrase, respectively) might motivate their respective functions. The difference between clause and phrase is whether they take a participial form or not. Compared to a phrase structure, a clause structure is more independent of its main clause in the sense that it has its own verb. Therefore, it is more related to the previous context. In contrast, AC2 takes the form of a phrase; therefore, it does not have its own verb and is more integrated with the main clause. Consequently, they show low topic continuity.

It should be noted that a parallel phenomenon is observed with respect to the position of the dependent structures such as conditional clause (Ford 1997) and purpose clause (Thompson 1985).[11] Here, the key contrast is not between phrases and clauses but between initial and final positions of the clause. These studies clarify that the dependent clause before the main clause is more likely to have a global function than the dependent clause after the main clause. In contrast, my study clarifies that the type of dependent structures in the *aside* constructions, phrase or clause, are also related to the discourse function, and clauses are more related to the previous contexts than phrases.[12]

6 Conclusion

The major findings of this study are the following two points. First, as the meaning of *aside* shifts from a semantically spatial one to a pragmatically

[11] This point was suggested by Mira Ariel at CSDL 9.

[12] This explanation cannot at present address the fact that pronouns such as *this* and *that* tend to be used in AC2. Although pronouns have already been mentioned in the previous context in many cases, they tend to appear in AC2.

This might be related to the length of NPs in the *aside* constructions. More specifically, two word orders within AC1, the sequential type and the insertion type, cause the discrepancy of the function and the word order. As shown in Table 8, the average count of NP in the sequential type is 8.71, while the average number of NP in the insertion type is 2.33. So, pronouns are supposed to be used in the insertion type. At the same time, as illustrated in Table 4, *aside* constructions with global functions tend to be used in the sequential type. Because of this crush, pronouns tend not to appear in the sequential type, even if the constructions with pronouns have global functions. Actually, in the previous studies of the verb-particle constructions, many researchers found a similar phenomenon. Pronouns do not appear in the sequential type.

(i) He put it off.

(ii) *He put off it.

discourse-organizing one, they behave differently with respect to both grammatical and semantic aspects. The *aside* constructions with a global function share a large number of properties with other discourse markers. Therefore, it can be concluded that the *aside* constructions are in the process of grammaticalization toward becoming discourse markers. Second, the two constructions, AC1 and AC2, have different discourse functions. That is, the function of AC1 is to exclude an old topic (=NP) which was mentioned in the previous context and introduce a new topic, while AC2 typically functions to exclude one crucial but unfavorable aspect of an anticipated new topic in advance for the specific purpose such as avoiding anticipated criticism. The different functions of AC1 and AC2 are motivated by their structures as either clauses or phrases. AC1's dependent clauses are more independent than AC2's dependent phrases with respect to the associated main clause. Therefore, AC1 shows higher topic continuity than AC2 does. This suggests that, even after the constructions are grammaticalized, the original meanings of each structure are preserved.

Though this study exclusively focuses on the *aside* constructions, the method used here can apply to the study of the static type of grammaticalization, i.e. the occasional functional use of lexical material. Mair (2004) notes that the static type of grammaticalization 'will usually not show up as a directed diachronic development in a historical corpus, nor are the phenomena concerned necessarily frequent in any statistical sense' (ibid. 123). This is true when only row frequency of instances is considered. However, as shown in this paper, detailed annotation of semantic and discourse properties allows us to discuss this type of grammaticalization with complementary quantitative and qualitative methods of investigation using large-scale linguistic corpora.

Furthermore, this study suggests the necessity of studying constructions from a discourse perspective, because most constructions have not only semantic meanings but also discourse functions. The discourse functions can never be discussed with data elicited independent of discourse. In the case of AC1 and AC2, they seem synonymous at the semantic level, but they have quite different functions at the discourse level. Therefore, it is necessary to discuss constructions within the context of discourse.

Author Note

I would like to express my sincere gratitude to Sandra A. Thompson and Masa-aki Yamanashi for their valuable comments. I am also grateful to Kiyoko Sohmiya, Yoko Iyeiri, Chie Fukada, Nobutaka Takara, Daisuke Yokomori, Natsuko Nakagawa and Jun Sawada. Special thanks also go to David Humphrey for his suggestions in stylistic improvements.

Naoki Otani
Center for English Education and Development, Saitama University, Japan
otani@mail.saitama.ac.jp

References

Bybee J. L. 1985. *Morphology: A Study of the Relation between Meaning and Form*. Amsterdam/Philadelphia: John Benjamins

Bybee, J. L. 2003. Cognitive Processes in Grammaticalization. *The New Psychology of Language*. vol.2, ed. M. Tomasello, 145-167, Mahwah: Lawrence Erlbaum Associates, Inc., Publishers.

Cheng, P. 1986. Discourse and Particle Movement in English. *Studies in Language* 10: 79-95.

Dixon, R. M. W. 2005. *A Semantic Approach to English Grammar*. Oxford: OUP.

Du Bois, John W. 2003. Discourse and Grammar. *The New Psychology of Language: Cognitive and Functional Approaches to Language Structure*. vol.2, ed. M. Tomasello, 47-87. Mahwah: Lawrence Erlbaum Associates, Inc., Publishers.

Fillmore, C. J., P. Kay & M. C. O'Connor 1988. Regularity and Idiomaticity in Grammatical Constructions: The Case of *Let Alone*. *Language* 64: 501-538.

Ford, C. E. 1997. Speaking Conditionality: Some Contexts for If-Clause in Conversation. *On Conditionals Again*, eds. A. Athanasiadou & R. Dirven, 387-413. Amsterdam/Philadelphia: John Benjamins.

Fraser, B. 1999. What are Discourse Markers?. *Journal of Pragmatics* 31: 931-952.

Givón, T. 1983. *Topic Continuity in Discourse: A Quantitative Cross-language Study*. Amsterdam/Philadelphia: John Benjamins.

Goldberg, A. E. 1995 *Constructions: A Construction Grammar Approach to Argument Structure*. Chicago: Chicago University Press.

Goldberg, A. E. 2006. *Constructions at Work: the nature of generalization in language*. Oxford: OUP.

Hopper, P. J. & J. L. Bybee eds. 2001. *Frequency and the Emergence of Linguistic Structure*. Amsterdam/Philadelphia: John Benjamins.

Hopper, P. J. & E. C. Traugott 1993. *Grammaticalization*. Cambridge: CUP.

Huddleston, R. & G. K. Pullum 2002. *The Cambridge Grammar of the English Language*. Cambridge: CUP.

Langacker, R. W. 1987. *Foundations of Cognitive Grammar,* vol. 1, *Theoretical Prerequisities*. Stanford: Stanford University Press.

Langacker, R. W. 1988. A Usage-based Model. *Topics in Cognitive Linguistics*, ed. B. Rudzka-Ostyn, 127-161. Amsterdam/Philadelphia: John Benjamins.

Langacker, R. W. 2008. *Cognitive Grammar: A Basic Introduction*. Oxford: OUP.

Lenk, U. 1998. *Marking Discourse Coherence: Functions of Discourse Markers in Spoken English*. Tübingen: Gunter Narr Verlag.

Mair, C. 2004. Corpus Linguistics and Grammaticalization. *Corpus approaches to grammaticalization in English*, ed. H. Lindquist & C. Mair, 121-150. Amsterdam/Philadelphia: John Benjamins.

Mann, W. C. & S. A. Thompson 1987. Rhetorical Structure Theory: A Theory of Text Organization. Available as *Information Sciences Institute Research Report* 87-190, 4676 Admiralty Way, Marina del Rey, CA 90292-6695.

Matthiessen, C. & S. A. Thompson 1988. The Structure of Discourse and 'Subordination.' *Clause Combining in Grammar and Discourse*, eds. J. Haiman & S. A. Thompson, 275-329. Amsterdam/Philadelphia: John Benjamins.

Quirk, R., S. Greenbaum, G. Leech & J. Svartvik 1985. *A Comprehensive Grammar of the English Language*. London: Longman.

Redeker, G. 1990. Ideational and Pragmatic Markers of Discourse Structure. *Journal of Pragmatics* 14: 367-381.

Schffrin, D. 1987. *Discourse Markers*. Cambridge: CUP.

Stefanowitsch, A. & S. T. Gries 2003. Collostructions: Investigating the Interaction of Words and Constructions. *International Journal of Corpus Linguistics* 8: 209-243.

Thompson, S. A. 1985. Grammar and Written Discourse: Initial vs. Final Purpose Clauses in English. *Text* 5: 55-83.

Thompson, S. A. & A. Mulac. 1991. A Quantitative Perspective on the Grammaticization of Epistemic Parentheticals in English. *Grammaticalization*, eds. E. C. Traugott & B. Heine, 313-339. Amsterdam/Philadelphia: John Benjamins.

Traugott, E. C. 1989. On the Rise of Epistemic Meanings in English: An Example of Subjectification in Semantic Change. *Language* 65: 31-55.

Traugott, E. C. 1995 Subjectification in Grammaticalisation. *Subjectivity and Subjectivization: Linguistics Perspectives*, eds. D. Stein & S. Wright, 31-54. Cambridge: CUP.

Zwicky, A. M. 1985. Clitics and Particles. *Language* 61: 283-305.

13

Talking Fast: The Use of Speech Rate as Iconic Gesture

MARCUS PERLMAN

In the recently popular country song "Our Song," Taylor Swift recalls a memory of talking to her high school boyfriend on the phone. She sings,

> When we're on the phone and you talk *reeeeal slow*,
> because it's late, and your mama don't know.

As Swift sings the phrase "real slow", she performs an interesting effect with her voice. Whereas the other words in these two lines last for an eighth or a sixteenth note, the word "real" is extended for a quarter note. It is, in fact, the only instance in the song in which the second to last word, opposed to the last, is the longest in the line. The listener is given the clear impression that Swift is using her voice to iconically depict the slow temporal quality of the phone conversation.

In another popular country song, Garth Brooks uses the pitch of his voice to create a similar sort of iconic vocal effect when he sings, "I've got friends in *low* places." Prior to "low," the line moves between small intervals: two major seconds and a minor third. However, as he sings the word "low," Brooks pushes the lower end of his vocal range by descending a much larger interval of a major sixth, thus creating an iconic emphasis on the sense of lowness he is expressing. It is also interesting in this example to note the metaphorical extension of the spatial word "low" to the target domain of social class. This metaphor is expressed linguistically and mirrored

Meaning, Form & Body.
Fey Parrill, Vera Tobin, and Mark Turner (eds.).

with the iconic drop in pitch, similar to how people often make metaphorical extensions with gestures (McNeill, 2005).

Casual observation reveals that the use of iconic voice is not isolated to country music, and indeed, seems to be a common occurrence within everyday, ordinary conversation. For example, it is easy to imagine a speaker lengthening vowel duration when describing a movie that was *sooo looong*, or perhaps deepening her voice when describing the movements of a large, lumbering animal. Yet, although scholars occasionally make reference to these phenomena (particularly as they relate to gesture, e.g., Emmorey, 1999; Liddell, 2003; Okrent, 2002), they have been the subject of little empirically study, especially regarding their occurrence within naturalistic discourse. Thus, the present study aimed to document whether people regularly produce iconic vocalizations when they talk, and additionally, to explore how these vocalizations are integrated within an utterance.

Guiding the study, iconic vocal behaviors are understood within a modality-independent framework of gesture, which is established in the first part of this paper (Emmorey, 1999; McNeill, 1992; 2005; Okrent, 2002). Then, after reviewing the limited empirical study on "vocal" gesture, I report findings that show that people frequently vary their speech rate in correspondence with the speed of an event they are describing. These findings are discussed with respect to implications for understanding how people integrate iconic speech rate within their linguistic utterance, as well as the cognitive processes that drive its production during communication. On this second point, I put forward the hypothesis that vocal gestures arise as a physical manifestation of the sensorimotor-based simulations that people enact as they communicate. According to this hypothesis, the voice is not just an arbitrary means to channel symbolic language. To the contrary, it is argued that vocalizations share a fundamental role along with manual gesture in structuring the embodied basis for how people actually understand and think about imagery-grounded concepts as they communicate.

1 Vocal Gesture

The sort of iconic vocal behaviors described above share many essential similarities to manual iconic and metaphoric gesture (Okrent, 2002). To illustrate this point, it is useful to consider them with respect to some of the prototypical properties of gesture as adapted from McNeill (1992, 2005). However, in making this comparison, it is critical at the outset to keep two principles in mind (see also Okrent). First, it is important to note that the properties represent the prototypical gestural end of a continuum, with prototypical linguistic properties on the other end. Thus, we are not looking to make absolute distinctions, but rather, wish to show that iconic vocal phenomena can be aptly treated within this framework and generally exhibit qualities that closely match those of gesture. The second principle to keep in mind is that the set of properties that distinguish gesture from more linguistic forms of communication are, in theory, wholly independent of modality. Just as language can manifest in sign, gesture can manifest in vocalizations.

McNeill (1992: 12) demonstrates the properties of gesture with the following example of a man describing a scene from a comic book story in which a character bends a tree back to the ground. The speaker describes the event:

> And he *bends it way back*

As he utters the words "bends it way back," the speaker gestures by using his right hand to demonstrate grabbing the tree, and then pulling his hand back, from high and in front of his body to back and down near his shoulder.

According to McNeill, one way gestures are distinguished from linguistic elements is by their structural form and their relation to other gestures. This is exhibited by three basic properties. Gestures are global, meaning that their form is primarily interpreted as a whole, rather than as a combination of morphological parts. In the example above, the parts of the gesture—for instance, the grab and the pull-back—are only interpretable after understanding the gesture's full form. In contrast, the linguistic meaning of the event requires the combination of morphological elements. Gestures are also synthetic—a single gesture can convey many meanings. The single gesture above expresses a meaning for which language uses four words to express. And finally, gestures are noncombinatoric and thus cannot be combined together to create a larger hierarchical meaning. Whereas the words above combine into a verb phrase, the parts of the gesture do not comprise any such organizational structure.

A second way gestures are distinguished from linguistic communication relates to how they express meaning. Unlike linguistic elements, gestures are not conventionalized and have no standards of form. Instead they are expressive by their iconic formal similarity to their referent. In our example, for instance, the speaker's gesture appears to imitate the act of bending the tree back. Related to this point, gestures exhibit meaningful gradience in their form. The speaker could have made subtle changes to the meaning of his gesture by making the movement the other way across his body, or faster, or at a sharper angle, etc.

A final defining set of properties has to do with gesture's relationship to speech. Gestures tend to be semantically coexpressive with speech and depend on context to be meaningful. Without the context of words, one would be hard-pressed to make sense of the speaker's bending-back gesture. McNeill also observes that the semantically coexpressive elements of gesture and speech tend to be synchronous in time; the bending-back gesture above was produced just as the speaker articulated the semantically-related words "bends it way back."

Together these modality-independent qualities characterize prototypical gesture. Now, for comparison, let us consider an example of the iconic use of speech rate. The following utterance was spoken to a person in an adjacent room to explain the source of a loud bang—a sound caused by a screen door blowing open by the wind and then slamming shut after the drop in pressure.

> The door did that thing where it *openns reeeally sloowly and then slamsshut*.

In this example, the speaker first slows and then increases his rate of speech to depict a change in the speed contour of the door-slamming event. The first verb phrase "opens really slowly" is stretched in duration to depict the slow manner in which the screen door was blown open. In contrast, the subsequent verb phrase "slams shut" is contracted to depict the high velocity with which the door slammed close, causing the bang that was heard in the next room.

So how does this use of speech rate measure up against the first set of form-related gestural characteristics? It appears to be global in that its meaning comes from tracing the holistic time contour of the event and is not built from any combination of parts. It is also synthetic—the single speech rate contour conveys multiple meanings including manners of movement and degrees of speed, whereas the linguistic message requires several morphological elements to express this information. Third, it is noncombinatorial, lacking any kind of hierarchical organizational structure.

With respect to how it expresses meaning, this use of speech rate also exhibits qualitative similarities to gesture. It is relatively unconventional, without any apparent regularities in use or form (but see Okrent, 2002), and it is also iconic and gradient. Meaning is conveyed by a graded contrast in speech rate and correspondence with the temporal contour of the described event, and not by categorical interpretations of 'slow' and 'fast'.

Lastly, this use of iconic speech rate is clearly semantically coexpressive and temporally synchronous with speech, and furthermore depends on the context of the speech to be meaningful. The speech rate modulations occur precisely as the speaker is describing each related component in the temporal sequence of the event, and would not be interpretable without the synchronous speech to contextualize them.

Because of these essential similarities to McNeill's notion of gesture, in the remainder of this paper, I refer to iconic vocal phenomena such as those described above, without qualification, as a fully fledged form of gesture.

1.1 Empirical Study of Vocal Gesture

While scholars occasionally make reference to vocal gesture as exemplifying the principle of modality independence when considering the status of gestural versus linguistic communication (E.g., Emmorey, 1999; Liddell, 2003; and see Okrent, 2002 for more detailed treatment), actual direct empirical investigation has been limited and amounts to only a handful of studies by Shintel and colleagues.

In the first of these studies, Shintel, Nusbaum, and Okrent (2006) investigated the use of speech rate and pitch to express information about speed and verticality. In one experiment, participants watched an animated dot move either left or right at different speeds across a computer screen, and were instructed to use the sentences *It is going left* or *It is going right* to describe its motion. It was found that the mean utterance duration was significantly shorter for fast animations than for slow animations. Moreover, when these utterances were replayed for listeners, it was found that listeners, presumably using information conveyed by speech rate, were significantly better than chance at guessing whether the speaker had watched a fast or slow animation.

In a second complementary experiment, Shintel and colleagues looked at whether people use fundamental pitch to convey information about verticality. Participants watched an animated dot move up or down and were instructed to describe its direction by saying *It is going up* or *It is going down*. The findings revealed that people used a higher fundamental frequency for upward compared to downward-moving dots. According to Shintel and colleagues, these results provide evidence for what they call "analog acoustic expressions", an analog prosodic feature of speech that communicates propositional information about external referents.

Two additional comprehension studies focused specifically on how the speech rate phenomenon is understood by listeners. In the first, participants listened to sentences spoken at varying speaking rates followed by a visually presented picture of an object, and had to make speeded judgments of whether the pictured object had been mentioned in the sentence (Shintel & Nusbaum, 2007). The critical manipulation was whether the mentioned pictures were in motion or at rest. For example, a participant might hear the sentence "The horse is brown" followed, in the matching condition, by a picture of a brown horse that was either running or standing still. Shintel and Nusbaum found that participants were faster to verify that the pictured object had been in the sentence when the motion implied by the picture matched the spoken rate of the sentence—a fast rate with a moving horse, a slow rate with a stationary horse, for instance. Based on this observation, the authors conclude that people integrate speech rate information into an online perceptually-based simulation that constitutes the meaning of the sentence.

In a second follow-up study, Shintel and Nusbaum (2008) looked at whether speech rate influences listeners independently of context, or alternatively, whether the effect occurs most strongly when it is contextually relevant. Participants read short scenarios ending either with or without an implication of urgency, and after each, they heard a recorded instruction to press a key, spoken at a fast or slow rate. The results showed that participants were faster to respond to the fast key press instruction specifically after having read the scenarios implying urgency. The finding suggests that speech rate influences listeners not through some automatic cross-modal speed-matching process, but instead functions like other communicative aspects of prosody, such as those related to syntax or discourse.

2 Study

Though interesting, it is unclear how the work of Shintel and colleagues relates to the use of vocal gesture within natural discourse, as is the focus of many manual gesture studies. Thus the present study aimed to systematically document and analyze the use of vocal gesture within a relatively unconstrained speech production task. The goal was first to see whether people would regularly produce vocal gestures within natural discourse, and second, to gain some understanding of how these gestures are integrated with the spoken language of an utterance. Participants watched video clips of various fast or slow-paced events and described them to an experimenter. The descriptions were recorded and later analyzed for the occurrence of speech rate effects that matched the speed of the described event. It was predicted that people would talk fast—i.e., increase their speech rate—when describing the fast events, and talk slow when describing the slow ones. More specifically, it was predicted that iconic speech rate would function like manual gesture with respect to how it is integrated semantically and temporally within an utterance. Since manual gestures tend to be semantically linked to concurrent speech, vocal speech rate gestures ought to function the same way. Based on this reasoning, speech rate gestures related to the speed of an event were predicted to cooccur with spoken linguistic expressions of speed, such as during the production of speed-related adverbial phrases.

2.1 Method

2.1.1 Participants

45 University of California, Santa Cruz undergraduates participated in the study in exchange for course credit. (However, as will be described below, data was used only from those 25 participants who made explicit mention of speed in their descriptions.) They were all native speakers of English.

2.2.2 Materials

The video stimuli consisted of trimmed video clips selected from the website http://www.youtube.com. Ten event themes were chosen (including *dog running*, *man juggling*, *couple dancing*, *girl bouncing on a ball, robot walking, man smoking, fish swimming, man eating, car driving, and man/woman boxing*), and videos were selected in pairs, with one item of the pair showing a fast version of the theme, and the other item a slow version. For example, in one fast video, a greyhound was shown racing around the beach with a ball in its mouth, whereas in the corresponding slow video, a large, shaggy dog was shown clumsily trotting along the beach. The clips were each edited to be within 10 to15 seconds in length, and then combined together into a single long movie of all 20 clips. Between each clip, 15 seconds of black screen was inserted to provide time for participants to describe the previous clip. The video clips were combined together into one of four counterbalanced orders, which were presented in equal proportions to participants. Videos of the same event theme were spaced maximally apart and the clips alternated in speed through the movie. (Despite the alternation between fast and slow videos, participants were generally unaware that speed was a factor of the study. This was indicated in postexperiment interviews, as well as evidenced by the fact that only about 20% of participants' descriptions made explicit mention to speed.) All four movies began first with two practice clips.

2.2.3 Procedure

Participants were seated by an experimenter at a table in front of a 16" laptop computer on which they watched the movie. They were told that they would watch and describe a series of video clips. To make the interaction more purposeful and natural, the experimenter explained that she had her own task to do, which was to check off each video from a list as it was described by the participant. The experimenter said that she was unfamiliar with the videos and would check off each video based on the participant's description.

After seating the participant, the experimenter sat down across the table a few feet away and gave spoken instructions. Seating position was selected so that the participant could easily make eye contact and talk to the experimenter without being obstructed by the computer screen. When the participant verified that she understood the task, she was told to click on the play symbol with the mouse, and the movie began (the movies were played with Windows Media Player). Throughout the movie, the experimenter acted out her end of the task, actively listening and, after each description, checking off an item from her list. The descriptions were recorded with a flat table microphone which was connected to a digital recorder and placed inconspicuously on the table about two feet in front of the participant.

2.2 Analysis and Results

Below are some representative descriptions produced by participants during the task. As will be described, analysis focused only on descriptions making explicit reference to speed, and so this is reflected in the examples:

> Umm some guy hitting a punching bag like really fast. Like it looks like in a boxing gym or something.

> This clip showed a fish, in what I can only assume to be like the natural environment not an aquarium, and it was swimming very slowly, and it was it wasn't a tropical fish like before it was- I don't know how to describe it.

> Uhh, someone was sitting at a table and there was some type of robot slowly walking across, but you couldn't see the person's face.

> Someone driving very fast in a suburban area taking a left turn, and then driving down a side street until making a stop.

The quantitative analysis consisted of two primary comparisons: A comparison between the overall spoken rate of descriptions for fast versus slow videos (measured in syllables per second), and a more specific analysis comparing the spoken rate of speed adverbial phrases (measured more precisely in phones per second). As discussed above, this second speed adverbial analysis was motivated by previous empirical findings that gestures tend to be semantically and temporally coexpressive with speech (McNeill, 1992; 2005).

All speech rate measurements, including the determination of speech onset and offset boundaries and the durations between them, were made using Praat phonetic analysis software. Statistical tests in both analyses consisted of within-subject paired t-tests comparing speech rates between the fast and slow video conditions.

2.2.1 Overall Description Rates

Analysis of overall description rates was conducted only on descriptions which made explicit mention of speed, thus assuring that speed was a salient aspect of how the participant perceived the event. Additionally, since the analysis was within-subject, only the descriptions from participants who referred to speed in both the fast and slow conditions could be used. This resulted in data from 25 participants, a total of 142 descriptions, 75 for fast videos and 67 for slow. Each participant produced a mean of 3.00 fast descriptions and 2.68 slow descriptions, with standard deviations of 1.58 and 1.68 respectively. All 20 video clips were represented in the descriptions.

Speech rates were measured in syllables per second. Utterance duration was calculated from the onset of any vocalization related to the description until the point of silence when the participant was finished. Mean description length was 7.83 seconds with a standard deviation of 2.58, with no difference in utterance duration between conditions. Syllables were counted based on written transcriptions of the descriptions.

Analysis showed that descriptions of fast events were spoken at a faster rate than descriptions of slow events, with means of 4.26 syl/sec and 3.91 syl/sec and standard deviations of 0.92 and 0.62, respectively. A paired t-test showed this to be a significant difference ($t(24) = 2.27$, $p = 0.033$).

2.2.2 Speed Adverbial Rates

This analysis focused on adverbial phrases which made reference to speed following the verb. Thus the analysis included adverbials in utterances like "He was throwing punches at a bag *really fast*" or "This was a black dog just kind of running *slowly* around on the beach." Comparatives such as "faster" or "more slowly" were not included. Again, within-subject analysis required that participants produce speed adverbials in both conditions for their data to be included. This resulted in data from 18 participants and a total of 94 descriptions, with 58 for fast videos and 36 for slow. Individual participants produced a mean of 3.21 fast adverbials and 2.05 slow adverbials with standard deviations of 1.51 and 1.13. Again, all 20 video clips were represented in the descriptions.

Because adverbial phrases generally consisted of only a few syllables, a more precise measurement of phones per second was used. So, for example, the phrase "super fast" was counted as 9 phones. In addition, to compensate for the high frequency with which participants produced the root word "slow" and its relatively long open syllable, the /o/ in these cases was counted as 1.5 phones. Thus, the phrase "really slowly" would be counted as containing 10.5 phones. Adverbial phrase boundaries were determined using phonetic cues such as the onset and offset of voicing, frication, and formant transitions.

The analysis found that fast adverbials were spoken significantly faster than slow adverbials, with means of 12.86 phones/sec and 10.54 phones/sec and standard deviations of 2.48 and 2.10, respectively (paired t-test, $t(17) = 3.19, p < 0.01$).

3 Discussion

The first goal of the study was to gain a general sense of how frequently people would produce vocal gestures when describing the fast and slow events shown in the videos. Specifically, how often would people increase or decrease their rate of speech when describing fast versus slow events? The second goal was to investigate more closely *how* people manipulate their speech rate to gesture about speed. For example, how are vocal gestures integrated within the spoken language of an utterance? Two relevant findings were made. First, people appear to modulate their overall rate of speech in correspondence with video speed throughout a particular description. Second, they also specifically alter the spoken rate of adverbial phrases used to describe the speed of an event, such as when they say "real slow" or "very quickly".

To interpret these two findings, it is first necessary to consider whether the difference in overall description rate is driven by the difference in adverbial rate, or whether they are two separate effects. Given the relatively short duration of the speed adverbial phrases in comparison to the overall duration of the full descriptions, it is unlikely that this second effect is the basis for the first. (The adverbial effect size amounts to roughly 0.15 seconds in comparison to a mean utterance duration of 7.83 seconds.) Thus, it appears that people are producing two different forms of speech rate gestures throughout their descriptions.

A second important question is whether these differences in speech rate between fast and slow descriptions are large enough to be communicatively meaningful. A useful starting point is to consider the just noticeable difference in speech tempo, estimated at 5% (Quené, 2007). In comparison, the effect sizes found in this study were 8.6% for overall utterance rate and

20.0% for speed adverbial rate—differences that certainly exceed the minimum criteria to be perceptually noticeable.

3.1 The Coordination of Vocal Gesture with Speech

In principle, as described above, gesture is characterized by a set of qualities that are independent of modality (McNeill, 1992; 2005; Okrent, 2002), and indeed we have seen that people appear to gesture quite naturally vocally. Yet clearly, there exist certain physical constraints when coordinating vocal gestures with speech that do not apply to the coordination of manual gestures. With manual gesture, the hands are free to function independently as the vocal apparatus articulates speech. Thus, though a gesture is constrained by the conceptualizing processes shared with linguistic communication, it is physically unfettered. In contrast, vocal gestures must be coordinated with and actually physically integrated with the articulatory movements involved in producing the linguistic stream of speech. How does this integration happen?

The finding in this study that people produce two different forms of speech rate gestures offers some initial ground for understanding this integration process. In one case, people modulate their speech rate through a relatively general and wide portion of their utterance. They appear to demonstrate the overall pace of the event with their rate of speech, more-or-less independently of the detailed semantics being directly expressed concurrently in the linguistic signal. In comparison, the second effect consists of a more specific change in the spoken rate of semantically-related speed adverbials. Here the gesture and linguistic semantics are tightly integrated together as the expression of speed is simultaneously expressed through both gesture and language.

Questions relating to more specific details of how vocal gestures take form and are integrated with speech remain to be addressed. One such question concerns which specific phonetic segments are subject to lengthening or shortening. Informal investigation of the "really" speed adverbial constructions produced in this study (e.g., "really quickly", "really slowly", etc.) reveals this to be quite variable. In some instances there was extension or contraction on the vowel of "really" without any apparent change to the speed adverb. In other instances the effect was on the speed adverb with little effect on "really." This was demonstrated in one case by a speaker describing a girl bouncing slowly on Yoga ball:

> There's another girl bouncing on a ball but really *sssslooowly*…

Interestingly, in this utterance, the word “slowly” is extended both across the initial frication of the /s/ as well as across the vowel. In fact, this sort of idiosyncratic variability is exactly in line with the characteristics of gesture described by McNeill. Yet, here we also see evidence of the physical constraints on coordination as a consequence of shared expression through a single modality. A particular vocal gesture is, by necessity, formally constrained as it is incorporated with the phonetic segments of the utterance.

Particularly with respect to the speed adverbial effect, we might also ask whether vocal gestures are marked in any special way, such as with a pause or a quotation device such as “like”, to indicate a transition in communicative style (cf. Clark & Gerrig, 1990). For at least some of the data from this study, this appears to be the case. Consider the following description of a man eating a cheeseburger at a fast food restaurant.

> This one’s a guy at McDonalds. He’s eating a cheeseburger, like, *reallyfast*. He just like downs the whole thing.

After the first “like” the speaker leaves a short pause before saliently speaking the phrase “really fast” at an increased rate. In a description by a different speaker, only pauses were used:

> This one’s like a man playing fetch with his dog on the beach and the dog is running around, *superfast,* with a red ball in its mouth.

Here the short pauses separating the speed adverbial phrase appear to mark the vocal gesture.

We may also gain insight from researchers of sign language, who have noted an analogous coordination problem for signers. For example, Emmorey (1999) observes that, as signers’ hands are involved in producing a linguistic utterance, there are constraints on bimanual coordination and motor resources that prevent signing on one hand while gesturing with the other. According to Emmorey, one way that signers gesture within these constraints is by alternating sign and gesture, using what Clark (1996) refers to as component gestures. In this process, a signer might temporarily break from signing, then gesture, and then continue back to signing, with the gestural meaning incorporated into the utterance. (Clark and Gerrig (1990) also offer examples of this sort of alternation between speech and manual gesture.) Though strictly speaking, component gestures, due to their independence from concurrent language, fall towards the linguistic end of the gesture-language continuum, it is nevertheless worthwhile to consider these model cases of how same-modality constraints are worked out during communication. It is interesting to note, for example, the similarities between the use of component gestures and the phenomenon described above in which the speaker uses pauses to mark vocal gestures within speech.

It is additionally interesting to observe that sign languages commonly integrate communication with more gesture-like properties into the linguistic signing system, such as with the use of classifier constructions of American Sign Language (Emmorey & Herzig, 2003; Liddell, 2003). In these constructions, handshape takes on the categorical, conventional form associated with a linguistic morpheme, yet location within signing space is gradient like gesture. A similar mixed system dictates the use of pronouns in ASL: Morphological handshape distinguishes case, orientation distinguishes person, and movement distinguishes number, yet these signs exhibit gradience in how they are directed towards their referent within signing space. A spoken parallel may be seen in the combination of a morphological word form with gradient gesture-like qualities manifesting in the prosody with which it is articulated.

Finally, a last question that remains to be examined is how vocal gestures, in addition to coordination with speech, are also executed in multimodal coordination with manual and other bodily gestures. One might predict, for example, that as imagistic aspects of a message are sufficiently activated to manifest as vocal gestures within speech, they are also likely to manifest in manual gestural movements. Thus, in the case of iconic speech rate, we might expect to observe faster and slower manual gestures in synchrony with speech rate modulations as the speaker describes the speed of an event. Furthermore, extending this point to an experimental perspective, relevant manual gestures may even be useful to predict when vocal gestures are likely to occur, thereby increasing the power of studies to identify and describe vocal gestures within natural discourse.

3.2 Vocal Gesture as Embodied Simulation

In this final section of discussion, I present a hypothesis for the underlying cognitive process that leads people to produce iconic speech rate gestures as they describe various fast and slow paced events. This point is particularly interesting because, for the most part, the vocal gestures do not seem to be produced with any special deliberateness. They are not, for instance, a product of elaborate vocal pantomimes or part of a purposefully crafted chorus to a Garth Brooks song. On the contrary, they seem most often to manifest as an ordinary part of the process of talking. Just as people are not aware of the extent to which they use their hands to iconically depict the subject of their speech, they seem similarly unaware that they also iconically represent their subject matter with the pattern of their voice.

My proposal is that vocal gesture arises so naturally as a part of spoken communication because it is a physical consequence of how people conceptualize action and other bodily-based domains as they communicate. A growing collection of experimental evidence shows that people make sense of language through the enactment of embodied, sensorimotor-based simulations created during online language processing (Glenberg & Kaschak, 2002; Stanfield & Zwaan, 2001), including metaphoric language (Bergen, 2005; Gibbs, 2006). Building on this, a recent hypothesis suggests that these sorts of sensorimotor simulations also provide the mechanism that leads to the production of representative manual gesture (Hostetter & Alibali, 2008). In their Gesture as Simulated Action framework, Hostetter and Alibali hypothesize that simulations of action-related thoughts lead to activation of neural premotor action states, which then has the potential to spread to motor areas. This spreading activation is realized as the overt action of gesture.

Hostetter and Alibali's exclusive focus on simulated *action* as the basis for representative gesture is questionable, and gesture scholars such as McNeill argue more broadly that sensorimotor imagery, including but not limited to action, forms the semantic basis of gesture. Still, it might be maintained that people activate cortical areas related to bodily movements and postures as part of the process of conceptualizing and communicating about a wide range of imagery-laden domains. Importantly, the findings from this study suggest that the embodied simulations enacted during communication additionally spread to motor areas related to vocalizing. Thus, given the characteristic iconicity of vocal gesture, it follows that the semantics of gestural communication—that is, how we use our bodies to understand and represent actions in the external world--is in part based on actions of the vocal tract, in addition to the hands.

With the simulation hypothesis in mind, we return again to the two forms of vocal gesture reported in this study. First, recall the finding that people specifically alter their speech rate as they articulate adverbial phrases about the speed of the event. As discussed above, in this case vocal gesture functions similarly to prototypical examples of manual gesture, occurring in semantic and temporal synchrony with concurrent speech. The gesture emerges precisely as the speaker is conceptualizing and communicating about speed as the profiled aspect of the message. In terms of a gesture as embodied simulation framework, the speed-related simulation processes that drive linguistic production of the adverbial phrase simultaneously lead to iconic vocal expression of speed manifesting in the speaker's speech rate.

In contrast, consider the other form of vocal gesture that was found, which differs from the previous more prototypical case. This form consists of a more general increase in speech rate throughout a wider description of the event—an overall shift in the rate at which the description is spoken. In this case, while speed is not actively profiled in language production, it appears that the speaker is more generally engaged with the pace of the action as she proceeds through her description. It may be argued, in this instance, that the speaker's speech rate reflects a backgrounded simulation of the event, as she scans and profiles specific details to highlight with linguistic communication (cf. Langacker, 1990). Though the speaker's attention is not focused enough to produce particular speed-related linguistic constructions and gestures, it is sufficient to more generally influence the overall rate of speech. Thus the wider modulation of speech rate might be considered as a vocal manifestation of simulated background.

4 Conclusion

It is fairly obvious that people occasionally use their voice for iconic communication, as demonstrated, for instance, by the introductory examples taken from popular country music. Yet, despite its commonplace appearance, there has been only limited empirical study directed towards understanding how vocal gesture functions within speech and especially within more natural discourse. In this paper, I have shown that such study is critical to our understanding of the relationship between speech, gesture, and language, and for informing theories of how the body and sensorimotor system contribute to cognitive processes related to conceptualization and communication. The preliminary findings reported here on the use of speech rate suggest that people, as with manual gesture, very naturally produce iconic vocalizations as they talk about imagery-grounded domains such as speed. In his seminal book *Hand and Mind,* David McNeill writes that "Gestures are like thoughts themselves" (1992: 12). Thus, it appears then that just as thoughts are rendered visible by the hands, they are also rendered audible by the voice.

Author Note

Marcus Perlman, Department of Psychology, University of California, Santa Cruz.

Many thanks to David Garner for contributing his musical expertise. I am also grateful to Ray Gibbs, Marlene Johansson Falk, and two anonymous reviewers for their helpful comments on previous drafts of this paper. And finally, Natalie Benitez deserves special mention for her tireless enthusiasm as she listened intently to the same video clip descriptions, over and over and over…

References

Bergen, B. 2005. Mental simulation in literal and figurative language understanding. *The Literal and Nonliteral in Language and Thought*. Eds. S. Coulson & B. Lewandowska-Tomaszczyk. 255-280. Berlin: Lang.

Clark, H. 1996. *Using Language*. Cambridge University Press.

Clark, H. & Gerrig, R. 1990. Quotations as demonstrations. *Language 66: 764-805*.

Gibbs, R. W. Jr. 2006. Metaphor interpretation as embodied simulation. *Mind & Language 21: 434-458*.

Glenberg, A. & Kaschak, M. 2002. Grounding Language in Action. *Psychonomic Bulletin & Rewview 9:* 558-565.

Emmorey, K. 1999. Do Signers Gesture? *Gesture, Speech, and Sign,* eds. L. Messing & R. Cambell. 133-159. New York: Oxford University Press.

Emmorey, K. & Herzig, M. 2003. Categorical Versus Gradient Properties of Classifier Constructions in ASL. *Perspectives on Classifier Constructions in Sign Languages,* ed. K. Emmorey. 221-246. Mahwah, NJ: Lawrence Erlbaum Associates.

Hostetter, A. B. & Alibali, M. W. 2008. Visible Embodiment: Gestures as Simulated Action. *Psychonomic Bulletin and Review 15: 495-514*.

Kendon, A. 1988. How gestures can become like words. *Cross-Cultural Perspectives in Nonverbal Communication*. Ed. F. Poyatos, 131-141. Toronto: Hogrefe.

Langacker, R. W. 1990. *Concept, Image, and Symbol: The Cognitive Basis of Grammar*. Berlin/New York: Mouton de Gruyter.

Liddell, S. K. 2003. *Grammar, Gesture, and Meaning in American Sign Language*. Cambridge: Cambridge University Press.

McNeill, D. 1992. *Hand and Mind: What Gestures Reveal about Thought*. Chicago: University of Chicago Press.

McNeill, D. 2005. *Gesture and Thought*. Chicago: University of Chicago Press.

Okrent, A. 2002. A Modality-Free Notion of Gesture and How It Can Help Us with the Morpheme Vs. Gesture Question in Sign Language Linguistics. *Modality and Structure in Signed and Spoken Language,* eds. R. P. Meier, K. Kormier, & D. Quinto-Pozos. 175-198. Cambridge: Cambridge University Press.

Quené, H. 2007. On the Just Noticeable Difference for Tempo in Speech. *Journal of Phonetics 35: 353-362*.

Shintel, H. & Nusbaum, H. C. 2007. The Sound of Motion in Spoken Language: Visual Information Conveyed by Acoustic Properties of Speech. *Cognition 105: 681-690*.

Shintel, H. & Nusbaum, H. C. 2008. Moving to the Speed of Sound: Context Modulation of the Effect of Acoustic Properties of Speech. *Cognitive Science 32: 1063-1074*.

Shintel, H., Nusbaum, H. C., & Okrent, A. 2006. Analog Acoustic Expression in Speech Communication. *Journal of Memory and Language 55: 167-177*.

Stanfield, R. A. & Zwaan, R. A. 2001. The Effect of Implied Orientation Derived from Verbal Context on Picture Recognition. *Psychological Science 12:* 153-156.

14

Werewolves in Epaulettes

ANNA PLESHAKOVA

This article presents a case study of the novel Russian metaphor *oborotni v pogonakh* (werewolves in epaulettes). The metaphor is analyzed using conceptual integration (Fauconnier and Turner, 2002) as a general model of cognitive framing with frame-blending (Turner, 2008), conceptual blending in discourse analysis (Oakley, 1998), and the 'rethinking of metaphor' (Fauconnier and Turner, 2008) forming the core research method. The approach to metaphor analysis in the case study will include the consideration of permanent features of cognition: integration networks, cobbling and sculpting, emergent structure, compression, and overarching goals other than projection of inference (Fauconnier and Turner, 2008). The study of this metaphor will be also based on the principles of conceptual blending in discourse analysis, central to which is "explaining how and why each linguistic cue prompts a certain kind of construction" (Oakley, 1998: 322; Coulson, 2001 and 2006; Lukes, 2007).

The central argument of this article is that conceptual integration can be successfully employed for the analysis of cognition and culture in their interrelation. The case study will provide an illustration of the utility of conceptual blending as a tool for cultural analysis through the construction of the multi-scope network 'werewolves in epaulettes'.

This particular metaphor is especially interesting for analysis within the conceptual integration framework for two reasons. First, this metaphoric structure emerged not long ago to reflect important aspects of the construction of post-Soviet Russian identity. Second, this metaphor is culturally specific. Initial research suggests that despite the individual presence of the concepts relevant for the construction of this metaphoric network, in other

Meaning, Form & Body.
Fey Parrill, Vera Tobin, and Mark Turner (eds.).

cultures there is no blending of these to produce an emergent structure and the linguistic realization equivalent to the metaphor 'werewolves in epaulettes'.

The blending analysis reveals the complexity of integrations underlying this metaphorical structure. The analysis of the respective conceptual integration network elucidates the metaphor's cultural specificity, its rhetorical capacity, its potential in motivating secondary metaphoric structures, the relation of metaphor to past cultural and ideological traditions, and the ideological implications of its usage in the contemporary Russian mass-media discourse. The conceptual blending analysis makes it evident that this metaphoric network becomes a new Russian national construal of the post-Soviet mythologized concept of enemy.

The study of this culturally-specific and highly creative metaphoric structure reveals the significance of accounting for both permanent features of cognition and metaphor's cultural and discourse history in the construction of metaphoric integration networks. The cultural specificity of input spaces and cultural models' motivational and 'adaptation' capacity have a crucial influence on the cross-space mappings and projections in the network. The case study will demonstrate that in the construction of such conceptual integration networks as 'werewolves in epaulettes', the overarching goal 'Achieve Human Scale' is complemented by a noteworthy sub goal 'Achieve Cultural Scale'.

1 Case Study

1.1 Material

The construction of the conceptual integration network behind the metaphor 'werewolves in epaulettes' is based on the analysis of Russian mass-media texts about 'werewolves' selected from: 1) Russian National Corpus 611 texts, including 1065 contexts for *oboroten'* (werewolf), 202 contexts for *vrag naroda* (people's enemy), 116 contexts for *vreditel'* (saboteur), and 8 contexts for *ubijcy v belykh khalatakh* (murderers in white gowns); 2) the online archive of the Russian national newspaper '*Kommersant*' for the period dating 2000-2008 (105 texts); on the text corpus[1] incorporating Russian news texts about local events for the period of 1994-1998 (180 texts); as well as the analysis of Russian mythological and literary texts and films,

[1] Created by Pleshakova A. for her doctoral research in 1994-1998

both conducted by the author of this article and taken from various books and articles in the fields of cultural studies and social sciences.

1.2 Werewolves in Epaulettes: Integration network

During the last eight years the Russian mass-media has offered its spectators and readers stories about corrupt officers of law enforcement agencies initiating events which have negative consequences for individuals and society. Such officers have often been named in these texts as *oborotni v pogonakh* (werewolves in epaulettes).

Let us consider the following examples.

[1] *Otdel'nye oborotni v pogonakh sdelali chechentsev istochnikom svoego vnebiudzhetnogo finansirovaniia. ... Dlia oborotnej glavnoe – podbrasyvanie narkotikov, potom vymogatel'stvo deneg. (Duma o Chechne // "Zhizn' natsional'nostej", 2001)* 'Individual werewolves in epaulettes have made Chechen people a source of their (werewolves' - AP)' off-budget funding. ... The main thing for werewolves is the planting of drugs, and then the extortion of money' (Duma about Chechnya)

[2] *Kak mogli militsionery, liudi, kotorye obiazany sledit' za sobliudeniem zakona, prevratit'sia v "oborotnej", to est' stat' prestupnikami? (Oborotni //Argumenty i fakty, 2001.03.07)* 'How could policemen, people, whose duty is to maintain law and order, turn into "werewolves", i.e. become criminals?' (Werewolves)

[3] *Vsiudu ved'my, kolduny i oborotni, i poka ne istrebim ikh – ne budet chelovechestvu pokoia. (Anatolij Kucherena[2]. Bal bezzakonia, 1999).* Everywhere there are witches, sorcerers and werewolves, and until we eliminate them – humankind will not get any peace.' (The ball of infinite lawlessness)

[4] *Pervonachal'naia informatsiia, vydannaia zhurnalistam nakanune i v khode operatsii s sovetskim nazvaniem "Oborotni", navodit na mysli ob usechennoj versii znamenitoj ital'ianskoj operatsii "Chistye ruki"" (Siloviki-zatejniki//"Novaja gazeta", 2003.01.02).* 'The preliminary information, released to journalists on the eve of and during the operation bearing the Soviet title 'Werewolves', prompts thought about a truncated version of the famous Italian operation "Clean Hands" (Officers of law enforcement agencies-entertainers)'.

[5] *"Edinaia Rossiia" sdelaet vse, chtob k wyboram ne ostalos oborotnej, vampirov, goblinov, orkov, kriugerov, ved'm i bab iag. (O khoroshem //Moskovskij Komsomolets, 2003.01.15)* '"United Russia" will do everything in order to eliminate all werewolves, vampires, goblins, orcs, krugers, witches and bab iagas (evil characters of Russian fairy-tales) by the time of election'.

---

[2] Russian lawyer and the Chairman of the Public Chamber Committee for controlling the activities of the law enforcement structures

These examples, as well as many others from the post-Soviet mass-media discourse and the emergent structures behind them, exploit the same systematic and elaborate conceptual integration network 'werewolves in epaulettes'. This metaphoric network involves mappings and bindings between many spaces, compression and the complex emergent structure in the blend. Let us start by considering the inputs and some vital relations central to the integration network.

Example 2 shows that one input space gets its structure from law and order: 'policemen, people, whose duty is to maintain law and order'. Example 1 provides the textual evidence that the second input is the event of a crime: 'the planting of drugs, and then the extortion of money'. There is also the input of corruption in this network: the operation 'Werewolves' - a truncated version of the famous Italian operation "Clean Hands" (Example 4). This sentence prompts the activation of a frame of corruption as an 'alien/other' cultural model. More simply, people know what corruption and the fight against it are about, but mainly understand them to be something of foreign origin and vital to people living in other countries. And yet they also need to be defined in relation to Russian socio-cultural reality and adapted to it through the construction of 'werewolves in epaulettes' as well as related conceptual networks. All our examples demonstrate that the fourth input space has the mythological creature of werewolf and potentially other mythological creatures (Example 3 and 5). Examples 4 and 5 indicate the network's other input spaces: one of the Soviet ideological 'werewolf' 'the Soviet title Werewolves', and the other of Russian political life (P) 'United Russia', 'the time of election'.

In the network configuration, shown in Figure 1, these input spaces are called M (mythological werewolf), S (Soviet werewolf), E (event of crime), C (corruption), L.O (law and order) and P (political life). The dashed lines indicate cross-space mappings between the spaces and the solid lines stand for selective projection to the blend and the mappings to the generic spaces (B).

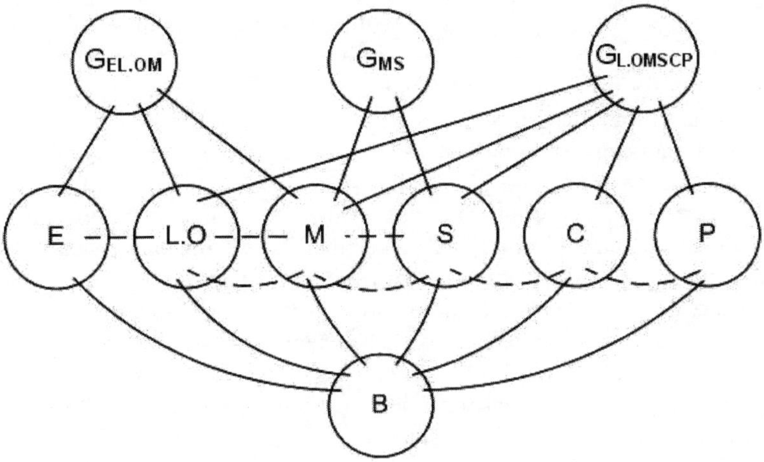

Figure 1 Werewolves in Epaulettes Network

In the cross-space mapping, the policemen are the counterparts of criminals and werewolves (Examples 2 and 3); and humankind, the Chechen people are the counterparts of victims of crime (Examples 1 and 3). They are mapped by *ANALOGY/DISANALOGY* and *ROLE-VALUE* outer-space relations. There is an *ANALOGY + VALUE* connector between policemen and criminals (the same people who act in accordance with different roles). At the same time these elements are disanalogous because of the *ROLE* the *VALUE* is attached to in each input. There are also analogical relations between these elements and the mythological werewolf and the Soviet werewolf. They are analogous in many respects and disanalogous in others. All of them metamorphose on a regular basis which results in leading a double-life but such metamorphosis has different natures and different physical and moral manifestations. *ANALOGY/DISANALOGY* and *ROLE-VALUE* relations compress into *IDENTITY + CHANGE* and further into *UNIQUENESS* in the blend. *ANALOGY/DISANALOGY* and *ROLE-VALUE* relations also compress into *REPRESENTATION* and further into *UNIQUENESS*. In the blend, there are the body projected from the 'mythological werewolves' input (that represents a number of characteristics of the mythological werewolf) and the officer's uniform projected from the law and order input (that represents the officer). There is also a *PART-WHOLE* relation which compresses into *UNIQUENESS*. In the blend, werewolves wear only epaulettes. *ANALOGY/DISANALOGY* is combined here with *CAUSE-EFFECT* vital relations. The causal chain in the mythological werewolf input is mapped into the causal chain in the crime input and into the causal chain in the Soviet werewolf-enemy input. A physical and magical action of metamorphosis involving a change in the appearance of a person – transformation into an animal or an object - is mapped into a physical/social/criminal action involving a change in a person's social role. Both magical and social/criminal actions involve a change in a person's state of mind and behaviour.

In the blend, the criminal action of the officer is blended with the mythological metamorphosis, thus fusing the cause from one space (E) with the counterpart effect from the other (M), linguistically realized in Example 2, where policemen turn into werewolves.

There are cross-space mappings between the mythological werewolves (M), the people's enemy/victim from the Soviet werewolf input (S), corrupt officials (C), an instrument for gaining political credit (needed to win elections) in the political life input space (P) and Italian corrupt officials in (C). The fight with corruption (L.O) is mapped into the 'Clean Hands' operation (C), the political PR in P, and further into the werewolf-hunting (M) and the witch-hunting in the Soviet werewolf/Stalinist repressions scenario (S). In the blended space, the corrupt officers are 'werewolves in epaulettes', who need to be eliminated as criminals-enemies in order to get peace (Example 1 and 3); who need to be eliminated in order to win elections and who become 'operation-werewolves in epaulettes' (Example 4 and 5); and who are victims (people's enemy) of the Kremlin's policies (Example 4 and 5).

The cross-space mappings indicate the existence of at least three generic spaces in this integration network. There are: a generic space with an enemy/metamorphosis scenario common to both the mythological and Soviet werewolves – G:MS; a generic space of 'actor/patient and normal event versus abnormal event plus evaluation' scenario common to the inputs of mythological werewolf, crime, and law and order - G:MEL.O; and a generic space linking ideological instruments from the Soviet epoch and the post-Soviet political life with mythological werewolves and the fight against corruption – the 'witch-hunting' scenario – G:PL.OCMS.

So far, we have established the main input spaces and some vital relations central to the multi-scope conceptual network 'werewolves in epaulettes'. We have observed the activation of the cultural model of Soviet repressions in the network 'werewolves in epaulettes'. We have also seen how the 'other' cultural model of corruption adapts to achieve the successful blend in this metaphoric network. As we continue our analysis in the next sections, we will be considering more examples from the post-Soviet mass-media discourse and Soviet ideological discourse, as well as the cultural and historical motivations behind the metaphor 'werewolves in epaulettes'.

Such consideration will allow us a deeper insight into the integrations of this metaphoric network.

1.3 Infinite Lawlessness and Responsibility

The construction of the post-Soviet concept of 'infinite lawlessness' versus the 'fight against corruption' (Example 3) central to the metaphoric structure 'werewolves in epaulettes' is rooted in the conceptual integration networks underlying the mass-media stories from the late nineties similar to the one we consider below.

> [6] *Pokupaia brillianty, prokurory vmesto deneg prediavili prodavtsu svoi udostoverenia. Starshij pomoschnik i nachl'nik otdela Tul'skoj prokuratury byli zaderzhany sotrudnikami ROOPa po rasporiazheniu prokurora oblasti Anatolia Sedukhina. V nachale 1997 goda rabotniki prokuratury kupili cherez posrednika tri brillianta. V moment sovershenia sdelki oni vmesto deneg dostali svoi udostoverenia vmeste s Ugolovnym kodeksom i, krepko napugav prodavtsa, "iziali" brillianty v svoiu pol'zu. Prodavets reshil poluchit' svoi $5 tys. s posrednika, dlia chego privlek "krutykh rebiat". Zapugannyj imi posrednik obratilsia v ROOP. Vchera prokuroram bylo prediavleno obvinenie v zloupotreblenii sluzhebnym polozheniem.* 'When buying diamonds, Prosecutors show the seller their identification instead of money. The Senior Assistant and the Head of Department of the Tula Region Prosecutor's Office were arrested by members of the Regional Department dealing with Organised Crime (RDOC) following a directive from Anatolij Sedukhin, the Regional Prosecutor. At the beginning of 1997 employees of the Prosecutor's Office bought three diamonds through a mediator. At the moment of purchase, instead of producing the money, they took out their identification along with the Criminal Code and, having thoroughly intimidated the seller, "confiscated" the diamonds for their own benefit. The seller decided to recover his $5,000 from the mediator and hired some thugs to that end. Frightened by them, the mediator turned to RDOC. Yesterday the Prosecutors were charged with abuse of office.'

From the outset, the frame of buy-sell (B.S) is evoked by the name of action central to this frame - the gerund 'buying' and the name of the participant, 'seller'. One of the central slots in this frame, however, is filled by an unexpected value - 'identification'. The unexpectedness of this infill is emphasized by the expression 'instead of money'. The buyer in this frame has a value of 'prosecutors' and along with the conventional expression 'showed their identification', it immediately activates the frame of law and order (L.O). The usage of a gerund construction in the title emphasizes that actions from both frames are happening simultaneously and have the same actor. There is *ANALOGY/DISANALOGY* and *ROLE-VALUE* outer-space relations between 'money' in the buy-sell input and 'identification plus the Criminal Code of the Russian Federation' in the law and order input, which compresses into *CHANGE* and further into *UNIQUENESS* in the blend. These elements are analogous because according to the text both are used for buying but the connection is disanalogous because the reader immediately realizes that what the seller is shown instead of money cannot be used as a substitute for it. The violation of the *ROLE-VALUE* vital relation prompts a frame-shifting and activates the frame of crime-robbery (C). Buyers are mapped into prosecutors and initiators of a crime by *ANALOGY/DISANALOGY*. There is an *ANALOGY + VALUE* connector between these elements in the inputs (the same people acting in different roles) but these elements are disanalogous because of the *ROLE* this *VALUE* is attached to in each input. *ANALOGY/DISANALOGY* is compressed into *IDENTITY + CHANGE* and further into UNIQUENESS in the blend. As the text comprehension continues, the *ROLE* of money acquires additional *VALUE* from the crime input - 'having thoroughly intimidated the seller' - which enriches the clash between the buy-sell, the law and order and the crime input frames.

The topologies of the inputs' clash on causality and intentionality: whereas buy-sell is a planned event, event-crime is unexpected; while buy-sell aims at achieving a positive goal, the crime leads to something which is evaluated negatively. The topologies also clash on participant roles, identity and internal event structure: the prosecutors are buyers in the frame of buy-sell but they are mapped to the role of initiators in the frame of crime, which is projected onto the blend along with their identity.

In Nineties' Russia, the scenario whereby prosecutors abuse their power to force the seller to give them something for free presents a blend reflecting a new level of norm violation. It seems that the high creativity in this text and the emergence of 'infinite lawlessness' in the blend is motivated by the fact that in the process of understanding this text, subjects have to deal with two levels of norms or their violation simultaneously. Initially norms in law and order are violated by the event-crime of robbery because of the nature of this event and then norms are violated again when the expectations of subjects about this type of crime are not confirmed. An event, such as the one constructed in the integration network for the news text about prosecutors, is defined as abnormal by Kahneman and Miller (1986). They argue that "an abnormal event is one that has highly available alternatives, whether retrieved or constructed; a normal event mainly evokes representations that resemble it". It can be suggested that in our case a conventional type of robbery as the crime input is considered to be a normal event in the sense that it confirms expectations about crimes in general. Defined as 'an unanticipated event' (Kahneman and Miller, 1986: 145), it is judged normal because it simply fails to evoke strong alternatives. A novel type of crime described in this text, however, is considered to be abnormal or violating norms for the second time on the next level of consideration, and thus, it is comprehended through the construction of a double-scope integration network and a new emergent structure in the blend.

There is a vital inner-space relation of *CAUSE-EFFECT* between the prosecutor/criminal/buyer and the victim/seller/criminal in the blend. It results from scaling down a long causal chain and its combination with the compression of analogous and disanalogous relations. The seller is mapped into the protected people in the law and order input space, the victim in the crime and 'cause/initiator' in the debt collection input (D) by *ANALOGY/DISANALOGY* and *ROLE-VALUE* outer-space relations, which compress into *IDENTITY + CHANGE*. Together with the tightened *CAUSE-EFFECT*, this vital relation is further compressed into *UNIQUENESS* in the blend. The unique criminal is a cause for the emergence of the unique victim. *CAUSE-EFFECT* compression is accompanied by the creation of a new *INTENTIONALITY*: a huge lack of trust and belief in law enforcement agencies is demonstrated here, linguistically marked by the phrase 'The seller decided to recover his $5,000 from the mediator and hired some thugs to that end'.

The 'mediator' in the buy-sell input is mapped into victim in the debt collection input by *ANALOGY/DISANALOGY* and *ROLE-VALUE*, which compresses into *IDENTITY+ CHANGE* and then further into *UNIQUENESS* in the blend. The role of the rescue team from the debt collection and crime-robbery inputs is mapped into the value of RDOC officers in the law and order input. There is also an analogous/disanalogous connector observed here: officers are analogous due to their main duties – protect people/deal with criminals – and disanalogous as RDOC officers can also deal with officers-criminals. Both *ROLE-VALUE* and *ANALOGY/DISANALOGY* relations are compressed into *UNIQUENESS*. In the blend, the unique victim-mediator knows how the unique criminals can be punished – with the help of the unique rescue team 'RDOC'.

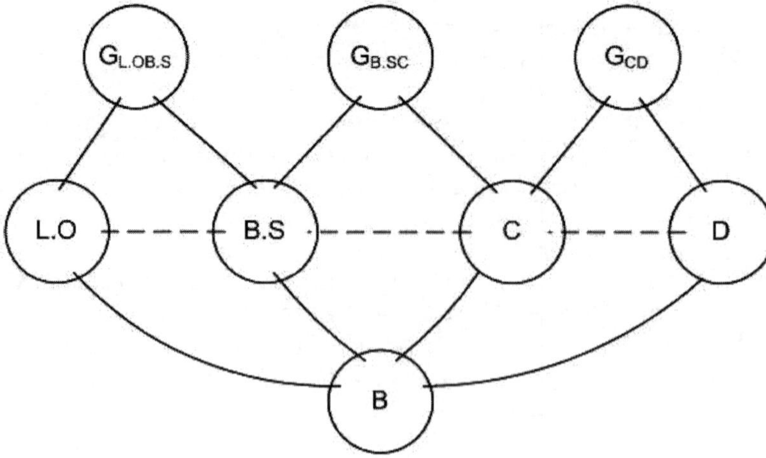

Figure 2 Prosecutors Network

The overall structure of the network is shown in Figure 2, where the dashed lines represent the cross-space mappings between the spaces and the solid lines indicate the mappings to the generic space and the selective projections to the blend. The generic space (G) is a schema common to all input spaces - 'actor/patient and normal event versus abnormal event plus evaluation'.

There is a concrete organizing structure of the buy-sell frame presented in the blend, with prosecutors buying diamonds, but at the same time the blend inherits causal, intentional and internal event structures from the crime and law and order input spaces. In the blend in this double-scope network, it becomes possible to buy diamonds by demonstrating power given to legal enforcement agencies. The rich clashes between the input spaces, compressions and integrations in the blend create the new *INTENTIONALITY* – 'the fear that bad officers are everywhere, lack of trust, the simultaneous necessity and impossibility of knowing who is an honest/good officer and who is a dishonest/bad officer, and the necessity of knowing how bad officers can be punished. Central to the blend is the action, linguistically marked by the verb 'to confiscate' in the speech marks. The action 'to confiscate' projected from the law and order input (where this action is a normal action), will project back to the buy-sell input (where it is perceived as an abnormal action). When 'to confiscate' is projected back to the crime input the suitable inferences related to the abnormality of this event are produced. This causes the extension of the category of crime in the blend. A single action *"to confiscate"* is the integration of events to buy, to rob and to confiscate, which remains linked to events in all input spaces. *"To confiscate"* in the text linguistically marks the new emergent structure in the blend with the new intentionality of infinite lawlessness: a new type of event involving officers-bandits and its evaluation as highly abnormal and unacceptable. Though *"to confiscate"* successfully manifests the uniqueness of criminals-prosecutors, it takes the whole text to prompt the construction of the conceptual integration network for these corrupt officers, their crime and its evaluation.

In the text, the event is also labeled as 'the abuse of office'. Events of this type can also be referred to using other judicial terms, for example 'fraud', but they appear to be insufficient in successfully categorizing this new range of events from the nineties and in highlighting their novel character. When such texts start to appear more frequently in the mass-media, a lack of a conventional word or expressions to refer to this new type of crime is felt especially acutely.

There is one more interesting facet observed for the analyzed emergent structure in the blend. The sentence 'The Senior Assistant and the Head of Department of the Tula Region Prosecutor's Office were arrested by members of RDOC following a directive from Anatolij Sedukhin, the Regional Prosecutor' prompts the emergence of the strong idea of responsibility for such a crime with the profiled role of the rescue team/saviours. The new *INTENTIONALITY* is created – 'the criminal should and will be identified and punished'. The structure of 'infinite lawlessness versus strong idea of responsibility' emerges in the blend. Though this structure is realized on the level of text, a lack of a conventional word or expression to name the new type of criminals, the new type of crime, as well as to emphasize its evaluation and the crucial role of the 'rescue team', creates the necessary prerequisites for continuing a search for an optimal blend.

1.4 Werewolves: Cultural History

The analysis of post-Soviet and Soviet discourse, socio-political events, literature and films as well as folk narratives allows us to define the most important concepts and events, which influence the emergence and maintaining of the metaphor 'werewolves in epaulettes'.

The instability of the nineties with their 'infinite lawlessness' led to 'nostalgia' for everything good and stable, which had existed in the Soviet period. Such nostalgia was often expressed in the reading of Soviet books and watching of Soviet films (see Oushakine, 2007). Different literary texts and films with relevant topics were easily available (on TV, on sale, in school and university programmes) and these will be considered during the process of constructing meaning. The concept of Russian *oboroten'* presents a main theme in many Russian and Soviet literary works. In the late Soviet period, an extremely popular Russian telenovela (10 episodes) 'Born by the Revolution' (1974) tells the history of Soviet criminal police. In this film bandits who used to dress in the Russian police uniform to commit their crimes are called 'werewolves'.

The loss of communist ideals led to searching for new beliefs and ideals, and motivated an increased interest in different supernatural matters including old myths about and beliefs in 'evil spirits' to rely upon in difficult situations and to blame for difficulties (see Kosareva, 2001, Yarskaia-Smirnova and Romanov, 2007). In the mid-nineties Russian authors started to develop the new literary 'mysticism' genre, guided by West European and American analogies (Kosareva, 2001). With the beginning of the stabilization process under Putin's government one could observe a rise in sentiments of Russian nationalism. A burgeoning feeling of patriotism was expressed by an interest in everything Russian, including folk traditions, narratives, etc. For example, there is an increased interest in Russian fairy-tale creatures. Stepanov (2004) devotes two articles to '*Baba Iaga*'[3] and '*Kashchej Bessmertnyj*' (Kashchej the Immortal),[4] analyzing these concepts in his "Dictionary of Russian Culture" as Russian 'constants' - the key national concepts of Russian culture. These concepts often feature in the texts about werewolves in epaulettes.

Under Putin and Medvedev one can also see the enhancement of law enforcement agencies' political and social role, which leads to the strengthening of the idea of 'infinite lawlessness versus responsibility'. Attempts to regain trust in Russian Law Enforcement Agencies and the State Authorities have resulted in well publicized cases against several high-ranking Russian officers (see e.g. newspaper stories dated back to 2003 devoted to the case of the Russian General of Police, Vladimir Ganeev – the first case in a series of 'werewolves in epaulettes' investigations).

1.5 Body, Metamorphosis and *Proisshestvie*

A human body motivates the emergence of countless metaphorical and metonymical structures in languages in the world (Lakoff, 1987, Frank, et al., 2007). One of reasons for this is that the interpretation of a complex phenomenon through a human body helps to satisfy the overarching goal of human cognition – 'Achieve Human Scale'.

---

[3] In Russian fairy-tales an ugly, evil and insidious old woman who has a great bewitching power and who always acts as an antagonist to a positive hero.

[4] In Russian fairy-tales an ugly, evil and insidious old man who has a great bewitching power and who always acts as an antagonist to a positive hero.

The metamorphosis involving the human body is central to the mythological werewolves input in the conceptual integration network 'werewolves in epaulettes'. The important characteristics of the concept of mythological werewolf are two-fold: the werewolf is both a creature and an event in which it participates. This creature undergoes a metamorphosis; it experiences an event – a regular change from one state to another, from one situation to another. Although the concept of werewolf tends to be perceived as a universal one, the Russian *oboroten'* (werewolf) presents a certain cultural specificity. It is derived from Russian verbs *oborachivat'sia – oborotit'sia* ('to turn over', 'to roll over'), whereas 'werewolf' is rooted in the conceptualization of a creature – half human, half wolf. As opposed to werewolves, Russian *oboroten'* can change into a variety of objects, not necessarily animals, e.g. a rug, scarf, utensils, etc. The Russian (Slavic) concept of *oboroten'* is different from other mythological werewolves in several respects, among which is a profiled 'function' and stress on actions of this creature, as opposed to a profiled 'hierarchal position', which characterizes the respective creatures from other European mythological traditions (see Levkievskaya, 2007; Nekliudov, 1992).

The metaphor 'werewolves in epaulettes' is used in the mass-media to refer to both corrupt officers and events in which they participate. Today one can find sub columns 'Werewolves' or 'Werewolves in Epaulettes' within a column *'Proisshestviia'* in major Russian newspapers, such as *'Kommersant'*. Various texts about *proisshestviia*[5] in such sub columns do not necessarily incorporate the word *oboroten'* or label it as a crime, although they are strongly felt to belong to one category, one class of events.

Proisshestvie can be used to refer to different events breaching norms, including crimes. However, where the crime is mainly about 'breaking norms in the Russian law domain', *proisshestvie* presents the framing of 'breaking norms in the various domains of Russian society'. While interpreting the mass-media texts about *proisshestviia*, people evoke conceptualizations of these norms. This makes them analyze and accept or reject

---

[5] *Proisshestvie* is defined in Russian dictionaries as an unexpected event which breaks the usual pattern of things and disturbs the usual course of life and as an unwanted and unpleasant event. Russian 'proisshestvie' can be translated into English using words 'accident', 'incident', 'event', 'adverse event', 'local event', etc. The central characteristic of 'Norm Violating' presents one very productive and universal cognitive principle behind both Russian *proisshestvie* and the respective English event. At the same time socio-cultural and national specificity of norms being violated, along with other cultural factors involved, significantly influence the way in which people produce, perceive and interpret such event in terms of Western and Russian mentality and culture. For the cultural and historical analysis of how Russian event-*proisshestvie* was used to create a well-known and highly influential Soviet myth about Pavlik Morozov, see Kelly 2005.

subconsciously the values, beliefs and attitudes which are shared by people in society. Our conceptual integration network has the input of *proisshestvie*. This input is evoked to allow integrations, which can both include or exclude the evaluation of 'werewolves in epaulettes' as a crime. When needed, this input permits a shift from the frame of crime to the frame of norm violation.

Using a name for participant(s) in realizing a type of event-*proisshestvie* in mass-media discourse linguistically presents a rather unusual situation for the Russian language (see Pleshakova, 1998). Our analysis shows that the ability of 'werewolves in epaulettes' to categorize a class of events is motivated by the cultural specificity of the Russian concept of *oboroten'*, with its profiled action/event/function and cultural model *proisshestvie*, and is rooted in the mappings between these two inputs.

In our integration network, a creature-werewolf in the mythological werewolf input has the counterpart of the initiator of norm violation in the *proisshestvie* input. The metamorphosis of the werewolf is mapped into the action violating a norm in the *proisshestvie* input. There are also patients in both inputs. The outer-space topologies here are defined by *ANALOGY/DISANALOGY*, *CAUSE-EFFECT* and *ROLE-VALUE* vital relations. The elements-counterparts in the inputs are analogous because in both inputs there are actors realizing the event-norm violation and patients. They are disanalogous because the werewolf's transformation is perceived as something magical and unreal while *proisshestvia* depicted in the mass-media are grounded in real events. At the same time, the very existence of a werewolf and its transformation can be understood to be a type of *proisshestvie*, and the role of initiator in the *proisshestvie* input can have a value 'werewolf', for example. Werewolf in its turn is a cause of *proishestvie* here: the transformation causes the norm violation. The vital outer-space relations between these inputs are compressed into *CATEGORY* in the blend.

> [7] *Ono i stalo: nu ne mozhet zhe s arestom bankira, oborotniami, zagovorom i skandal'noj pokupkoj "Chelsi" konkurirovat' rutinnaia gibel' polutora desiatkov chelovek v Tushine! (O chem molchat oligarkhi? // "Moskovskie novosti", 2003.04.01)*'So it became: it is absolutely impossible, isn't it, for the routine death of a few dozen of people in Tushino to compete with the arrest of a banker, werewolves, conspiracy and the scandalous purchase of "Chelsea"'.

In this example 'werewolves' are listed equally among the other events, and therefore comprise a name for a category of events. The analogous and disanalogous connections between the inputs of events in the integration network behind this example - arrest, werewolves, conspiracy, and purchase - compress into *SIMILARITY* and *PROPERTY* 'event' in the blend.

The blend in the 'werewolves in epaulettes' network inherits the central frame topology of metamorphosis from the mythological werewolf input. In particular, there is an inner-space frame-metonymic relation. This is automatic, rich in potential and pervasive in cognition[6] in the blend projected from the mythological werewolf input. The emergent structure in the blend has werewolves in epaulettes as participants, a new type of event in which they participate and a class of mass-media stories about such events. Speaking in traditional linguistic terms, we can say that 'werewolves in epaulettes' is both a metaphor and a metonymy. The analysis of our conceptual network shows that both types cannot be separated as they are the product of the same integrations emerging under the same constitutive, governing principles and overarching goals.

1.6 Soviet Werewolves

There is a cultural memory of Soviet werewolf as an enemy, double-dealer and killer. As described by Lotman:

> Deeply mythological in its nature theme of "enemy double dealer", "who has changed his face" and who has no identifying features, the mythological concept of werewolf, who cannot be identified using rational methods and is recognized only through magical fighting, is very representative. This appeal to methods of exposure of "the crafty designs of the devil" had a notorious impact on the juridical thinking of Vyshinsky and was almost an idée fixe of Soviet literature of the late 30s, particularly developed in Gaidar's work. (Lotman, 1997)

The analysis of the Soviet newspaper texts shows that the Soviet concept of enemy is described as: *vrag naroda* (people's enemy), *vreditel'* (saboteur), *predatel'* (traitor), *shpion* (spy), *diversant* (subversive), etc. Although our analysis of Stalinist ideological discourse does not show the usage of the name *oboroten'*, the relation of the novel Russian concept of 'werewolves in epaulettes' to the concept of Stalinist werewolf is obvious. The cultural memory of such Stalinist concepts is reactivated with a new double power after *Perestrojka* and the collapse of the Soviet Union when the Russian public becomes familiar with many literary works and films on Stalinist themes, which had, until then, been prohibited by the Soviet censorship (see Yurchak, 2004).

Here is one example from the contemporary Russian discourse.

> [7] *Teleprogrammy perepolnilis' reportazhami o murovskikh zagorodnykh osobniakakh i inomarkakh, SMI prinialis' publikovat' obshirnye spiski prodazhnykh militsionerov i firm, kotorym oni pokrovitel'stvovali, a v gosucherezhdeniiakh, ne tol'ko , silovykh, razvernulas' masshtabnaia okhota*

---

[6] See Sweetser and Dancygier (2005) for exploration of frame-metonymic relation in the analysis of conditional constructions.

> *na samykh raznykh oborotnej – v pogonakh, meditsinskikh khalatakh, strogikh kostiumakh (Oborotnyj protsess. Vlast', no. 36, 2006).*'Tele programmes are over flooded with reports about criminal policemen's villas in the country and cars produced abroad, mass-media has started publishing long lists of corrupt policemen and firms that they are patronizing, and has unfolded a large-scale hunt for various kinds of werewolves – in epaulettes, doctors' coats, formal suits, in state institutions, not only in legal enforcement agencies.

The input of the Stalinist werewolf is evoked by such linguistic triggers as 'a large-scale hunt for various kinds of werewolves – in epaulettes, doctors' coats'. The latter presents the novel metaphor 'werewolves in doctor's coats', a multi-scope conceptual network integrating two metaphoric blending networks: 'werewolves in epaulettes' and '*ubijtsy v belykh khalatakh*' (murderers in white gowns). 'Murderers in white gowns' emerged at the time of a famous Stalinist case, the 'Doctors' plot'. Central to the case was the execution of doctors, who had been on trial for the attempt to poison Soviet leaders, including Stalin himself. In Russian cultural memory the doctors are perceived as victims of Stalin's repressions. In the blend of the integration network 'werewolves in doctor's coats', there is the emergent structure of the unique werewolves-doctors, who are corrupt, enemies and victims. There are analogous and disanalogous connectors between the mythological werewolf (a creature which lives among us, which is hard to identify, dangerous and harmful', needs to be identified and treated and eliminated by means of some magical rules), the doctor-murderer (which is hard to identify, very dangerous, an enemy, a killer, needs to be identified and eliminated in accordance with some ideological rules), the corrupt doctor and the doctor-victim of Stalin's repressions, that routinely compress into *UNIQUENESS*. Here we can observe 'cobbling and sculpting' – a mix of the novel metaphoric structure 'werewolves in epaulettes' and the conventional structure of 'murderers in white gowns'. Various examples of the discourse usage of 'werewolves in epaulettes' suggest that one of the building techniques for this metaphor is borrowed from 'murderers in white gowns'. A building technique for 'werewolves in doctor's coats', in its turn, is transmitted from the 'werewolves in epaulettes'.

In addition to the inputs of the political life, the mythological werewolf and Soviet werewolf, and the input spaces of corruption, crime and *proisshestvie,* we bring in the input of mass-media. The mass-media input plays a significant role in the emergence of 'werewolves in epaulettes' as the political PR and propaganda scenario and victims in the blend. Example 7 shows that in the blend, the mass-media's excessive reports fuse with the political will from the political life input and oppressors from the Soviet werewolf input and constitute the cause for the large-scale 'werewolf-hunting' in the hunting' in the various sectors of the post-Soviet society. Such 'werewolf-hunting' leads to an oppression of victims.

1.7 Post-Soviet Mythologized Concept of Enemy

The function of this particular network is to structure the Russian political life scenario rhetorically and conceptually. The metaphor of 'werewolves in epaulettes' tells us about the political will of the Russian authorities to fight corruption, suggests that they are doing this to gain political credibility, and warns us about the dangers of adopting Soviet methods in so doing.

The topologies of the input spaces clash on causality, intentionality, participant roles, temporal sequence, identity, and internal event structure. These rich clashes allow for the highly creative complex structure with the newly created *INTENTIONALITY* to emerge in the blend: 'werewolves in epaulettes' - the post-Soviet mythologized enemy.

Criminals break norms and that is why we do not like them. We do not necessarily perceive them as enemies as we are used to having crimes in our society and they do not present something 'abnormal' for us as a phenomenon as soon as we know how to address them. The knowledge of the rules brings us inner peace. Werewolves, on the contrary, are perceived as enemies as they present a highly abnormal phenomenon. The rules helping to deal with them are 'magical' and only the select few know how to identify and deal with these creatures. Werewolves are our enemies. The select few save us from enemies and they are good ones and they talk to us and we should listen to them - otherwise, we may get in big trouble. The search for an enemy may result in the wrong person being identified as an enemy and this is dangerous because we know from our cultural memory of Soviet experience what such 'mistakes' can lead to.

Let us call the input spaces P (political life), C (corruption), M (mass-media), E (crime), L.O (law and order), A (*proisshestvie*), WML (werewolf in myths and literature) and WSLF (werewolf in Soviet ideological discourse, literature and films). The overall configuration of the conceptual integration network 'werewolves in epaulettes', shown in Figure 3, has the dashed lines as indication of the cross-space mappings between the spaces and the solid lines standing for the mappings to the generic spaces and the projections to the blend.

Because there are the multiple cross-space mappings, our network has at least six main distinct generic spaces. The generic space common to WML and WSLF is an enemy/metamorphosis scenario depicted in Russian myths and Russian/Soviet literature and films (G:W). The generic space of 'actor, patient, normal event versus abnormal event, evaluation' scenario is common to E, A, WSL and WML inputs (G:EAW). The generic space for

E, L.O and A presents the idea of responsibility common to these spaces (G: EL.OA). The generic space for A and M is the evaluation of *proisshestvia* through the mass-media (G:AM). The generic space common to L.O, WML, WSLF, C and P is the 'witch-hunting' scenario (G: L.OWMLWSLFCP). The generic space of 'PR' schema is common to P, C and M (G:PCM).

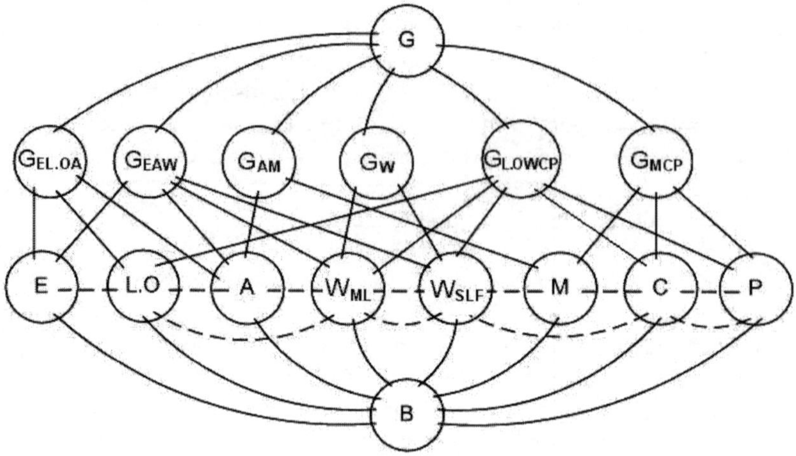

Figure 3 Werewolves in Epaulettes Network

In the blend, there is first, the newly created *INTENTIONALITY* of criminals being exceptionally dangerous due to the difficulty of their identification and the scale of potential damage they can cause to both the victims and the system of law and order. This judgment about dangers is projected from the mythological werewolf input space and will project back to the crime and law and order inputs. In turn, this will produce suitable inferences about the character of such criminals - criminals are our enemies - which in turn serves to heighten fear related to this type of crime, and the difficulty of identifying such criminals and the necessity of knowing special rules in order to deal with such crimes.

Second, there is the newly created *INTENTIONALITY* of the legal enforcement agencies and the leading political party using the 'werewolves in epaulettes' for gaining political credit. They are saviours, but they save people from enemies for their own benefit. Third, there is the structure of 'witch-hunting' projected from the mythological werewolf and the werewolves as an ideological technique projected from the Soviet werewolf input space. Both of the latter will project back to the crime, law and order and the political life inputs to produce such inferences as: the fight with corruption may be for show only; and there are potential dangers related to legal enforcement agencies adopting Soviet ideological/repression techniques.

The network of 'werewolves in epaulettes' includes a single schematic generic space (G) common to all other spaces, and relates to the general schema of enemy. Nevertheless, it is also necessary to account for the more specific generic spaces. The resulting blend includes at least three potentially separate blends with their own intentional structures and the network needs a detailed and refined organization of generic spaces to ensure the successful running of the network. At the same time the pressure is put on the specific generic spaces to achieve G, common to all inputs. For example, the generic space of 'PR' schema (G:PCM) adjusts to include propaganda 'bring salvation from enemy', which is not its necessary component.

However, only when three potentially distinct metaphoric networks are blended, there is the result 'werewolves in epaulettes' with a new meaning of the mythologized concept of enemy.

2 Conclusion

We have shown in some detail how the conceptual blending analysis of the novel Russian metaphorical structure 'werewolves in epaulettes' allows a deeper insight into the cognitive and cultural processes underlying the construction of this metaphorical meaning. The complexity of integrations leads to the construction of a multi-scope network with potentially multiple blends. The integration of 'werewolves-corrupt officers/criminals', 'werewolves-ideological instruments' and 'werewolves-victims of oppression' presents a formation of a new national concept of mythologized enemy. This concept of enemy is constructed to strengthen the 'national unity' and becomes an important part of the Russian 'imagined community' (Anderson, 2006; Fritzsche, 2004). The conceptual blending analysis of the post Soviet discourse about 'werewolves in epaulettes' shows an explicit reference to the Stalinist concept of 'enemy-werewolf'. However, by presenting such references in the light of criticism towards the Stalinist (Soviet) regime and alerting the public about possible analogies between the present Russian (Kremlin) and past Soviet ideologies, the contemporary discourse demonstrates the difference between the 'Soviet enemy-werewolf' and today's Russian 'werewolves in epaulettes'. Today's 'werewolf' cannot and must not be physically eliminated and the danger of punishing the 'werewolf' - who is not a true enemy - is being explicitly realized at the level of discourse. The emergent structure in the blend with all its interesting properties discussed above is the product of the formation of the mythologized concept of enemy as a new Russian national construal. Our case study shows that the new concept appears to be manifestly different from its Soviet predecessor due to its heterogeneousness and the high variety of morals that emerge in the blend[7].

The conceptual blending analysis in this study demonstrates that the new metaphorical meaning of mythologized enemy ensures the high productivity of 'werewolves in epaulettes', and motivates the emergence of secondary metaphors: e.g. werewolves in doctor's coats.[8] Both the rhetorical and productive capacities of the metaphor 'werewolves in epaulettes' is based on the cultural specificity of the input spaces and their 'adaptation' capacity, e.g. the cultural models of 'Russian mythological werewolf', 'Soviet werewolf', *proisshestvie*, the input of the Russian political life, which on the one hand, define to a considerable degree the selection of projections to the blend and the integrations in the blend, but on the other hand, adapt to achieve the optimal cultural blend and successful running of the conceptual network. Coulson points out that the role of conceptual blending in the adaptation and perpetuation of cultural models becomes especially evident in the persuasive texts dealing with such serious socio-cultural, political and ideological issues as the ones presented in the 'werewolves in epaulettes' texts. She argues that "that real persuasion depends on the motivational capacity of the cultural models themselves" (2006: 188).

Our case study demonstrates the utility of conceptual blending as a tool for cultural analysis. The integrated 'cognition and culture' approach based on conceptual integration allows us to take into consideration both the important principles of cognitive and cultural theoretical approaches and to pay attention to both innate cognitive abilities and cultural variation. Palmer (2006) points out that although many categories are universal to a certain extent, as they are constrained by universal biological and physical experiences, because shared frames are predominately cultural, they present important differences. Our case study shows that such differences may lead to the construction of a culturally specific metaphor that becomes a new, very important national construal of reality.

---

[7] The formation of a new mythologized concept of enemy manifests a rise of nationalism in post-Soviet Russia, the phenomenon which despite being extremely vital and influencing modern Russian culture, language, economy, politics, etc. and having received much attention in academic literature and beyond, still remains insufficiently explored and understood. One of the recent attempts to elucidate the background of this problem has been an on-going large international research project "National Identity in Russia from 1961: Traditions & Deterritorialisation" (http://www.mod-langs.ox.ac.uk/russian/nationalism/index.htm).

[8] Other examples include *oborotni v shokolade* (werewolves in chocolate) - oligarchs, *oborotni Chechni* ('werewolves of Chechnia') - bandits, terrorists acting in Chechnia, etc.

The principles of conceptual integration behind the construction of the meaning of 'werewolves in epaulettes-mythologized enemy' conspire to achieve the overarching goal 'Achieve Human Scale' and its noteworthy sub goals: compress what is diffuse; obtain global insight; strengthen vital relations; come up with a story; go from many to one (Fauconnier and Turner, 2002). Our analysis suggests the existence of an additional sub goal—'achieving a cultural scale'. This sub goal, in our opinion, ensures the activation of inputs and selection of mappings and projections which make the blend culture-friendly. Making the blend more intelligible, blazing and memorable, and useful to us as human beings thinking in culture, this sub goal contributes to the goal 'Achieve Human Scale'. The importance of this sub goal must not be underestimated, since accounting for 'achieving cultural scale' helps to elucidate the metaphor in its full capacity. Our analysis shows that human-friendly and perfectly suited to Russian culture, the concept of 'werewolf in epaulettes' is unlikely to be constructed in other cultures, even assuming that they have concepts of werewolf, crime, corruption, etc.

Central to the application of conceptual blending as a tool for cultural research is the analysis of cultural models and their capacities. According to Lukes (2007) it is crucial for successful discourse analysis to determine conceptual patterns (frames), as constituents of a conceptual space – text, through identifying and analyzing the potential textual evidence for them. He refers to Lakoff (1987, 1996) to emphasize the importance of looking for the linguistic evidence for frames at all levels of language – from phonetics to text. Shore emphasizes that "the idea of cultural models is a useful alternative to dissolving the concept of culture altogether into vague notions of power or discourse" (1996: 45). In our opinion, the concept of 'cultural model' presents a technique based on the analysis of textual evidence or linguistic triggers for various conceptual structures, which accounts explicitly for the cultural and historical dimensions of the conceptual blending analysis.

Author note

I would like to thank two anonymous reviewers for their helpful and constructive comments. I am also grateful to Mark Turner for his thoughtful comments on an earlier version of this paper that I received during the CSDL9 conference. Address for correspondence: Anna Pleshakova, School of Interdisciplinary Area Studies, University of Oxford, 12 Bevington Road, Oxford, OX2 6LH, UK; email: anna.pleshakova@area.ox.ac.uk.

References

Anderson, B. 2006. Imagined Communities: Reflections on the Origin and Spread of Nationalism. London New York: Verso.

Couldon, S. 2001. Semantic Leaps: Frame-Shifting and Conceptual Blending in Meaning Construction. Cambridge: Cambridge University Press.

Couldon, S. 2006. Conceptual Blending in Thought, Rhetoric, and Ideology. *Cognitive Linguistics: Current Applications and Future Perspectives,* eds. G. Kristiansen, et al., 187-211. Berlin New York: Mouton de Gruyter.

Fauconnier, G., M. Turner. 2002. The Way We Think: Conceptual Blending and the Mind's Hidden Complexities. New York: Basic Books.

Fauconnier, G., M. Turner. 2008. Rethinking Metaphor. Cambridge Handbook of Metaphor and Thought, ed. R. Gibbs. Cambridge: Cambridge University Press. Available at SSRN: http://ssrn.com/abstract=1275662

Frank, R. et al. 2007. Body, Language and Mind: Sociocultural Situatedness, eds. Berlin New York: Mouton de Gruyter.

Fritzsche, P. 2004. Stranded in the Present: Modern Time and the Melancholy of History. Cambridge: Harvard University Press.

Kahneman, D., D. Miller. 1986. Norm Theory: Comparing Reality to its Alternatives. *Psychological Review,* vol. 93, 2: 136-153.

Kelly, C. 2005. Comrade Pavlik: The Rise and Fall of a Soviet Boy Hero. London: Granta Books.

Kosareva, A. 2001. Mirivozrencheskie paradigm fantastiki. *Tossijskaja massovaia kul'tura kontsa 20-go veka.* Sankt-Peterburg: Sankt-Peterburgskoe Filosofskoe Obshchestvo.

Available at: http://antropology.ru/ru/texts/gathered/masscult/index.html

Lakoff, G. 1987. Women, Fire, and Dangerous Things: What Categories Revealabout the Mind. Chicago: University of Chicago Press.

Lakoff, G. 1996. Moral politics: What Conservatives Know that Liberals Don't. Chicago: University of Chicago Press.

Levkievskaya, E. 2004. Mifologicheskij personazh: sootnoshenie imeni i obraza. *Khrestomatiia po fol'kloristike*. Sankt-Peterburg: Proppovskij Tsentr.

Lotman, Yu. 1997. Sovremennost' mezhdu Vostokom i Zapadom. Znamia 9. available at: http://vivovoco.rsl.ru/vv/PAPERS/Lotman/Lotman07.HTM

Lukes, D. 2007. What Does it Mean When Texts "Really" Mean Something?: Types of Evidence for Conceptual Patterns in Discourse. *Cognitive Linguistics in Critical Discourse Analysis,* eds. Ch. Hart and D. Lukes, 180-207. Cambridge Scholars Publishing.

Nekliudov, S. 1992. Oborotnichestvo. *Mify narodov mira.* 2. Moskva.

Oakley, T. 1998. Conceptual Blending, Narrative Discourse, and Rhetoric. *Cognitive Linguistics* 9:321-360.

Oushakine, S. 2007. "We're Nostalgic but We're Not Crazy": Retrofitting the Past in Russia. *Russian Review* 66, 3: 451-482.

Palmer, G. 2006. Energy through Fusion at Last: Synergies in Cognitive Anthropology and Cognitive Linguistics. *Cognitive Linguistics: Current Applications and Future Perspectives,* eds. G. Kristiansen, et al., 263-300. Berlin New York: Mouton de Gruyter.

Pleshakova, A. 1998. Issledovanie freimov "proisshestvie" na materiale russkikh i anglijskikh gazetnykh tekstov zhanra "informacionnoe soobshchenie". Doctoral dissertation.

Romanov, P., E. Jarskaia-Smirnova. 2007. Sotsial'noe kak ratsional'noe? NLO 83. Available at: http://magazines.rus.ru/nlo/2007/83/ro14.html

Shore, B. 1996. Culture in Mind: Cognition, Culture, and the Problem of Meaning. Oxford: Oxford University Press.

Sweetser, E. and B. Dancygier. 2005. Mental spaces in Grammar: Conditional Constructions. Cambridge: Cambridge University Press.

Stepanov, Yu. 2004. Konstanty: Slovar' russkoj kul'tury: M.: Akademicheskij Proekt.

Turner, M. 2008. Frame blending. *Frames, Corpora, and Knowledge Representation*, ed.. R. Favretti, 13-32. Bologna: Bononia University Press.

Yurchak, A. 2006. Everything Was Forever, Until It Was No More: the Last Soviet Generation. Princeton University Press.

15

It's Not All About the Brain: A Cross-Linguistic Exploration of Body Part Metaphors in Chess

JUDIT SIMÓ

1 Introduction

The investigation of the figurative uses of body part terms constitutes a central part of cross-linguistic research motivated by the conceptual theory of metaphor (Lakoff & Johnson, 1980, 1999). With the idea of embodiment, body parts, which supposedly function more or less the same way in all healthy humans, are a good candidate to show a high degree of universality in their metaphoric and metonymic uses. Also, since we are experiencing the world through our bodies, it should be a salient source domain in every culture. Body parts or functions that can unequivocally be related to a body part (e.g. seeing to eyes) feature in cross-linguistic studies in two ways.

The first, more direct line of research starts out with a body part or body parts, examining its/their figurative uses in two or more languages. Most of these studies focus on perception verbs or body parts that are related to perception, and although they vary in methodology and also in the extent of their emphasis on conceptual metaphors, they usually agree on the most common metaphorical uses. Most notably, vision is related to mental processes like knowledge, understanding, thinking and attention (Deignan & Potter, 2004; Ibarretxe-Antuñano, 2002a; Yu, 2004), taste to the affective domain, including manner and likes/dislikes (Charteris-Black, 2003; Ibarretxe-Antuñano, 2002a), and smell to suspicion, guessing and investigation

Form, Meaning & Body.
Fey Parrill, Vera Tobin, and Mark Turner (eds.).

(Ibarretxe- Antuñano, 1993, 2002a). Studies that are not concerned with perception per se also find a big overlap in the figurative uses of body parts between languages, for example mouth (or tongue) standing for speaking (Charteris-Black, 2003; Deignan & Potter, 2004) or hand (or palm) for control (Yu, 2000).

A second type of studies focuses on conceptual metaphors describing a certain phenomenon (most often an emotion), and analyzes the linguistic instantiations of the metaphor, noting the body parts that are used to depict the phenomenon. Apart from the similarities (attributed, in the case of emotions, mainly to the universal physiological symptoms accompanying the emotion; Kövecses, 2002), an important difference is pointed out in describing the emotions of anger and happiness in Chinese (Yu, 1995), Tunisian Arabic (Maalej, 2004) and to a lesser extent, Hungarian (Kövecses, 2002); namely, that these languages seem to make use of more body parts than English to metaphorically talk about these emotions. In spite of the shared conceptual metaphors, a non-emotion, thinking, also shows substantial differences in the metaphorical usage of body parts (Yu, 2003). Overall, with both types of studies, a great number of similarities in the figurative usage of body parts are found, which is considered the 'normal' state of affairs. At the same time, the observed remarkable variation is explained most often by cultural differences. Also, in general, though a few studies use naturally occurring data, most of them are concerned with what is possible, as opposed to what is probable, in a language.

The present study falls in line with the second group in that its starting point is a phenomenon. However, the purpose of the study is the identification of all body part metaphors of chess, with conceptual metaphors being of less concern. Apart from this, the study aims to widen the scope of existing research on body part metaphors in two ways. First, untraditionally, the object of the investigation is a human artifact, namely, chess. This game has so far received scant attention in research on metaphors. Richie (2003) uses it as an example to challenge Lakoff's ARGUMENT IS WAR conceptual metaphor. Most importantly, this study is an extension on an earlier investigation of the source domains that are drawn on to describe a chess event or game metaphorically in American English and Hungarian (Simó, 2009a). That study found that although there is about a fifty percent overlap in source domain usage, substantial differences could also be detected between the two languages, the most prominent of which were the more frequent usage of the domain 'supernatural/gambling' in the Hungarian, and of 'confining actions' in the American data. Also, some expressions in the domain 'violent act/violent movement' carried a strong sense of brutality only in the Hungarian articles. These observations were attributed to cultural and linguistic differences. A second aim of the present study is to, rather than relying on purely cultural considerations when explaining the results, connect the metaphorical uses of body parts to the cognitive concept of chess in the two cultures. A Roschian (e.g. Rosch & Mervis, 1975) investigation of *game* as a prototype concept showed that both American and Hungarian college students viewed chess as a game of medium typicality. At the same time, there were significant differences in the attributes that were listed for chess: Americans named 'strategy', 'checkmate', 'nerds', and 'old' much more often than Hungarians, while Hungarians mentioned 'logic', 'competition', 'time', and 'tactics' to a much greater extent [46 and 42 participants, respectively, with 60% of both populations reporting knowing how to play chess] (Simó, 2008). We can speculate that these differences may partially be a reflection of chess's differing status in the two countries. In Hungary, chess is an important and popular sport, with events extensively covered on the sport pages of daily papers and in the sport news on television and radio. Cities and most towns have at least one chess club, and members form a team and play in leagues organized at different national and regional levels. On the other hand, in the United States, chess seems more to be the pastime of a few intelligent people, some of whom take it to a very high level. The biggest events are covered but to a much lesser extent than in Hungary, and often not among other sports. These differing views of chess may result in a more dynamic concept of the game in Hungary, which may have evoked the attributes 'competition' and 'tactics' in the survey. The American attributes hint at a less alive activity.

To find possible connections between cognitive concept and metaphors, this study sought to answer two questions:

1. Which body parts do American and Hungarian reporters draw on in their metaphors when commenting on a chess player or a chess game?
2. How do the similarities and differences in the metaphorical usage of body parts in the two languages relate to the cognitive concept of chess in those two countries?

2 Method

Data for this study come from print as well as online sources in both languages, American English and Hungarian. Both data sets included about 20,000 words. Specifically, the American data come from the March 2008 issue of the monthly magazine *Chess Life* (4929 words), the online version of the two daily papers *Washington Post* and *New York Times* (September-October 2004; 8276 words) and the website of the United States Chess Federation, uschess.org (between July-October 2008; 6482 words). Altogether, eleven authors contributed to these articles. The Hungarian data come from the April 2004 issue of *Sakkvilág* ('Chess World', 4628 words), the online versions of the two dailies *Nemzeti Sport* (a sport daily; from October 2004; 4488 words) and *Népszabadság* (a political daily; from October 2004 and March 2008; 945 words) and the sport news website sporthirek.hu (from March-April 2008 and October 2004; 9209 words). Twelve authors penned these articles. Moves (e. g. 29. Bf3) were not included in the word count. Table 1 displays this information.

Table 1. Number of words from each source in the two languages

American data **Total: 19687 words**	**Hungarian data** **Total: 19270 words**
Chess Life: 4929 words	Sakkvilág: 4628 words
New York Times, Washington Post: 8276 words	Nemzeti Sport, Népszabadság: 5433 words
Uschess.org: 6482 words	Sporthirek.hu: 9209 words

Articles were searched for body part metaphors, where 'body part' was understood in a broad sense. Thus, in addition to metaphors that named a specific, 'well-established' body part (e.g. 'head', 'hand'), less typical body parts, for example, 'nerve', as well as the substance 'blood', were also included. Moreover, metaphors that could unequivocally be related to a body part (*remiszagú- 'draw-smelling'*, i.e. likely to lead to a draw, related to nose or *hungry grandmaster*, related to stomach) were also analyzed. Verbal and other derivative forms were included as well. Thus, 'head', for example, featured as a noun (*fejjel megy a falnak - 'run at the wall with his head'*, i.e. rush headlong into the wall), adverbial (*UTB-A, headed by ...*) and verb (*the knight is heading to f4*). Metaphors were grouped based on which body part they named or could be related to and also whether they described the player or the game (pieces or position). Metaphorical descriptions of players were included because chess games are possible only if there are players (except for computers playing chess, which, admittedly, is of little interest to the present author). Also, the attribute lists mentioned in the introduction indicate that people do invoke the players when thinking about chess, even if to a smaller extent than the specifics of the game. The number of times the same metaphorical expression emerged was not tracked; therefore, numbers about the frequency of usage is not provided in the table; however, type frequency is discussed in the running text. Sometimes it proved problematic to decide whether a certain metaphor described the player or the game. For instance, in the expression 'a heavy-handed performance', the adjective describes the game metaphorically, but it is the player who committed the action. These cases were resolved in two ways: I followed the syntactic clues (and thus grouped the above example under 'game', since that is what the adjective modifies) and also asked for uninvolved parties' opinion and made a decision after weighing both. These ambiguous examples are pointed out in the text.

3 Body parts used metaphorically to describe a chess game or a chess player

Table 2 lists the body parts that were used in each language and provides an answer for the first research question.

Table 2. List of body parts in the two languages

	USA		**HUN**	
	Game	Player	Game	Player
1. Leg	√	√	√	√
2. Hand	√	√	√	√
3. Eyes	√	√	√	√
4. Mouth	√	√	√	√
5. Stomach		√		√
6. Head	√	√		√
7. Spine	√		√	√
8.Breathing system	√			√
9. Blood			√	√
10.Tongue			√	√
11. Nose			√	√
12.Nerves			√	
13. Neck			√	
14.Shoulder				√
15.Buttocks				√
16.Uterus	√			
17. Face		√		
18. Nail	√			
19. Hair	√			

As can be seen from the table, altogether, the two languages make use of nineteen body parts; eight of these overlap. Breaking down by languages, American articles make use of twelve body parts, whereas the Hungarian, fifteen. The eight body parts used in both languages are 'leg', 'hand', 'eyes', 'mouth', 'stomach', 'head', 'spine', and 'breathing system'. Seven body parts –'blood', 'tongue', 'nose', 'nerves', 'neck', 'shoulder', and 'buttocks'- were used only in the Hungarian articles, and four-'uterus', 'face', 'nail', and 'hair'- only in the American articles. Moreover, American articles used ten body parts to describe the game and seven to describe the player, whereas the Hungarian articles used ten body parts to describe the game and thirteen to describe the player.

The next sections provide examples of the most important and interesting metaphorical usages of some body parts. First, examples for 'leg', 'hand', 'eyes' and 'mouth' are discussed as these were used the most often in both languages; also, they were used in the most similar ways. This is followed by a discussion of 'stomach', which was used less frequently but in a similar way in the two languages; 'head', 'spine', and 'breathing system' are used in both languages but less similarly. Finally, four body parts that came up only in one of the languages will be discussed: 'blood', 'tongue', and 'nose' from the Hungarian data and 'face' from the American articles. 'Neck', 'shoulder', 'buttocks', 'nerves', 'uterus', 'nail', and 'hair' each gave only one example and thus are not discussed this time. Example sentences are numbered and prefixed with H for Hungarian and A for American. The word-for-word translation of the Hungarian sentences is given only where it is necessary to show metaphoricity.

3.1 Leg

This body part gave the most numerous examples (about twenty types) in both languages, mainly metaphorical usages of a number of verbs related to the movement of legs. The bulk (about 70-80%) of the expressions describes the player in both languages.

Player:

In both languages, when used in connection to a player, the metaphorical uses of 'leg' most often express the results of a game or tournament (A1 and H1). Most of the examples include a verb related to the movement of the legs, some exceptions being one use of the noun leg- láb in Hungarian (H2), 'stroll' used as a noun in American (A2) and some expressions with the nouns 'step'/'lépés', which appears in both languages (A1 and H3):

A1: Black *stumbles* when only a *step* from victory.

H1: Hatodik helyre *futott be* honfitársa, Oleg Kornyejev nagymester.

Sixth place-to *ran in* his countryman, grandmaster Oleg Kornyejev.

His countryman, Oleg Korneiev, came in sixth.

H2: A harmadik menetben *vetette meg* egyébként a *lábát* az élbolyban-Malahov és Alexej Drejev.

It was in the third round that Malahov and Alexej Dreiev *cast their legs* in the front bunch (came up to the top of the standings).

A2: Viswanathan Anand's *stroll* to the World Championship title in Mexico City could turn into a nail-biter after victories for Anand's main rivals in round 12 on Thursday.

H3: Tartotta velük a *lépést* az orosz ex-egyéni bajnok, Konsztantyin Szakajev is.

Kept the *step* with them the Russian ex-individual champion, Konstantin Sakaiev, too (kept pace with them).

An interesting, though not very common, use of leg-related verbs appears in idioms, which help describe the mental state of a player (A3 and H4):

A3: Morozevich praised Kramnik's sacrifice but *was kicking* himself for missing a chance to launch a counter-attack late in the game.

H4: Lékó Péter és az érte szurkoló népes magyar csapat *megjárta* a mennyet és a poklot.

Peter Leko and his many fans *have gone through* heaven and hell.

Game:

Legs are also used in a similar way in the two languages in relation to the game in that these expressions comment on the movement of the pieces (A4 and H5):

A4: The queen *goes* pawn hunting.

H5: Hiába *szaladt* az 'a' szabadgyalog.

The passed 'a'pawn *was running* in vain.

3.2 Hand

'Hand', together with 'eye', was the second most often used body part in both languages, with about ten types. Again, most of the examples use verbs related to the functions of hands and describe the players' actions; nevertheless, the noun 'hand' and its derivative forms also appear.

Player:
The most typical usage of 'hand' in both languages is to describe players' efforts or actions (see A5, A6, A7, H6, and H7). This usage resonates with Yu's (2000) observation of hand's role in having control over something.

> A5: Instead "Moro" decided to sacrifice the exchange with Rxe3 but was unable to *hold* the endgame.

> A6: Leko begins to *lose his grip* on the game.

> A7: A draw would have made Leko the winner, but he decided to play the better position for a win and *mishandled* the complications.

> H6: Sokat kivett belőlem, hogy a mérkőzéssorozat végéig *tartani* tudjam magam.
>
> It took a lot of my energy to be able to *hold* myself until the end of the match.

> H7: Világos masszív centrumot épít ki, ami a lavírozó harcmodort kedvelők *kezében* nagy előny.
>
> White builds a solid center, which is a big advantage *in the hands* of those who prefer a slower fight.

Both languages also use 'hand' to comment on the manner of the playing or performance (A8 and H8).

> A8: Unfortunately for UTD, history did not repeat itself and UMBC-Awon *handily* with a score of 3-1.

> H8: A szupernagymesterek nem bántak *kesztyűs kézzel* egymással.
>
> The super GMs did not handle each other with *gloved hands* (with kid gloves).

Game:
'Hand' is also used metaphorically to talk about the game, though to a lesser extent, in both languages (A9 and H9; see the discussion of the former's ambiguity in the Methods section).

A9: Of course, Kramnik can still win brilliantly today and we may forgive him his previous *heavy - handed* performance.

H9: Fenyeget g4 tiszt*fogás*sal.

Threatening is g4 with a piece-*grab* (trapping a piece).

3.3 Eyes

Eyes are used roughly to the same extent in both languages, but whereas 70% of the expressions describe the player in the Hungarian data, the rate is the opposite in the American articles, with 70% of the expressions being related to the game.

Player:
Again, in relation to players, the most common usage of the body part 'eye' is identical in the two languages- verbs related to the function of the eyes are used to comment on the ability of players, making use of the KNOWING IS SEEING conceptual metaphor (A10, H10):

A10: Svidler *overlooked* an elegant counterblow.

H10: Sahriyar Mamedgyarov *elnézte* a kötést.

Sahriyar Mamedarov *awaylooked* (overlooked) the pin.

There are two additional usages of eyes describing players in Hungarian; one of them, though related to knowing, comments more on the mental state of the player (H11):

H11: Ezt Vlagyimir Kramnyik nehezen *látta be*, sokáig hasztalan próbálkozott.

This-Acc Vladimir Kramnik hard-way *saw in*, (Kramnik had a hard time coming to terms with this), he was trying for a long time in vain.

The other usage more or less corresponds to the American expression 'facing somebody' (H12):

> H12: A Horváth József által irányított hölgyek egyértelmű esélyesként *néztek farkasszemet* a lettekkel.
>
> The women, directed by Joseph Horvath, as the unequivocal favorites *looked wolf- eye* (faced) with the Latvians.

Game:
Verbs of eye function (American) as well as the noun itself (Hungarian) are also made use of in both languages to describe the position (A11, A12, H13):

> A11: On 14...exd5 Karpov's suggestion of 15.Bd2! and 16.Bf4 *looks* s-trong.

> A12: Kramnik gained half an hour with his quiet 11.a3 move and another half an hour with the *dangerous-looking* 13.Qc7.

> H13: Látszólag világos nyerte a párbajt, az e6 ló azonban csak *szemre* veszélyes.
>
> On the surface, White has won the duel, but the e6 knight only *eye-to* dangerous (only looks dangerous).

An interesting difference here is that whereas the Hungarian expression conveys a negative meaning and thus hints at the deception our eyes can cause, the American metaphor suggests more that whatever looks good is in fact good. This Hungarian usage seems to be a variation on the KNOWING IS SEEING metaphor.

3.4 Mouth

One more body part that both languages used in relation to both player and game was 'mouth', with less numerous examples than the previous three body parts. 'Mouth' gives twice as many different expressions in the American articles than in the Hungarian ones, thanks to its more ubiquitous use in describing the game.

Player:
Both languages had only two different expressions in this category. 'Mouth' features as the organ of speaking, resulting in expressions that refer to the actions of players (A13, H14):

A13: However Kramnik's actions *spoke* louder than his words.

H14: A Juzsnij Ural Cseljabinszk a 77 éves Viktor Korcsnojnak *köszönheti* győzelmét.

The team Juzhny Ural Cheljabinsk *can thank* its victory to the 77 year-old Viktor Korchnoi.

Game:
In both languages, one category of these expressions is when the speech act verb 'promise' is used to describe a possible outcome of the game (A14, H15):

A14: Black's weak squares don't *promise* him an easy game.

H15: Bf3 többet *ígért*.

Rf3 *promised* more.

Games and moves are also characterized with the word *quiet* in the American data, giving four different expressions (A15, A16). This usage did not come up in the Hungarian articles.

A15: Aronian [....] chooses the *quieter* Moscow variation.

A16: The *quietest* game of the day was Gelfand-Grischuk.

3.5 Stomach

'Stomach' was used in both languages for the description of players, more precisely, to comment on player's mental states (A17, H16, H17). The first two of these expressions fall under the DESIRE IS HUNGER conceptual metaphor. This body part gave only one type in the American and two types in the Hungarian articles. It is interesting to note that in Hungarian, *megemészt* (digest) refers more to emotions, whereas in American English, it is used more to describe the processing of information.

A17: The Hungarian grandmaster was *hungrier*.

H16: És akkor még nem beszéltünk [...], a játékosok megalkuvás nélküli *győzeleméhségéről*, ami még a szicíliai védelemben is a spanyol hódítás korát idézheti.

Not to mention the [..] the players' *hunger for success* without appeasement, which can evoke the era of the Spanish conquest even in the Sicilian defense.

H17: Nem lehetett könnyű *megemészteni* Morozevicséknek az óriási botlást.

It was probably not easy for Morozevich and his team to *digest* (get over) the huge stumble.

3.6 Head

Both languages make use of 'head' to describe the player, but only the American articles use it in relation to a game. One language-specific morphological aspect that makes this body part more productive in the American articles is its usage as a verb.

Player:
In relation to a player, both languages comment on the result of a game or a tournament (A18, A19, H18):

A18: Bachmann wisely *heads* for a draw.

A19: After Anand had taken the *crown*, attention turned to the prospect of an Anand-Kramnik match ... .

H18: Megszerezte első nagy *skalp*ját a holland Loek van Wely.

The Duch Loek van Wely collected his first big *scalp*.

'Mind', which is often considered a physical part of the head, (Ibarretxe-Antuñano, 2002b) is also used in the American data to describe the mental state of a player (A20):

A20: Gelfand won a counter-attacking game against an *aggressively minded* Aronian.

'Head' also symbolized the most important player of a team in the American data (A21):

A21: The action began to heat up in round three when UTB-A, *headed* by GM Axel Bachmann and IM Dan Fernandez took on UTD-A ….

An interesting usage in Hungarian is when doing something with the head implies a negative meaning (H19):

H19: Világossal *fejjel ment a falnak* Vaszilij Ivancsuk.

With White, Vasili Ivanchuk *ran at the wall with his head.* (rushed headlong into the wall).

Game:
To describe the game, the American articles use 'head' in the verb form to comment on the movement of a piece (A22):

A22: The knight *is heading* to f4.

3.7 Spine

This body part gave only one example in the American data, and two in the Hungarian. It is discussed because of the vividness of the expressions and also to highlight a methodological concern in the grouping of the expressions. All three examples use the verb '*paralyze*'. The first Hungarian example (H20) unequivocally describes the game, more specifically, the unfortunate position of some pieces:

H20: A huszárok *bénasága* miatt sötét állása reménytelen.

Because of the *paralysis* (lameness) of the knights, Black's position is hopeless.

In the next two examples, the same noun (Black/Sötét) is used in the two languages; nevertheless, the American sentence (A23) was deemed to be describing the game, whereas the Hungarian (H21), the player:

A23: Black is *paralyzed*.

H21: Sötét *bénultan* várja a halált.

Black is waiting *paralyzed* for death.

The rationale for this grouping was that the American example seems to be more of an evaluation of the configuration of the pieces, whereas the Hungarian sentence, by using the verb 'wait', involves the player to a bigger extent, and thus describes his/her helplessness. This is so even if this state emerges as the result of the pieces' awkward position.

3.8 Breathing system

Each language had one expression that referred to breathing; the American one describes the position of the pieces (A24), and the Hungarian, the mental state of the player (H22):

A24: After 34...fxg4 35. hxg4 White keeps the grip on the *suffocated* black pieces.

H22: 26. ...Va8?!-re 27. Bb5! (27. Fxb6 Vxc6 és sötét *föllélegezhet*!) ... .

If 26. ...Qa8 ?! 27. Rb5! (27. Bxb6 Qxc6 and Black *can up- breathe*! ... . (Black can breathe a sigh of relief).

3.9 Blood

Metaphorical uses of the vital body substance 'blood' ('vér') came up only in the Hungarian articles. There, it was quite widely used, describing mainly players (5 types), and to a lesser extent (3 types), games.

Player:

To describe a player, both cold and warm blood is used positively, the former expressing a mental state, levelheadedness (H23), the latter, the result of effort (H24):

H23: A 17 éves norvég titán *hidegvérrel* védekezett.

The 17 year-old Norwegian titan defended *in cold blood*. (in a calm, collected manner).

H24: Döntetlen- *vért izzadva*.

A draw- *sweating blood*.

Game:
When describing a game, 'vér' symbolizes the results or the intensity of a fight (H25, H26):

H25: *Ezer sebből vérző* állás.

Thousand wound-from bleeding position.

A position full of weaknesses.

H26: *Véres harcok* után, másfél-két év múlva a zónaközik legjobbjai elkezdték a világbajnokjelöltek küzdelmét.

After *bloody combat*, in one and a half to two years, the best players from the interzonals started the battle of the world champion candidates.

3.10 Tongue

The sense organ of taste, tongue, was also used only in the Hungarian articles, giving five different expressions, describing both player and game.

Player:
With players, tongue is mostly used to describe the negative mental state of players drawing on the taste of bitterness (H27):

H27: Veszelin Topalov villámgyors vezérmanőverei *megkeserítették* a tulipánosok legjobbjának életét.

Veselin Topalov's lightning-quick queen maneuvers *embittered* the life of the best players of the tulip-team.

Game:
Sometimes moves are described with adjectives expressing taste (H28). This usage falls in line with the MANNER IS TASTE metaphor (Charteris-Black, 2003).

H28: Nagyon *finom* lépés!

A *delicious* (subtle) move!

3.11 Nose

The organ of smelling, nose, gives two expressions in the Hungarian data; both are derived from the verb for smell, 'szag'. One expression describes the mental state of the player (H29); here, the power of the metaphor is enhanced by the object of smelling, blood. The other expression is a speculation about the possible outcome of the game (H30), and exemplifies the SUSPECTING IS SMELLING metaphor (Ibarretxe-Antuñano, 1993).

> H29: Rublevszkij [...] gyalogot áldozott Henkinnek, s miután az *vért szagolt*, minőséget szedett le róla.
>
> Rublevski [...] sacrificed a pawn for Henkin, when, *smelling blood*, the latter picked up an exchange.

> H30: Lékó egyiket sem teszi meg, helyette egy *remiszagú* folytatásra szavaz.
>
> Leko does neither, instead he chooses a *draw-smelling* (likely to lead to a draw) continuation.

3.12 Face

Face was used only in the American articles, and only in relation to the player. The two expressions that came up both draw on the image of facing a difficulty that has to be overcome (A25, A26):

> A25: ... UMBC-A *faced* a tough Miami Dade College-A team with GM-elect Renier Gonzalez on first board.

> A26: So I am *faced* with a Sicilian Najdorf.

4 Discussion

As Table 2 and the above discussed examples show, both languages use a host of body parts or body-related actions to talk about a chess game or a chess player metaphorically. Even though chess is a highly cerebral game, this is not surprising, if we endorse Sweetser's (1990) mind-as-body metaphor. Previous studies have in fact shown that different body parts are handily drawn on to describe a gamut of experiences. The present exploration has verified most of the earlier findings on body parts' function in metaphorical expressions, for example, mappings of hand for control, eyes for knowing, hunger for desire, or smell for suspicion. At the same time, less discussed mappings of body parts also emerged; for example, hand's usage for manner, or the function of eyes, and, through taste, of tongue for mental state. Also, body parts that have been given less attention so far, for example, leg, head, or blood, proved important in relation to chess. This suggests that an inclusive investigation of body part metaphors in the description of a specific target in naturally occurring data may help illuminate less-explored areas of the figurative uses of body parts. Conversely, examining a target in a bottom-up fashion, starting from the source body parts as opposed to pre-selected conceptual metaphors, can shed light on details of conceptualizations that may otherwise eschew the researcher. Cross-linguistic comparisons, where the effects of factors influencing conceptualization can become even more complex than in the case of one language, may especially benefit from this approach.

Comparing the two languages, we find the biggest similarities in the metaphorical uses related to 'leg', 'hand', 'mouth', and 'stomach'. 'Leg' in both languages is used most often to talk about result or to describe the movement of the pieces; hand movements imply control and manner; 'mouth', as the organ of speech, is used in the production of speech act verbs, describing possible outcome; and functions of the stomach is related to players' mental state. Both languages also draw on the KNOWING IS SEEING conceptual metaphor, and 'spine' shows a similar usage in relation to a game.

Apart from the fact that both languages make use of a range of body parts and related expressions, and use many of these the same way, conspicuous differences also emerge. Chief among these is the fact that whereas the American articles use more body parts to describe the game than the player, the reverse is true for the Hungarian articles. Both languages use ten body parts to talk about the game; of these, the five overlapping ones,- 'leg', 'hand', 'mouth', 'eyes', and 'spine'- are mostly used similarly, with some interesting differences in the usage of eyes and mouth. The most important body part that was used only in one language in relation to a game is 'head' in the American, and 'blood' in the Hungarian data. On the other hand, American articles use seven body parts to talk about the player; Hungarian, thirteen. Six of these overlap, with 'head' and 'eyes' showing remarkable differences in usage. Of the seven body parts that were used only in the Hungarian articles, 'blood' and 'tongue' gave several expressions. Moreover, 'eyes', 'breathing system', 'blood', 'tongue', and 'nose' were used only in the Hungarian articles to talk about the mental state of players. Only 'head' did the same in the American articles. Another difference is that the 'Hungarian-only' body parts seem to be used more extensively than the 'American-only' ones: three of the seven, -blood, and two organs of perception, nose and tongue- appear in relation to both the game and the player there.

These differences offer an answer to the second research question. The more widespread use of sensory organs and blood, as well as Hungarian articles' usage of more body parts to comment on the player, seems to be in synch with the view of chess in this country. As mentioned in the introduction, chess is considered as a highly competitive sport in Hungary, and this study provides converging evidence for this more dynamic, alive, and flesh-and-bone image of the game. A tentative link that may be established between the findings of the present study and those mentioned in the introduction is the connection between the attributes 'competition' and 'tactics' (Simó, 2008), the usage of the source domains 'violent act/violent movement' and 'supernatural/gambling' (Simó, 2009a), and the frequent metaphorical use of 'blood', and the higher usage of sensory organs, in the present study. A tactical battle on the board often involves sacrifices, which is a forceful way to decide a game. This may thus conjure up the image of a violent competition, resulting in bloodshed. Moreover, the usage of more sensory organs in Hungarian, revealed by the present study, suggests an image of chess as a live entity that can be got at through our senses. Such strong correspondences between the findings for the American concept is harder to pinpoint, apart from the negative evidence, that is, the systematic lack or lesser importance of the above mentioned characteristics. Nevertheless, we may recognize a relation between the attribute 'strategy', the source domain 'confining actions' and the metaphorical usage of the verbal 'head' and the spine metaphor of 'paralyze' in that the notion of space (or the lack of it) is a prominent feature of all of these concepts.

A debatable point in the current analysis of the metaphorical usages of body parts and their relation to the concept of chess is whether the observed trends really have to do with this game, or whether they are true in the two languages in general. Whereas conventions of a language at large will undeniably appear in any specific usage of that language, as was shown, for example, in relation to 'head', there are two counterarguments to this challenge. First of all, the connection between cognitive concept and metaphorical expressions is based on an aggregate of observations about a host of source domains and body parts emerging in naturally occurring data, and not on a couple of hand-picked examples. Secondly, even if some of the metaphorical expressions are indeed more frequent in one language, it does not necessarily weaken the link. An example for this is the blood metaphor "in cold blood." An ongoing corpus investigation of mine (Simó, 2009b) indicates that this expression is in fact more frequently used in Hungarian, and especially its positive meaning (levelheadedness) is more prominent than in the American data. At the same time, 29% of this usage occurs in the commentary of a sport event, which implies that chess, by being talked about in a similar way, belongs to this category of competitive, dynamic events in Hungarian.

5 Conclusion

This study is first of all an extension on the scarce previous cross-linguistic research on metaphors of chess. The examination of multiple different data sources has shown that, as could be expected, both American English and Hungarian use numerous body parts metaphorically to talk about a chess game or a chess player, with about a 40% overlap. At the same time, apart from the similarities, striking differences also emerge in the way certain body parts are used as well as in the importance of some of them. I have intended to provide a less usual explanation for the findings.

It was suggested that rather than just speculating about the effects of cultural and linguistic differences, the cognitive concept of chess, shaped by different views of this game in the two cultures, may offer a more tangible link between metaphor usage and cognition. To find evidence for any such link is I believe rather remarkable and makes explanations based on culture more plausible.

The study also aimed at using a somewhat new approach to body part metaphor research in that the starting point was the phenomenon, as opposed to some pre-selected body parts, and all body part metaphors were analyzed regardless of their fitting into conceptual metaphors. This necessarily called for an examination of naturally occurring data. I hope to have shown the benefits of this form of analysis in that it may lead to the emergence of less explored body parts as well as less explored functions of well-established body parts.

The limitations of the study call for more research. First of all, naturally, bigger corpora would give more reliable results. Moreover, it may be of interest to separate texts into those specifically from a chess medium and those written for a more general audience. This may help to determine to what extent the concept outlined here is a 'folk-theory' of chess, and whether and how this theory differs from the expert one. Also, although there was substantial overlap in the events that the two sets of data covered, this could be controlled even more. Possessing this baseline data which emerged from an inclusive understanding of body parts, it would also be interesting to narrow down the focus and do a more extensive research on the usage of those body parts that appeared the most interesting. The study may spark an interest in examining these not only in chess, but other competitive events as well.

Author note

Affiliation: Case Western Reserve University
Acknowledgments: I am most indebted to Carol Moder for her invaluable insights on the ideas presented here. The paper has greatly profited from the discussion with the participants of the CSDL 9 conference. I want to thank the two anonymous reviewers for their very useful comments and the organizers of the conference for this wonderful event. All errors remain solely mine.

References

Charteris-Black, J. (2003). Speaking with a forked tongue: A comparative study of metaphor and metonymy in English and Malay phraseology. *Metaphor and Symbol, 18,* 289-310.

Deignan, A., & Potter, L. (2004). A corpus study of metaphors and metonyms in English and Italian. *Journal of Pragmatics, 36,* 1231-1252.

Ibarretxe-Antuñano, I. (1993). Metaphorical mappings in the sense of smell. In R.W. Gibbs, Jr., & G. J. Steen (Eds.), *Metaphor in cognitive linguistics* (pp. 29-45). Amsterdam: John Benjamins.

Ibarretxe-Antuñano, I. (2002a). Mind-as-body as a cross-linguistic conceptual metaphor. *Miscelánea: A Journal of English and American Studies, 25,* 93-119.

Ibarretxe-Antuñano, I. (2002b). The conceptual structure of Basque buru 'head.' *Fontes Linguae Vasconum, 34*(91), 463-491.

Kövecses, Z. (2002). *Metaphor: A practical introduction.* Oxford: Oxford University Press.

Lakoff, G. & Johnson, M. (1980). *Metaphors we live by.* Chicago: The University of Chicago Press.

Lakoff, G. & Johnson, M. (1999). *Philosophy in the flesh.* New York: Basic Books.

Maalej, Z. (2004). Figurative language in anger expressions in Tunisian Arabic: An extended view of embodiment. *Metaphor and Symbol, 19*(1), 51-75.

Ritchie, D. (2003). "Argument is war"- or is it a game of chess? Multiple meanings in the analysis of implicit metaphors. *Metaphor and Symbol, 18,* 125-146.

Rosch, E., & Mervis, C. B. (1975). Family resemblances: Studies in the internal structure of categories. *Cognitive Psychology, 7,* 573-605.

Simó, J. (2008). *The cognitive concept of game in American English and Hungarian.* Doctoral dissertation, Oklahoma State University, 2008. Dissertation Abstracts International-A 69/04.

Simó, J. (2009a). Chess metaphors in American English and Hungarian. *Metaphor and Symbol, 24*(1), 42-59.

Simó, J. (2009b). Metaphors of *blood* in American English and Hungarian (upcoming colloquium presentation). Corpus Based Approaches to Figurative Language (Endorsed by RaAM), July 2009, Liverpool, UK.

Sweetser, E. (1990). *From etymology to pragmatics*. Cambridge: Cambridge University Press.

Yu, N. (1995). Metaphorical expressions of anger and happiness in English and Chinese. *Metaphor and Symbolic Activity 10*, 59-92.

Yu, N. (2000). Figurative uses of *finger* and *palm* in Chinese and English. *Metaphor and Symbol, 15*(3), 159.175.

Yu, N. (2003). Chinese metaphors of thinking. *Cognitive Linguistics, 14*(2-3), 141-165.

Yu, N. (2004). The eyes for sight and mind. *Journal of Pragmatics, 36,* 663-686.

16

Is “Generic is Specific” a Metaphor?

KAREN SULLIVAN & EVE SWEETSER

Debate has raged for decades over what counts as metaphor. Do proverbs, such as *better the devil you know than the one you don't*, involve metaphor? When we refer to a generic-brand tissue as a *Kleenex*, is that a metaphor? In this paper, we observe that controversial examples such as these fall into the class of structures called “Generic is Specific” in Conceptual Metaphor Theory (Lakoff & Johnson 1980).

We argue that “Generic is Specific” examples have complicated the debate between proponents of a conceptual theory of metaphor (Lakoff & Turner 1989) and detractors of this type of theory (McGlone 2007, Sperber & Wilson forthcoming). Furthermore, we suggest that Blending Theory (Fauconnier & Turner 2002) has the explanatory power to supersede this debate, and to show that “Is this structure a metaphor?” may be a less meaningful question than “How does this structure work?”

Blending Theory can represent the ways in which “Generic is Specific” blends look more or less like metaphor. In this paper, we find that these blends resemble metaphor to a greater or lesser degree depending on the similarity of the blends' input spaces, the extent to which these spaces are structured by the same organizing frames, and the complexity of the blends' mappings. According to our analysis, “Generic is Specific” blends map the family resemblances characterizing a category prototype to other category members. Some of these blends give the impression of metaphor, as in McGlone's (2007) example *this journal is a gem*, which ascribes the qualities of a prototypical valuable object to a journal; while others appear less metaphoric, such as Sperber and Wilson's (forthcoming) example of *here's a Kleenex* used in reference to a generic-brand tissue.

Meaning, Form & Body.
Fey Parrill, Vera Tobin, and Mark Turner (eds.).

Blending diagrams illustrate that in examples such as *this journal is a gem,* qualities related to gems (namely, their high value for a particular purpose) are projected to the blended space. Similarly, in *here's a Kleenex,* qualities related to Kleenex are projected to a blend involving the generic-brand tissue. The major difference between the two blends is that in the *Kleenex* blend, both input spaces belong to the same low-level category (tissues), and therefore necessarily share an organizing frame (in that both types of tissues are used for the same purposes). This causes the *Kleenex* blend to appear less metaphoric than *this journal is a gem*, as the latter relates two very different concepts, each structured by an assortment of frames, which therefore may or may not project the same organizing frames to a blended space.

Another variation on "Generic is Specific" has been identified in proverbs (Lakoff & Turner 1989) and indeed, many proverbs, such as *better the devil you know*... share the defining characteristics of blends such as the one involved in *this journal is a gem*. A major difference between these blends is that proverbs tend to map relations, scales, and temporal and causal sequences in addition to the qualities found in other "Generic is Specific" examples. In other words, their organizing frames are more complex; and as we will see, these complex frames are projected only from one input space. This paper will conclude by extending its Blending Theory analysis from "Generic is Specific" blends such as *here's a Kleenex* and *this journal is a gem* to the more intricate structures blending found in proverbs.

1 "Generic is Specific": Much Attention, Little Analysis

Arguments against a conceptual view of metaphor tend to use and re-use certain types of examples, such as *she/Joan is an angel* (in both Thomas & Mareschal 2001 and Sperber & Wilson forthcoming), and *this journal is a gem* (McGlone 2007). A disproportionate number of examples used by metaphor critics fall into the category labeled "Generic is Specific" in Conceptual Metaphor Theory. What makes these particular examples so attractive to opponents of conceptual metaphor?

In fact, "Generic is Specific" examples demonstrate several characteristics that make them easy targets for opponents of a conceptual view of metaphor. The first charge leveled against these examples is that these "metaphors" lack the systematic mappings required of conceptual metaphors. Regarding the sentence *this journal is a gem,* McGlone (2007:109-110) asserts: "...your understanding of this sentence did not hinge on a literal reading of the sentence – e.g., at no point in your reading did you wonder about the journal's carat weight or how it might look in an engagement ring". These observations, by themselves, represent a defective argument, in that conceptual metaphors necessarily involve partial mappings (Lakoff & Johnson 1980). The absence of particular mappings in no way indicates the absence of conceptual metaphor.

However, when applied only to examples of "Generic is Specific," McGlone's observations have some merit. The structure of "Generic is Specific," as in *this journal is a gem,* does seem impoverished compared to that of more prototypical metaphors such as the Location Event-Structure Metaphor (see Lakoff & Johnson 1999) or the Conduit Metaphor (Reddy 1979). What, after all, is really mapped from Gem to Journal when we say *this journal is a gem*? This statement does little more than assert the high value of the journal in question. This minimal structure stands in stark contrast to metaphors with dozens of mappings, entailments and inferences, such as the Location Event-Structure Metaphor.

McGlone (2007) and others (see Glucksberg & Keysar 1993, Glucksberg et al. 1997, cf. Sperber & Wilson forthcoming) analyze statements such as *this journal is a gem* as "category-inclusion assertions," in this case including Journal in an "attributive category" exemplified by Gem, allowing "properties" from this category to be "attributed" to Journal. In this paper, we argue that this argument is relatively on-track insofar as it applies to the structures called "Generic is Specific," and that the applicability of this argument to "Generic is Specific" has paved the way for the overextension of McGlone-style analyses to metaphor in general.

This type of analysis, even as applied to "Generic is Specific," has two faults that need to be corrected. First, extensive research on category structure has shown that natural categories do not themselves have properties – category members have properties (see Rosch 1973, 1975, 1983, Rosch & Mervis 1975). Attributing characteristics from a category is meaningless unless we know the specific category members from which we are attributing family resemblances, and the reasons underlying the choice of both these category members and the relevant family resemblances.

McGlone's lack of attention to category structure leads to a second flaw in his analysis of *this journal is a gem*. If properties of an "attributive category" are simply assigned to Journal, how do we know which properties should be "attributed"? Salience of characteristics alone is not the answer, since (among other problems) salience can vary depending on context, as will be shown in the following section.

All in all, a more nuanced explanation of these examples is called for. Blending Theory, as employed here, is one framework within which such an explanation can be presented. A Blending Theory analysis of "Generic is Specific," while in some senses similar to McGlone's explanation, offers three advantages in addition to the resolution of the two problems described above. First, a Blending Theory analysis can account for the more complex

"Generic is Specific" found in proverbs (see section 4), which we argue cannot be modeled as "attributive categorization".

Second, a Blending Theory analysis demonstrates graphically the impoverished structure of "Generic is Specific" compared to more prototypical metaphors. Since these metaphors have also been represented using Blending Theory (see Turner & Fauconnier 1995, Grady et al. 1999), this framework provides the optimal perspective from which to understand how "Generic is Specific" deviates from prototypical metaphor.

Finally, Blending Theory illustrates why "Generic is Specific" has been analyzed as metaphor in Conceptual Metaphor Theory; and additionally, why some examples of "Generic is Specific" are the focus of analyses by metaphor theorists, while others are of greater interest to opponents of a conceptual view of metaphor. While we argue that it is impossible to provide a simple answer to the question "Is 'Generic is Specific' a metaphor?", we suggest that Blending Theory nonetheless provides the means to view exactly when, and to what extent, "Generic is Specific" looks more or less like prototypical metaphor.

2 A Blending Theory Account of "Generic is Specific"

The analysis of "Generic is Specific" given here, like the "attributive categorization" model of metaphor (and Relevance Theory analyses such as Sperber & Wilson forthcoming), recognizes the central role of categorization in generating the meaning of statements such as *this journal is a gem*. However, Blending Theory is able to offer a more precise representation of the conceptual structure of these statements – one which is also more in keeping with the results of category structure research.

According to the current analysis, the statement *this journal is a gem* does not re-categorize the concept "Journal". Rather, this statement makes use of the status of Gem as an ideal, or a paragon prototype of the category of valuable objects (see Lakoff 1987). Here, this category roughly corresponds with the generic space. In "Generic is Specific," the structure of the generic space often corresponds to that of the category encompassing both inputs, as this allows for easy recognition of the relevant category prototype. However, the generic space may also be more complex than a single category, as is normally the case in "Generic is Specific" in proverbs (section 4).

Journal does not to be re-categorized as a member of the category of valuable objects, as a journal is already an object that will have some degree of value (positive or negative) assigned to it. The value, or the usefulness of an item for a purpose, is one frame associated with Journal (as with all members of the category of valuable objects). However, Journal lacks the prototype status of Gem, and does not necessarily share the High Value that is crucial to the status of Gem as a paragon prototype. The assertion *this journal is a gem* maps the High Value role of Gem to the Value role of Journal, as illustrated in the blending diagram in Figure (1).

Although the "value/usefulness for a purpose" frame is arguably not the most salient frame structuring the concept Journal, this frame is part of the concept Journal and is not projected solely from the Gem space. As can be seen in the blend in Figure (1), all relevant roles (such as Value) and relations (such as between an Object and its Value) are present both in Journal and in Gem, as well as in the generic space. Therefore, all spaces in Figure (1) share an organizing frame, rendering these blends *mirror networks* (as described in Fauconnier & Turner 2002:122-25). If other frame structure in Journal or Gem besides "value/usefulness for a purpose" is projected to the blend, the "mirror" is no longer a perfect one, and the blend must be considered a single-scope or double-scope network. We will return to this possibility when comparing more and less "metaphoric" forms of "Generic is Specific".

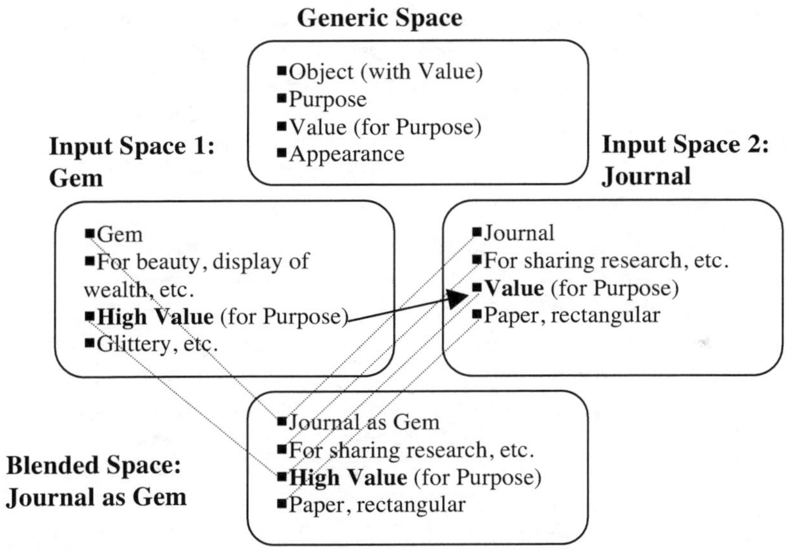

Figure 1. In understanding *this journal is a gem,* the High Value of Gem is projected to the blended space.

The blend in Figure (1) has only one mapping (shown by the arrow), which maps a Gem's value (for its purpose) to the Journal's value (for its purpose). Gem, as a paragon prototype in the category of valuable objects, is characterized by the family resemblance of an extraordinarily high value. This "High Value" filler of the Value role is projected to the blended space.[1]

Although the High Value of Gem projects to the blended space, the other fillers characterizing Journal, rather than those of Gem, project to this space. This induces "High Value" to be interpreted somewhat differently in the blended space than in the "Gem" space, since the Purpose of a Journal is different from that of a Gem. As a result, the High Value in the blended space refers to readability, sound methodology, and all the other elements of a valuable journal – rather than to glitter, carat weight, and the other attributes that contribute to the value of a gem.

This representation of the structure underlying *this journal is a gem* differs from the analysis proposed by McGlone in several ways. First, the "attributes" (or fillers) that are assigned to Journal come from the Gem space, rather than from a category to which Gem belongs. Second, Journal is not assigned to a new category; instead, its placement within an existing category is recognized and is taken advantage of in the construction of the blend. These differences render the above model more realistic than "attributive categorization" in terms of what is known about category structure, the importance of prototypes, and the locus of the family resemblances that structure categories. These differences give the Blending Theory representation explanatory power that the "attributive categorization" theory lacks. For example, Blending Theory explains why certain attributes and not others are mapped, as explored in the next subsection.

2.1 Mapping from Prototypes of Multiple Categories

"Attributive categorization" and related theories fail to satisfactorily explain why certain characteristics are "attributed" and others are not. However, research on category structure and prototype theory sheds light on these issues. According to current models of human categorization, prototypes in a given category are characterized by certain family resemblances, by which the prototypicality of other category members can be judged (see Rosch & Mervis 1975). When a "Generic is Specific" blend uses a prototypical category member in an input space, the blend maps the resemblances that are most important for the member's prototype status.

The relevant prototype is not necessarily a paragon. For example, the blend in Figure (1) could equally well involve an anti-paragon of the category of valuable objects, that is, an object with outstandingly low value, as

[1] Spaces with roles/fillers could each be depicted as a simplex blend between a space with roles and a space with fillers (see Fauconnier & Turner 2002:120-22), but this structure has not been represented here. Additionally, lines denoting correspondences with the generic space have been omitted from the diagrams in this paper.

in *this journal is a piece of filth*. Here, the (very bad) filler of the Value role in Filth is mapped to Journal and projected to the blended space, just as the (excellent) filler of the Value role for Gem is mapped to Journal courtesy of *this journal is a gem*. Category members must be some kind of prototype in order to produce this type of blend. For example, everyday objects such as *apple, desk, coffee mug* are not considered to have an outstandingly high or low value. For this reason, *this journal is a coffee mug* fails to provide the useful inferences of *this journal is a gem* or *this journal is a piece of filth*.

The explanatory advantages of the Blending Theory model are especially apparent when we look at an input that is a prototype of more than one category. In this case, the input will normally be considered as a member of one category or the other, but not as a member of both. For example, the sentence *she/Joan is an angel* has been examined repeatedly by critics of conceptual metaphor, yet these critics have all overlooked the sentence's two available meanings, roughly paraphrased as *Joan acts like an angel* and *Joan looks like an angel*. Though both these meanings are possible, the default interpretation of *Joan is an angel* refers to moral nature (as in *Joan acts like an angel*), not appearance (as in *Joan looks like an angel*). The "moral nature" interpretation of the sentence *Joan is an angel* is given in the blend shown below.

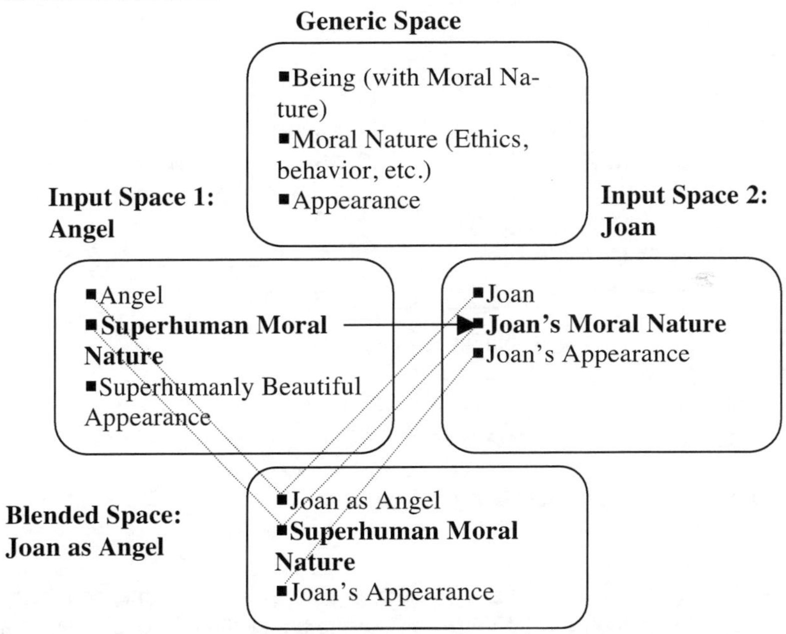

Figure 2. The blend evoked by *Joan is an angel / Joan acts like an angel*

Figure (2) represents one interpretation of the sentence *Joan is an angel,* in which Joan's moral nature is interpreted as angelic. Angels are paragon prototype moral beings, whereas the human Joan is not a prototype of this category. If the status of Angel as a prototype of moral beings is most relevant in context, then the superhuman moral nature of Angel will be mapped to Joan, and projected to the blend. Joan's other characteristics will be projected to the blended space: in this blend, Joan looks like Joan, has Joan's phone number, etc., but she has the superhuman moral nature of an angel.

However, angels are prototypes of more than one category. In the appropriate context, angels' superhuman beauty may be more relevant than their status as moral paragons. As a result of the dual category membership of Angel, the sentence *Joan is an angel* may also refer to Joan's appearance, rather than her moral nature. This interpretation is diagrammed in Figure (3).

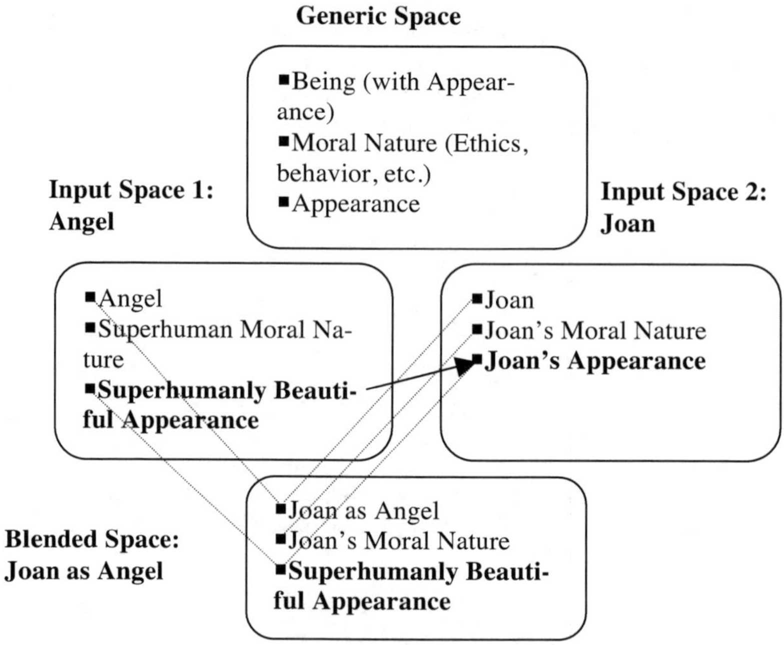

Figure 3. The blend evoked by *Joan is an angel* / *Joan looks like an angel*

In Figure (3), the filler of the Appearance role in Angel is mapped, rather than the filler of the Moral Nature role. In the blend, Joan has her own Mor-

Moral Nature (she may be ethical, cruel, indifferent, etc.). However, in the blend she has the superhuman beauty of an angel.

In the blends in Figures (2) and (3), Angel is treated either as a paragon of beauty or a paragon of ethics – not both. Additional space-builders are needed to bring in the characteristics associated with Angel as the prototype of both categories, as in *Joan acts like an angel, and she looks like one too.*

If we follow the "attributive categorization" model and add *Joan* to a category instantiated by Angel, we wouldn't know which category, nor would we know which properties to "attribute". The above model, in contrast, predicts exactly which categories we will be able to draw on when we use Angel as Input Space 1 in a "Generic is Specific" blend. We may use precisely those categories of which the Input 2 is a member, and of which Angel is a prototype. The family resemblances of Angel that are mapped will be those that characterize it as a prototype in its category, and all other projected information will come from Input 2. This predictive capability is not supplied by other accounts of "Generic is Specific".

3 A Cline of Metaphoricity in "Generic is Specific"

If "Generic is Specific" isn't "attributive categorization," is it metaphor? Many examples of "Generic is Specific" are almost universally termed "metaphor," and yet we might balk at assigning this label to other examples that demonstrate the same blending structure, such as when someone hands over a generic-brand tissue and says, "Here's a Kleenex". However, using brand names with generic reference is structurally identical to more figurative-seeming usages, such as calling a journal a "gem". This is shown in Figure (4) on the following page.

As in the blend evoked by *this journal is a gem,* shown in Figure (1), the blend in Figure (4) involves the mapping of family resemblances from a category prototype to a non-prototypical category member. Due primarily to advertising by its manufacturers, the Kleenex brand of tissue has become a prototype of the tissue category. As such, the qualities of Kleenex can be attributed to other category members via a "Generic is Specific" blend. This possibility upsets the manufacturers of Kleenex and other brand-name products, who are rightly concerned that by using the brand name to refer to generic products, consumers will map the perceived qualities of the brand-name products to generic-brand products. Ironically, however, this blending is possible only because the brand-name manufacturers have worked hard to make their products the category prototype. Non-prototypical brand-name products are not used as Input 1 in "Generic is Specific" blends.

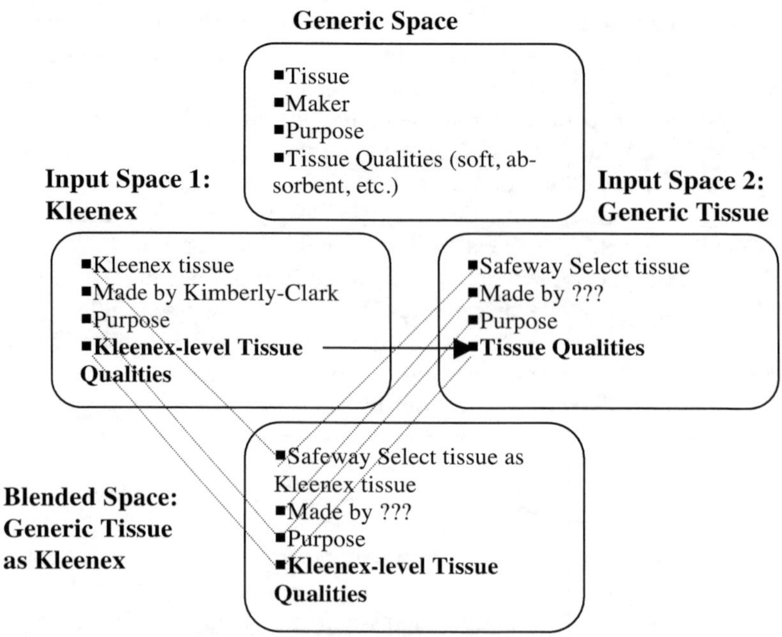

Figure 4. The blend evoked by *Here's a Kleenex* (referring to generic tissue)

If we compare the structures in Figures (1)-(4), we find them to be virtually identical. In each case, a characteristic or set of characteristics is mapped from a prototype to a non-prototypical category member, resulting in a blended space which contains all the characteristics of the non-prototypical category member except for the family resemblances that characterize the category prototype. This can result in a blended space juxtaposing the Purpose of a Journal with the Value of a Gem, as in Figure (1); or the Moral Nature of an Angel with the Appearance of a human being, as in Figure (2); or the perceived high quality of Kleenex with the attributes of generic-brand tissue, as in Figure (4). All of these blends can be considered mirror networks, in that the spaces in each blend share an organizing frame and differ only in the fillers of their frame roles. In each case, Input 1 provides the fillers associated with a category prototype, and Input 2 provides all other fillers. Why, then, do some "Generic is Specific" blends intuitively seem more metaphoric than others? This question can be resolved if we examine these blends in terms of the various attributes that characterize prototypical metaphor.

3.1 "Generic is Specific" and the Characteristics of Metaphor

Is "Generic is Specific" a metaphor? Some signs point to "no". First of all, the popularity of "Generic is Specific" with opponents of conceptual metaphor suggests, in and of itself, that these blends make easy targets for critics of conceptual metaphor. Second, some instances of "Generic is Specific," such as the *Kleenex* example in Figure (4), seem less figurative than others despite similarities in their blending structure, indicating that it may be counterproductive to uniformly assign or deny the label of "metaphor" to all examples of "Generic is Specific". To pinpoint the source of these impressions, "Generic is Specific" can be examined in a step-by-step comparison with the characteristics of prototypical metaphor.

The most detailed list of criteria for the identification of prototypical conceptual metaphor remains that of Lakoff and Turner (1989:103), which provides three general criteria for distinguishing metaphor from metonymy (and presumably, from other non-metaphoric processes). First, metaphor involves "two conceptual domains, and one is understood in terms of the other". Second, "a whole schematic structure (with two or more entities) is mapped onto another whole schematic structure," and third, "the logic of the source-domain structure is mapped onto the logic of the target-domain structure".

We need look no further than the first of these three criteria to see why some instances of "Generic is Specific" seem more metaphoric than others. In the *Kleenex* example in Figure (4), are Generic Tissue and Kleenex "two conceptual domains"? The term "domain" is a slippery one, but most researchers would probably find Kleenex and Generic Tissue too similar to constitute two separate domains. One way to capture the similarity of the two concepts is to notice that the lowest-level category to which both belong to is very specific: the category of tissues. As a result, the generic space in the blend evoked by *here's a Kleenex* is also very specific, as shown in Figure (5).

- Tissue
- Maker
- Purpose
- Tissue Qualities (soft, absorbent, etc.)

Figure 5. The generic space of Generic Tissue as Kleenex (see Figure 4)

Another way to capture the similarity between the input spaces is to recognize that these inputs necessarily have the same organizing frames. The blend in Figure (4) can hardly be extended in novel ways, because there is little structure that can be projected from either input space which is not shared by the other input. This type of "Generic is Specific" is therefore necessarily a mirror network.

The specificity of the generic space in Figures (4)-(5), the low-level status of the category it represents, and the perfect fit of the inputs' organizing frames, render Kleenex and Generic Tissue too similar to qualify as separate domains, according to most definitions of "domain".

In the more metaphoric-seeming example *this journal is a gem,* on the other hand, are Journal and Gem different enough to constitute "two conceptual domains"? These inputs may seem more like "domains" than do Kleenex and Generic Tissue. For one thing, the lowest-level category that both belong to, valuable objects, is very general, and the generic space evoked by *this journal is a gem* is consequently equally general (as in Figure 6).

- ▪Object (with Value)
- ▪Purpose
- ▪Value (for Purpose)
- ▪Appearance

Figure 6. The generic space of Journal as Gem (see Figure 1)

Inputs that belong to the same low-level category, and take part in blends with relatively specific generic spaces, seem less like separate domains, and result in less "figurative," less "metaphoric" blends.

Additionally, the Journal as Gem blend in Figure (1) can be extended in ways unavailable to the Generic Tissue as Kleenex blend in Figure (4). In the Journal as Gem blend, frame structure can potentially be projected from only one input space, rendering the blend something other than a mirror network. For example, "this journal is a gem in the rough" recruits not only the value of gems, but also their lapidary process, which is not part of the Journal input. The blend therefore maps the physical process of refining and polishing a gem, and the resultant increase in the gem's value, onto the process of revising, reformatting, and so forth, which can allow a journal to achieve its potential. This blend is clearly a single-scope network and not a mirror network, in that the organizing frame structure of Gem projected to the blend includes material not found in Journal. The availability of frames such as the lapidary process is only possible because of the structural differences between Journal and Gem. Blends with more similar inputs, such as Kleenex and Generic Tissue, cannot be extended in this manner.

It appears, then, that some "Generic is Specific" blends fare better than others in fulfilling the two-domain criterion of metaphor. How well, then, do these blends fit the other two characteristics of metaphor in Lakoff and Turner's list (1989:103)? According to this list, in a prototypical metaphor, "a whole schematic structure (with two or more entities) is mapped onto another whole schematic structure". Here, most "Generic is Specific" examples fail miserably. "Generic is Specific" generally maps only one quality of a prototype, or at most, a set of related qualities, such as those characterizing a "Moral Nature" or the qualities of a good tissue. This is a far cry from the dozens of systematic mappings that make up conceptual metaphors such as the Location Event-Structure Metaphor. "Generic is Specific" blends, then, are inherently different from prototypical metaphors, in that their mappings are more limited. In this sense, "Generic is Specific" can be said to look more like metonymy rather than metaphor.

"Generic is Specific" fares better on the third characteristic, which stipulates that in metaphor, "the logic of the source-domain structure is mapped onto the logic of the target-domain structure". Here, "Generic is Specific" measures up insofar as it always generates at least one unidirectional inference, ascribing the mapped quality of a category prototype to another category member.

Note that when Generic is Specific is elaborated into a single-scope network, it immediately picks up all the traits of metaphor. For example, the blend evoked by "this journal is a gem in the rough," as described above, includes numerous mappings, rather than the simple mapping of family resemblances. It also recruits the structure of a conventional blend (the Object Event-Structure Metaphor, a "primary metaphor" that includes the mapping Ideas are Objects) in order to complete the mappings from elements in Gem to Journal, and to generate new inferences, such as the inference that revising a journal will allow it to realize its high potential (as polishing a gem brings it to its highest potential value). Elaborating a mirror network, then, can turn it into a single-scope network that clearly fits the criteria of metaphor (different domains, multiple mappings, and inferences). This elaboration may occur in mirror networks with highly different inputs, such as Journal and Gem, but cannot occur in mirror networks with nearly identical inputs, such as Kleenex and Generic Tissue. The potential for creating a single-scope network, which easily fits any and all criteria for metaphor, may contribute to the "figurative" interpretation of blends such as Journal as Gem.

Whether "Generic is Specific" should be considered a metaphor depends on the value placed on the various characteristics of metaphor. If, for example, a researcher finds it most useful to limit the term "metaphor" to conceptual blends with multiple mappings, then "Generic is Specific" examples such as those in Figures (1)-(4) should not be considered metaphoric blends. At the same time, the potential of certain "Generic is Specific" blends to be extended into single-scope networks, and the consequent increase in the features of prototypical metaphor, should not be ignored.

Finally, any definitive conclusions about "Generic is Specific" must take into account its instantiations in proverbs, many of which are more nuanced than the examples we've seen so far.

4 "Generic is Specific" in Proverbs

The question of whether "Generic is Specific" should be called "metaphor" is complicated by the variations of "Generic is Specific" found in proverbs (see Lakoff & Turner 1989). In another sense, though, these examples clarify the status of "Generic is Specific," in that they completely defy an "attributive categorization" explanation.

This section will focus on the "Generic is Specific" proverb *better (deal with) the devil you know than the one you don't,* as used in this quotation from Paul Nisbet, a defense analyst (boldface ours).[2]

> "There are reasons why the Navy might not be as delighted with having Northrop as the preeminent shipbuilder rather than GD," Nisbet said. "They know GD; they've dealt with them for years and decades. Northrop is a 'Johnny Come Lately.' **Better deal with the devil you know than the one you don't**."
>
> ("Northrop Bid Likely to Fail, But So What?", *Los Angeles Business Journal*, May 14, 2001).

The "Generic is Specific" blend evoked by this proverb is shown in Figure (7), in which it can be seen that dealing with GD (as opposed to Northrop) is conceptualized in terms of dealing with a known devil (as opposed to a new devil). (Note that the lines indicating projections to the blend have been omitted from this diagram in order to limit clutter.)

[2] This example was chosen for the instantiation of "Generic is Specific" with minimal influence from more prototypical metaphors. Many proverbs combine prototypical metaphor and "Generic is Specific," as in *you can lead a horse to water, but you can't make it drink*, which involves the Location Event-Structure Metaphor (in which guiding a horse to a goal maps to assisting someone in the accomplishment of a purpose, among other mappings).

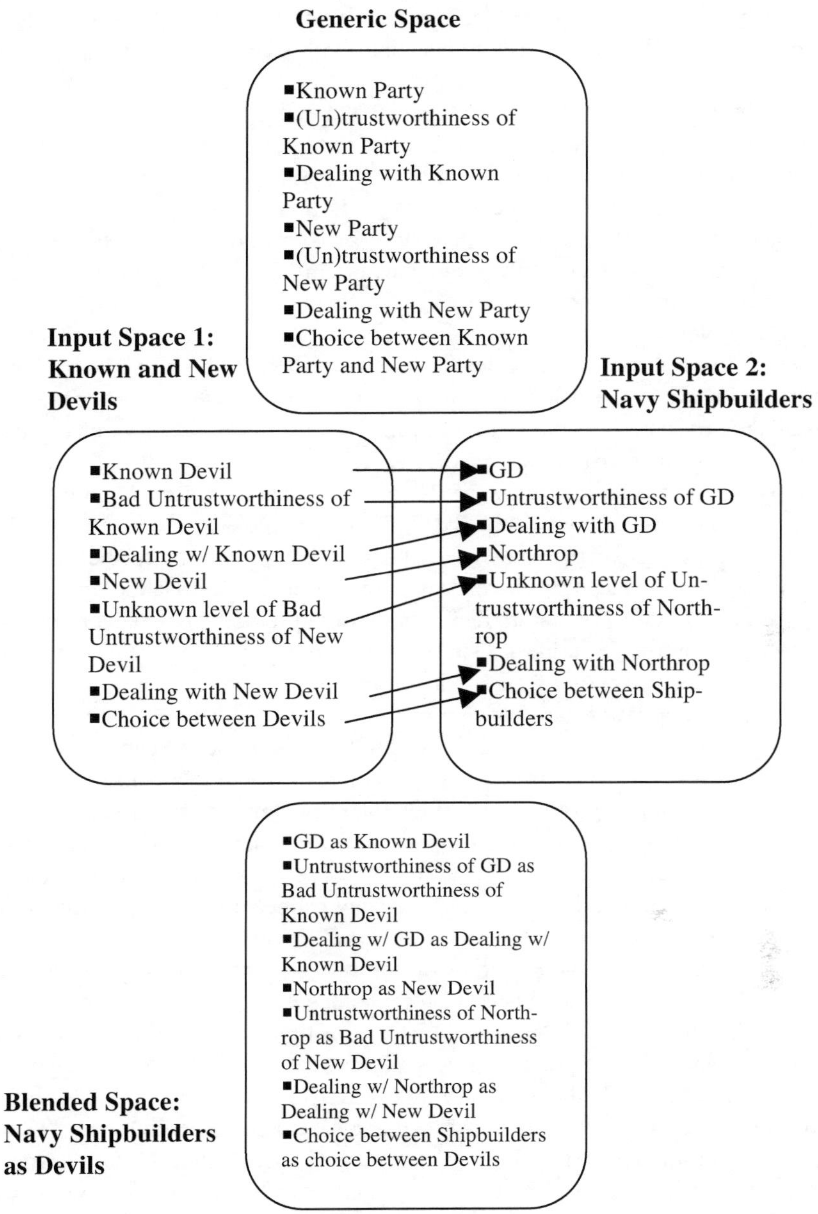

Figure 7. The blend evoked by *better (deal with) the devil you know than the one you don't* (in reference to Navy shipbuilders GD and Northrop)

Clearly, the structure of the blend evoked by *better the devil you know than the one you don't* is more complex than the "Generic is Specific" blends evoked by expressions such as *Joan is an angel*. However, it is equally clear that the blend in (7) draws on some of the same blending strategies. For example, the use of the term *devil* here generates inferences in much the way that *angel* does in *Joan is an angel*, in that the Untrustworthiness of the devils is projected to the blended space, as the Moral Nature of angels is projected to the blended space in Figure (2). Since Nisbet refers to both GD and Northrop as "devils," this generates the inference that both are untrustworthy to some degree.

The blend in (7), however, contains a great deal of structure besides the mapped characteristics of a prototype. In addition to the untrustworthiness of the known and new devils, the *relative* untrustworthiness of these two devils is preserved in the blend. In other words, an entire *scale* of untrustworthiness/trustworthiness is projected to the blend. A scale of familiarity/newness is also projected, as this is necessary in order to compare the relative newness of the two devils/shipbuilders. Additionally, temporal relations are projected: the known devil was dealt with prior to the decision between devils, etc. Causal relations are preserved, in that the choice between devils will precipitate dealings involving either a greater or a lesser extent of untrustworthiness. These scales, relations, etc., can be said to compose the organizing frame structure of Input 1 which is projected to the blend. These relations are not part of Input 2, so the blend cannot be said to be a mirror network like the earlier examples of Generic is Specific.

It seems, then, that the type of "Generic is Specific" in Figure (7) involves the mapped prototype qualities found in simpler examples such as in Figures (1)-(4), but additionally maps more complex structures, including scalar, temporal, and causal relations. Because more than prototype qualities are mapped, and because the organizing frame structure is not shared by all spaces, this type of "Generic is Specific" involves a generic space that does not align with the structure of a single category. In fact, the generic space in this type of blend is quite complex, as is apparent in Figure (7).

The complexity of the generic space in this type of "Generic is Specific" renders it completely incompatible with an "attributive categorization" explanation. If this structure involved category inclusion, then Input 2 would be included as a member in a category called something like: "Dealing with a known party of some level of (un)trustworthiness, faced with a decision between a known party and a new party of unknown (un)trustworthiness ..." and so forth. This type of structure would be a cognitively implausible category. Category members have family resemblances, but they do not include structures such as causal sequences. The type of "Generic is Specific" in Figure (7) involves the blending of structures that simply cannot be accounted for as "attributive categorization".

If this type of "Generic is Specific" cannot be "attributive categorization," can it then be "metaphor"? Returning to the criteria used earlier, are there "two conceptual domains, and is one understood in terms of the other"? The inputs in Figure (7) are highly distinct, especially given that they do not belong to a common category or share the same organizing frames, so they seem like good candidates for "domains". Next, does a "whole schematic structure (with two or more entities)" map onto another whole schematic structure? In this respect, the example in Figure (7) looks more like metaphor than examples such as (1)-(4), in that the blend in (7) involves numerous mappings. Finally, is "the logic of the source-domain structure ... mapped onto the logic of the target-domain structure"? Again, yes: the blend gives us unidirectional inferences regarding the high untrustworthiness of the two shipbuilders, and the superiority of the one over the other. The proverb diverges from prototypical metaphor in that its organizing frame structure is a matter of convention, rather than embodiment or world experience, but it certainly generates inferences.

It seems, then, that the most metaphor-like instances of "Generic is Specific" are those in which the inputs do not share the same organizing frames, as in proverbs such as *Better the devil you know* ... Examples in which the inputs are substantially different, even if they do share organizing frames, also resemble conceptual metaphors to a certain degree (as in *this journal is a gem*). Both of these types look like metaphor in that their inputs are more "domain"-like than those in examples such as *here's a Kleenex*. Moreover, when "Generic is Specific" lacks shared organizing frames, it looks more like metaphor in that it involves multiple (usually numerous) mappings. And finally, all "Generic is Specific" examples behave like metaphor in that they produce inferences. Overall, then, we see a cline of metaphoricity in "Generic is Specific" examples, from highly metaphoric proverbs, to blends such as *this journal is a gem,* down to examples such as *here's a Kleenex*.

5 Conclusions

The present analysis of "Generic is Specific" has implications for both opponents and proponents of a conceptual view of metaphor. First, this analysis suggests that opponents of conceptual metaphor are not justified in using instances of "Generic is Specific" (and especially the least metaphor-like types of "Generic is Specific") as counterexamples to a conceptual theory of metaphor. To a greater or lesser extent, all types of "Generic is Specific" differ in their structure from more prototypical metaphors, and cannot be legitimately used to attack conceptual metaphor as a whole.

Second, even if "attributive categorization" theorists limit the scope of their argument to "Generic is Specific," their model needs refinement before it can adequately account for structures of this type. These theorists need to recognize that categories do not have "properties"; they need to reshape their theory so that it is capable of predicting which "properties" would be "attributed," and from which categories; and they need to revise their theory so that we are not forced to call some strange things "categories," such as "Dealing with a known party of some level of (un)trustworthiness, etc."

Even though "attributive categorization" does not adequately represent "Generic is Specific," Conceptual Metaphor Theory cannot yet fully account for this process, either. This paper has shown that "Generic is Specific" may look more or less like metaphor, depending on how much structure is mapped, the lowest-level category to which both inputs can be assigned, and whether these inputs share the same organizing frames.

The Blending Theory analysis given here has the advantage of capturing both the metaphor-like and the category-based aspects of "Generic is Specific". In answer to the question, "Is 'Generic is Specific' a metaphor?" then, the best response might be "Does it matter?" Human beings use many types of conceptual structures in reasoning and in language. We cannot expect that these structures will belong to hard-and-fast categories, any more than we can expect to find hard-and-fast categories in most other areas of human cognition. Identifying, modeling and understanding the structures that occur, then, may be more productive than assigning labels and trying to confine these conceptual structures to artificially invented categories.

Author Note

Karen Sullivan is a Postdoctoral Fellow at the Autonomous University of Barcelona. Eve Sweetser is Professor of Linguistics at the University of California, Berkeley.

References

Fauconnier, G. 1997. *Mappings in Thought and Language*. Cambridge: Cambridge University Press.

Fauconnier, G. & M. Turner 2002. *The Way We Think: Conceptual Blending and the Mind's Hidden Complexities*. New York: Basic Books.

Glucksberg, S. & B. Keysar 1993. "How Metaphors Work". In A. Ortony, ed., *Metaphor and Thought*. Cambridge: Cambridge University Press, 401-424.

Glucksberg, S., M. S. McGlone, & D. Manfredi 1997. "Property Attribution in Metaphor Comprehension". *Journal of Memory and Language 36*, 50-67.

Grady, J. E., T. Oakley & S. Coulson 1999. "Blending and Metaphor". In: R. Gibbs, ed., *Metaphor in Cognitive Linguistics*. Amsterdam: John Benjamins, 101-124.

Lakoff, G. 1987. *Women, Fire and Dangerous Things*. Chicago: University of Chicago Press.

Lakoff, G. & M. Turner 1989. *More Than Cool Reason*. Chicago: The University of Chicago Press.

Lakoff, G. & M. Johnson 1980. *Metaphors We Live By*. Chicago: University of Chicago Press.

Lakoff, G. & M. Johnson 1999. *Philosophy in the Flesh*. New York: Basic Books.

McGlone, M. S. 2007. "What is the Explanatory Value of a Conceptual Metaphor?". *Language and Communication 27,* 109-126.

Reddy, M. J. 1979. "The Conduit Metaphor: A Case of Frame Conflict in our Language about Language". In A. Ortony, ed., *Metaphor and Thought*. Cambridge University Press, 164-201.

Rosch, E. H. 1973. "Natural Categories". *Cognitive Psychology* 4, 328-350.

Rosch, R. H. 1975. "Cognitive Reference Points". *Cognitive Psychology* 7, 532-547.

Rosch, E. H. 1983. "Prototype Classification and Logical Classification: The Two Systems". In E. K. Scholnick, ed., *New Trends in Conceptual Representation: Challenges to Piaget's Theory?*, Hillsdale: Lawrence Erlbaum Associates, 73-86.

Rosch, E. H. & C. B. Mervis, 1975. "Family Resemblances: Studies in the Internal Structure of Categories". *Cognitive Psychology* 7, 573-605.

Sperber, D. & D. Wilson *forthcoming*. "A Deflationary Account of Metaphor". In: R. Gibbs, ed., *Handbook of Metaphor (3rd edition)*. Cambridge: Cambridge University Press.

Thomas, M. S. C. & D. Mareschal 2001. "Metaphor as Categorization: A Connectionist Implementation". *Metaphor and Symbol* 16 (1&2), 5-27.

Turner, M. & G. Fauconnier 1995. "Conceptual Integration and Formal Expression". *Metaphor and Symbolic Activity*, 10:3, 183-203.

17

Grammatical and Rhetorical Consequences of Entrenchment in Conceptual Blending: Compressions Involving Change

VERA TOBIN

1 Introduction

It is a commonplace of blending theory (e.g. Fauconnier and Turner 2002: 260) that "no one is deluded" by the conceptual integrations involved in many creative blends. This paper examines a number of cases in which it seems that people are, in fact, "deluded"—that is, cases where a given blending structure is sufficiently highly entrenched that it becomes routine, automatic, and relatively opaque to self-reflection. Specifically, I present a cluster of phenomena in which variability across a group is compressed (Fauconnier and Turner 2002) into, or conceptualized as, change in an individual.

The starting point of this paper is a new observation about English grammatical constructions for expressing change in an entity over time. Constructions that are canonically limited to expressing change in an individual turn out to show more flexible patterns of use with certain content domains. These exceptions seem to reflect a high degree of entrenchment, not of the expression, but of an underlying conceptual mapping.

Meaning, Form & Body.
Fey Parrill, Vera Tobin, and Mark Turner (eds.).

Analysis of these examples suggests that the semantics of certain constructions can be usefully analyzed in terms of whether they do or do not prompt for decompression of an expressed relation. This account is further supported by their use rhetorically to influence conceptualization, as seen in examples such as Kenner 1967 and Hirshman 2008 (below). The resulting account points to new ways that grammatical data can provide evidence for blending structures, and new ways that blending theory can explain grammatical phenomena.

2 Ways of Expressing Change

It has frequently been noted (e.g. Fodor 1970, Shibatani 1976, Haiman 1983, Sweetser 1997) that the variety of situations that can be described by lexical change predicates and lexical causative expressions are subsets of the range of situations that can be expressed by their periphrastic counterparts.

Typically, lexical causatives, as in (1a), are used only to express cases of direct causation, while periphrastic causative expressions like (1b) can be used to express either direct or indirect causation.

(1) a. Helen moved the book.

b. Helen made the book move.

Similarly, as observed in Sweetser (1997), both (2a) and (2b) can be used to express literal change to a single room, but only (2b) can be used to express fictive change.

(2) a. My cubicle shrinks every year.

b. My cubicle gets smaller every year.

However, under the right circumstances, both of these lexical constructions can license interpretations usually reserved for their periphrastic cousins, as seen in (3).

(3) a. Moore shortened the poem for every new edition.

b. Edward cut his hair. [A stylist actually did the cutting.]

I will be arguing that these apparent exceptions to the usual constraints are a consequence of a critical degree of entrenchment of underlying conceptual compressions.

Exceptions of the second sort have received a fair amount of attention from linguists (e.g. Croft 1991, Goldberg 1995, Woolf 2003). In these cases, the represented causal relation seems to be indirect, in that there is an intermediary cause. But events, and their component chains of causation, can always be construed at different levels of granularity, so that a given causal chain can potentially be construed as a unified single event. Further, Woolf (2003: 5-6) proposes that causal chains with intermediate entities at the same level of granularity as the initial causer or final recipient (as in our hair-cutting example) can be viewed as direct if those intermediaries can be construed as "enabling conditions" rather than salient causal agents in their own right.

Most relevant to the current analysis is the explanation of such examples proposed by Goldberg (1995: 169)—namely, that the acceptability of such constructions depends on how "conventional" the causal scenario in question happens to be:

> It is a conventional way to have one's hair cut to go to a salon, a conventional way to have one's house painted to have professional painters do it, and so forth. That is, simple causatives can be used to imply *conventionalized* causation that may in actuality involve an intermediate cause. It seems that conventionalized scenarios can be cognitively "packaged" in such a way that their internal structure is ignored.

Specifically, I propose that the particular kind of "packaging" on display here is the result of the entrenchment of patterns of compression across vital relations.

3 Compressions and Vital Relations

Conceptual blending theory (Fauconnier and Turner 2000, 2002; Fauconnier 2005; Turner 2006) argues that our understanding of the world is crucially structured in terms of twenty or so vital relations, such as Cause-Effect, Analogy, Time, Space, Change, Identity, and Uniqueness. Reducing complexity to a conceptually manageable scale involves frequent *compressions* across those relations: from many elements to few, from diffuse connections to tight.

In a conceptual integration network, some mental spaces serve as "input spaces" that selectively project structure to a new, "blended" mental space, where these projected elements are integrated, and new structures emerge. Mappings between input spaces are compressed, selectively, within a single blended space. Relations can be compressed into human-scale versions of the same relation, or into different vital relations. These compressions are memorable, intelligible, and manipulable, because they are concise and at human scale.

When we imagine our current selves answering an old criticism, we are compressing over time, so that events separated by many years can be conceptualized as nearly simultaneous in the compression. When we see an actor on stage and say, "Hamlet is dead," the link of representation between the thing being represented and the thing representing it is being compressed into uniqueness. While we still understand perfectly well that the actor and Hamlet are not one and the same, we can think about and refer to the situation as if they were.

The role reading of sentences like *My cubicle gets smaller every year*, then, can similarly be analyzed as the product of a conceptual blend in which analogies between many specific individuals are compressed into an identity relation, and further to uniqueness, producing a single individual in the resulting blend. Disanalogies across those specific individuals are then understood in terms of changes to that unique individual, so that the blend presents one individual participating in a dynamic scene. Figure 1 presents a schematic representation of these compressions.

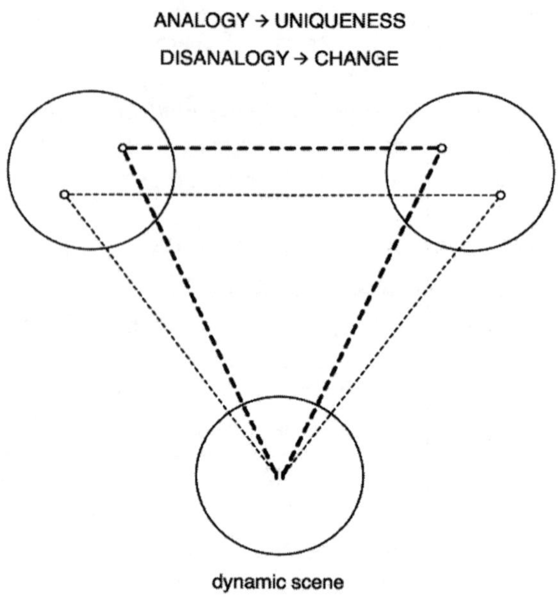

Figure 1: The compression of outer-space relations to inner-space relation

Fauconnier (2005: 524) observes that this general pattern of compression is an especially common one, indeed "one of the most common." Its archetypal illustration in the blending literature involves the theory according to which birds are the evolutionary descendants of dinosaurs. This evolutionary story covers a vast span of time, during which a great many animals lived, reproduced, and died, without changing into anything else. However, we can and do think about this story as one of change, and we can, for instance, say that some scientists believe that "dinosaurs turned into birds." In this blend, millions of years are compressed into the single lifetime of a single animal. Again, analogies between individuals—in this case, offspring and their ancestors—are compressed to produce a single entity in the blend, while disanalogies are compressed into change: at the beginning, this entity is a dinosaur, and at the end, it is a bird.

The blending literature often notes that these kinds of compressions are so prevalent that "Everyday language includes expressions for automatically compressing Disanalogy into Change" (Fauconnier and Turner 2002: 94), with sentences like *My tax bill gets bigger every year* presented as illustrative examples. However, as we have seen, not all change-of-state predicates are equally amenable to interpretations of this sort. Observing when and how the more restrictive constructions for expressing change do appear will provide useful evidence about how conventionalized and "packaged" a given compression is in conceptualization.

4 Constraints on the Expression of Compressed Relations

Sweetser (1997) observes that there are a number of related, semantically close pairs of predicates that differ according to whether they do or do not permit a role reading for their subjects, and identifies a general trend: periphrastic change predicates allow both role and individual readings, while monolexemic change predicates are more restrictive. By way of illustration, consider the different interpretations of the subject noun phrases suggested by the following sentences (examples taken from Sweetser 1997: 119).

(4) a. His kids keep getting taller.

b. His kids keep growing. (easy to contextualize)

(5) a. His lovers keep getting taller.

b. # His lovers keep growing. (more difficult to contextualize)

(4a) and (4b) seem to be paraphrases of one another, while (5a) and (5b) are not. Why is this?

Sweetser explains that *grow* demands an "individual" reading, in which the subject noun phrase is taken to refer to an individual or (in the case of a plural noun phrase, as in these examples) or set of individuals that undergo an actual change in size. The periphrastic *get taller*, on the other hand, permits either this reading or a "role" interpretation, where the noun phrase can be understood to refer to a succession of individuals, each one taller than the last. It is unremarkable to think of children as individually growing taller, while we are less likely to expect lovers, who are generally adults, to be doing the same. (Sweetser's original analysis is too polite to mention it, incidentally, but there is indeed a natural, if prurient, reading for (5b) that preserves the requirement for an individual interpretation: *his lovers* can be taken as a *totum pro parte* synecdoche referring to the gentlemen's most salient body parts.)

Examples (6) and (7) illustrate the same contrast in other cases involving a set of temporally successive fillers of a single role:

(6) a. Your apartment gets bigger every time I visit.

b. Your apartment expands every time I visit.

(7) a. The students make their uniforms shorter every year.

b. The students shorten their uniforms every year.

The sentence in (6a) can be used to refer to a sequence of progressively larger apartments, while (6b) strongly invites an interpretation in which "your apartment" refers to an individual apartment that is being remodeled. Example (7a) could be used in a situation where one set of (individual) students alter the hems of their (individual) uniforms annually, or to describe a sequence of students (different individuals filling the same role) whose uniforms are sequentially shorter than the set of uniforms on display the year before. (7b) prefers the former reading.

The general pattern is that periphrastic change predicates permit a role reading, while (with certain exceptions) their monolexemic counterparts do not. We can recast this distinction in blending theory in terms of two alternate conceptual structures, one of which involves overt compression, and the other of which does not. Figure 2 illustrates the role reading that is available, and indeed preferred, for the periphrastic *My cubicle gets bigger every year*.

The grammar of the sentence presents a blend in which there is one cubicle, growing bigger over time. Recognizing this sentence as referring to a succession of progressively larger cubicles which fill the role of "my cubicle" requires the hearer to unpack this blend—in other words, to recognize it *as* a blend, and to construct an integration network in which an inner-space relation of uniqueness is decompressed into a cross-space connection of analogy, and the inner-space relation of change is decompressed into a cross-space connection of disanalogy.

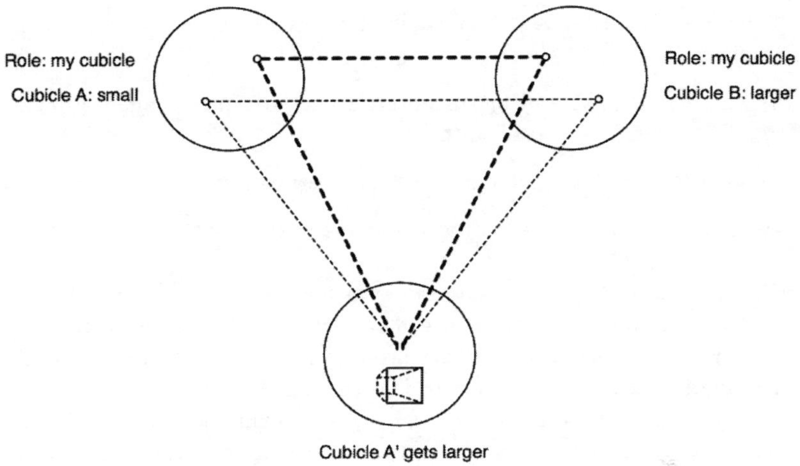

Figure 2: Role reading: *My cubicle gets bigger every year.*

By contrast, as illustrated in figure 3, in the individual reading permitted by *My cubicle gets bigger* and demanded by its counterpart *My cubicle grows* (or, alternately and perhaps more naturally, *My cubicle is growing*, *My cubicle keeps growing*, and similar constructions), there is only one mental space.

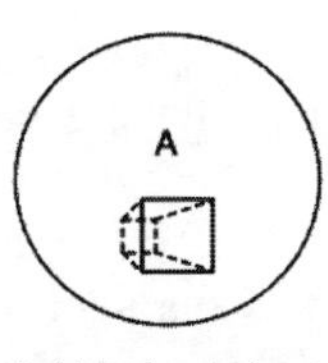

Figure 3: Individual reading

In this construal, there is just one cubicle, which undergoes a change over time. There is nothing to decompress; there are no predecessor cubicles linked to the present one by analogy and identity.

5 Exceptions: The LITERARY WORK Compression

A set of interesting possible exceptions to the generalization cited above arises in the case of noun phrases referring to artistic or literary works, or portions thereof. It is not immediately clear whether the ordinary readings of these sentences should be described as involving an "individual" interpretation.

(8) The text shrinks and the manuscript becomes predominantly pictorial. (Henderson 1967: 116)

(9) She shortened/expanded the poem in every edition.

(10) Can you enlarge this photograph in the next issue?

The sentence in (8) is from an article on multiple 13th-century illuminated manuscripts presenting the text of the New Testament book of Revelation. Over time, new manuscripts were produced, and the textual component of each book takes up less space in later manuscripts than it does in earlier ones. Example (9) presents a similar case, with the difference that the change predicate appears in a transitive (causative) construction. I introduce this example in order to point out that the role/individual contrast between monolexemic and periphrastic predicates does ordinarily obtain in these contexts as well. In the parallel sentences below, for instance, we see that a role reading is available for a sentence like (11) but not for (12).

(11) The estate manager made the flagpoles shorter in every yard. (Said of a manager who put up successively shorter flagpoles.)

(12) # The estate manager shortened the flagpole(s) in every yard.

All of the sentences in (8-10) rest on compressions in which many individuals and diffuse causal structure are compressed to uniqueness in the blend. In these cases, however, the compression is far less amenable to introspection than are the compressions that underlie the role readings of periphrastic sentences in the previous section.

Most hearers of *My cubicle gets smaller every year* are not deluded into thinking that the speaker's cubicle is "really" growing. It is less obvious that *She shortened the poem in each new edition* does not, in fact, refer to a poem that has "really" changed or that Edward in *Edward cut his hair* did not "really" cut his hair. This conceptual entrenchment is reflected in and evidenced by the expressions available for referring to these relationships.

Example (13) follows the same pattern. It comes from a critical discussion of one of the most famously revised poems in modern English, the twentieth-century American author Marianne Moore's "Poetry."

(13) The poem initially expands from thirteen lines... to thirty-eight lines... but then shrinks to a lonely three. (Conley 2003: 26)

Here, the monolexemic change predicates *expand* and *shrink* invite a reading in which *the poem* is taken to refer to an individual that changes, rather than to a succession of individuals filling a role identified by the noun phrase. In other words, multiple, non-identical documents are taken to be merely versions or manifestations of one actual literary work.[1]

This compression can also be extended such that a number of such "individual" works can serve as successive values for a role, as seen in the following set of examples from Sweetser (1997: 116). A frustrated editor might say either (14) or (15) of a situation in which an author has been refusing to settle on a final version of her contribution to an edited volume, sending new manuscripts each month, every one longer than the last. Meanwhile, the same editor might exclaim something like (16), but *not* (17), of an author who has published a new paper in each volume in a series, and each successive contribution has been longer than the one that appeared the year before.

(14) Higgenbottom's paper gets longer with every month of delay.

(15) Higgenbottom's paper grows with every month of delay.

(16) Higgenbottom's paper keeps getting longer every year.

(17) # Higgenbottom's paper keeps growing every year.

In Sweetser's original formulation, only the second scenario involves a role interpretation of *Higgenbottom's paper*, but in fact both, at their base, refer to a succession of individuals filling a role identified by the phrase. The

[1] A particularly influential articulation of this construal is put forward in the editorial theories of G. Thomas Tanselle (1975), which distinguishes between a "work" and "expressions" of it. The "work" is the true, idealized form of a piece of literary art, while any realized instantiation of an artwork—in print, performance, manuscript, or otherwise—is merely an "expression" of that ideal. Alternate approaches to scholarly editing, such as the "social text" approach associated most famously with Jerome McGann (1983, 1991), sometimes attempt to jettison this distinction, but they are swimming upstream. The work/expression distinction is alive and well, not to mention officially ratified, in the practice of both editors and librarians, as seen for example in the International Federation of Library Associations and Institutions' *Functional Guidelines for Bibliographic Records* (1998), as well as in the everyday linguistic and social practices discussed here.

difference is that the former rests on a cultural pre-compression that is highly conventionalized. The latter takes that pre-compressed conceptualization and parlays it forward into a new role-value relationship.

Some other compressions that follow the general pattern in which analogy compresses to uniqueness and disanalogy compresses to change are even more deeply entrenched in conceptualization than the LITERARY WORK compression is. Indeed, highly entrenched compressions to uniqueness underlie any conceptualizations of an entity as "one thing" persisting over space and time. We integrate over multiple encounters and variable perceptual input, understanding disanalogies between these experiences as symptoms of changes to some unique individual. These compressions are not just second nature to us, but first nature. It is vastly more natural for me to think of myself, for example, as an individual persisting over time, than as a succession of similar but not identical collections of organic matter.

These sorts of highly entrenched compressions are a fundamental part of our experience, what Fauconnier and Turner (2002:83) call "living in the blend." Some compressions need to be experienced as the basic essence of our experience, so that we can make use of them quickly, easily, without conscious thought. The apparent exceptions to Sweetser's rule seen in (8-10) are interesting because they illustrate what can happen when compression to uniqueness is moderately well entrenched, but not so entrenched as to be obligatory. This degree of entrenchment is sufficient to license the use of monolexemic change predicates seen here (or, to put it another way, the availability of these predicates constitutes evidence for the claim that this compression is well entrenched). However, as we will see, there are circumstances where hewing to the compression seems to generate mistakes, or at least vexing presumptions.

The LITERARY WORK compression on display in these examples is a very ordinary, everyday way of talking and thinking about texts, one so common that it hardly seems noteworthy or troublesome at all. But it bears greater consideration.

6 Case Study: "Poetry"

Let us take up the case of Marianne Moore's "Poetry," the poem in (13) that "expanded" to thirty-eight lines, before "shrinking" to "a lonely three." Moore was a frequent and prolific reviser, and the quantity and magnitude of her revisions present a special challenge to scholars of her work. There are many authors for whom revisions are largely a matter of editorial interest: a single definitive edition with a few explanatory footnotes is perfectly adequate for scholars not specifically concerned with publication history. But no one who hopes to write seriously about Moore's poems can ignore her revisions and re-revisions. They are simply too numerous and, in many cases, too dramatic to be glossed over. Furthermore, many of her poems take poetry and communication themselves as their subject, making the process of their construction particularly relevant to analysis of their structure and content. Little surprise, then, that critics agree that Moore's poetics are inextricably "entwined with their printing history" (Kenner 1969: 161).

"Poetry" presents an especially compelling locus for this discussion. The many texts that have appeared under this title represent at least six major variations and many dozens of printings over sixty-three years.[2] The first version, published in 1919, was five stanzas long. Other versions included one organized in a single stanza of thirteen unrhymed lines and one of fifteen lines in three stanzas. Finally, in 1967, Moore produced a version that consisted of a mere three lines, with a lightly revised take on the original five-stanza version included in an endnote. Variants of the five-stanza version were published many more times in Moore's lifetime than any other version, and she went on revising this longer version even as she produced the shorter alternates, making various small adjustments right up until the final endnote version (1967: 266-7), which reads:

POETRY (page 36)

Longer version:

I, too, dislike it: there are things that are important beyond all this fiddle.
    Reading it, however, with a perfect contempt for it, one discovers in
    it, after all, a place for the genuine.
        Hands that can grasp, eyes
        that can dilate, hair that can rise
            if it must, these things are important not because a

high-sounding interpretation can be put upon them but because they are
    useful. When they become so derivative as to become unintelligible,
    the same thing may be said for all of us, that we
        do not admire what
        we cannot understand: the bat
            holding on upside down or in quest of something to

eat, elephants pushing, a wild horse taking a roll, a tireless wolf under
    a tree, the immovable critic twitching his skin like a horse that feels a flea,
            the base-
    ball fan, the statistician—

---

[2] Detailed accounts of the complete publication history of these variants can be found in Honigsblum (1990) and Schulze (2002). A similarly complete transcript would, unfortunately, take up far more room than I have here;

nor is it valid
to discriminate against "business documents and

school-books"; all these phenomena are important. One must make a distinc-
tion
however: when dragged into prominence by half poets, the result is not poetry,
nor till the poets among us can be
"literalists of
the imagination"—above
insolence and triviality and can present

for inspection, "imaginary gardens with real toads in them," shall we have
it. In the meantime, if you demand on the one hand,
the raw material of poetry in
all its rawness and
that which is on the other hand
genuine, you are interested in poetry.

This five-stanza poem stands in stark contrast to the version that appears in the main body of the collection (1967: 36):

POETRY

I, too, dislike it.
Reading it, however, with a perfect contempt for it, one discovers in
it, after all, a place for the genuine.

Yet more variations have appeared since Moore's death. These include scholarly editions that present partial or complete "variorum" overviews of the entire history of the poem, as well as numerous editions in anthologies designed for students and casual readers. The latter most commonly present a five-stanza version in the main text, sometimes accompanied by a footnote or endnote that includes the three-line version.

Critical responses to "Poetry" often treat its history of revisions as a sequence of damages or losses. The critic Hugh Kenner was a particularly dramatic perpetrator of this approach, referring for example to the five-stanza version as "the one scarred by all those revisions" (1967: 1432). Here the many variations published under the title "Poetry" are (as we would expect) presented as a single, concrete entity that the poet has altered many times. This entity is also metaphorically characterized as a living body, and the alterations that remove material from that body as violent mutilations. In this way, even a new, intact printing of an earlier version can be "scarred" by the publication of shorter variations.

The availability of such construals is subject to complex social and conceptual conditions. Various *versions* of a literary work—that is, texts that the relevant community takes to be variations of the same work—are related by identity across the mental spaces that correspond to their time and mode of production. Culture affords some participants special social authority to decide that two given texts are manifestations of the "same" poem, novel, textbook, article, or what have you. Marianne Moore has the authority to decide that POETRY_1 (thirteen lines), POETRY_2 (thirty-eight lines), and POETRY_3 (three lines) are all manifestations of a single poem, in a way that is difficult for others to resist or undo without her ratification.

Thus, the editor and theorist Jerome McGann is welcome to argue that editors and readers would "probably do well to regard it [the three-line POETRY] as a new and separate poem rather than as a revision of the earlier work" (1992: 86), but the publication history and Moore's public characterizations of the works in question make this treatment all but impossible in practice. Nor do such decisions rest only in the hands of authors. Exactly which participants in the creation and dissemination of texts have this authority, and to what degree, is historically contingent and varies across genres and media. Early modern print culture in England, for instance, famously accorded primary authority in such matters to printers, rather than composers (Saunders 1951; Marotti 1995).

Culture also adjudicates the "sameness" of texts by external legislation. Some differences are held to be more substantive than others, and the author does not necessarily have any say in the matter. For instance, my own culture will assuredly insist that two texts are the same even if they are set in different typefaces. These rules and their enforcement have material consequences. I may consider a chapter of my book to be a new and separate text from an article that I published in a journal the year before, but if they are similar enough (according to the mores and laws of my culture), I must obtain permission from the journal to "reprint" that material or face sanctions. Screenwriters in the United States may receive "story by" credit (and monetary compensation to match) on films that bear little resemblance to their original scripts, under circumstances constrained by rules laid out by the Screenwriters' Guild of America and enshrined in contracts with the motion picture studios.

Compression to uniqueness is necessary to produce the emergent structure borrowed from the frame of single entities undergoing change. But not all identity connections, including other identity connections involving literary texts, result in the ultimate compression of identity into uniqueness. Multiple copies of a book, for instance, like the multiple drafts of Higgenbottom's article, are linked by identity connections. In a classroom, it is common for each student to have his or her own copy of the assigned text, and to treat each of these separate physical objects as common possessors of a shared identity. These individual objects have a great deal in common.

Their covers probably look extremely similar. The printed text inside them is also very similar, though there may be slight variations, perhaps in the color of the ink or the number of printings indicated on the copyright page.

When they emerged from the printer and binder, these books were very similar indeed. Since then they may have become less similar. Some have been marked by pens and highlighters. Some are grubbier than others. Some may be torn. These effects will be understood, however, as changes to individual copies, and as disanalogies between entities that are linked by identity, not uniqueness. For instance, we wouldn't say that one of the figures in the current paper was "destroyed" if you, the reader, altered or annotated your copy with a ballpoint pen; but we might if I, the author, made a similar alteration before publication.

The notion that Moore's revisions somehow damage or detract from the five-stanza version follows naturally from the LITERARY WORK compression. And yet, nothing has actually been destroyed—many copies of the original printings of previous versions exist, and there is nothing stopping anyone from re-reading or even re-printing whatever version they please. The very collection that presents the traumatizing three-line revision includes a complete instantiation of the "scarred" five-stanza version in every copy.

What's more, the variation that is surely most in danger of vanishing from readers' experience is not the five-stanza version, but the thirteen-line version in free verse, which was apparently a one-time experiment appearing only in the second (1925) edition of *Observations*. The three-stanza version has not fared much better, published only five times in Moore's life, in three editions of an anthology edited by Harriet Monroe and Alice Corbin Henderson, *The New Poetry* (1932, 1934, 1938) and two editions of Louis Zukofsky's anthology, *A Test of Poetry* (1948, 1952). Still, even these versions, which had all but vanished in the last decades of the twentieth century, do remain in print to some degree, quoted in critical essays and in the endnotes of Grace Schulman's epic collection *The Poems of Marianne Moore* (2003), as well as Robin Schulze's (2002) variorum edition of Moore's early poetry.

What's going on here? Kenner's dismay seems genuine, and he was certainly not alone in expressing such a sentiment. Critics have characterized Moore's edits variously as "revision by subtraction" (Willis 1986), "revisionary chopping" (Hicok 2000), or a series of "drastic fits of rectitude" (Kenner 1975). Moore herself seemed to take special pleasure in telling friends about the "drastic cut" (Gregor 1984) she had made for the 1967 volume, then savoring their shocked reactions. Why, given the continued existence and frequent reproduction of the five-stanza poetic utterance quoted above, have these readers persisted in feeling that something has been lost?

7 Constructions of Non-Decompression

In short, these examples are the progeny of a deluded blend, in the sense so often invoked in the negative by Fauconnier and Turner. This characterization is not intended to insult the intelligence or insight of Hugh Kenner or any other reader who feels a sense of loss when she encounters the three-line "Poetry." Rather, it is to say that the LITERARY WORK compression is both conventional and persuasive, and that these conclusions arise from the conviction that this framing is basic and true. With enough work it is possible, at least temporarily, to unpack the compression, but most of the time, there is no need, and we do not. (Indeed, as discussed in Section 5, sometimes it is much more useful not to—on the flip side to resisting being "deluded" by these compressions are the benefits of "living in the blend.")

Thus, the compressions that motivate a given conceptualization may or may not be decompressed in the moment. Furthermore, certain grammatical constructions do not admit, or do not encourage, that decompression. Some relations are conventionally pre-compressed in culture and experience, making them conceptually "packaged" enough to license the use of such constructions to express them. The use of these constructions can reinforce that packaging.

This phenomenon extends beyond the specific case of the change predicates discussed above. Haiman (1980, 1983) influentially observed that there is a general, iconically motivated, cross-linguistic pattern in which single lexemes tend to refer to single, well-integrated events, while lexically complex forms tend to refer to more diffuse, complex, indirectly linked sequences of events—which is to say, exactly the kinds of relationships that compression serves to mediate.

We should therefore expect many single word expressions denoting change to encourage interpretations in which the referenced scenario is taken to be "naturally" compressed—i.e. it is conventionally construed as involving actual, direct, unmediated change to an individual—and indeed they do. If Edwina takes up a knife and uses it to stab Frank seven times in the lungs, and as a result Frank suffers from a Class IV hemorrhage, goes into shock, and dies, we are certainly licensed to say that *Edwina killed Frank*. When we do, it seems natural and correct to consider Edwina as the simple agent of Frank's death, and the act of killing as a single event. The expression does not invite the hearer to decompress this tight cause-effect relation and unique event into something more diffuse.

Single word, adjectival predicates whose lexical semantics centrally denote a significant change to an entity's physical or essential form, such as *mutilated*, *shrunken*, or *transformed*, or Kenner's *scarred*, similarly discourage decompression of the expressed relations of uniqueness and change. So too do those that denote a quality of changeability, such as *erratic*, *fickle*, or *variable*.

As a result, any of these constructions of non-decompression can, by virtue of this feature, be used rhetorically to influence conceptualization. Kenner's description of Moore's publication history persuades in part by taking advantage of this inclination away from decompression. The following example illustrates how the same quality can be exploited in political discourse.

8 Rhetorical Exploitation

The United States Democratic presidential primaries of 2008 pitted Senator Hillary Clinton of New York, a white woman, against Senator Barack Obama of Illinois, a black man. The possibility of electing either the first African-American president or the first female president raised issues of demographic solidarity for many voters struggling to choose between the two. In March of that year, the Washington Post columnist Linda Hirshman wrote the following, from a position of apparent exasperation:

> [E]ven though this is also a year with the first major female presidential candidate, women are split every way they can be. They're the only voting bloc not voting their bloc. For the Clinton campaign, this is devastating. A year ago, chief strategist Mark Penn proclaimed that the double-X factor was going to catapult his candidate all the way to the White House. Instead, the women's vote has fragmented… I can imagine the strategists for the senator from Illinois thinking, "What's that song in Verdi's 'Rigoletto'?" Women are fickle. Turns out it's true.

In the final lines of this passage, variability across a group is again figured as change in each individual in a newly conceptualized version of the group. Here, however, both ways of considering the facts are overtly, even forthrightly, available for the reader's consideration: first, women voters are first presented as a group whose votes vary synchronically. It is only after this explanation that the *Women are fickle* compression appears. An ideally alert reader should then respond to this passage with full cognizance of the relationship between the ingredients in the input spaces and their compressed counterparts in the blend, so that we could say, with Turner (2004)

"Of course, we are not deluded in the least," or with Fauconnier and Turner (2002) "No one is deluded." But sometimes one is deluded, after all.

The grammar of *Women are fickle* does not encourage decompression or the construction of a multi-space blending network—it prompts, instead, the construction of (or collapse down to) a single mental space structured by inner-space relations. This makes it a good way to smuggle in a claim rhetorically, encouraging readers to attribute structure directly to the source domain, concluding that women *are* fickle. Now Democratic women "not voting their bloc" are not only failing to exhibit desired solidarity in the deployment of their votes, but also letting down the side by individually manifesting the stereotypically feminine fault of fickleness.

9 Conclusions

This paper has suggested that compressions across vital relations can be more or less entrenched for a given conceptual domain, and that this degree of entrenchment has both grammatical and rhetorical consequences. The semantics of several constructions can be usefully analyzed in terms of whether they do or do not invoke, or permit for, a decompression of the expressed relation. Grammatical structures canonically limited to expressing change in an individual can thus serve as tools to encourage moderately entrenched conceptualizations.

These findings, and their particular relevance to the domain of literary works, have interesting applications for professions with a substantial stake in questions of textual identity, such as archival studies, bibliography, and the law. Librarians and legislatures alike do their best to codify precisely when revisions to a document do and do not constitute the creation of a "new" text. Similarly, they must decide and enforce how members of the profession are to treat mechanical reproductions of a document. If certain conceptualizations of these relationships are strongly entrenched in grammatical structure and social practice, it should perhaps not be surprising that some approaches—for instance, the *variorium* edition endorsed by social-text approaches to editing—are much more widely appreciated than used.

Finally, the phenomena described here are difficult to explain without recourse to a theory including compressions or similar conceptual processes. This analysis suggests new ways that grammatical data can provide evidence for the theoretical constructs of compression and vital relations, and new ways that blending theory can explain grammatical phenomena.

Author Note

Vera Tobin is a lecturer in the Department of Cognitive Science at Case Western Reserve University. Thanks to Eve Sweetser, Adele Goldberg, and anonymous reviewers for their comments and suggestions regarding earlier presentations of this work. The errors and infelicities that remain are, of course, entirely my own.

References

Conley, T. 2003. *Joyces Mistakes: Problems of Intention, Irony and Interpretation.* Toronto: University of Toronto Press.

Fauconnier, G. 2005. Compression and Emergent Structure. *Language and Linguistics* 6.4: 523-538.

Fauconnier, G. & Turner, M. 2000. Compression and Global Insight. *Cognitive Linguistics* 11: 283-304.

Fauconnier, G. and Turner, M. 2002. *The Way We Think.* New York: Basic Books.

Fodor, J. A. 1970. Three Reasons for Not Deriving "Kill" from "Cause to Die." *Linguistic Inquiry* 1:429-38.

Goldberg, A. E. 1995. *Constructions: A Construction Grammar Approach to Argument Structure*. Chicago: University of Chicago Press.

Gregor, A. 1984. "Omissions Are Not Accidents": Reminiscences. *Twentieth Century Literature* 30: 150-159.

Haiman, J. 1980. The Iconicity of Grammar: Isomorphism and Motivation. *Language* 56: 515-40.

Haiman, J. 1983. Iconic and Economic Motivation. *Language* 59: 781-819.

Henderson, G. 1967. Part II: The English Apocalypse. *Journal of the Warburg and Courtauld Institutes* 30: 104-37.

Hicok, B. 2000. To Work "Lovingly": Marianne Moore at Bryn Mawr, 1905-1909. *Journal of Modern Literature* 23: 483-501.

Hirshman, L. 2008. For Hillary's Campaign, It's Been a Class Struggle. *Washington Post* (March 2)

Honigsblum, B. 1990. Marianne Moore's Revisions of "Poetry." *Marianne Moore: Woman and Poet*, ed. P. C. Willis. 185-222. Orono, ME: National Poetry Foundation.

IFLA Study Group on the Functional Requirements for Bibliographic Records. 1998. *Functional Requirements for Bibliographic Records: Final Report.* München: UBCIM Publications.

Kenner, H. 1967. Artemis and Harlequin. *National Review* 19: 1432-1433.

Kenner, H. 1969. Meditation and Enactment. *Marianne Moore: A Collection of Critical Essays*, ed. C. Thomlinson. 159-64. Englewood Cliffs, N.J.: Prentice Hall.

Kenner, H. 1975. *A Homemade World: The American Modernist Writers*. New York: Alfred A. Knopf.

Marotti, A. 1995. *Manuscript, Print, and the English Renaissance Lyric*. Ithaca: Cornell Univ. Press.

McGann, J. 1983. *Critique of Modern Textual Criticism*. Charlottesville, VA: University Press of Virginia.

McGann, J. 1991. *The Textual Condition*. Princeton, NJ: Princeton University Press.

Monroe, H. and Henderson, A. C. 1932/1934/1938. *The New Poetry*. New York: Macmillan.

Moore, M. 1924. *Observations*. London: Egoist Press. Reprinted in facsimile in Schultze, R. (Ed.) *Becoming Marianne Moore*.

Moore, M. 1967. *Collected Poems*. New York: Macmillan and The Viking Press.

Saunders, J.W. 1951. From Manuscript to Print: A Note on the Circulation of Poetic Manuscripts in the Sixteenth Century. *Proceedings of the Leeds Philosophical and Literary Society* 7.5: 507-28

Schulze, R. G. 2002. *Becoming Marianne Moore: The Early Poems, 1907-1924*. Berkeley: University of California Press.

Shibatani, M. 1976. The Grammar of Causative Constructions: A Conspectus. *Syntax and Semantics, Vol. 6: The Grammar of Causative Constructions*, ed. M. Shibatani. 1-40. New York: Academic Press.

Sweetser, E. 1997. Role and Individual Readings of Change Predicates. *Language and Conceptualization*, eds. J. Nuyts and E. Pederson. 116-36. Oxford: Oxford University Press.

Tanselle, G. T. 1975. Greg's Theory of Copy-Text and the Editing of American Literature. *Studies in Bibliography* 28, 323–60.

Turner, M. 2004. The Origin of Selkies. *Journal of Consciousness Studies* 11: 90-115.

Turner, M. 2006. Compression and Representation. *Language and Literature* 17-27.

Willis, P.C. 1986. *The Complete Prose of Marianne Moore*. New York: Viking Press.

Wolff, P. 2003. Direct Causation in the Linguistic Coding and Individuation of Causal Events. *Cognition* 88: 1-48.

Zukofsky, L. 1948/1952. *A Test of Poetry*. New York: The Objectivist Press.

18

Perception by Body versus Mind: An Alternative Analysis of 'Things' (*MONO* and *KOTO*) in Japanese Discourse

NINA AZUMI YOSHIDA

1 Introduction

This paper presents an alternative, unitary analysis to account for the discourse pragmatic functions of the formal nouns (=*keisiki meisi*)[1] ***mono*** and ***koto*** in Modern Japanese, when employed as sentence[2]-final complementizers/nominalizers in the ***mon(o)****da*[3] and ***koto****da* constructions to express speaker (deontic, epistemic, and evaluative) modality. It will propose the existence of two distinct ***mon(o)****da* and ***koto****da* constructions, one which results in a 'referential' (Yoshida, 2009) reading, and the other, a 'non-referential' interpretation of the elements ***mono*** and ***koto*** within them. Based on an examination of their current, grammatical uses in Japanese

[1] 'Formal nouns', or *keisiki meisi* in Japanese, refer to those morphological items which possess significance as nouns in formal terms only. The meanings signaled by such formal nouns are often opaque and lacking in substantial significance.

[2] The term 'sentence', usually employed in specific reference to an established unit of written data, is being employed here generically to refer synonymously to the notion of 'utterance' in spoken data.

[3] In colloquial or informal discourse contexts, ***mono*** may be further contracted to ***mon***, resulting in the semi-fixed, or 'grammaticalized' sentence-final form ***monda***.

Meaning, Form & Body.
Fey Parrill, Vera Tobin and Mark Turner (eds.).

discourse, a primary semantics of 'physically-perceived existence' versus 'cognitively-conceived existence' is posited, respectively, for ***mono*** and ***koto***, one that is alternative to those claimed for these formal nouns in past studies (e.g. Tsubone 1994, Agetsuma 1991, Fujii 2000). It will be hypothesized that the pragmatic messages signaled by these within the ***mon(o)****da* and ***koto****da* constructions represent secondary meanings that arise through metaphorical (SPACE>TIME) and metonymical (PHYSICAL>SOCIAL) processes applying to their 'core' or primary semantics. Namely, it will be claimed that a continuity exists in the semantics born by ***mono*** and ***koto*** in the ***mon(o)****da* and ***koto****da* constructions, and that these represent inferable extensions of their primary meanings that occur as a result of reanalysis (Hopper and Traugott, 1993; 2000) due to the grammaticalization of these constructions in Modern Japanese. Furthermore, it will be suggested that ***mon(o)****da* and ***koto****da*'s striking formal resemblance to the commentary predicate--namely the *B [da]* portion of a topic-comment type construction--is a key structural factor contributing to their pragmatic capabilities.

A brief overview of the main grammatical uses of ***mono*** and ***koto*** in Modern Japanese, followed by a look at the discourse modal functions of the ***mon(o)****da* and ***koto****da* construction, is provided in the next section.

2 *Mono* and *Koto*: Grammatical Uses

2.1. *Mono* and *koto* as head nouns

Roughly speaking, both the formal nouns ***mono*** and ***koto*** express the meaning 'thing' of English. Reference grammars for students of Japanese commonly explain the choice between them as being governed by the opposing semantic notions of 'concrete' versus 'abstract' (Naganuma 1970, Martin 1975, McGloin 1989), or 'tangible' versus 'intangible' (Makino and Tsutsui 1989).

The example below from McGloin (1989) neatly illustrates an instance where the choice of ***mono*** or ***koto*** would render a meaning difference in a pair of otherwise identical sentences.

(1a) *Kakitai* ***mono*** *ga* *aru.*[4]
want to write *MONO* NOM exist:NPST
'There is (some)thing I want to write.'

[4] The following list of abbreviations were employed in glossing the Japanese data: ACC=Accusative; ASP=Aspect; CONJ=Conjunctive; COP=Copula; DAT=Dative; GEN=Genitive; NEG=Negative; NOM=Nominative; NPST=Non Past; PST=Past; QT=Quotative; TE= *Te* Connective; TOP=Topic

(e.g. a book, diary, or letter)

(1b) *Kakitai* **koto** *ga* *aru.*
want to write *KOTO* NOM exist:NPST
'There is (some)thing I want to write (about).'
(e.g. a topic or idea)

In (1a), ***mono*** might refer to a book or a diary, or similar literary medium, whereas ***koto*** in (1b) would more likely indicate a subject matter, topic, or idea that one wants to write about.[5] Thus, Japanese possesses a lexical means for differentiating between or marking 'things' which individuals should perceive as being either a ***mono*** or ***koto***.

2.2 *Koto* as a Nominalizer

Koto is often preceded or modified by a verb or verbal clause in the non-past or imperfect form to indicate 'the activity of'. When this ***koto*** is replaced by ***mono***, it indicates the object upon which the act takes place or the performer of the act. Examples of such usage, employing a transitive verb, are given in (2a) and (2b):

	Verb	Verb +***koto***	Verb + ***mono***
(2a)	*<kaku>*	*<kaku**koto**>*	*<kaku**mono**>*
	'to write'	'writing'	'(some)thing to write on' (paper, desk, etc.) '(some)thing to write with' (pen, crayon, etc.) '(some)one who writes'
(2b)	*<tukuru>*	*<tukuru**koto**>*	*<tukuru**mono**>*
	'to make'	'making'	'(some)thing to make' '(some)thing to make (something) with' '(some)one who makes (something)'

Koto together with ***no*** are the two most commonly recognized nominalizers in Japanese. Though their uses are mutually interchangeable in many cases, as pointed out in Akatsuka-McCawley (1978), ***no*** tends to be employed when the nominalized clause expresses a directly perceivable event,[6] whereas ***koto*** would indicate the absence of direct or personal involvement

---

[5] Examples from McGloin 1989: 110

[6] Example given in Akatsuka-McCawley 1978:
Watasi wa zibun ga hurueteiru ***no/*koto*** *o kanzita*
I TOP self NOM shaking;NPST **NO/KOTO** ACC feel:PST
'I felt my body trembl**ing**.'

by the speaker in the event named by the marked clause. Such connotational differences might surface in situations where both ***no*** and ***koto*** are grammatically possible, as in the (constructed) example below:

(3.) *Syoosetu o kaku* ***no/koto*** *wa muzukasii.*
novel ACC write ***NO/KOTO*** TOP difficult
'Writing a novel is difficult.'

In this example, the use of nominalizer ***koto*** indicates that the speaker of the sentence is somewhat detached and not personally involved in the expressed activity of writing a novel, whereas ***no*** gives an implication of personal involvement.

2.3 Prenominal/Preadjectival Uses of *Mono*

Mono possesses a grammatical use whose equivalent is not found in the case of ***koto***. When ***mono*** is attached pre-adjectivally or pre-nominally, it imparts an added sense of indefiniteness or vagueness. It functions to increase the ambiguity or the inability to pinpoint the underlying source of the sensation or phenomenon to which it is prefixed, with an effect equivalent to the 'somehow' or 'somewhat' of English:

(4.) (a) *kanasii* / ***mono****-ganasii* 'sad' / 'somehow sad'
(b) *sizuka* / ***mono****-sizuka* 'quiet;serene'/'strangely quiet'

(5.) (a) *oto ga suru* / ***mono-****oto ga suru*
'hear sounds' 'hear the sounds of something'
(b) *kage ni kakureru* / ***mono-****kage ni kakureru*
'to hide in the shadows' 'to hide in the shadows of something'

2.3 Modal Uses: The *Mon(o)da* and *Kotoda* Construction

The ***mon(o)****da* construction, in particular, has been identified by a number of modern Japanese grammarians (e.g., Martin 1975, Mizutani and Mizutani 1977, Makino and Tsutsui 1989) as possessing the linguistic capacity to imbue an otherwise neutral or 'objective' statement with various degrees of the speaker's subjective or emotive affect, ranging from conviction toward an unquestionable/natural truth, nostalgic reminiscences, long-nurtured desires, deep wonder/amazement, as well as to indirect commands. Below is a representative set of examples illustrating the diversity of these affective effects[7]:

---

[7] Examples adapted from Martin 1975: 725-6

(6.)*Inu wa hoeru* ***mon(o)****da.*
dog TOP bark:NPST *MONO*:COP
'Dogs naturally bark./It's expected that dogs bark.'

Emotive affect: conviction toward (an unquestionable/natural) truth

(7.)*Mukasi wa yoku kono kooen de asonda* ***mon(o)****da.*
long ago TOP well this park at play:PST *MONO*:COP
'Back then/Long ago, I sure used to play at this park alot.'

Emotive affect: nostalgic reminiscence/recollection

(8.)*Konna rippa-na uti ni itido wa sumitai* ***mon(o)****da.*
like this magnificent house in once TOP want to live *MONO*:COP
'Just once, I sure would want to live in a magnificent house like this.'

Emotive affect: deep-seated/long nurtured desire

(9.)*Yoku yatta* ***mon****(o)da.*
well do:PST *MONO*:COP
'How well you did!/It's amazing that you did (so) well.'

Emotive affect: deep wonder/amazement

(10.) *Hito ni wa amari meiwaku o kakenai* ***mon(o)****da.*
people DAT TOP too much trouble ACC cause:NEG:NPST *MONO*:COP
'You shouldn't cause too much trouble to others.'

Pragmatic effect: indirect command

In contrast, the uses of ***koto****da* to mark speaker affect extend only to exclamations of mild wonder,[8] or indirect commands of an instructive nature, as exemplified in (11) and (12)[9].

(11.) *Huyu no umi ni otite,*
winter GEN sea into fall:CONJ
yoku sinzoo mahi de sinanakatta ***koto****da.*

---

[8] Such exclamatory ***koto****da* expression are regarded as slightly obsolete and/or dialectal in present-day Modern Japanese discourse.
[9] Examples from Nagara et al. 1987: 29-30

well heart attack from die:NEG:PST *KOTO*:COP
'It's a wonder that s/he/you fell in to the sea in winter, and didn't die from a cardiac arrest.'

Emotive affect: mild wonder/surprise

(12.) *Yasumi ni wa benkyoo no koto nado wasurete,*
day off on TOP studies GEN about such as forget:CONJ
zyuubun-ni tanosimu ***koto**da.*
fully enjoy:NPST *KOTO*:COP
'On days off, you should forget about such things as studying, and fully enjoy (yourself).'

Pragmatic effect: indirect command/instructive warning

There exist a number of past studies on this linguistic phenomena (Teramura 1981, 1984; Agetsuma 1991; Tsubone 1996; Fujii 1998 inter alia); however, the question of what particular semantic and structural features of the ***mon(o)**da* and ***koto**da* constructions enable them to reference their range of pragmatic implications remains to be unitarily answered.

It is suggested that ***mon(o)**da* and ***koto**da*'s striking formal resemblance to the commentary predicate—namely, that of a nominalized predicate occupying the comment position of a topic-comment type construction-- is a key structural factor contributing to such pragmatic capabilities. Structurally-speaking, ***mon(o)**da* and ***koto**da* constructions may be analyzed as consisting of the formal nouns ***mono*** or ***koto*** immediately preceded by a clause or declarative sentence in the *rentaikei* 'attributive' form and followed by the copula *da*, as shown in (13):

(13.) TOPIC COMMENT
[Noun Phrase^{A} -*wa*] [Noun Phrase^{B} + copula *da*]
[(clause)^{attributive} + ***mono*/*koto*** + copula *da*]

It is furthermore hypothesized that two variant ***mon(o)**da* and ***koto**da* constructions exist in Japanese, one which generates what is termed here a 'referential' reading of the ***mono*/*koto*** and the other, a 'non-referential' (i.e. modal) one. Moreover, as elements within these two distinct constructions, it is the primary semantics of ***mono*** and ***koto*** (to be proposed) which is claimed to be referenced in the former, whereas their secondary, or extended, meanings are what arise in the latter.

3 The *Mon(o)da* and *Kotoda* Construction

3.1 'Referential' vs. 'Non-referential' Nominalized Predicates:

As initially noted in Yoshida (2009), there exists two types of topic-comment (or A *wa* B *da*) sentences consisting of a nominalized predicate ending in *da:*

i.) Those which may be interpreted as containing 'regular' nominalized predicates, in that the nominal element serving as the head noun retains its nominal status as the referential object of the *wa*-marked topic, and

ii.) Those which have become formulaic or 'grammaticalized' to the extent that the head noun has lost its nominal status and bears only a non-referential or 'modal' meaning.

Using this criterion, I wish to differentiate between what I am labeling here a fully 'referential' nominalized predicate and its grammaticalized, 'non-referential' counterpart. For example, in the absence of further context, the following sentence (14) may be considered 'ambiguous' with at least two possible readings, as given in (14a) and (14b):

(14)	*(O)hasi*	*wa*	*taberu*	*toki ni*	*tukau*	***mon***(*o*)*da*.
	chopsticks	TOP	eat:NPST	times on	use: NPST	*MONO*:COP

(14a) Reading 1:'Chopsticks are (some)thing (one) uses when (one) eats.'

(14b) Reading 2: '(You) are supposed to use the chopsticks *for eating*.'
Lit. (when [you] eat)

In the first reading (14a), the head noun ***mono*** takes on a referential reading in that it refers semantically to a 'thing' modified by the clause *taberu toki ni tukau* 'use when (one) eats', which in turn serves to comment on, or define the *wa*-marked topic *(o)hasi* 'chopsticks'. In the second reading in (14b), however, the formal noun ***mono*** is no longer functioning as a nominal with a referent, but simply as a modal marker, in this case, to mark it as an indirect command with the deontic modality of obligation.

As initially noted by Givon (1982), the propositional contents of a clause modifying a nominal element have been shown cross-linguistically in both Japanese, English, and other languages to be 'nonchallengeable'.[10] A speaker is likely to present as background, and as 'information that is shielded from challenge'—i.e., nonchallengeable--that which he considers presupposed, assumed, shared, or believed in by the hearer (Givon 1982: 100).

[10] Givon 1982: 100.

3.2 The topic-comment [*A wa B (da)*] construction

One of the intrinsic messages coded by the *A wa B (da)*[11], or topic-comment construction is that some sort of relationship exists between A and B; however, the type of relationship that exists is not specified. Observe the following pair of examples illustrating this construction type:

(15a.) *Boku wa gakusei (da).*
I TOP student COP
'I am a student.'

(15b.) *Boku wa unagi(da).*[12]
I TOP eels COP
'I will have the broiled eels.'

It is unclear, unless the context in which it is uttered is known, whether the concept expressed by the sentence is simply indicative of a connotative relationship between the *wa*-marked topic A and its comment B (that is, A is B, or A connotes B, as in example 15a.), or whether an 'appropriate' interpretation (i.e., an interpretation appropriate within the context of the current discourse) involves inferencing an additional unexpressed main idea from the minimal pair of concepts A and B. For example, if (15b) is uttered in a restaurant or store, from A, *boku* 'first person pronoun (used by males)', and B, *unagi* 'eel', will be inferred the reading 'I am <u>going to eat/buy/order</u> the <u>broiled</u> eels.', and not 'I am an eel', which would also be an entirely possible interpretation of this sentence, given it's structural properties.

Only after the sentence has been fully uttered and contextualized, can it be determined whether the *wa* -marked topic noun has been topicalized as an entity to be referenced by the predicative noun, or whether it has been topicalized in allusion to some conceptual aspect of it embodied by the commentary predicate itself.

---

[11] The copula *da* is enclosed in parentheses to indicate that it is an optional element in this construction. I claim that *da* encodes an additional feature here that is compatible with, but not essential to the topic-comment (i.e. A wa B) type utterances; namely, that it marks for what Narahara (2002) terms the "anti-ignorative mode" (Narahara 2002: 165-6). Overt marking by *da* instead of its covert implication by a zero-morpheme indicates that the speaker has knowledge of some information; namely, the truth-value of the sentential content. The copula form *da* expresses the speaker's explicit assertion of his certainty in his knowledge and his belief in his affirmative judgement about the truth of the sentential content so marked. Hence, when the assertive or authoritative effects of *da* are perceived to be inappropriate for the speaker's gender or the hierarchical interpersonal relation between the discourse participants, it is proposed that the speaker will chose the zero-copula-- i.e. "*da*-less"-- form over its overt use.

[12] Example from Okutsu (1978: 8).

Similarly, nominalized predicates such as ***mon(o)**da* and ***koto**da* share the same formal patterning; hence, it is only possible to comprehend the relationship between topic A and its comment B upon knowledge of the discourse context in which it occurs.

I claim that the nominalized predicate takes the propositional contents of what appears, superficially, to be an objectivized event or state, and 're-packages' it as either a ***mono*** or ***koto*** in indication of how these contents are to be received. This repackaged proposition, made non-challengeable through its nominalization and embellished with the speakers attitudinal stance in the form of either ***mono*** or ***koto***, is what is then presented to the hearer when a non-referential type nominalized predicate, such as ***mon(o)**da* or ***koto**da*, is uttered.

I moreover propose that the various attitudinal stances of the speaker—either, deontic, epistemic, or evaluative--signaled by the ***mon(o)**da* and ***ko-to**da* constructions, derive themselves from the underlying meanings the formal nouns ***mono*** and ***koto*** possess as nominals in this construction. Next, I present what I hypothesize to be the primary, or 'core', semantics of ***mono*** and ***koto***, followed up by how these 'propositional attitudes' (Fujii 2000) arise and are inferenced within these constructions.

4 The Semantics of *Mono* and *Koto*

As previously stated, reference grammars commonly explain the choice between ***mono*** and ***koto*** as being regulated by such opposing semantic notions as 'concrete' versus 'abstract' or 'tangible' vs. 'intangible'. Although this simple and seemingly clear-cut rule holds up well in the majority of instances where ***mono*** and ***koto*** tend to occur, the distinction becomes difficult to account for when confronted by the acceptability of sentences such as in (16) and (17), where the logical referent of ***mono*** does not appear to possess any obvious features of 'concreteness' or 'tangibility':

(16.) *Ano hito wa yasasisa to iu **mono**/****koto*** *ni kaketeiru.*
that person TOP kindness QT say MONO DAT lack:TE-ASP:NPST
'That person is lacking in (the thing called) kindness.'

(17.) *Hito no kokoro o ugokasu **mono**/****koto*** *wa netsui da.*
people GEN heart ACC move:NPST MONO TOP ardor COP:NPST
'Ardor is what (lit. the thing that) moves people's hearts.'

Teramura (1981) provides the insight that ***mono***'s most typical definition is that it signals an object, or a category thereof, possessing some type of 'physical concreteness' that can be perceived by one of the five bodily senses. Additionally, it's meaning encompasses those phenomena having 'a reality (capable of being) sensed psychologically' (Teramura 1981: 754). ***Koto***, on the other hand, represents 'the object of one's thought and discourse, such as (informational) content that can be expressed by a topic', or 'an act, action, situation, change of state or general quality which may be expressed by a verb or adjective' (Teramura 1981: 754).

Past studies on ***mono***'s functions as a discourse modal, have ascribed such meanings as *ippansei* 'generality' (Tsubone 1994, 1996), *ippanteki* 'general/generic' (Agetsuma 1991), as well as pointed out the 'set-evoking effect' of constructions involving ***mono*** as a element (Fujii 1999, 2000). Moreover, in their deontic uses of marking for speaker modality, Noda (1995) has noted that ***mon(o)****da* is employed for conveying obligations that are generally or collectively acknowledged by a group or community, whereas ***koto****da* may be used when the speaker alone feels justified in its necessity or importance. (Noda 1995: 258-9).

Based on such past accounts, I propose a more unitary semantic analysis of the formal nouns ***mono*** and ***koto*** in Modern Japanese. It is termed 'unitary' in suggesting that the seemingly multiple meanings born by ***mono*** and ***koto*** in each of its different modal uses are the result of polysemy, and that they represent extensions of ***mono***'s and ***koto***'s core semantics inferred by metaphorical and metonymical means. Namely, the following 'primary' semantics for ***mono*** and ***koto*** are suggested:

(i.) ***Mono*** signals an existence that is 'sensorily' perceptible (i.e. through the bodily senses of sight, smell, sound, taste, and touch—as well as one's inner state experiences, such as pain, hunger, emotions, etc.); hence, ***mono*** is indicative of a physically perceived, and by token of this notion, an 'unrationalized' phenomenon, an existence that can be directly sensed without the aid or use of one's mind and its rationalizing powers.

In contrast,

(ii.) ***Koto*** refers to an intellectually or cognitively perceived existence; namely, marking an existence as a ***koto*** signals that it will require processing within one's mental faculties and that one's powers of rationalization must be called in to enable this ***koto*** to become perceptible.

These opposing semantics of 'physically sensed/unrationalized' existence versus 'cognitively conceived/rationalized' existence—namely, perception by body versus mind--are hypothesized as being the key, definitive features distinguishing ***mono*** from ***koto*** in instances when they are to take on a referential reading.

Because ***mono***'s semantics denote a phenomenon whose actual existence can be validated by sensory means alone (i.e., without the need for mental processing), it prototypically indicates a physical entity or material object. However, because its meaning also signals that whose perceived presence is to remain 'unrationalized', it connotes an existence that 'somehow exists', and by token of this, is unidentified, undifferentiated or unindividuated; namely, a 'generic', 'general', or 'collective' entity. In this respect, ***mono*** may reference a substance having an (actual or construed) internal homogeneity, such as in the case of abstract nouns (e.g., *yasasisa* 'kindness'), or may potentially reference a person, albeit in a generic, physical sense, and would thus be inappropriate in referring to a uniquely identified individual or one meriting distinction and respect.[13]

Moreover, since ***mono***'s meaning typically references a physical object, a proposition presented as a certain type of ***mono*** may be assumed to occupy a three-dimensional area of space, an assumption that would necessarily be absent in the case of one marked by ***koto***, a phenomenon that only comes into existence in one's mind at the moment of its conception.

5 How Speaker Modality Arises in the *Mon(o)da* and *Kotoda* Constructions

5.1 The Deontic Reading of Nominalized Predicates

As pointed out by Lyons (1977), when we impose upon someone the obligation to perform (or to refrain from performing) a particular act, we are describing the desirable results that will obtain if the act in question is performed (Lyons 1977: 823). Deontic necessity, moreover, typically proceeds or derives from some source or cause. If we recognize that we are obliged to perform some act, then we usually acknowledge that someone or something is responsible for our obligation (Lyons 1997: 824).

In Yoshida (2008), it has been claimed that the deontic interpretation of predicates nominalized by ***mono*** or ***koto*** typically emerges (i) when the clause modifying ***mono*** or ***koto*** contains a verb with nonpast (i.e. future) inflection denoting an agent-controllable action, and (ii) the utterance containing this nominalized predicate is directed toward an overt or implied

---

[13] When employed as a bare noun, the Japanese *kanji* orthography allows a distinction to be made between the ***mono*** meaning 'person' from that of 'physical object', using 者 for the former, and 物 for the latter, respectively. However, as claimed above, ***mono*** (者) refers to a person, but to one lacking distinction; hence, its common use in the expression used to humbly introduce oneself (e.g., *Yosida to iu mono desu ga.*/Lit. 'I am a ***mono*** (=person/[some]one) named Yoshida.')

second-person referent. The fact that the propositional content expressed by the modifying clause has been made nonchallengeable through its nominalization is what structurally imbues this construction with the illocutionary force of a directive. (Yoshida, 2008: 375)

The speaker's embellishment of this nominalized clause with the choice of either ***mono*** or ***koto*** functions not just to indicate to the hearer that he has an obligation to carry out the designated action, but to direct him to the authoritative 'source' or basis behind why he is obligated to perform it. Thus, the function of ***mono*** or ***koto*** in a nonreferential nominalized predicate, when employed in this directive sense, is to denote the existence of this authoritative 'voice' behind utterances so marked (Yoshida, 2008: 375).

It is further suggested that the differences in the type of authoritative source they each reference derive themselves from the degree of epistemic truth value, and thus deontic necessity, accorded to an existence marked as either a ***mono*** or ***koto***. Moreover, this 'existence = obligation' interpretation arises in part as a result of the metaphorical extension (i.e. SPACE > TIME) of the underlying or primary meanings of ***mono*** or ***koto*** as nominals. Hence, ***mono***, whose original, referential meaning as a nominal denotes an existence that occupies a vaguely defined, but constant, area in three dimensional space, is reinterpreted in its non-referential use, as denoting a proposition with temporal persistence, or has persisted throughout time, namely a 'general, universal, or consensual truth'.

5.2 How the Deontic Stance Arises in *Mon(o)da* and *Kotoda* Constructions

When the speaker marks a clause denoting the performance of a future act with ***mon(o)da***, he is presenting the obligation the hearer has toward carrying out the designated act as finding its grounds in a general norm that has persisted throughout time. The existence of the obligation is true and compelling for the hearer because it corresponds to what has been traditionally and socially regarded as proper, natural, or normal behavior by others. The truth or legitimacy behind a ***mono***-marked obligation is something to be accepted 'as is', without any attempt to rationalize the logical reasoning behind its necessity; hence, it represents something that appeals to 'common sense' or constitutes a social norm.

Thus, in a situation where example (14) is directed toward a child who is using his chopsticks to play drums (instead of eating) with them, its utterance would be interpreted as a directive stating 'You're supposed to use (the) chopsticks for eating!' It is an "indirect" command in that the speaker is merely stating what the norm or desirable action should be, and it is up to the hearer to then determine how their behavior or actions (as they relate to the current discourse context) deviates from it. Such overtones of a desirable action grounded in a social norm or common sense are similarly found in example (10).

It was earlier claimed as well that the semantics of referential ***koto*** denote a 'cognitively conceived/rationalized' existence. When ***koto*** takes on a nonreferential interpretation as in the ***koto**da* construction, metaphorical inferencing causes it to take on the extended meaning of connoting a proposition that only comes into existence at the specific instance of its conception; hence, it indicates a 'particular truth', or one whose validity applies only to a specific time or situation.

Accordingly, when the speaker marks a clause denoting the performance of a future act with ***koto***, he is presenting the obligation the hearer has toward carrying out the designated act as finding its basis in something that was conceived within the speaker's mind. Thus, the existence of this obligation is true and valid because its necessity is known solely to the speaker, or 'source', of the utterance. This results in the effect of an instructive warning, as it marks the utterer of the ***koto**da* directive as being the more 'knowing' or authoritative party.

5.3 How Epistemic Stance Arises in the *Mon(o)da* Construction

According to Bybee and Pagliuca (1985), a common tendency regarded as metaphoric of meaning change is the development of meanings related to deontic obligation into that of epistemic possibility and probability. The epistemic sense is a metaphorical extension of obligation being made to apply to the truth of a proposition; namely, that a particular proposition is "obliged" to be true (Bybee and Pagliuca 1985: 73).

It is suggested that from ***mono***'s underlying semantics (i.e., physically-perceived/unrationalized existence) is inferentially derived the epistemic stance that existence = truth, and physically-perceived/ unrationalized = general/natural, resulting in its secondary meaning of a 'general/natural truth'. A definition is typically that which provides the most commonly recognized description of an entity's qualities or characteristics, namely the one most generally or naturally associated with it. As for the definitional reading of (14), the proposition 'use when (one) eats', made nonchallengeable through its nominalization, is being presented as a generally-known truth regarding the *wa*-marked topic, 'chopsticks', and moreover, as one without need of further explication (i.e., unrationalized). This results in the 'definitional' interpretation, as given in (14a) above, although somewhat colored with the speaker's subjective affect that this is an expected or natural truth is to be accepted 'as is', as likewise seen in example (7).

5.4 How the Evaluative Stance Arises in *Mon(o)da* and *Kotoda* Constructions

By token of its underlying semantics (i.e. physically-sensed/unrationalized) ***mono*** potentially references an existence that is unidentified, undifferentiated or un-individuated; namely, a generic, general, or collective entity possessing an internal homogeneity. Such an entity would necessarily be one lacking in agency as such individual agents would be subsumed and obfuscated within the collective whole. From this, it is hypothesized that one of the major functions of presenting a propositional content as a certain type of ***mono***, when employed to mark the speaker's evaluative stance, is to present it as one which lacks individual (human) agency.

By extension of this meaning, a proposition so marked is also considered one that is 'uncontrollable'. It is this secondary meaning of uncontrollability, coupled with that of temporal persistence (inferred from ***mono***'s semantics of spatial persistence by metaphorical extension), which gives rise to the evaluative stance ***mono*** takes on in Examples (6) and (9), where it serves as the head noun of a proposition predicated by a verb in the past tense indicating a past event or action, or in the desiderative (i.e. *–tai*) form. The function of ***mono*** in such instances is to give the effect of emotional and temporal 'depth' to the proposition so marked, resulting in the nostalgic recollections and deep-seated desire readings, respectively. An unrationalized sensation is also one that escapes one's mental grasp or comprehension; this is rendered as the evaluative stance of deep wonder/amazement, as in Example (8).

Such features of uncontrollability and temporal persistence or depth are absent with the use of ***koto***, resulting in the milder or more muted overtones of wonder/surprise seen in example (11).

6 Conclusion

The aim of this study has been twofold:

I.) To show that a continuity exists in the semantics born by the formal nouns ***mono*** and ***koto*** in its uses of marking speaker (deontic, epistemic, and evaluative) modality (as elements within the ***mon(o)****da* or ***koto****da* constructions), and

II.) To point out that these represent inferable extensions of ***mono***'s and ***koto***'s primary meaning (as proposed—namely, physically-perceived or cognitively-conceived existence), that arise by metaphorical (SPACE>TIME) and metonymical (PHYSICAL>SOCIAL) means when

mono and ***koto*** occur as elements in such grammaticalized constructions as ***mon(o)**da* or ***koto**da* in Japanese discourse.

Author Note

University of California, Los Angeles
(Department of Asian Languages & Cultures)

I wish to thank Prof. Robert S. Kirsner and the two anonymous reviewers for this volume for their constructive and thought-provoking comments on an earlier version of this paper.

References

Agetsuma, Y. 1991. Zissitu meisi 'mono' to keisikiteki yoohoo to no imiteki tunagari. *Toohoku Daigaku Bungakubu Nihongogakka Ronsyuu* 1: 2-11.

Akatsuka-McCawley, N. 1978. Another look at *no, koto,* and *to*: Epistemology and complementizer choice in Japanese. *Problems in Japanese Syntax and Semantics*. eds. J. Hinds & I. Hayward , 178-212. Tokyo: Kaitakusya.

Bybee, J. & W. Pagliuca. 1985. Cross-linguistic comparison and the development of grammatical meaning. *Historical Semantics, Historical Word Formation*. ed. J. Fisiak. 59-83 The Hague: Mouton.

Fujii, S. 1999. What can 'things' (*'mono'*) do for propositional attitudes in Japanese discourse?. *Pragmatics in 1998: Selected Papers from the 6th International Pragmatics Conference, Vol. 2*. ed. J. Verschueren, 159-171. Antwerp: International Pragmatics Association

Fujii, S. 2000. Incipient Decategorizaion of MONO in Japanese Discourse. *Pragmatic Markers and Propositional Attitude*. eds. G. Andersen & T. Freitheim, 83-118. Amsterdam/Philadelphia: John Benjamins Publishing Company.

Givon, T. 1982. Evidentiality and Epistemic Space. *Studies in Language* 6: 23-49.

Hopper, P. & E. C. Traugott. 1993. *Grammaticalization*. Cambridge: Cambridge University Press.

Lyons, J. 1977. *Semantics*: *Volume 2*, Cambridge: Cambridge University Press.

Makino, S. & M. Tsutsui. 1986. *A Dictionary Of Basic Japanese Grammar*. Tokyo: The Japan Times.

Martin, S. 1975. *A Reference Grammar of Japanese*. London: Yale University Press.

McGloin, N. H. 1989. *A Student's Guide to Japanese Grammar*. Tokyo: Taisyuukan Publishing Company.

Nagara S., Hirota, N. & Nakanishi, Y. 1987. *Japanese for Foreigners: Innovative Workbook in Japanese: Volume 2*. Tokyo: Aratake.

Narahara, T. 2002. *The Japanese Copula: Forms and Functions*. New York: Palgrave Macmillan.

Noda, H. 1995. Monoda to kotoda to noda: meisisei no zyodoosi no tooiteki na yoohoo. *Nihongo ruigi hyoogen no bunpoo*. eds. T. Miyajima & Y. Nida, 253-262. Tokyo: Kurosio Syuppan.

Okutsu, K. 1978. *'Boku wa unagi da' no bunpoo*. ('The grammar of "*Boku wa unagi da*" [type sentences]') Tokyo: Kurosio Syuppan.

Sweetser, E. 1990. *From Etymology to Pragmatics: Metaphorical and Cultural Aspects of Semantic Structure*. Cambridge: Cambridge University Press.

Teramura, H. 1981. Mono to koto. ('*Mono* and *koto*') *Mabuti Kazuo hakase taikankinen kokugogaku ronsyuu*. 743-762.

Teramura, H. 1984. *Nihongo no sintakusu to imi* ('Japanese syntax and meaning'), Volume 2. Tokyo: Kurosio Syuppan.

Tsubone, Y. 1994. 'Monoda' ni kansuru ichi koosatsu. ('A study of *monoda*') *Nihongo Kyooiku* 84: 65-77.

Yoshida, N. A. 2008. Nominalized Predicates as Directives in Japanese Discourse. *Japanese Korean Linguistics 13*. eds. Endo Hudson, M., Jun, S., Sells, P., Clancy P. M., Iwasaki, S. & S. Sohn. 371-383. Stanford: CSLI Publications.

Yoshida, N. A. 2009. How 'Things' (*mono*) Get Reanalyzed in Japanese Discourse. *Japanese Korean Linguistics 16*. eds. Takubo, T., Kinuhata, T., Grzelak, S., and K. Nagai. 329-343. Stanford: CSLI Publications.

Author Index

Subject Index